The Battlecruiser *New Zealand*

THE
BATTLECRUISER
New Zealand
A GIFT TO EMPIRE

MATTHEW WRIGHT

Oratia Seaforth
PUBLISHING

Visit Matthew Wright online at: www.matthewwright.net
Read Matthew Wright's blog: www.mjwrightnz.wordpress.com
Like Matthew Wright's Facebook page: www.facebook.com/MatthewWrightNZ

Copyright © Matthew Wright 2021
First published in Great Britain in 2021 by
Seaforth Publishing,
A division of Pen & Sword Books Ltd,
47 Church Street,
Barnsley S70 2AS
www.seaforthpublishing.com
and
Oratia Books, Oratia Media Ltd,
783 West Coast Road, Oratia, Auckland 0604, New Zealand
www.oratia.co.nz

British Library Cataloguing in Publication Data
A catalogue record for this book is available from the British Library

ISBN 978 1 5267 8403 2 (HARDBACK)
ISBN 978 1 5267 8404 9 (EPUB)
ISBN 978 1 5267 8405 6 (KINDLE)

Pen & Sword Books Limited incorporates the imprints of Atlas,
Archaeology, Aviation, Discovery, Family History, Fiction, History, Maritime, Military,
Military Classics, Politics, Select, Transport, True Crime, Air World, Frontline Publishing,
Leo Cooper, Remember When, Seaforth Publishing, The Praetorian Press, Wharncliffe
Local History, Wharncliffe Transport, Wharncliffe True Crime and White Owl

Typeset and designed by Ian Hughes, Mousemat Design Limited

Printed and bound in Great Britain by TJ International Ltd, Padstow

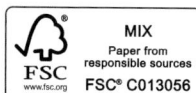

MIX
Paper from
responsible sources
FSC
www.fsc.org
FSC® C013056

CONTENTS

Colour plate section between pages 144 and 145

FOREWORD

by Nick Jellicoe

It is with great pleasure that I write the foreword for Matthew Wright's *Battlecruiser New Zealand: A Gift to Empire*. The battlecruiser's story was intimately bound together with that of my grandfather John Jellicoe before, during and after the Great War. As Controller and Third Sea Lord, my grandfather played a key role in her design and construction; at the battles of Heligoland Bight, Dogger Bank and Jutland, she came under Jellicoe's wings as the Grand Fleet's first wartime C-in-C; her last great voyage carried the admiral, newly promoted Admiral of the Fleet, around Britain's dominions to set the stage for naval co-operation in the next war. At Jutland, HMS *New Zealand* expended more ammunition than any other British ship but – unfairly, I think – was widely criticised. Her final shots, as the last light of day was falling, at SMS *Schlesien*, bravely protecting Hipper's badly damaged battlecruisers, were among the last shots exchanged between the opposing lines and were the last she fired in the war.

Jellicoe was much-loved by his men: the small admiral had the weathered face of a sailor and sported a recognisably prominent nose around whom others always felt the humour in his warmly sparkling eyes. After being aboard *New Zealand* for more than a year, he was moved to tears when the time came to part company. He was keenly aware of the huge debt that Britain owed New Zealanders after the slaughter of the Great War. When the great ship arrived in Auckland on her second dominion tour, Jellicoe asked to meet the father of the gallant Q-ship commander, William Sanders VC, to whom he gave some watercolours of his son's ship, the *Prize*. While in Takapuna, unveiling a memorial, his wife, Gwen, announced that she had lost her gold net purse. It was found that evening by the son of a local grocer and Jellicoe was alerted. Apparently, she was rather 'shocked that the boy wanted a favour for finding the purse'. When Jellicoe found out that all he wanted was to come aboard HMS *New Zealand*, he sent his cutter to Takapuna's Bayswater Quay to collect the lad. After being met as he boarded the ship and being taken around personally by the admiral, he was given a small 'many bladed' pocket knife as a memento.

The admiral's tenure as Governor-General of New Zealand counted, I think, as some of the family's happiest days, marred only by the ever-present shadow of Jutland and the need to defend his record. It was a pity that he felt the need to cut his New Zealand stay short to return to England in the midst of the Jutland controversy: for one, he was not able to take up a Māori title that, family lore has it, he was to be offered.

During my first visit to New Zealand, I went to the small museum at Devonport where the massive shell splinter from X turret was held. With me was a copy of a two-volume collection of photographs from the ship's later 1919 dominion tour that once again took her around the world. I had hoped to get back to the land of the long white cloud this last September – it was the centenary of Jellicoe's tour as Governor General – but Covid-19 prevented me. Here, at home, I am lucky enough to be able to keep those memories alive: my father left me a beautiful painting of the ship at anchor done by the great marine watercolourist, A B Cull. She rests at anchor: serene and majestic.

Wright skilfully uses the ship as the mouthpiece through which to tell a fascinating story of the age – the dreadnought age. Through her conception, design, building and short life, he has been able to set the stage on which his main protagonist played. While many thought that the New Zealand premier Joseph Ward's offer of a gift dreadnought 'impetuous' and a 'knee-jerk reaction' to Britain's 1909 naval estimates crisis, what he did pushed Australia to a similar decision. The new ship also suited Jackie Fisher's purpose: it allowed him to build more of what he called his 'New Testament' ships – the battlecruiser – and, since as First Sea Lord he had stripped away much of Britain's imperial naval arsenal, to use the new ship as a worthy counter to his critics, even if the British weren't prepared for either Australia's or New Zealand's to be gunned with the higher 13.5in weapon such as ships like HMS *Iron Duke* were being given.

I agree wholeheartedly with Arthur Marder's dictum (quoted by Wright) that history is an evolving discussion: I have learned much in these wonderfully written pages. HMS *New Zealand* was a ship whose crew and country stood solidly behind with deep pride. When the ship first toured the world in 1913, nearly half a million people went aboard and in New Zealand an astonishing third of the new nation took the opportunity to visit their ship. In the words of her first captain, Lionel Halsey, the tour became 'the means of creating a great wave of imperial loyalty'. It was a public relations triumph, though one not without its challenges and diplomatic difficulties.

Writing the foreword to Matthew Wright's *Battlecruiser HMS New Zealand: A Gift to Empire* feels like closing a circle; it is an honour to have been asked to do so.

Nick Jellicoe
Jongny, Switzerland, February 2021

INTRODUCTION

In March 1909 New Zealand's Premier, Joseph Ward, offered Britain 'one first-class battleship of the latest type' and, 'if subsequent events show it to be necessary', a second.[1] It was an astonishing gesture by a colony whose population stood at under a million – on the face of it a grand show of loyalty at a time when Britain was suffering a public crisis of confidence over the scale of its naval forces. The gift catapulted New Zealand to brief prominence across the Empire, momentarily capturing the moral high ground in an age of social militarism, a time when fantasies of battlefield glory had yet to be blown out of the public imagination by the hard realities of industrial-age warfare.

This book is the story of that gift; the story of the human shapes and patterns that drove a major warship into existence and then shaped her career. Along the way we shall meet the politicians whose dreams created her and the naval officers whose arguments shaped her. We shall explore how the ship was paid for and built, then follow her career from her world-spanning public relations tour of 1913 through the key battles of the First World War, to her final hurrah as a home and office for Admiral of the Fleet Sir John Jellicoe.

We shall also explore some of the myths and legends that swirl about this vessel. HMS *New Zealand*'s political origins and intended purpose, in particular, have been subject to ongoing misapprehension, including the curious assertion that the New Zealand government intended the ship for local service but belatedly realised it could not be maintained.[2] This was simply untrue. Other accounts misrepresent the order of events.[3] In and around these stand a plethora of other long-standing mythologies, such as the notion that the purchase was unaffordable for a small dominion; or that the gift was financially constrained, which is why it was built as a battlecruiser; or that the ship was funded by a single loan, not paid off until two decades or so after she had been scrapped.[4] Some of this is outright wrong and none of it, as we shall see, is strictly true.

One of the persistent stories remains the cause of *New Zealand*'s extraordinary luck in the North Sea battles. Despite being amidst some of the most intense fighting of Britain's naval war, she was scarcely damaged. Her deliverance was usually put down, sailor chat insisted, to a hei tiki (pendant) and piupiu (warrior's skirt) given to the ship's captain, Lionel Halsey, during the 1913 visit to New Zealand, on promise that it would protect the vessel from danger if worn in battle.[5] This legend – which, as we shall see, was primarily generated aboard the ship itself – masked the circumstance of the gifts from the Māori and their intended local function as political devices. We shall explore that issue in this book.

Ultimately – as with all history – the story of HMS *New Zealand* is a human tale: the story of the people whose work and lives entwined with the ship, from the politicians that drove her into being, to the men who built her; from her first captain, Lionel Halsey, to officers and crew such as Midshipman Edmund Coore, the New Zealand-born officer Lieutenant Alexander David Boyle and others. At a time when 'great men' could contribute a flavour to socio-political events, a key player remains Joseph Ward, the ambitious Liberal party politician whose personal papers were burned on his death in 1930. Another major figure was Admiral Sir John Fisher, the controversial naval reformer who fancied himself England's second Nelson.[6] There was also Winston Churchill, the mercurial, ambitious politician whose place as First Lord of the Admiralty from 1912 gave him a significant role in *New Zealand*'s fortunes.

Perhaps the main character remains Admiral of the Fleet Sir John Jellicoe, Earl Jellicoe of Scapa; the professional and thoughtful officer responsible for maintaining Britain's First World War supremacy at sea. His career was entwined with the ship in surprising ways. As Controller in 1909 he was responsible for *New Zealand*'s building contracts; in his various duties with the Admiralty he was behind some of the technologies aboard – and his service career concluded with *New Zealand*'s last voyage, when the ship became his home for a year.

This book is written for a general readership as well as those whose interest is more focused on naval matters. As such it includes explanations of naval terms and history that are perhaps already familiar to some. It is also intentionally broad. History demands context, and the story of *New Zealand* is no exception. In 1996, James Goldrick suggested that a new approach was required for 'industrial era' naval history: one that embraced the financial, policy, personal and strategic sides of the field; was technically informed; and with methodologies able to achieve a synthesis of both archival and 'other sources'. This historiographical revolution was, as Goldrick observed, on its way in that field at the time.[7] Such an approach had long been understood to be true generally of wider study; and the advent of the 'information revolution' has, if anything, amplified the point.

Goldrick's formula is not the only way of approaching the breadth required of a ship's 'biography'. In this book the focus is initially on the origins of the ship, the social and political forces that drove her existence, her role and popular reception. We then turn to the tale of her construction and how she was paid for – a story wrapped in politics and the intricacies of government debt funding, a story that engaged a wide swathe of British industry – revealing how well integrated shipbuilding was with Britain's economy of the day. The last third of the book explores the ship's main battle experiences. We close with the story of her last voyage, as transport, office and home for Jellicoe on his mission to offer naval advice to a changed Empire; and with the way both the debt and memorabilia were handled by the New Zealand government. To this extent the story of *New Zealand* is a case study, a lens through which to view the rise and fall of the 'dreadnought' era.

Throughout we have to remember that the documents by which we capture glimpses of the past are products of human endeavour and, by that nature, subjective. In the case of *New Zealand* even statistical data – such as the number of shells fired by particular guns – varies depending on the account. The official record, for instance, indicates a dozen shells were fired by X-turret at the Battle of Heligoland Bight, but the records of the turret commander listed fourteen.[8] And that is without considering the variable times logged during naval battles for events that were clearly simultaneous.[9] Put another way, humanity intrudes at all levels – including record-keeping. The issue reinforces the point that the study of history must be a reasonable discussion.

Times are given per the twelve-hour clock. Military time was adopted by the Royal Navy in mid-1915, but the older form was used by participants in personal letters and even official records afterwards, including some of *New Zealand*'s formal documents. Later, the twelve-hour clock was used in Britain's official 1920 publication of the Jutland despatches.[10] Measurements are similarly given in period terms. Another point to note is the way the British formally named their naval guns, by bore, in decimalised inches.

Photographs have been selected for purpose. In an age when archives are putting their holdings online – and where these are increasingly being circulated on social media – there seems little to add by repeating better-known images of *New Zealand*. During research for this book, however, I was offered glass plate negatives and located ephemera – including diagrams drawn aboard the ship itself – which had not previously been published. The main exception is the superb portrait of *New Zealand* at Lyttelton in 1919, which remains one of the most sublime images of any warship of the period, and for which associated information is published here for the first time.

Sources include manuscripts and files held by Archives New Zealand and the National Library of New Zealand, notably *New Zealand*'s Captain's Ship's Book; the builders' drawings; and selected Admiralty records, along with academic literature and selected secondary publications where relevant. Challenges along the way included the Covid-19 pandemic and lockdowns.

I am grateful to Julian Mannering and the team at Seaforth publishing; and to Peter Dowling of Oratia Books, for making this book possible. I also thank my colleagues and others in the field who have so generously given their time, expertise and resources throughout the project, particularly Nick Jellicoe for his kind offer to read the draft manuscript and write the foreword. Bill Jurens offered valuable thoughts on the loss of HMS *Queen Mary* and the subsequent mystery 'explosion' felt aboard *New Zealand*. Ian Johnston kindly provided pictures of *New Zealand*'s launch and offered useful insight into Fairfield's operations. Richard Brook kindly gave permission for use of a manuscript in his family collection by Arthur Smith, *New Zealand*'s gunnery officer at Jutland, for facilitating which I am also grateful to Stephen Clifford. Lemuel Lyes generously supplied a range of *New Zealand* ephemera and glass plate negatives, published here for the first time. Rachael Stallard of the Royal New Zealand Navy Museum at Torpedo Bay, Devonport, generously assisted with photographs. The staff of the Alexander Turnbull Library and Archives New Zealand were, as always, supportive in my quest for both records and images.

Matthew Wright

CHAPTER 1
THE PRUSSIA OF THE PACIFIC

Around noon on 28 August 1914, nineteen-year-old Edmund Coore waited at his action station aboard the battlecruiser *New Zealand*. He was a 'snotty', a midshipman – a young trainee officer who was required to know about the ship and its systems. But he had no precedent for what was about to happen. War had broken out three and a half weeks earlier, and the ship was pushing into a misty Heligoland Bight, home waters of Germany's High Seas Fleet. Light cruisers and destroyers from the Royal Navy's Harwich-based forces had gone in earlier in the day to engage German light forces, and had called for help. Now five British battlecruisers were racing in, under command of Vice-Admiral Sir David Beatty aboard his flagship *Lion*,[1] followed by *Queen Mary*, *Princess Royal* and *New Zealand*, with the slower Invincible trailing behind.[2]

In theory these ships were about to dominate a battlefield that, the British expected, would consist only of light ships.[3] It was a moment to savour. To the public, battlecruisers were the cavalry of the fleet and Beatty their dashing hero commander.[4] Just five days earlier the British Expeditionary Force, despatched to the Continent to join the French, had engaged the huge First Army of *Generaloberst* Alexander von Kluck at Mons in south-western Belgium and been forced to retreat. British papers were abuzz with the moment, the first time British soldiers had confronted an enemy on continental soil since Napoleon's day.[5] But now, as the British plunged deep into German home waters, the navy seemed about to even the score.

There was only one problem. Certainly, the battlecruisers racing through the Heligoland Bight that day in 1914 were among the largest warships afloat, faster than some crack transatlantic ocean liners of the day. They carried some of the most powerful weapons yet built in the history of the world, with precision-engineered guns that could hurl shells weighing around half a ton or more to the horizon.[6] They were protected by steel armour that stretched period chemistry. They deployed the latest technology of the age, everything from electric lighting and telephones to complex electro-mechanical computing devices. None of this was cheap. Most of the heavy ships plunging into German home waters that day had cost British taxpayers sums approaching 2 million pounds sterling – except for *New Zealand*, whose cost was levied against New Zealand taxpayers; and this in an era when a pound of flour could be got for ninepence.[7] Yet, for all the wealth and ingenuity poured into them, the battlecruisers had never been used in combat. Britain's Napoleonic-era naval commanders such as Richard Howe, George Rodney and Horatio Nelson could draw on around two centuries' worth of active experience with ships of the line. In August 1914, by contrast, actual combat experience with industrial-era warships was minimal. In theory, David Beatty's battlecruisers were going to perform well. In practice, nobody knew.

Edmund Coore's main problem – shared with most of the 789 officers and men on board *New Zealand* – was that he could not see what was going on. His action station was in the closed confines of the aft gun house, 'X-turret', a claustrophobic space dominated by the breeches of two Mk X 12in guns and their loading equipment. The only people with a direct view were the gun layers, including the turret commander, Lieutenant Alexander David Boyle – a New Zealander, known to his friends as David – who was peering through a protective hood poking through the roof at the front of the gun house. Even then, instructions as to where to point the gun came from the Transmitting Station, the heart of a fire-control process that began with the

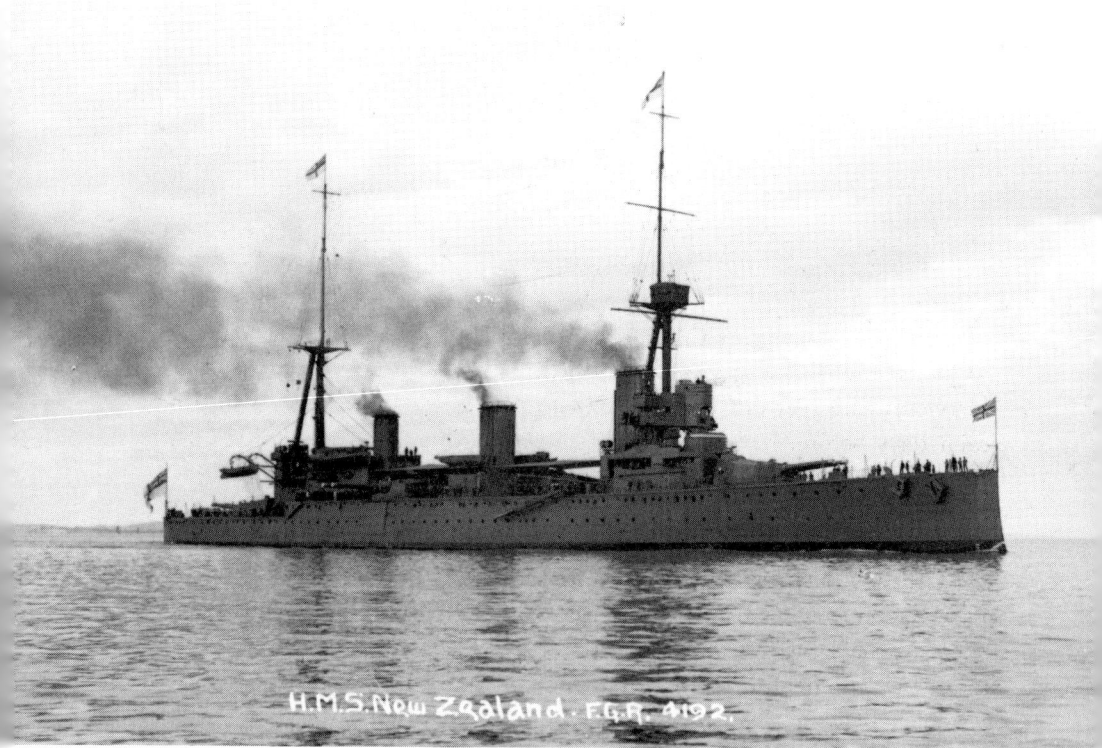

Period postcard of HMS *New Zealand*.
(*Lemuel Lyes Collection*)

team in the ship's spotting top, high on the foremast.[8] Coore's lack of view rankled, perhaps the more so because the gun crews were idle.[9] However, none of the officers and men working the munition supply system that stretched down to the shell rooms and magazines in the depths of the ship had a view either.[10] Their task was to feed the guns in a multi-step process designed to bring 850lb shells and 65lb cordite propellant charges – four per shot – to the breeches while keeping the gun house isolated.[11] Fire could not be allowed to spread to the cordite magazines; this would destroy the vessel.

For Coore, in the aftermost turret, the only sign that the ship was entering battle was the way the deck was shaking. Pre-war publicity had called the way *New Zealand*'s stern oscillated at speed a 'slight tremor'.[12] But in the waters of the bight, Coore's gun house was vibrating so much that, as both he and the official ship's report noted, the crew had trouble hearing instructions coming through their Graham Navyphones.[13] Coore, who had filled his midshipman's workbook with diagrams of the ship's systems,[14] knew what this meant. *New Zealand* was surging through the water, her propellers spinning at something over the design maximum of 275rpm and – as a side effect – slamming water against the bottom of the hull in a succession of quick-fire blows that resonated into the structure.[15] This also meant the ship was doing a little over 26 knots.[16]

That speed was slightly more than she had been designed for,[17] a feat all the more remarkable because the coal that made it possible was delivered to the fire boxes by human muscle power. Some 335 men out of the ship's official complement of 789[18] were dedicated to working the engines and boilers.[19] Of these, around 200 were stokers who fed the furnaces whenever the gongs and lights of the Kilroy stoking indicators demanded it.[20] They were often young men, among them twenty-two-year-old John Cottier, who had joined the ship seven weeks earlier; eighteen-year-old Aaron Cunane; and twenty-one-year-old Robert Emberson, who had joined the ship just eleven days before.[21] But he was an old hand by comparison with John Hudson and Ernest Hepburn, both aboard less than a week, and both twenty-six years of age.[22]

Those in charge were more experienced. Thirty-nine-year-old Stoker Petty Officer Thomas Taggart had been aboard since the ship commissioned. So had Stoker Petty Officer Francis Veal, also thirty-nine.[23] One of the chief stokers, Michael Griffith, was an Irishman hailing from Donegal, and he was almost ancient – by stoking standards – at forty-two years of age.[24] Such was the human shape of this world of dust and labour in the bowels of the ship, cut off from the outside, working to what by later standards was the dim and distinctly yellow glow of electric lamps.

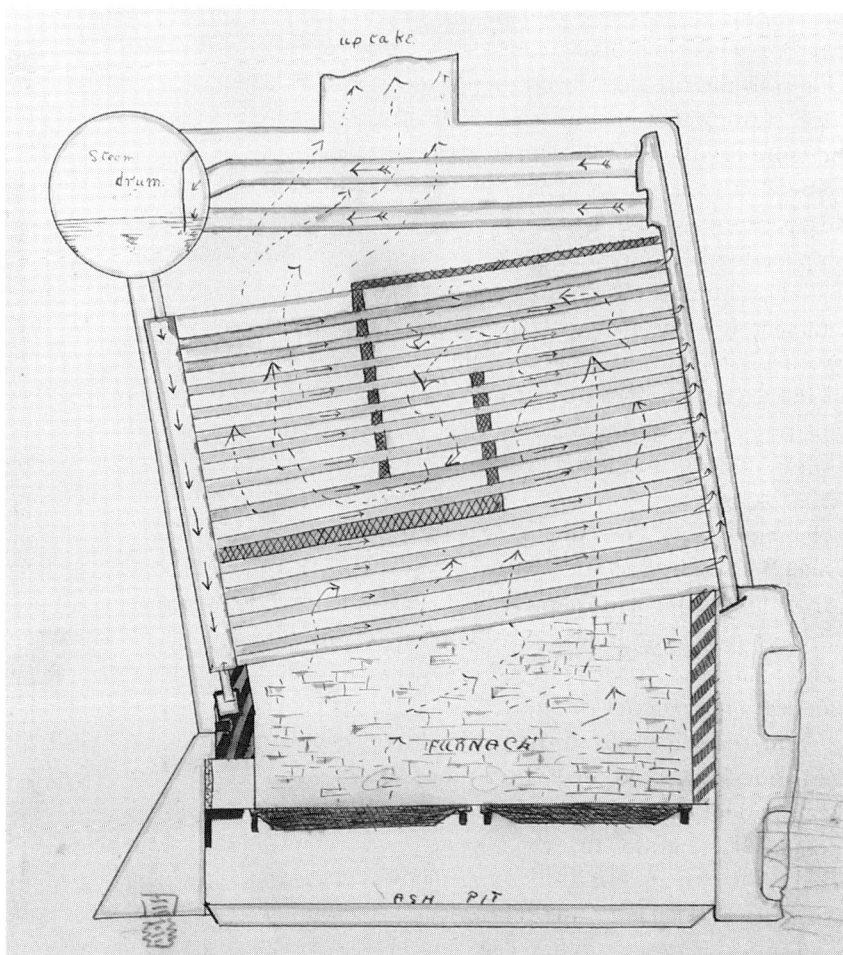

Midshipman Edmund Coore was required to understand and draw *New Zealand*'s systems as part of his training. This is a detail from his diary, showing a Babcock & Wilcox boiler.
(*Detail from qMS-0545, Coore, E G B, fl.1913–1914: Journal, Alexander Turnbull Library*)

Now, Cottier, Emberson, Cunane and their colleagues were working like Trojans. The furnaces – three to each of the thirty-one boilers – were roaring. The coal, dug out of the rich seams of Wales,[25] burned hot under sprays of oil and a fan-driven forced draft that pushed oxygen into the fire.[26] Eventually, the stokers knew, the mix of coal and oil would generate a tarry residue that was difficult to clean off.[27] But for now the men feeding those fires were enduring the labours of Sisyphus. The 'trimmers', as they were called, brought coal from the bunkers on trolleys and dumped it on the foot-plates;[28] at once the stokers scooped it into the grates, aiming for any place inside the fire box where the blaze seemed low. They were bathed in heat: the men closest to the fire doors were hosed to keep them cool.[29] Their efforts sent 'dry' steam – hot enough to lack water droplets – into the turbines at a pressure of around 250 pounds per square inch. The result was an output somewhat over the designed 44,000 horsepower,[30] sending *New Zealand* surging forwards at the maximum velocity that water depth, hull fouling and ship loading allowed that day.[31]

These numbers were, of course, academic: the more important issue in the moment was the fact that the ship was going into action, and the men labouring to feed the boilers – more than a third of the crew – knew their chances would be bleak if the ship went down. Nor could they see out: their sole knowledge of the battle came from the engine telegraph orders and the thump of their own guns. Yet ironically, even those with a view could see little that day, as Coore discovered when the gun crew went outside during a brief stand down. He found it 'very hard to distinguish anything owing to the haze'.[32] Visibility was apparently between 6,000 and 8,000yd,[33] well inside the range of the main armament. Around 1pm, by Coore's recollection[34] – 12.50pm according to another account[35] – the flash of enemy guns became visible and *New Zealand* opened fire. Coore's turret did not: their guns could not bear on the target.[36]

Still, the ship's part in the battle had begun – and for the fifty-odd New Zealanders on board, that was a moment to remember. The ship may have been part of the Royal Navy and primarily crewed by Britons, but *New Zealand* was emotionally 'their' vessel, a gift from the government of New Zealand to Britain. For the New Zealanders aboard it was the chance to show what their dominion – the self-styled 'best' of Britain's children – could do for Empire at a time when, social priorities insisted, heroism, glory and social honour were due rewards of war.[37] And in August 1914 that mindset had yet to be blasted out of society by the brutal human truths of the First World War, both on land and at sea.[38]

We shall return to the First Battle of Heligoland. *New Zealand*'s presence in those waters was no accident. She was a gift: a gift to Empire by a dominion of just on a million souls. She was also a gift without strings attached. And all this demands explanation. Why did New Zealand, one of Britain's smaller dominions, make such an expensive offering to their parent?

In this sense the gift was founded in more than a particular ship or a knee-jerk effort to support Britain. At heart it was about a *concept* of Empire held in New Zealand, a concept that stood against thinking in the Admiralty specifically, and in Imperial official circles generally. The gift was also about how New Zealand's political leaders pursued their concept of Empire by exploiting a social naval 'panic' in an effort to hijack pro-Imperial sentiment that, elsewhere, was filtered through very different local lenses. To explain the gift, then, we must begin by briefly exploring this environment and the principle Joseph Ward's government exploited – social militarism.

Social militarism – the popular adulation of military action, personnel and hardware, and the entanglement of this mix with national identity – had long been around by the nineteenth century.[39] However, it was given new life by the Crimean War of the mid-1850s and gained pace over the next few generations, driven in part by a significant hardening of attitude towards Empire that came with the Indian uprising of 1857–58.[40] Britain had not fought a major war since Napoleon's time, and the Crimean struggle was large enough to seem exciting, far enough away to pose little danger at home. It was socially promoted through photography, a wonder technology of the day that seized public imagination.[41] All this helped reinforce and embed the long-standing notion by which the battlefield was an exalted sports ground where status could be gained by heroic deed.[42] Even a disaster such as the charge by the Light Brigade at Balaclava could be redeemed by such imagery.[43] Over the next decades this style of thinking became part of British life. Vicarious military glory was seductive, compelling and – ultimately – patriotic to a population who had not known a major war in their lifetimes. 'Who would not die for England!' Alfred Austin eventually declared, '… Stern to every voice but Hers …'[44]

A public ideology that glorified military action, idolised military hardware, and entwined the whole with patriotic fervour soon gained a name: jingoism, from a word coined in 1878 by G W Hunt for a music hall song riffing on the Russian 'war scare' that year.[45] The same year, William Booth's Christian Mission became the 'Salvation Army'.[46] By the 1880s military symbolism was everywhere. Children were being dressed up in sailor suits. There was a roaring trade in 'cigarette cards', often printed with pictures celebrating the latest battleships, cruisers guarding the Empire's seaways, portraits of senior officers, or some other expression of Britain's military might.[47] When W S Gilbert and Arthur Sullivan lampooned Major General Sir Garnet Wolseley as the 'very model of a modern Major General', they knew everybody would get the joke.[48]

These developments shifted popular focus towards military power as a definition of national strength and security,[49] entwining it with identity and – as has been argued – definitions of masculinity.[50] It was socially seductive; and the fact that Britain's true power rested on the scale of the merchant marine, trade, and the economy mattered little.

This style of social militarism gained further focus in Britain during the last decades of the nineteenth century as new European rivalry erupted. This was most loudly expressed in Africa, where Britain's interests were championed by Cecil Rhodes in the south and – after 1882 – by the British establishment in Egypt,[51] fuelling ambitions for a 'Cape to Cairo' rail link.[52] However, Britain was only one of several European nations scrabbling to intrude into the continent.[53] And while Europe's national rivalries were sublimated away from their own borders, the underlying drivers – industrialisation, Europe's economic growth, and with that a rising challenge to Britain's pre-eminence as a global power – were clear enough.

This mix of social expectation and political rivalry was given spice by a raft of new military technologies. Iron, steel and steam revolutionised warfare on land and at sea. Weapons gained power that could only be dreamed of in Napoleonic times. By the 1870s there was debate over whether it was better to build battleships or swarms of 'torpedo boats'.[54] But if battleships were to be built, how were they to be designed? Even gun mountings – turreted or in open barbettes – were up for debate.[55] Then there was the problem of technological pace, rendering major warships obsolete before they were completed. When such issues were combined with years-long construction times and government parsimony, battleship construction became halting.

Public unease across Britain gained further power in 1884 when government dithered over the naval estimates and the Royal Navy responded by trying to swing popular opinion.[56] The charge was led by Captain John Fisher, the navy's *enfant terrible*, who lobbied the cause through the *Pall Mall Gazette*.[57] It was a radical shift: Nelson's 'band of brothers' were meant to remain politically aloof and silent. The eventual outcome – to which the Prime Minister, William Gladstone, objected but had to buckle[58] – was the 'Northbrook Programme'. This committed £3,100,000 over the next five years on warships, and a further £2,400,000 for static naval works that included developing a global network of coaling stations.[59] This last was salutary: for all the panic, the Admiralty had longer-term goals in mind. Coal was boring by comparison with the glory the public assigned to a naval battles, but by the 1880s such battles could not occur without it.

The outcome was remarkable given that Britain was in the economic doldrums during the 1880s.[60] A further naval 'scare' in 1888 – again with service voices clear in the media – led to the 1889 'Naval Defence Act'. This committed the British government to spending £21,500,000 over the next three years on a range of new vessels, including eight first-class battleships. It also came with a clincher: a standard by which the Royal Navy was to be maintained to 'such a scale that it should be at least equal to the naval strength of any two other countries'.[61]

This 'two power standard' was a signal to Germany, France and Russia that Britain was prepared to meet their economic challenge. Inevitably it fuelled French and Russian responses that, in turn, triggered a further British naval 'scare' in 1893.[62] Gladstone was opposed to further large-scale new construction, and the result was a fracas in which officers such as Beresford waded into the fray. When opposition politician Lord George Hamilton proposed increased naval funding in November, Gladstone decided to turn the issue into a no confidence vote, which his administration won. On the back of that he rubbished public 'panics' and told Hamilton that nobody need 'entertain the smallest apprehension' over British naval superiority.[63] There was, he insisted during Parliamentary debate on 19 November, no emergency.[64]

Others begged to differ, and matters came to a head in December, when the First Lord, John Spencer,[65] proposed a five-year programme featuring nine battleships and other vessels. At £31 million, this new scheme was vastly more expensive than the one authorised by the 1889 Defence Act.[66] Gladstone dragged the chain, addressing Parliament on 8 January 1894 with a plan for slower construction.[67] But he came under pressure. There was talk of his resignation through the first weeks of 1894, and on 27 February he told the Queen he would go. He announced his departure to what he called his 'blubbering Cabinet' on 1 March.[68]

The crisis – the third in nine years – underscored the new pattern. In this age of politicised social militarism, when the British public panicked over naval matters, government had to listen. The details varied each time, but the outcome usually did not.

The public mindset that buoyed this trend was broadly shared across the British Empire, further flavoured by local perceptions. One of the variations was in New Zealand, where the final two decades of the nineteenth century brought a significant reinvention of self-image. British settlers had flooded into New Zealand from 1840,[69] but early ambitions for a 'bigger' and socially 'better' Britain in the South Pacific were dashed. It was hard to attract settlers: the nineteenth century was Britain's great age of migration, but it was expensive to get to New Zealand.[70] Nor did ambition meet reality. There was brief prosperity on the back of gold in the early 1860s, joined by a wool boom driven by the Civil War in the United States; but both then stalled. Then, in the 1870s, government tried to boost the colony by spending on a grand scale. One of the strategies was a push for new colonists, by social legend from Scandinavia; but by numbers, mainly from Britain.[71]

The result was a socially significant influx of migrants through the 1870s and 1880s for whom Britain was 'home'. One outcome was a renewed focus on Britain as parent and validator. At the same time, New Zealand's colonial-age power structures faded as the colony grew, supplanted by a world of bureaucracies, town councils and political parties. At first there was one party, the Liberals, who came to power in 1890, introduced wide-ranging reforms designed to break the hegemony of colonial-age landed elites, and who recast older colonial ambition into one that portrayed New Zealand as Britain's best child. The champion of it from 1893 was Richard Seddon, the colourful Premier and former rough-house publican from Kumara whose nickname, 'King Dick', summarised his power and repute.[72]

With this came a notion that New Zealand was vulnerable. At the time naval defence was provided by the Australasian Squadron, based in Sydney, whose heaviest ships were cruisers. Admiralty opinion was that any large-scale intrusion into Australasian waters would be cut off by British naval forces based in Hong Kong. The problem was that the perception in Wellington, and around the various Australian colonial capitals, differed from the way things were seen in London; and the New Zealand sense of vulnerability was further driven by the 1,200-mile width of the Tasman. This point needs explanation, because this dissonance – at heart – is what then drove the gift ship.

During the last decades of the nineteenth century New Zealand's expected enemy was Russia, a vision shaped by British perspectives and the so-called 'great game' being played out between British and Russian Empires. Popular alarm was first triggered in 1873 when Aucklanders reading their *Daily Southern Cross* discovered that their city had been held to ransom by a captured British warship. With the help of 'mephitic water-gas' and a 'submarine pinnace', the Russian cruiser *Kaskowiski* had apparently taken control of a British cruiser visiting Auckland's Waitemata harbour, and demanded a £250,000 ransom from the authorities to stop the city being bombarded. The joke was obvious to anybody who read the name aloud, but the brief furore that followed triggered a new debate over defence – as the editor, David Luckie, intended.[73] The Empire-wide Russian 'war scares' of 1878 and 1885 intensified these fears. They were shared by Britain's other Australasian colonies, and one outcome was a brisk discussion over naval defence at the 1887 Colonial Conference, Britain's regular forum for discussion with her Empire. Here the Admiralty agreed that the seven Australasian colonies could pay for five cruisers and two torpedo boats to supplement the Australasian Squadron.[74] New Zealand's contribution began in the 1891–92 financial year and varied from £20,304 to £21,534.[75]

The flip side of New Zealand's self-image was an effort by the government to act on behalf of what it imagined Britain wanted in the South

Pacific. Germany, France and the United States were expanding into the region by the turn of the twentieth century. Seddon began doing the same in the name of Mother England. He even coveted Hawai'i. In the event, Fiji turned down Seddon's offers of annexation in 1900–01,[76] but he brought the Cook Islands and Niue under the New Zealand – hence, to his mind, British – wing. None of this went down well in London, and Seddon's subsequent efforts over Samoa were not welcomed by the Foreign Office.[77] This single-minded push did, however, give New Zealand the repute of being the 'Prussia of the Pacific', betraying a mindset that even the British felt was jingoistic. When Queen Victoria's last 'little war' broke out in South Africa in 1899,[78] members of New Zealand's Parliament stood and sang the British national anthem. There was a scrabble to join the fighting; an initial contingent of 204 men and eleven officers were rushed to South Africa.[79] In the end more than 6,000 Kiwis reached the war zone, and at least one wrote to his mother wishing for death as a road to better glory than being captured.[80]

All this came at a time when Britain's seven Australasian colonies were wobbling towards union, New Zealand among them. Australia's reasons for

An official Christmas card from 1899 from Premier Richard Seddon to
the first contingent to be despatched to South Africa.
(*Eph-A-CARDS-Christmas-Seddon-1899-cover. Alexander Turnbull Library,
Wellington, New Zealand*)

local federation have been described by one analyst as an intersection of nationalism and imperialism that gained ground from the 1880s.[81] The politics run outside the scope of this book: but the key point is that, in the end New Zealand – as Frank Wood put it – teetered away.[82] When it came to a Parliamentary vote over joining the new Commonwealth of Australia there were more abstentions than other voices. Exactly why has been subject to academic debate; but New Zealand had its own subculture, its own sense of identity, and Seddon thought his colony would be run from across the Tasman.[83] In the end, when the Commonwealth of Australia came into being on the first day of January 1901, New Zealand went from being one of seven roughly similar Australasian colonies, to the smallest of two. It was a pivotal change that, as we shall see, played a large part in the origins of the gift ship.

This, then, was the relationship between New Zealand and the British Empire by the first years of the twentieth century. It was an Empire at the zenith of its economic and naval power, but an Empire under challenge, whose populace feared nemesis. It was also an evolving Empire: its major colonies – Canada, the new Commonwealth of Australia, South Africa and New Zealand – were offered independent status within the structure. New Zealand procrastinated, not joining the dominion club until 1907, and even then portraying it as an act of loyalty to the parent. It was an empire where the trappings of military life had been adopted as badges of status and identity by the public, where naval power – particularly – was viewed as a gauge of imperial strength, and where by the early twentieth century there was a history of governments being swayed by public agitation whenever that strength was supposed to have fallen short.

All this meant that New Zealand was going to respond – somehow – to the way the first decade of the twentieth century changed Britain's naval defence position; and was going to do so from the perspective of being the smallest child in the Australasian room, desperately eager to have its voice heard. However, that did not automatically mean gifting a warship. Why, then, did Joseph Ward feel impelled to make the offer? It is to these dramatic interplays of politics and people that we now turn.

CHAPTER 2

AN IMPETUOUS OFFER?

To his critics and many historians alike, the offer by New Zealand Premier and Minister of Defence Joseph Ward to buy a dreadnought for Britain was the impetuous child of his jingoism and erratic policy making, a knee-jerk reaction to a naval crisis, given personal force by his desire for public profile. His successor as Minister of Defence, Colonel James Allen, denied that Ward had any consistent naval policy.[1] This view has been echoed by historians who have often portrayed Ward's 1909 offer as little more than an impulsive response to the latest panic over Imperial security.[2] The first New Zealand naval defence policy has generally been seen as originating with the government of William Massey, which succeeded Ward's in 1912.[3] Arguably, as we shall see, Massey's government also lacked coherent policy; and Ward's was always going to fail, meaning it was the interwar years before anything other than stopgap efforts emerged.[4]

Either way, there was more to Ward's motives than a simple response to a London naval panic, as we shall explore. Much of it, in the end, came down to the way the British Empire evolved against the backdrop of changing world politics as the nineteenth century drew to a close and the twentieth began to unfold. Internal issues included the ongoing devolution of power to some of the larger colonies, now styled self-governing dominions. There were other issues meeting defence costs, which the First Sea Lord from 1904 – the volcanic and combative Admiral Sir John Fisher – met with new strategies that, as we shall see, fed directly into Ward's lap. New external challenges included the economic power of a unified Germany. That crept up slowly, in part masked by close family ties between the nations. Some Germans – including Prince Louis of Battenberg – were naturalised British and high-ranking officers in the Royal Navy. His eldest son George served aboard *New Zealand*.[5]

Britain's main problem by the late 1890s was what George Foster called 'splendid isolation'[6] in a world where central Europe was rising. This complicated Britain's long-standing policy of nudging continental power balances so that no one group dominated. The Triple Alliance of 1882 brought Germany and Italy together with the Austro-Hungarian Empire to create a significant power bloc. French unease at these developments prompted them to seek alliance with Russia in 1894. Although colonial rivalries in Africa proxied many of Europe's rivalries away from the Continent, the Far East became a further trigger point, as European interests in China vied with those of a rapidly industrialising Japan.

Britain declined to join an ad hoc power bloc formed by France, Germany and Russia to knock Japan out of the Liaodong peninsula and the harbour of Port Arthur in 1895. However, British backing for Japan, captured in such arrangements as the 1895 Anglo-Japanese Treaty of Commerce and Navigation, offered direction. As a result, for the first time since the Napoleonic wars Britain sought an alliance, signed with Japan on 30 January 1902. Neither party was obligated to join the other if war broke out, and its role was partly geo-political, removing Japan from European rivalries in Korea and China. It relieved Britain of a defence burden across the Far East and western Pacific. And, as we shall see, it was pivotal to the chain of events that led to *New Zealand*.

Possible alliance between Britain and France had been on the table since the early 1880s, though barriers included competing interests in Africa, Southeast Asia, the Pacific and elsewhere. Britain declined to join the Triple Alliance in 1901. However, the Russo-Japanese crisis over Manchuria, which erupted in the wake of the Boxer rebellion of 1900, gained new intensity during 1903. Neither Britain nor France were prepared to support their respective allies by going to war themselves. Instead they finalised a 'cordial agreement' to support each other. This was signed on 8 April 1904, two months after war broke out between Russia and Japan. The *Entente Cordiale* was less alliance than a platonic dance between John Bull and Marianne, and it highlighted another reality. Germany and Britain were being pushed to opposite sides of a growing divide in power balances.

These developments gained intensity from naval rivalries. Here, Britain kept ahead of the game for a while. From the Naval Defence Act of 1889 to the Estimates of 1903–04 inclusive, the British government authorised forty-five battleships in several major classes, most of them representing variations and incremental improvements on the theme set by the *Royal Sovereign* class of 1889–90.[7] Their names were redolent of an Empire that drew inspiration both from the classical world and from its own place in history: *Caesar*, *Mars*, *Jupiter*, *Majestic*, *Goliath*, *Hindustan* and *Formidable* among them. This armada and their five 'second-class' associates – including two building for Chile, which were purchased in 1903 at £949,900 each to keep them out of Russian hands[8] – were backed by thirty-one armoured cruisers laid down from 1895.[9] They were joined by smaller vessels and by the older ships built in prior decades. Many of the older warships were small and obsolescent, but they were fixtures of harbours around the globe and made the Royal Navy ubiquitous. If trouble brewed, a gunboat with its crew of bluejackets was never far away.[10] Beyond these forces lay the reserve fleet, older ironclad battleships and cruisers rendered obsolete by the march of technology, but allowed to swing around their moorings with maintenance crews, preserved from the scrappers – for a while – just in case.

In 1903–04 no other navy came close to the power of the Royal Navy. But the effort had been expensive, and successive British governments – Liberal and Conservative alike – remained uneasy about the 'two-power' measure when there were other calls on the government budget. In May 1904, when William Palmer, the Second Earl of Selborne and First Lord of the Admiralty, informed Admiral Sir John Fisher that he was to be appointed First Sea Lord, the news came with a clear rider. Fisher's job was to cut naval spending.[11]

Described by Prime Minister H H Asquith as 'domineering and combative',[12] Fisher was the *enfant terrible* of the service. His writing was laced with acronyms he often concocted on the spot, multiple underlinings and Biblical quotations.[13] He was addicted to dancing, particularly with attractive women; and he fancied himself Britain's second Nelson – this to the point where, eventually, he found his own Lady Hamilton.[14] And he pursued his goals with relentless drive. As First Sea Lord, Fisher intentionally cultivated his favourites, regarding them as trustworthy and competent protégés – a policy that gave rise to criticisms of nepotism.[15] The 'optics' of this behaviour were not helped by the fact that Fisher did not hesitate to ruin the careers of junior officers who crossed him, and to pursue vendettas against his equals.[16] His motto became 'Fear God and Dread Nought', but perhaps it should have been the phrase with which he prefaced his 1904 reform scheme: 'we must be ruthless, relentless and remorseless!'[17]

Fisher decided to take up his position on Trafalgar Day – 21 October[18] – and meanwhile produced his blueprint for change, a heady document he titled 'Naval Necessities'. In a sense he was simply building on the modernisation that had been under way for some time. A new education system designed to provide officers with skills fitted to modern warships had been under development since 1902 – at Fisher's own hands, in point of fact, as Second Sea Lord.[19] The Admiralty followed this, in 1903, with a 'nucleus crew' system, a way of keeping ships partially commissioned with a core of experienced sailors who could be supplemented if the vessel was required for service.[20]

Now, as First Sea Lord, Fisher took these initiatives and ran with them, eventually encompassing the whole navy, from its hardware to its culture.[21] The Royal Navy of the First World War era was not called the 'fleet that Jack built' for nothing. Maurice Hankey described Fisher as a 'hurricane'.[22] As First Sea Lord, Fisher brought everything under scrutiny from flogging –

suspended in 1881 and abolished under his administration – to uniforms and food.[23] Still, old social traditions died hard. Many long-standing issues survived into the First World War, not least the problem of officer initiative when faced with tactical awareness that might not be shared by the Commander in Chief.

Public attention was seized by Fisher's two big-ticket items. The first, keenly felt in New Zealand, was a radical fleet reorganisation. Against the shifts in Europe's power balances, changes were necessary in arrangements that had, for decades, been directed against France, Russia and – vaguely – other enemies. This was already under discussion when Fisher became First Sea Lord. What emerged, however, was shaped by Fisher's vision, a 'great scheme' that he had Battenberg review on 22 October 1904, the day after he took office.[24] Fisher had been a long-standing advocate of the 'blue water' school by which sea force was concentrated in key areas. Such ideas had been bandied about in the Admiralty since the 1880s; and arguably Fisher drew in part from the work of both Captain Colombs and the United States naval strategist Rear Admiral Alfred Thayer Mahan.[25] He visualised concentrations in five locations – the 'five keys [that] lock up the world'.[26] Three – Portsmouth, Gibraltar and Malta – were to be occupied by battle fleets. They would seal enemy fleets in the North Sea and the Mediterranean, securing the British Empire against all but a few raiding cruisers. One key to the system was radio, then known as 'wireless', by which the Admiralty could instantly order fleets to any location. Just half the ships in the fleet had wireless sets by 1904, and transmitters were still being distributed around shore stations.[27] But radio was, nonetheless, on its way.

The flip side was that Fisher could do away with the ships scattered about the globe and slash the Estimates by 30 per cent. Maurice Hankey thought the scale of Fisher's scrapping programme – some 156 vessels – was a ploy to gain approval of his scheme by Cabinet.[28] Fisher knew it would be opposed within the service, however, and implemented it by stealth. By chance, the 'battle of Dogger Bank' – where a Russian battle fleet mistook British trawlers for Japanese torpedo boats and attacked them – sent tensions skyrocketing just as Fisher took office.[29] Although ill and confined to bed in his Charing Cross hotel, Fisher signalled all foreign stations that war with Russia was imminent and sent lists of ships to pay off, after which the crews would be sent to Britain.[30] The ploy largely worked: some of the overseas ships were saved, but many were not. Fisher also wanted to withdraw the heavier ships from the China Station, but the First Lord William Palmer, Second Earl of Selborne, blocked it.[31] Instead, in the face of the Russo-Japanese war, Selborne managed to persuade Fisher to reinforce the British fleet at Hong Kong. But before these reinforcements arrived, the Japanese victory at

Tsushima broke Russian naval power. Fisher immediately withdrew all British battleships from the Pacific.[32]

There was an outcry. The power of technology to send heavy ships skittering about the globe did not compensate for the moral effect of cruisers disappearing from everyday sight in far-flung harbours. And that was apart from the bitterness felt by officers who lost their commands.

The outcome was not helped by Fisher's style. His mantra, 'instant readiness for war',[33] did not identify which enemies he had in mind, or what the British fleets would do when war broke out. Nor was he prepared to explain. Instead he hedged, arguing that, 'Russia might ... call on her ally France, and at the same time give Germany the opportunity for which Russia's secret ally is eagerly waiting.'[34] Taking as precedent the manoeuvring that followed the Sino-Japanese war of 1894–95, he wrote that a 'Franco-German-Russian coalition of powers ... it is as well to remember, *did actually combine* ... to rob Japan of the fruits of victory.'[35] Such utterances have fuelled suggestion since that Fisher was using the Royal Navy as a weapon of deterrence against Germany as early as 1904.[36] However, remarks to that effect may also have been bargaining points within the Admiralty and Cabinet: he did not openly see Germany as pre-eminent until later in 1907, when they became the 'only possible foe'.[37] This meant a greater concentration in the North Sea.[38] However, Fisher refused to release specific war plans, arguing this would merely inform the Germans.[39] The most plausible explanation for his conduct – proposed in 1973 by Paul Haggie – was that Fisher saw war planning as his prerogative, and his alone.[40] Such observation, generally, seems compelling: as always, both for Fisher and others, to reveal information associated with the assertion of power was also to concede that power. And Fisher was not one to relinquish power without a fight.

None of this was obvious to the public, and the perception of weakness created by mass scrapping and redistribution joined the other major shift Fisher brought to the navy: two new types of heavy warship. This resolved the problem of perceived weakness in one sense but compounded it in another – creating a stepping stone on New Zealand's path to the gift.

In some ways the story of Fisher's introduction of dreadnoughts and battlecruisers scarcely needs retelling. And yet, in other ways, it does if we are to understand why *New Zealand* was offered as a dreadnought, then built as a battlecruiser. In this, we have to understand the historical orthodoxy by which both types – *Dreadnought* especially – have since been seen as a discontinuity, dividing naval engineering and history like a guillotine. This idea was cultivated by Fisher, picked up as a popular truth by the public, and became a historical truism that has been reinforced since by specialist publications that typically 'break' at 1904 or 1905, splitting heavy warships into 'before' and 'after' Fisher's *Dreadnought*.[41]

The public power of Fisher's narrative was such that the idea of *Dreadnought*-as-revolution was not seriously questioned within the academy until the turn of the twenty-first century. History – as a field of research and endeavour – is always a process by which the meanings attributed to empirical data are discussed. These often change through time as new questions are posed, and ideally the discussion is civil and constructive. When it comes to the meanings of HMS *Dreadnought*, however, the historical debate can best be described as vigorous, underscoring both the socio-political impact of this ship, and the way Fisher visualised dreadnoughts, 'fusion' fast battleships, and battlecruisers.[42] We will look into this in more detail in the next chapter, because it is one of the key reasons why the New Zealand gift emerged as a battlecruiser. For now, the question is how the social notion of *Dreadnought* as a discontinuity gained public traction in 1907–08, because this was a key factor behind New Zealand's gift.

Heavy warship designs were in transition by the first years of the twentieth century, driven in part by the rise in battle ranges that came with an increase in heavy weapon capability. This range increase reduced the effectiveness of 6in batteries that, in the 1890s, had been seen as vital because of their ability to smash lightly armoured structures with a 'hail of fire'. Delivering longer-range metal through 'intermediate' weapons such as Britain's 9.2in gun was one answer, but homogenous main armament was another. This last had wide currency in naval circles worldwide by 1904. Fisher had been proposing such ships for a while, as had the Constructor's department. Both the United States and Japan were known to be considering them.[43] The approach offered advantages beyond simplified fire control. A single type of heavy ammunition also created on-board stowage efficiencies and – because of the logistic rationalisation – better cost control.[44]

One of Fisher's first actions as First Sea Lord was to appoint a committee to define what would be built for the 1905–06 programme. The numbers had been approved before the committee met, in part on Fisher's recommendation, at one battleship and three armoured cruisers. The committee met in ten sessions under Fisher from late 1904 into January 1905, and among other things developed two new types of capital ship: an all-big-gun battleship and its armoured cruiser homologue. Both were fast by 1904–05 standards, and Watts, for his part, anticipated Fisher's need, asking the Admiralty Experimental Works to produce estimated power curves for various hull forms.[45]

Fisher's speed was made possible without unacceptable rise in displacement thanks to turbine propulsion. Fisher had wanted steam turbines aboard heavy warships for some time, and they were adopted now with advice from Engineer Vice-Admiral Sir John Durston.[46] It was a gamble. Charles Parsons had set up a company to develop turbines for marine use in 1893. However, although results with the destroyer *Viper* and light cruiser *Amethyst* were promising, none had yet been fitted to a large warship when Fisher's committee met.[47] Fisher accepted the risk. There were two other downsides. One was that turbines, at this time, were less fuel efficient at lower speeds than triple-expansion engines. The other was that they still relied on steam from coal-fired boilers fed by human labour, a resource that could tire. Sustained turbine-driven cruise was possible. However, thanks to the draconian power-speed curve, sustained tactical sprint speeds over more than a few hours – the other implicit rationale for the system – were another matter.

Fisher insisted that details of the three cruisers authorised in the 1905–06 programme be kept secret.[48] By contrast, he lost no time promoting the battleship, even as it was under lightning-fast build. This was part of Fisher's propaganda mix: he insisted that the ship, dubbed *Dreadnought*, be completed in the Biblical timing of a year and a day, and pushed the Portsmouth dockyard hard to get it. They almost succeeded. The ship was laid down in October 1905, and a basin trial some 366 days afterwards sufficed for Fisher to declare completion. The results were reported around the world.[49] In reality the ship was not completed until early 1907, but the practical building time of around fourteen months was still astonishing. The fact that her main armament was prioritised over that of the earlier *Lord Nelson* class helped,[50] as did an effort to stockpile steel in anticipation of the build. But much was also down to the efforts of the labourers, whose working week expanded to sixty-nine hours.

The immediate impact of *Dreadnought* was certainly social: the media lapped up Fisher's words and passed them on to a military-minded public. His spicier leaks were often prefixed 'Burn and Destroy', which confidantes such as the journalist Arnold White knew meant 'publish', as long as Fisher was not implicated.[51] It did not take long for praise of *Dreadnought* to become hyperbolic. When announced in May 1905, the ship was described by the Press Association as a 'combination of battleship and cruiser' that was 'equal in fighting power to any two warships afloat'.[52] This was essentially true. But by early 1906 the *Engineer* insisted she could 'probably tackle the entire German battle fleet single handed'.[53] That was a stretch, but the popular idea of *Dreadnought* being an invincible super-ship gained pace, including in New Zealand. In May 1906 Fisher released details of her firepower.[54] Her launch and commissioning became headlines, and her trial trip to the Caribbean was followed eagerly around the Empire.[55]

Fisher's masterful promotion had its effect: *Dreadnought* gave her name, generically, to battleships of similar type that were emerging worldwide. This masked the fact that the older ships were still effective and largely up to date in 1906–07. From an engineering perspective, *Dreadnought* had many equipment commonalities with older ships, and – as the proposed X-4 'fusion' design of 1906 showed, the all-big-gun concept was clearly only at the start of its own development curve. The First Lord of the Admiralty, Edward Marjoribanks, second Baron Tweedmouth, made the Admiralty's position clear at the annual dinner in Sheffield's Cutler's Hall in October 1906, the month *Dreadnought* was splashed to the world as complete. The Royal Navy was 'immensely stronger than any other navy', whether 'in point of numbers of ships or in armament, armor [sic] and tonnage'.[56] However, his remarks did little to reduce the emotionally framed mix with which *Dreadnought* was otherwise generally received.

The public perception of *Dreadnought* as discontinuity was particularly awkward when set against emerging Anglo-German naval rivalry. That had been brewing for some time, but gained pace in the first years of the twentieth century. Although a *Kaiserliche Marine* (Imperial Navy), was authorised on German unification in 1871, the new German government – confronted by land enemies on both sides – was not eager to spend on a seagoing branch of the military. That stood against the ambition of Kaiser Wilhelm II, who came to power on the death of his father in 1888. Wilhelm gained an ally in the form of *Konteradmiral* Alfred Peter Friedrich von Tirpitz (1849–1930), who was appointed Secretary of the *Reichsmarineamt* (Imperial Naval Office) in 1897 and able to get a force authorised, by statute, the following year.

Enshrining the scale of the German fleet in legislation made it difficult for subsequent governments to cut construction without political debate. It also created the illusion of a closed programme, although this was sophistry. The British seizure of German mail steamers in 1900, a little after the outbreak of the Second Anglo-Boer War, gave Tirpitz some of the ammunition he needed to push a new fleet law through that year. This authorised what Tirpitz called a '*riskflotte*'. By this concept, Germany had merely to construct a fleet big enough that the Royal Navy could not fight it without denuding the Empire of protection.[57]

To Britain and its Empire the likely naval threat offered by Germany grew with their fleet; and thanks to Fisher's promotion of *Dreadnought* as a wonder vessel, the public perception grew that he had hurled everything back to the starting gate. Into this fed a notion that war might begin as a 'bolt from the blue'. Suddenly, the number of dreadnoughts available or under construction became a matter of public concern, irrespective of the fact that naval officials, politicians and diplomats alike had more informed views about the workings of diplomacy.

Britain's public thinking was broadly shared in Australasia, with a twist shaped by local perspectives. By the first years of the twentieth century, governments in both Melbourne and Wellington saw themselves – in subtly different ways – as integral parts of Empire. Both leaned towards London, and aside from ties of culture, origin and people, both knew that their own prosperity relied on the British place in the world. However, distance from Whitehall counted. New Zealand and Australia had shared views about local security, but neither were privy to discussions in British diplomatic and naval circles. One result was a widening gap between the scale of force Britain supplied for the Australasian Squadron, and what was perceived as necessary by governments in Melbourne and Wellington.

Where the two Australasian governments came apart was over how that gap was to be addressed. New Zealand's problem was that Britain saw Australasia as a single strategic unit, where the lion's share of practical power and money rested in the Commonwealth of Australia. This was given intensity by the fact that Australia's vision of an Imperial future focused on local self-identity within the umbrella of Empire.[58] This differed from New Zealand's. A corollary to the Australian view was a local naval force. The sceptre was brandished by Captain William Rooke Creswell. The Gibraltar-born officer had joined the Royal Navy in 1865, aged thirteen. His career took him through the ranks, but he retired in 1878 to become a pastoralist in Australia. In 1885 he was appointed to the South Australian Defence Forces, and the following year began advocating for local naval forces as an alternative to subsiding the British squadron in Australian waters.[59] He found listeners in the state governments. By 1902, when he penned a paper to guide approaches in the upcoming Colonial Conference, he had become one of Australia's influential naval voices. To him, the naval subsidy was a road to stagnation and 'continued naval impotence for Australia'.[60]

That did not go down well in Melbourne, the Commonwealth capital.[61] While Australia's sense of vulnerability was real, the Minister of Defence, Sir John Forrest, felt it 'beyond the power of the Commonwealth ... to create a force adequate for the naval defence of Australia ... the cost of the annual maintenance of the *Royal Arthur* alone is more than our whole contribution'.[62] His answer to the gap between what Britain supplied and what Australia felt it wanted was to ask for eight *Highflyer*-class cruisers to supplement the Imperial squadron, of which Australia could support up to six in service. The cruisers would become part of the Australasian Squadron in wartime.[63]

Australasian concerns were intensified by Britain's pivot towards Japan.

Local fear of Russia had been framed by the latter's economic and territorial opposition to Britain, but fear of Japan was further fuelled by period attitudes to race, provoking fears across Australia and New Zealand that it would free up migration to their own territories. One of the first actions by Australia's new Commonwealth government, based in Melbourne, was to pass the Immigration Restriction Act of 1901. The racism was blatant even by period standards, and Japanese negotiators working on the alliance made it clear they meant no harm to Britain's South Pacific possessions.[64]

The Admiralty rejected independent forces, but accepted the locally perceived defence gap, and at the 1902 conference agreed to augment the Australasian Squadron with the enormous protected cruiser *Powerful*, two second-class and four third-class cruisers, and four sloops. Two of the additional ships were stationed in New Zealand waters. To compensate, the annual subsidies of the two dominions were increased to £40,000 for New Zealand,[65] and £200,000 for Australia.[66] That did not, however, hose down Australasian worries about Japanese ambition, which were fanned into flame by Japan's war with Russia from 1904. To observers in Australia, that made Japan an existential threat.[67] 'Australia must make up her mind to part forever with a past of most absolute security,' warned the *Sydney Morning Herald* as early as February 1904.[68] Such sentiments got worse with every

HMS *Powerful*, flagship of the Australasian Squadron, in New Zealand waters.
(*Lemuel Lyes Collection*)

Japanese military success, a mood again given power by entrenched period racism. The *Bulletin* wrote of Japanese victories at Mukden as the 'gravest cause for anxiety ... it would be long before Asiatic power could so grow as to threaten the territory of Europe ... but Australia is a lonely outpost of the white race on the very borders of Asia'.[69] Neville Meaney has argued that the Japanese victories in 1905 caused the Australian government to sense for the first time the 'possibility of a primary threat to their territorial integrity and national security'.[70] Certainly the Australian government was swift to reflect public concern.

This was an embarrassment for both Britain and Japan, not helped in April 1905 when Vice-Admiral Arthur Fanshawe, then in command of the Australasian Squadron, penned an inflammatory memorandum. His motive was partly his opposition to Fisher's reforms. What Fanshawe titled 'Australia and New Zealand's real and only danger from an enemy' warned of 'other' Pacific powers, where the only real protection either dominion had was the 'capacity of the Royal Navy to maintain command of Eastern seas'.[71] He never named Japan, but pointed out that Tokyo was closer than any major British naval base except Hong Kong.[72] The implication was clear; Japan had won significant victories over the Russians just as the Royal Navy's 'capacity ... to maintain command' of the South Pacific had been reduced.[73]

The view from New Zealand was similar, although some opinion differed, made clear when New Zealand's former Premier Sir Robert Stout published an article discussing what he called the 'eastern menace'. To Stout, Japan was an economic competitor. Increased efficiency, he insisted, was the answer.[74] But the elephant in the room remained the Anglo-Japanese alliance. An editorial in that paper a few days later argued that since the Japanese victory at Tsushima had eliminated Russian sea power, the alliance could be terminated at no loss to British interests.[75] All these views were awkward in London, although the Prime Minister of the day, Arthur Balfour, was 'doubtful whether this is a subject on which we either can, or ought, to coerce our self-governing colonies'. Still, he felt it 'obvious that if we permit them to differentiate against the Japanese immigrant, we can raise no objection to the Japanese differentiating against the British trader, whether he comes from Australia or from England'.[76]

By mid-1905, then, Australia and New Zealand saw a new naval threat, one Britain could not share. It stood on top of the perception of German naval ambition, widening the local defence gap. Where Australia and New Zealand came apart was over how to deal with it. New Zealand could not match Australia's financial resources, but the greater issue was ideological. New Zealand's Liberal government was initially happy with the naval subsidy because it engaged their federal concept of Imperial defence. By contrast, Australia had no truck with an Empire-wide concept, but saw the subsidy as an affordable answer to their own immediate defence issues.

In Australia, Creswell – now Director of Naval Forces – continued to press for a locally controlled navy. After the Japanese victory over the Russians at Port Arthur he penned a memorandum for the Committee of Imperial Defence (CID), in London, proposing a 'line necessary to us within the defence line of the Imperial fleet – a purely defensive line, that will give security to our naval bases, populous centres, principal ports and commerce'.[77] The CID pooh-poohed the notion. A successful invasion could be achieved only by a nation with command of the sea. This rested with Britain.[78] New Zealand was part of the mix; here, the CID judged the highest risk to be attacks by 'at most, two or three cruisers' landing no more than 400 men'.[79] Creswell responded by forming a committee to analyse Australia's needs and now argued for destroyers.[80] He hoped this 'torpedo defence' would begin a longer-term policy.[81] He also suggested that Australia should develop its industrial base to meet wartime needs. 'An axiom of our defence should be the production in Australia of every war requisite.'[82]

The scene was also changing in New Zealand. Seddon died in mid-1906 and his deputy, Joseph Ward, became Prime Minister on 6 August and took up the Defence portfolio on 23 November. Ward – Australian-born, a New Zealander by migration – was widely viewed as weak, although that was likely to happen to anybody who followed the rumbustious former publican. More to the point was the perception of little policy direction. One critic, A R Barclay, insisted Ward's government was like 'indiarubber'.[83] This was not wholly fair. For much of his time as Prime Minister, Ward and his Cabinet had to face major internal issues. Unionised and largely urbanised labour movements, drawing place and strength from the mining and waterside industries, stood at odds with rising 'small holder' farmers, represented in Parliament by the opposition political grouping under William Massey.[84] As one historian has argued, Ward had 'little room for manoeuvre.'[85] He was not helped by his long-winded jingoistic speeches, for which he was repeatedly lampooned. Through all the flummery, though, Ward's naval ideas were clear. Too high a level of local Australasian defence would weaken links with Britain.[86] And the Imperial future, as far as he was concerned, was federal. In this he was very much a lone voice. The concept of Empire-wide federation had been bandied about in British circles since the 1880s, but had never gained traction.[87] In New Zealand, however, the idea carried the potential to enhance New Zealand's place within the greater structure.

By early 1907, then, the forces behind New Zealand's gift of a dreadnought had come together. The Royal Navy was in the throes of a revolution, but not prepared to relinquish administrative control across the

Joseph Ward (1856–1930), Liberal party leader and Premier of New Zealand, seen here turning the first sod of the East Coast Railway in 1912.
(*PAColl-6075-57. Alexander Turnbull Library*)

Empire. Australia and New Zealand saw threats that Britain did not – and a 'defence gap' on the back of it. Both had different ways of tackling it, but neither were acceptable in London. Meanwhile, the public around the Empire had found a new way to measure naval strength: dreadnoughts, which engaged with their sense of Imperial identity. And the concept of Germany as the main threat was gaining pace.

A gift ship was still far from inevitable, but a succession of events began nudging Ward down that path. The first was the Colonial Conference of April 1907. This get-together of Britain's children covered the gamut of Imperial business, and the Australian government asked to discuss the 1902 Naval Defence Agreement.[88] It was a pretext to bring up Creswell's ideas: the Australian Prime Minister, Alfred Deakin, warned the First Lord of the Admiralty, Tweedmouth, that his people viewed the naval subsidy as a 'tribute'.[89] All this stood against Ward's thinking. New Zealand, he told delegates, was a frontier society with minimal population and expensive public work schemes. Any increase would have to be made up for in men, docks and coal.[90] But in any case, he insisted, the future of Imperial defence was federal. To this end he argued for an 'imperial council'.[91] His pleas fell on deaf ears. From the British perspective, Australasia was a single strategic entity and the major voice was Australian. Tweedmouth made clear that the Admiralty position had not changed. There was 'one sea, one Empire, and … one Navy'.[92] Still, in admission of the political realities in Melbourne, he agreed to a small Australian fleet.[93]

This was a significant defeat for Ward. However, while the Admiralty opposed federal contributions to central defence, they also objected to independent local navies. Both dominions, in short, were out of line. The Admiralty initially tried to deal with the Australian agreement by ignoring it. Late in the year Deakin offered to replace the naval subsidy with 1,000 sailors, in return for which two P-class cruisers – along with 400 seamen – would be kept in Australian waters.[94] The Admiralty turned him down.[95] Deakin warned that it would be 'dangerous for the Admiralty to insist upon a supremacy which, if mis-adventure fell, would place the whole responsibility on them'.[96] With support from the Opposition leader, Andrew Fisher,[97] he put the proposal back to the Admiralty, now calling for four P-class cruisers. This time the Colonial Office stepped up: Admiralty stone-walling interfered with the fact that the dominions were self-governing. The Admiralty had to back down and, in February 1908, agreed to Deakin's proposal.

New Zealand's problem was that the government had to either follow Australia, or do without. Either way it was a defeat for Ward's concept of a federalised defence, and he responded with a left-field ploy. At the Colonial Conference he had insisted New Zealand had no more money for the naval subsidy. Now, suddenly, he raised it to £100,000, without strings.[98] In this Ward had an unlikely ally in the Admiralty, who were not going to let Australia have its own navy if they could help it. The Admiralty managed to drag the Australian request through 1908, delaying responses to correspondence and even introducing the idea that under international law Australian-flagged warships might be considered pirates, because only Britain – as the parent – was recognised as an authority. Deakin's government begged to differ. In September the Colonial Office again stepped in, telling the Admiralty that to prove Deakin wrong might 'require the intervention of the Privy Council'.[99] The Admiralty replied that they intended 'taking the matter up with their own legal advisors'.[100]

Amid these political gyrations the United States sent a battle fleet – the 'Great White Fleet' – on a world tour, mainly to assert American interests in the Philippines against the Japanese. When the prime ministers of both Australia and New Zealand invited the Americans to visit, the gestures were seen as evidence that the United States was being wooed as an ally against the Japanese.[101]

Into this mix now crashed a new factor: a fresh naval 'scare' that brewed up on the back of a rising Germany and the increasing popular belief that only dreadnoughts offered Britain's Empire any guarantee of safety. Tirpitz spent the latter part of 1907 pushing for a further amendment to the navy law. The British naval attaché in Berlin, Philip Dumas, alerted the Admiralty in October.[102] It was passed by the Reichstag on 27 March 1908. On the face

Early twentieth-century enthusiasm across New Zealand for matters military – and the way it was entangled with patriotism – was reflected and promoted in schools. Material made available for children included a series of postcards showing life aboard the *King Edward VII*-class battleship *New Zealand*, completed in July 1905. Although carefully staged for the camera, these images capture details such as the way food was distributed to each mess for cooking. The officers and crew of this ship, too, intentionally forged links with New Zealand: the portrait of the New Zealand Premier, Richard Seddon, is noteworthy. Life aboard the battlecruiser of the same name was very similar.
(*Torpedo Bay Navy Museum ABT0086*)

(*Torpedo Bay Navy Museum ABT098*)

(Torpedo Bay Navy Museum ABT0090)

(Torpedo Bay Navy Museum ABTY0093)

A promotional postcard of *New Zealand* produced as part of her 1913 world tour.
(*Lemuel Lyes Collection*)

of it this *novelle* looked innocuous. All it did was reduce the age of battleships and large cruisers from twenty-five to twenty years before they were replaced. Arguably, Tirpitz's target was as much his own government as the British: the Chancellor, Bernhard von Bülow, was reluctant to fund the navy when the primary call on military funding, as he saw it, was the army. However, the outcome was that Tirpitz increased the rate from three to four major ships annually. And the new battleships and 'large cruisers' were the all-big-gun variety.

Admiralty efforts to look behind the veil were complicated by intelligence gathering. This rested in part on visits to the shipyards by Dumas and his successor Herbert Heath, which were strictly controlled. However, Dumas deduced that Germany could build up to nine battleships and three cruisers 'of the largest size' in thirty-three months, and that their primary gun and armour manufacturer, Krupp, had capacity to supply weapons for them.[103] The fact that Krupp were expanding their Essen works was well known. Tools had even been ordered from Britain, and the Admiralty estimated that Germany might be able to arm up to eight dreadnought-type ships a year.

This highlighted the fact that Britain's construction programmes had been relatively relaxed. In 1906, Fisher set up a new committee to consider future designs, including a warship that combined the speed of his all-big-gun armoured cruiser with the protection and guns of the *Dreadnought*; in effect, a fast battleship.[104] But it was larger than *Dreadnought* and unacceptable, even to Fisher's committee, in the face of Liberal pressure to reduce naval spending. This party gained a majority after the 1906 election; and the Prime Minister, Henry Campbell-Bannerman, was determined not to be profligate. Even the annual programme of four heavy ships recommended by Lord Cawdor's 1905 'Statement of Admiralty Policy' – the so-called 'Cawdor memorandum' – seemed too large.[105] The 1906–07 programme simply authorised three near-repeats of *Dreadnought*. So did the 1907–08 programme.[106]

Fisher continued to agitate for his all-big-gun armoured cruisers, but got nowhere until the 1908–09 programme, when he was allowed one. Fisher touted this ship as another wonder-vessel, hinting at improved armour and new propulsion technology.[107] Actually, and largely for financial reasons, she was a development of the *Invincible* of 1905, with midship turrets spaced to allow cross-deck fire from the offside turret.[108] Fisher deliberately obscured the point, even getting false data about the armour published.[109] A misconception about the guns – often considered to be the Mk XI/50-calibre 12in – might have been less deliberate. As Norman Friedman has noted, the accepted design, 'E', specified such weapons: but the weapon was downgraded to the earlier Mk X/45 when the plan was detailed.[110] This was the design used, with minor changes, for *New Zealand*.

Late in 1908 the Admiralty began considering their recommendations for the 1909–10 programme, which had to be approved by March the following year. This was subject to a good deal of public speculation across the Empire, even in the most ruralised corners of Britain's reach. 'In spite of the German Emperor's protestations of friendship towards Britain,' the *Wairarapa Age* mused in December 1908, 'Germany is steadily increasing its strength in those great battleships which alone can count for much in the naval battles of the future.' Such comment made clear how effective Fisher's propaganda had been. To the public, only dreadnoughts mattered.[111] The fact that Britain's naval programme was under such earnest discussion in a rural part of New Zealand, on the very fringe of Empire, underscored the strength of the message, which engaged closely with social militarism and local senses of patriotic identity. It was also clear that to the Imperial public, *Dreadnought* defined military strength. Indeed, the *Wairarapa Age* classified anything older as 'inferior British battleships, which necessarily compose the bulk of the Imperial battle-fleets'.[112]

What alarmed the Admiralty in late 1908 was less Tirpitz's *novelle* as what was imagined to be game playing.[113] Patchy reports seemed to add up to an effort by the German shipbuilding industry to expand its capacity.[114] This implied that the four heavy ships now allowed for each of Germany's 1908–09 and 1909–10 programmes would be completed early.[115] The picture built by the Director of Naval Intelligence, Rear Admiral John Slade, led to calculations that Germany might have seventeen to twenty-one dreadnoughts in commission by February 1912.[116] Even the budget-minded Fisher, as Matthew Seligman has since pointed out, was brought around to this view and – with it – the need for a response.[117] The Admiralty now wanted six dreadnoughts for the 1909–10 programme.[118]

Getting six when Prime Minister H H Asquith was leaning against four was another matter. Just before New Year 1909, the First Lord of the Admiralty, Reginald McKenna, put the question of German acceleration to the Foreign Secretary, Sir Edward Grey.[119] A few days later, on 4 January, Grey tackled the German ambassador, Count Paul Wolff Metternich; but he got the standard answer: the German fleet was fixed by law. Metternich thought Grey's figures 'excessive', nor was sudden acceleration credible. Yes, Metternich admitted, the shipyards had accumulated material in advance, but this was 'at their own risk' because it was 'more convenient to buy at leisure'.[120] This was not diplomatic utterance. By stretching construction, major private yards were maximising profits, in part by cutting labour costs through not paying overtime, in part by buying steel at optimal prices.[121] The only part Metternich did not mention was that Tirpitz had provided some contracts early.

However, in early 1909 the Admiralty saw more sinister overtones. Opinion among the Board was hardening around six ships for the 1909–10 programme, and this on calculations that included twenty-five older battleships. Government opinion was more sanguine. Winston Churchill, then in his 'small navy' phase, thought Tirpitz could never hide an accelerated building programme from the Reichstag. Four British battleships would be enough.[122] The debate continued into February, and not just behind closed doors in the Admiralty and Cabinet. Public argument was driven by the Navy League, whose calls for more dreadnoughts gained a media profile across the Empire.[123]

The growing sense of crisis gained pace when Vickers employee and Admiralty confidante Trevor Dawson made a clandestine foray over an ice-bound Danzig harbour to get a better view of the Schichau yard. What he saw, with other information, seemed to confirm that German battleships were being begun ahead of authorisation.[124] Fisher now decided Britain needed eight for the 1909–10 programme.[125] That went down badly with Asquith, whose Cabinet was deadlocked between six or four. There was talk of resignations. However, at a meeting on 24 February between the Board of Admiralty and key Cabinet members, Asquith managed to sell a compromise. Four dreadnoughts would be authorised. There would be provision for a further four as a contingency, if – but only if – further evaluation showed it necessary.[126]

Fisher continued to agitate for a guaranteed eight. His vision of German duplicity was not helped when, at the beginning of March 1909, an Argentine delegation arrived in Britain on a fact-finding mission, ahead of ordering their own dreadnoughts. They had just come from Germany, where they had been given better access to naval yards and plant than British attachés, telling Fisher they had counted around 100 heavy naval guns under construction along with a dozen large ships.[127] That, to Fisher, was confirmation of Tirpitz's clandestine acceleration. But still Asquith would not buckle. The fact that the issue was being debated in the media added a sense of popular drama. Although journalists were not privy to back-room Admiralty debates, any perceived threat to British naval superiority was a guaranteed headline grabber. When the public announcement of the naval estimates was delayed a week on 2 March it became national news in New Zealand, as elsewhere around the Empire.[128]

The crisis finally broke when McKenna introduced the proposed estimates to the Commons on 16 March, with Asquith's compromise. His speech was inflammatory:

> The difficulty in which the government finds itself placed at this moment is that we do not know, as we thought we did, the rate at which German construction is taking place … If the construction of these ships were to be accelerated I understand the four ships of the 1909–10 programme would be completed by April 1912, and at that date Germany would have seventeen *Dreadnoughts* and *Invincibles*. But even if no acceleration takes place before April 1910 this number would be completed in the autumn of 1912. This is a contingency which the government have to take into account. We cannot afford to run risks.[129]

Public alarm was already rumbling in Britain and across the Empire. Now it flared, adding to the pace in Australasia, where the differences between New Zealand and Australian thinking were coming to a head for other reasons. A minority Australian government under Andrew Fisher had been elected in late 1908. Like his predecessor Deakin, Fisher was a proponent of local defence,[130] and there was wide expectation of new local fleet proposals. McKenna's speech crashed the party. 'Naval Supremacy. Germany's strength in Dreadnoughts. Can construct as fast as Britain',[131] *The Age* declared in headlines on 18 March. To the *Sydney Morning Herald* the fact of McKenna's utterances coming from a Liberal administration in London – whose 'traditional policy' was to 'retrench' naval spending – made his claims an act of 'bowing only to inexorable necessity'.[132] Similar sentiments were published in the New Zealand media the same day, where the *Evening Post* speculated on German motives, repeating warnings from the *Pall Mall Gazette* that new Austrian dreadnoughts should be included in the German tally.[133]

So the new naval panic, borne on the singing lines of the telegraph, spread like wildfire across Britain's Empire. As in the 1880s and 1890s, the media focused and guided public opinion. In Australia, any local response was spun as a matter of loyalty by a prodigal child. A lengthy editorial in *The Age* on Friday, 19 March pondered the issue of Imperial naval defence. A 'crisis without parallel', they insisted, was upon the Empire in which 'a single extra dreadnought possessed by one or other of the contestants might well decide the victory'. Then the paper laid down the challenge. Was Australia, the editorial asked, 'rich enough and loyal enough to provide a dreadnought … whose possession by Britain in an hour of supreme need might determine the existence of the Empire?' They felt there was 'but one answer to that question'. The people of Australia would be 'eager to make the gift, if their rulers will but offer it to Britain'.[134] Of course this was without compromising local naval forces:

> The Imperial naval crisis … demonstrates beyond dispute that our naval beginning has not been made a day too soon. Indeed, the probabilities are that before long we shall be compelled to add greatly to our present programme …What concerns us to-day is that Britain is in grave danger of losing her old proud position as Keeper of the Trident, and that we can help her to retain it, if we will.[135]

The Australian dreadnought concept, in other words, was purely framed by period social militarism and its entanglement with Imperial patriotism. This drew attention in New Zealand, where Ward had a problem. Irrespective of a dreadnought gift, the fact was that Australia, whether under Andrew Fisher or Deakin, was going down the track of local naval defence. New Zealand was going to be obliged to follow, or do without. The weekend was upon him, but that meant nothing. On Saturday, 20 March he penned a memorandum for his Cabinet. There was a 'crisis in the affairs of the Empire', he declared, and:

> … the time has arrived when New Zealand should do something more than it is now doing to show its practical assistance and support of the British Navy in such a way that the moral effect of New Zealand's co-operation would, quite irrespective of the money value, be of more than ordinary moment … For your consideration I propose that we should offer to the British Government at least one, and, if necessary, two first-class battleships of the Dreadnought or latest types

... to be controlled both in peace and war time absolutely by the British Admiralty.[136]

This, he insisted, would create a 'moral effect' that 'would, in my opinion, have a great and far-reaching influence'.[137] His motive was transparent: he was using the naval crisis and associated patriotic sentiment as a device to sway Imperial opinion towards federal defence. And he had reason for haste. If an Australian dreadnought offer emerged over the weekend it would turn New Zealand into a follower and, with that, dissipate much of the moral leverage. As Ward saw it, he had no time to put the issue before Parliament, telling Cabinet that if the house refused to sanction it they would have to resign: but he felt confident that 'the loyalty of the people of New Zealand' would 'indorse [sic] the action of the Government'.[138] In short, the social legacy of New Zealand's pro-British jingoism would save them.

Ward still had to wait until the following Monday, 22 March, before Cabinet could meet. His offer was unanimously endorsed.[139] The Governor, Sir William Lee Plunket, was away in southern Hawke's Bay – hardly a place to engage in a significant matter of state. But Ward could not wait. The Governor passed the offer on, he insisted to Ward, with 'pride and satisfaction'.[140] The Secretary of State for the Colonies, Robert Crewe-Milnes, the First Marquis of Crewe, received it at 9.50am:

> Government of New Zealand offer to bear cost of immediate building and arming by the British government of one first-class battleship of the latest type. If subsequent events show it to be necessary will also bear cost of second warship of same type.[141]

The term Ward and his Cabinet used was archaic; the British had classified their heavy ships as 'first-', 'second-' and 'third-' class battleships in 1887.[142] By 1909 the term 'first-class battleship' had been supplanted in popular use by 'dreadnought'. Still, there was no mistaking the meaning. Ward intended to give Britain the most powerful warship available – possibly two.

CHAPTER 3

POLITICS OF CONSTRUCTION

Joseph Ward's haste to seize the political high ground on that weekend in late March 1909 was, it seemed, on point. Sentiment in Australia – fuelled by distinctly different criteria – was growing. On the morning of Monday, 22 March, the *Sydney Morning Herald* backed the idea of Australia making such a gesture.[1] Next day the editorial spoke of a 'deep and almost unanimous movement of public opinion' in which 'a great majority of Australians' were 'ready to commit themselves now to some considerable sacrifice in order to assist the mother country'. Of course, this did not mean discarding the local fleet concept: a dreadnought gift was 'something apart from, and in addition to' the 'schemes for home defence'.[2] And in that lay the essence of Ward's urgency: the context of his own gift was to undermine that policy and assert his federalised defence ideal.

News of the New Zealand offer broke across Australia on 24 March with electric effect in local terms, where the idea was seen as purely patriotic. A public meeting in Sydney's Town Hall on 25 March resolved to follow the 'splendid example of New Zealand'.[3] The Lord Mayor of Sydney, Sir Allen Taylor, opened a 'dreadnought fund' which received £55,000 within twenty-four hours. A few days later he called for a public subscription of £250,000. In Perth, there were heated scenes at another public meeting, where a motion was passed to the effect that Australia should do all it could to help British supremacy. The Premier of New South Wales, Sir Charles Wade, was more sanguine, but that only got him criticised by the media.[4] Both Wade and his opposite number in Victoria, Sir Thomas Bent, shortly announced that if the federal government did not make a dreadnought offer, they would.[5] They formalised the gesture a few days later with a telegram to the Colonial Office.[6]

None of this joyous enthusiasm for Empire dislodged Australia's local fleet policy. Even the Sydney meeting on 25 March looked on a gift ship as a way to meet an immediate defence emergency, not 'an alternative to an increased subsidy or a rational local defence'.[7] The Prime Minister, Andrew Fisher, nailed the message home at the end of the month. He made no gift, instead proposing to spend £5 million on a local Australian naval force, initially twenty destroyers.[8] The Admiralty would periodically inspect the fleet to ensure it came up to their standards.[9] There would, the Prime

Minister declared, be no Australian dreadnought, a decision that was promptly attacked by local Australian papers. The *Daily Telegraph* argued that such a local force would be useless if not attached to an overseas squadron; while the *Morning Herald* argued that destroyers did not give local immunity.[10] The *Evening Post* questioned the decision on the basis that Australia's real defence would still rest with the Royal Navy.[11] The idea of a gift dreadnought floated around the debate as a popular catch call. Ward's offer had, at least, achieved this small redefinition of the argument.

Ward's 'moral effect' also referred to the potential the gift had to inspire copycat offers across the Empire, particularly Canada. Like Australia, Canada had its own defence perspectives and was close to authorising a local navy.[12] But, like Australia, Canada was doing so within the ambit of Empire. Ward's offer struck a small chord, and on 26 March the Vancouver Board of Trade resolved that Canada should 'at once offer to the Imperial authorities a sufficient sum to build a Dreadnought of the strongest type'. As in Australia, the media leaped into the fray, but opinion was mixed, with pro-gift voices less strident. The *Toronto Globe* urged an offer, only to be attacked by the *Ottawa Free Press* for going off 'at half cock'.[13] The *Montreal Gazette* labelled a government discussion 'Dreadnoughtitis'.[14] Colonies such as Malaya began contemplating dreadnought gifts of their own. But the frenzy did not last. On the 29th the Canadian government confirmed its own local navy,[15] joining Australia, where Andrew Fisher was resolute over having a fleet and not a gift dreadnought, despite the public clamour.

New Zealand's gift, in short, was received in the key dominions as patriotism for Britain filtered by local frameworks – which was very different from the political intent with which it was offered. The British public, too, received it in purely patriotic terms. Harvey Holyoake even penned the 'Song of the Dreadnought', dripping with Imperial pride. The first stanza set the tone:

> *'Well done! New Zealand, bravo to you'*
> *Loudly we all do say*
> *Sir Joseph Ward, your Premier true,*
> *Great Britain loves today*[16]

The London Chamber of Commerce also passed a vote of thanks.[17] However, Ward's underlying motive was clear enough to contemporary observers. On 29 March the New Zealand journalist Guy Scholefield, London correspondent for the New Zealand Associated Press,[18] wrote at length in the *Times* on the New Zealand offer. To his mind, dominion navies were inevitable. Why did New Zealand have a different attitude? Scholefield felt it was purely timing. 'The native born of New Zealand are two generations less remote from the parent stock than those of Australia, and the feeling of nationalism is accordingly less mature.' To him, New Zealand's greater contribution to Empire was manpower.[19]

The defence model that Ward was trying to foist on the Admiralty was also not widely shared across New Zealand, where the gift was again seen as a patriotic gesture. Few dissented in those terms. The loudest was the MP for Christchurch North, Thomas Taylor, a well-known pacifist, who telegraphed British Prime Minister H H Asquith to directly express his opposition.[20] That prompted public protest meetings among his electorate condemning his 'unconstitutional, unjustifiable and unstatesmanlike' gesture.[21] Taylor was undeterred, moving a resolution against the offer at a public meeting held to discuss it. The resolution was carried by the gathering of perhaps 2,000; but that provoked 'pandemonium, applause and hooting' among those who favoured the ship.[22] In mid-May there were media calls for his resignation,[23] and Taylor was confronted outside his own home at midnight a few days later, when 'nine or ten young men … called him out'. This nearly turned into a brawl: according to the newspaper report, Taylor gave one a 'smart cut with a cane', and 'two constables' intervened. Taylor refused to have the men

THE MAN WHO GAVE THE DREADNOUGHT.
Vide London Graphic.
The Rt. Hon. Sir J. G. Ward, Bart., M.P.,
K.C.M.G., P.C., LL.D., &c., &c.

THE MEN WHO WILL HAVE TO SPEND THE NEXT 15 YEARS IN PAYING FOR IT.
Wright & Carman, 148, Featherston Street, Wellington.

The cost of *New Zealand*, although significantly less than that of New Zealand's major public works of the day, provoked outcry at a time when labour unions were agitating for workers' rights.
(*PUBL-0220-1. Alexander Turnbull Library*)

prosecuted.[24] The incident provoked more media criticism, and he was condemned by the Christchurch *Press* for, supposedly, being a 'socialist'.[25] In Britain, the fact that some in New Zealand were opposed to the gift occupied just a few column inches in the *Times*.[26]

Ward's gesture made no difference to the 'dreadnought panic' that flared across Britain through late March and into April. The naval estimates were due to be debated in the Commons on 29 March. That provoked the Conservative party to action, and on the 27th there was a vigorous meeting in the New Pavilion in Wigan, organised by the Lancashire and Cheshire Workingmen's Federation and chaired by the explorer and Conservative MP Sir Henry Seton-Karr. His fellow MP, George Wyndham, member for Dover, spoke passionately. 'If we lost one sea fight within 48 hours we should be lost for ever, we should be faced by starvation, we could not even fight for national existence.' The answer was to build the four 'contingent' dreadnoughts. 'We want eight,' he declared, 'and we won't wait.' The call was taken up by the crowd and reported in the *Times* the following Monday, becoming a wider catch call among the Conservatives and the Navy League.[27]

Other voices that weekend included the MP Keir Hardie, who informed constituents at Merthyr Tydfil that their priority was the upcoming Mines (Eight Hours) Bill, not the 'naval scare'.[28] However, government was more interested in social policy. The Chancellor of the Exchequer, David Lloyd George, introduced the so-called 'people's budget' in April, with a significant social component and shift in the taxation system to pay for it. This was opposed by conservative groups and has been seen as a device for provoking a showdown with the House of Lords over social reform. This was a far larger issue than the dreadnought debate. The 'naval panic', however, continued to grind away, pushed by the Admiralty, Navy League and Conservative party. 'War would never be forced upon us while we were strong enough to win,' Conservative MP Arthur Lee told a meeting in the Portsmouth Town Hall, 'but it would be as soon as we were weak enough to be beaten.'[29]

The 'panic' was shortly tangled with the other great naval scandal of the day, the Fisher–Beresford feud. Although an ally during the 'naval panics' of 1888 and 1893, Beresford had been at odds with Fisher for years before being appointed Commander in Chief of the Channel Fleet, Britain's premier sea force, in 1907.[30] Fisher promptly stripped that fleet in favour of a new Home Fleet in the Nore, mostly made up of nucleus-crew ships, but with a number of full-commission warships that included *Dreadnought*. Beresford was left with a handful of older battleships and an insignificant number of supporting vessels. Nor would Fisher give Beresford detailed war plans, and to add insult to injury, Fisher then appointed Beresford's enemy, Vice-Admiral Sir Reginald Custance, as his second-in-command.[31] The feud became public in early 1908 over the 'paintwork' incident, when Fisher supporter Rear Admiral Percy Scott made a signal implicitly critical of Beresford,[32] provoking a media scandal. Warfare within Admiralty factions was fuelled by the fact that Beresford was independently wealthy and ran an 'open home' in London, which became the centre of intrigue against Fisher.[33]

Beresford restrained his response while a serving officer, but his tenure at sea ended on 24 March 1909, just as the 'dreadnought crisis' reached new heights. Fisher immediately got rid of Beresford's Channel Fleet and put British forces in home waters under a single command.[34] It was not subtle. On 2 April, Beresford told Asquith he intended to have Fisher held to account.[35] The link with the 'naval panic' was made explicit at the beginning of April when Sir George Armstrong – former naval officer and now MP – addressed a meeting of the Navy League at the Constitutional Club. The dreadnought problem, he declared, was purely of the Liberal government's making: they had interfered with the Cawdor programme. Then Armstrong attacked Fisher who, he declared, had personal control over the 'whole of our organisation for war', duties 'humanly impossible for any one man to carry out', coupled with 'autocratic power' that 'could not fail to have the most evil consequences', all buoyed on a 'system of favouritism and cliquism' that had 'never existed' in the navy before.[36]

Amidst the furore, Asquith decided he had little option but to give Beresford a hearing. Fisher called it 'treachery'.[37] The enquiry unfolded between 27 April and 13 July – the key period during which the 'dreadnought crisis' played out. The net outcome was that Britain was awash through April and May 1909 with public meetings, media reports, letters to the editor and political arguments, all just as the Admiralty was being forced to air its dirty laundry.

All this did not reduce the political problem Ward's gift posed for Fisher's Admiralty. It stood outside the political debate in Whitehall – there was no question of considering it a substitute for one of the 'contingent dread-noughts' – and in any case the Board, particularly under Fisher, had little truck with anything other than centrally managed building programmes. The situation was complicated by the ripples the offer created across the Empire. Asquith's answer was a further Imperial conference, specifically to look into Imperial defence and dominion naval aspiration. It would be 'held in private' and be 'purely consultative'.[38] He hoped to host it in early July, but Ward needed to bring his own Parliament together to debate the offer, and the earliest he could do that was 10 June. This meant he could not get to London before late July.[39] That did not go down well with the Colonial Office, which had to juggle delegates from Canada, Australia and South Africa.

Meanwhile, calls in Australia to make a dreadnought offer were answered when Andrew Fisher's Labour government fell on 2 June, toppled by a new 'fusion' government assembled by opposition Liberal leader Alfred Deakin. He was able to cobble this together in part on promise of a dreadnought offer, and promptly honoured it, hedged with the qualifier that the specific gift would depend on the outcome of the conference.[40] But it was also an extra: he did not resile from the plan to develop a local Australian navy.

Deakin's move compounded the issues the Admiralty had to manage. They had two dreadnought offers to deal with – essentially, products of a collision between trans-Tasman differences in defence thinking and the Imperial mindset – along with Australia's local naval aspirations, now joined by a resolution in Canada for the same thing. Fisher's answer was bold, manipulative, and well removed from Ward's thinking. He seems to have come up with the idea in late June, possibly with input from his friend William Thomson, Lord Kelvin,[41] then sold it to the Admiralty. However, neither Ward nor any of the other dominion delegates attending the Imperial Conference at were aware of Fisher's machinations until just before the conference began.

This was not the only way the conference was politicised. Most of the dominions sent lower-ranking representatives, underscoring the importance it had to their governments. However Ward – who told Plunket he 'intended "going for the two ships"'[42]– refused to delegate. Nor was he prepared to leave New Zealand while Parliament was sitting, in part because he was coming under increasing pressure over the gift. The issue, as he explained to Plunket, was getting the House to agree to rise during his absence.[43] That delayed the conference, because he could not offer a confirmed travel date.

Ward's problem was that members on both sides of the House felt the decision should have been debated in Parliament first. The Liberal member for Nelson, John Graham, scoffed at Ward's 'moral effect' and told the House that Britain was in a position to pay for 'any number' of dreadnoughts in a genuine emergency.[44] Now it was too late to back out. Ward's position was not helped by the fact that he had told newspaper editors he had 'confidential information relating to the pressing danger of the situation'.[45] This was revealed as a lie when the correspondence was published in Australia. In the end Ward was not able to get the vote to prorogue Parliament until 12 June, when it passed forty-five to twenty-nine.[46] Then he had to wait for the debate over the offer, two days later, which went into early evening. The tenor was again summed up by Reform party member for Manukau, Frederic Lang: nobody objected, but Ward had set poor precedent by not calling Parliament.[47] This became the political narrative, brought up like a tolling bell whenever the offer was discussed afterwards.[48] Indeed, opposition leader William Massey was referring to it as late as 1913, when he had become Prime Minister and joyous crowds were flocking to see the gift ship on her New Zealand tour.[49]

As a result of these gyrations Ward did not leave for London until Friday, 18 June, on passage via Egypt.[50] The Colonial Office got the news the same day and only then were they able to finalise timing for the conference, held in the Foreign Office under Crewe, as chairman.[51] Ward arrived in London on 24 July, by chance just three days after the end of the 'dreadnought crisis' that had given framework to his gift.

That crisis came to a close when Asquith's Cabinet gave in and authorised the 'contingent' dreadnoughts.[52] But it was not quite the concession it seemed: the arrangement came ahead of the vote on Lloyd George's social budget. The tax reforms that were going to pay for the social component also provided for the 'contingent' dreadnoughts.[53] It was not subtle. So ended Britain's largest 'naval scare' in over a decade. The irony was that the Germans had not suddenly accelerated their building rate. Tirpitz had indeed contracted two of the 1909–10 programme ships early, largely for the commercial reasons Metternich outlined to Grey. Heath had given Tirpitz a copy of Britain's proposed 1909–10 estimates on 28 March and, despite the friendly atmosphere, left with the 'impression that the Admiral is nursing a personal grievance' over the issue of his word being doubted.[54]

Britain was now committed to eight dreadnoughts for the 1909–10 programme, plus two gift ships. Fisher had plans for the latter, a proposal he formally raised with the Imperial conference delegates on 3 August. Instead of building dreadnoughts, Fisher intended to have the gifts commuted to armoured cruisers of what he called the 'new "Indomitable" class'. Each would form the nucleus of two 'fleet units', one based at Hong Kong, the other in Sydney.[55] The latter would become the Australian local navy and come under Royal Navy control during wartime.

From the British and Australian perspectives this was a brilliant scheme. It gave Australia what it wanted – resolving the issue the Admiralty had with the Colonial Office, and without losing wartime control of the force. From Fisher's perspective he got two of his favoured 'New Testament' vessels.[56] Because the scheme put heavier units into the Pacific, it also addressed criticism that his reorganisation had denuded the Empire of protection. This

Joseph Ward was ruthlessly lampooned for his pomposity by the New Zealand media.
Cartoonist Malcolm Melvin had this to say about Ward's journey to London in 1909 to
discuss the 'dreadnought' gift.
(*Eph-A-POLITICS-1909-01. Alexander Turnbull Library*)

had an immediate purpose. The Beresford enquiry – a sub-committee of the CID led by Asquith himself – was still sitting when Fisher came up with the fleet unit idea in late June, and its brief included determining whether Fisher had, in fact, left the Empire vulnerable.[57] The likelihood that Fisher saw his 'fleet units' as a device for deflecting criticism of his fleet distributions – both to the Beresford enquiry and otherwise – seems clear from the fact that, part-way through discussions at the conference, he then hit upon the idea of using them as the core of a whole new 'Pacific fleet', paid for by the dominions.[58] As always, his thinking evolved over time.

The only one left out in the cold was Ward, who responded with long and waffling monologues attacking the fleet units on multiple grounds. Germany was a clear enemy: two or three dreadnoughts in the Pacific would not alter matters if a victorious German fleet emerged to attack them.[59] As for the Australian fleet unit, the sheer size of Australia made it impracticable for a squadron stationed at Sydney to protect the entire coastline.[60] His real problem was that the plan defeated his concept of federal defence, and he said so directly:

> If we are going on with this piece-meal disintegrating system of trying to create a local Navy for the purpose of conceding to the demand by local people of having ships built locally … we are not going to do in the eyes of the world what I think this conference should do if it were to arrive at a decision as to providing a unified Navy.[61]

While, he argued, the immediate threat was Germany – who he felt would 'endeavour to starve England', not invade,[62] a centrally reinforced Royal Navy would, as he put it: 'Be best for us in the days to come, when … a great Power in the East, now happily attached to England … may be detached from it.'[63] To Ward, in short, a Royal Navy built by federal contribution from Britain's Empire was both an immediate and future solution to the changing strategic situation – especially, of course, as seen from Australasia.

He was, once again, a lone voice, but he was so strident that Fisher took him aside for 'a few momentous words'. We have only Fisher's account, but he apparently presented the fleet units to Ward as the beginning of a new Pacific fleet that would be paid for and supported by the dominions. Once portrayed in those terms, Fisher's vision engaged sufficiently with Ward's ideas to get him on board; as Fisher exulted a few weeks later to his friend Esher, 'He saw it!'[64]

Ward's concession may have satisfied Fisher. However, from Ward's perspective it did not disguise the fact that his gamble had failed. He had not forestalled Australia's plans, and the 'fleet unit' scheme left New Zealand reliant for local protection on the Australian ships, over which government in Wellington had no authority. That gave Ward a new problem. He could not return empty-handed, so he arranged a separate meeting with Fisher; McKenna; the DNI, Rear Admiral Alexander Bethell; the Assistant Secretary of the Admiralty, William Graham Greene;[65] and the Secretary to the CID, Rear Admiral Sir Charles Ottley. Once again Ward outlined his vision: 'I favour one great Imperial Navy with all the Overseas Dominions contributing.' That was never a starter, but the Admiralty officials agreed to divert part of the China–Pacific fleet unit to New Zealand waters: two *Bristol*-class light cruisers, three destroyers and two submarines.[66] McKenna confirmed the deal a week later, making clear they were eager to help due to the 'patriotic action taken by yourself and your Ministers in March last'.[67]

Fisher's scheme explains why both *New Zealand* and HMAS *Australia* were built as battlecruisers, and why the Australian ship became part of the Royal Australian Navy (RAN). But that begs questions of its own. Why did Fisher not specify dreadnoughts? The Australian gift was qualified, but the New Zealand gift was explicitly a 'first-class battleship' – explicitly, in 1909, a dreadnought. As usual, Fisher kept his reasoning to himself – his motto 'never explain' intrudes. Still, we can broadly reconstruct his logic. One factor was the expectation that, as long as potential British enemies were bottled up in European waters by his fleet distributions, the Pacific was likely to be threatened only by armoured cruisers, notably the German East Asiatic Squadron then based at Tsingtao. A 'fleet unit' therefore needed a speed advantage over armoured cruiser forces, so it could not be based around a dreadnought. Into this came a political factor: heavy ships intended for Far Eastern and Pacific service had traditionally been a grade lower than those of the main battle fleet.

Arguably, though, both reasons were pretexts from Fisher's perspective. For all the splash he had given *Dreadnought*, he openly considered his all-big-gun armoured cruiser to be the ideal warship. He had picked the second-class battleship *Renown* as his flag when Commander in Chief of the Mediterranean Fleet in 1899, because of her speed. As early as 1902 he was insisting the armoured cruiser was a 'swift battleship in disguise'.[68] This notion was not original to Fisher: a combination of speed and big guns had been a feature of Italian naval thinking for years, and Vickers began offering 'cruiser battleships' – large and powerful armoured cruisers – for the export market in 1900. Japan, meanwhile, was ordering battleships and armoured cruisers in approximately equal numbers, apparently for fleet work.[69]

Fisher was, however, clearly captured by the concept and soon began taking it in his own direction. The turbine-driven, 25-knot, all-big-gun armoured cruisers that emerged from his 1904–05 Committee on Designs became, to Fisher, 'New Testament' ships.[70] His chosen terminology alone underscores the place they held for this devout admiral. Fisher's concept was further underscored by an early name change to the first class. Initially the first three were to have been called *Invincible*, *Immortalite* and *Raleigh*, the latter two names more closely associated with cruisers. In December 1905, however, they were switched to the more prestigious *Inflexible* and *Indomitable*, which as one analyst has shown, were traditionally associated with first-class ships.[71] Fisher seems to have seen them as such, telling the journalist Arnold White they were 'stronger than dreadnoughts'.[72]

The problem for historians is that Fisher never made the role he envisaged for his wonder vessels explicit. His initial vision, which he brought to his committee at the end of 1904, was for a 25-knot armoured cruiser with homogenous 9.2in armament. This could outgun and outrun any prior armoured cruiser. But that did not mean he saw such ships as second rate: he also wanted 10in guns for his ideal battleship, seeing both weapons as superior thanks to their rate of fire and the fact that they could penetrate virtually all armour of the period at the expected battle ranges of the day. Fisher was persuaded to give the battleship 12in guns, but only accepted the same for the cruisers under pressure. The problem then was keeping displacement within financially acceptable bounds.[73] The calculation was not simply picking any two out of guns, speed and armour. Other factors included – but were not limited to – cruising range, munitions stowage, habitability, sea-keeping, ability to enter particular docking facilities, and performance in specified states of hull fouling. The expected role of the vessel was also a factor.

What emerged had similar scale of protection to the prior *Defence* class of armoured cruiser, but greater speed and firepower. This was partly made possible by a jump in displacement, partly by the switch to the more weight-efficient turbine. What role these ships would fill, though, was as unclear as that already wrapping the armoured cruisers. The committee envisaged, in general, that the new ships would primarily be used to overwhelm armoured cruisers posing threats to British trade routes – at the time typically French. As with earlier armoured cruisers, there was also talk of using the new ships in fleet action to harry the enemy van, or to scout.[74] This was not unique: United States War College studies during 1904 had suggested that a fast armoured cruiser wing would be effective in a fleet action.[75]

Whether Fisher had the same idea is unclear. Historians have since proposed that the targets Fisher had in mind included German liners converted to trade warfare.[76] It is difficult to be certain as, despite his apparent transparency, Fisher kept the reasoning behind most of his decisions to himself. One hypothesis is that Fisher saw his all-big-gun armoured cruisers as a complete replacement for battleships, but could never get the idea accepted.[77] This has some merit. As early as May 1904, when he was told he would be First Sea Lord, Fisher argued that battleships were not needed – that armoured cruisers could do the job.[78] Then in 1906 he declared that his new cruisers were 'more correctly described as battleships which, thanks to their speed, can drive anything afloat off the seas'.[79] In the face of Liberal-era programmes that focused solely on limited numbers of battleships, he began blurring the lines, referring to all new heavy vessels collectively as 'capital ships' from late 1906,[80] then having the all-big-gun armoured cruisers officially classified as 'battleship-cruisers' in 1908.[81]

To give this perspective we have to remember that although Fisher liked portraying his achievements, post-fact, as having emerged full-blown from his imagination, his thinking actually evolved over time. Until late 1904 his 'ideal' ships combined speed with medium-calibre guns, but the 1904–05 Committee on Designs swung him towards the bigger gun. The X-4 design of 1905–06 then showed that a vessel of scale to carry heavy guns, with cruiser speed and battleship-scale armour was politically unaffordable.[82] But to Fisher the combination of speed and heavy guns – even at the expense of armour – became seductive, an idea he eventually took to an extreme in 1914–15, partly due to political constraints, but also reflecting the way his thinking shifted over the period.[83]

In this context, Fisher's immediate problem while First Sea Lord in the 1904–10 period was that dilatory Liberal building programmes had been disastrous for his favoured ships. Nobody wanted to abandon battleships, and by mid-1909 only two of his 'battleship-cruisers' had been authorised since the 1905–06 programme.[84] On this basis, when Fisher saw an opportunity to get two further examples of the type, he took it. The more useful question is not why the two gift ships were built as battlecruisers, but why they were both built to a slightly altered *Indefatigable* design. In one sense it was reasonable. *Indefatigable* was the latest type in early 1909, only laid down in February that year. However, as Fisher well knew when he came up with his 'fleet unit', larger designs were already in hand, designed to carry the new Mk V/45-calibre 13.5in gun.

The Admiralty had ordered this weapon in October 1908 after the relative failure of the Mk XI/50-calibre 12in, initially asking Vickers to produce designs for 13, 13.5 and 14in guns.[85] The 13.5in was picked for further development and seemed so promising that Jellicoe, as Controller, decided that all heavy ships after the *Colossus* class – themselves under construction – would carry the new guns.[86] By early 1909 Watts and his team had a 13.5in battleship and its 'battleship-cruiser' homologue under design. The Admiralty intended to order one of each to complete the guaranteed four-ship 1909–10 programme.[87] A final legend design for the 'battleship-cruiser' was circulated to the Board for approval on 7 June,[88] well ahead of the Imperial Conference. For the first time it was heavier than its equivalent battleship, with a proposed displacement of 26,350 tons. Armour was significantly better than earlier 'battleship-cruiser' types, and Watts planned a speed of 28 knots.[89]

Fisher was in no doubt as to the place of the 13.5in gunned ships, later telling Arnold White that they were 'as beyond the *Dreadnought* as the *Dreadnought* was beyond all before her!'[90] For once he was not being hyperbolic. The combination of all-centre line armament and new gun, with increased protection and jump in displacement underscored the point that the 'dreadnought revolution' was, itself, also evolutionary. There was no question about the superiority of the 13.5in gunned 'battleship-cruiser'. *Lion* had longer-ranged guns firing shells half as heavy again, materially better armour than the *Indefatigables*, and higher design speed.[91] Fisher laid it out to White: '70,000 horsepower!!! And guns that will gut them!!!'[92]

The only downside was the price tag, a liability in the political context of 1909. That became clear when Watts suggested that by lengthening the new cruiser design by 9ft he could add a fifth turret for a ten-gun broadside.[93] He was declined; it would bump the price by 7 per cent, which the Board judged prohibitive.[94] The point for our story is that *Lion* was largely designed ahead of the Imperial conference and laid down on 29 September,[95] barely five weeks after Ward's private meeting with key members of the Board and well ahead of formal arrangements to contract the gifts. Those were not concluded until early 1910. By then, Britain had six 13.5in gunned ships confirmed via the expanded 1909–10 programme, and five more to improved designs planned for 1910–11.[96]

In short, the Admiralty foisted outmoded designs on both dominions. Why? Historians can only deduce the reasons. The only certainty is that the problem was *not* financial: Ward explicitly offered the latest possible vessel – or two – and, as we will see, New Zealand had no issues meeting that cost. But a raft of other reasons for limiting the gifts floated in and around the offers, including the ongoing reluctance of the Admiralty to permit interference with their shipbuilding programmes and the strategic position in the Pacific as seen from London, coupled with the politics of the Australian fleet. This last was perhaps the most significant factor, and in that calculation – as we shall see later in this chapter – the Admiralty saw both ships as a job lot. There was no question of building them to different designs.

Australian officials in London initially questioned having an *Indefatigable* as part of their force.[97] Despite voices in Australia favouring a capital ship locally, the 'dreadnought' was officially separate. But Fisher would not be moved. During a private meeting on 10 August, he told Australian delegates that the type he proposed was necessary to deal with the enemy forces likely to reach Australian waters.[98] This was in line with Admiralty risk assessments that identified cruisers alone as a threat outside European waters, and also consistent with the usual British policy of posting second-rate capital ships overseas. Fisher's proposals for an *Indefatigable* were accepted.

A degree of passive-aggressive obstruction cannot be ruled out. The Admiralty were allowing Australia its own navy only under protest, under pressure from the Colonial Office. Providing one of Britain's latest 13.5in gunned warships with it was potentially too great a concession. Into that mix came a political calculation: the 'fleet units' were being proposed in the context of the Anglo-Japanese alliance and the known objections to it in Australasia. While Fisher apparently had longer-term plans in mind, including a hedge against the risk of the alliance not being renewed in 1915,[99] to allow Australia to have a *Lion*, then one of the most powerful capital ships in the world, was arguably a political signal Britain could not send in 1909.

Against these political constraints other factors were less crucial; but one likely issue was security. There had been public talk of 13.5in guns,[100] but the Admiralty did not want Germany discovering the status of the weapon before they had to. The 13.5in gun was designed under a cover name, and *Orion*'s design was classified.[101] In this context the special Imperial Conference of 1909 was hardly clandestine, and its associated discussions were all going to be published widely.[102]

Practical constraints probably also played a part. British industry could only build enough heavy guns and mountings to equip about eight dreadnought-type ships in any year. The switch to the 13.5in gun came amidst the 'panic', with its resolution of eight ships for the 1909–10 programme. Of these, two were the *Colossus* class, which carried the problematic Mk XI/50-calibre 12in weapon.[103] The rest – two *Lion*-class 'battleship-cruisers' and four 'super-dreadnought' battleships – were 13.5in armed ships.[104] Some 206 13.5in barrels were eventually made by a range of companies,[105] but in 1909–10 British industry was only beginning to tool up for these weapons and the mountings that carried them, a process that included hand drawing multiple copies of the plans. By early 1909 orders for

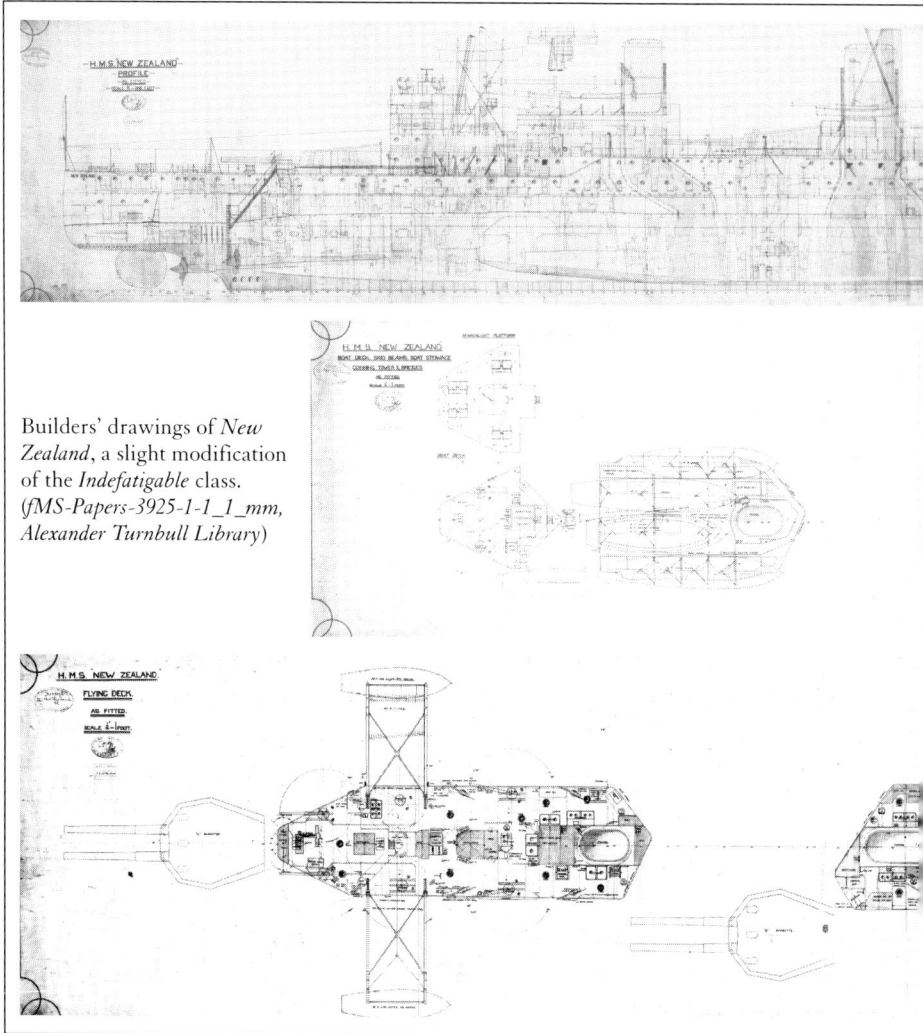

Builders' drawings of *New Zealand*, a slight modification of the *Indefatigable* class. (*fMS-Papers-3925-1-1_1_mm, Alexander Turnbull Library*)

13.5in mountings were already placed with Armstrong Whitworth's Elswick works and the Coventry Ordnance Works.[106] Rendering the gift vessels as the earlier *Indefatigable*, with Mk X 12in/45-calibre weapons for which tooling and blueprints were available across the industry, potentially eased bottlenecks. Armour was a separate issue but, again, there was a maximum capacity. In point of fact, the armour for *Australia* was caught up by that issue, delaying her completion some months beyond that of *New Zealand*.

It was December before the gift ship was put on a legislative basis in New Zealand. A Naval Defence bill capped costs at £2 million and authorised the Minister of Defence to borrow up to that figure under the New Zealand

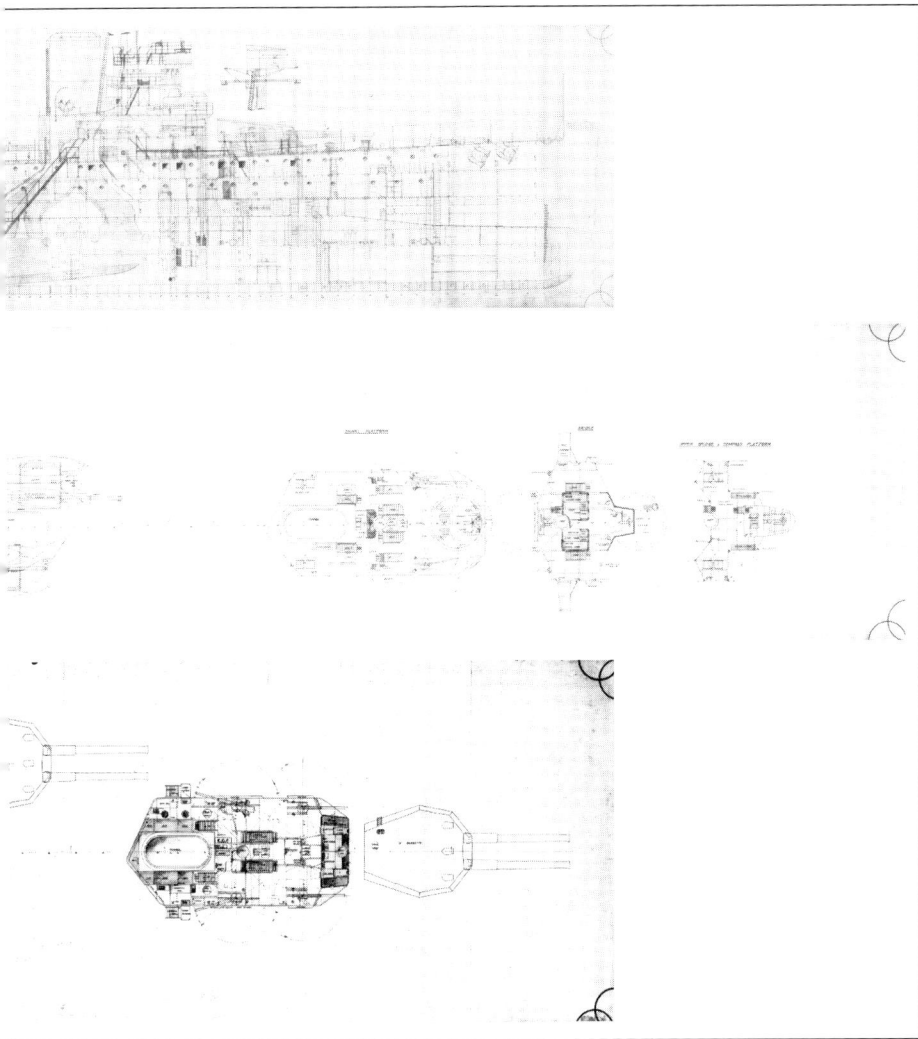

Loans Act 1908.[107] It did not pass without debate, partly flowing from Ward's prior failure to consult Parliament, but most of it a consequence of the agreement he had reached to have part of the China fleet unit stationed in New Zealand waters. By the time of the third reading on the evening of 9 December the argument in the house was intense. The opposition defence spokesman, James Allen, picked relentlessly at Ward's policy and costs. Ward bit back.[108] Debate continued into the early hours of 10 December before the Bill was voted for a third and final reading.[109] The House finally rose at 2.20am.[110] After going through committee stage, the Naval Defence bill 1909 was finally passed on Christmas Eve.[111]

The Admiralty had decided to treat the two Australasian gift ships as a unit, and the job of organising construction fell to the Controller, Rear Admiral John Jellicoe, and his staff. Early in 1910 his office issued ten requests to competing shipyards for tenders to build the hulls and machinery as a pair. This fell flat: nobody wanted to commit to more than one, and Harland and Wolff turned the invitation down altogether.[112] In the end Jellicoe picked two tenders; one from upper Clyde-based company John Brown & Co., and a cheaper offer from the Fairfield Shipbuilding and Engineering Company, a little further upstream at Govan on the southern bank of the river.

Ward knew the wheels were in motion, and on 10 March telegraphed the High Commissioner in London, William Hall-Jones, for a cost estimate. This, Hall-Jones reported, was likely to be about £1.8 million, 'including guns and first outfit of ammunition'.[113] Ward initially picked John Brown's tender, despite acknowledging it might be difficult to get them to reduce the price to Fairfield's. Then he discovered the John Brown offer had been snapped up by the Australian government, who decided to pay the higher figure.[114] That left Fairfield. Ward was happy enough, telling Hall-Jones he was 'very glad' New Zealand had 'the cheapest vessel'.[115]

Fairfield were one of Britain's premier shipbuilders, managed by former naval architect William Gracie.[116] They had been founded by Charles Randolph, Richard Cunliff and John Elder, and constructed their first vessel in 1864. The enterprise was incorporated under the Fairfield name in 1886, going on to build a variety of cruisers for the Royal Navy alongside an extensive civil shipbuilding programme. In 1905 they partially amalgamated with Cammell Laird and Company, which opened doors to the armaments industry through Cammell Laird's share in the Coventry Ordnance Works. Fairfield had built one of the first trio of battlecruisers, HMS *Indomitable*;[117] and *New Zealand* was their second capital ship of the dreadnought era.

Jellicoe met Hall-Jones on 15 March 1910 to discuss the details. The Admiralty drew up a standard contract with Fairfield, but included clauses levying the charges to the New Zealand government. The cost included the first stores fit out, with coal and ammunition. All stores bar the coal were offered from Admiralty stocks at the 'Rate Book' price. This was extended, later, to small items such as electro-plated cutlery, made for the Admiralty by Walker & Hall, supplied 'from Admiralty stocks'.[118] There was no charge for the Admiralty's oversight of the estimated thirty-month building process. However, the contract also included nebulous 'extras', which Hall-Jones told Ward usually amounted to £15,000.[119]

Admiral Sir John Jellicoe was closely involved with *New Zealand* from her inception –
when, as Controller, he was responsible for her building contracts – to the end of her career.
This photo, by Herman Schmidt, was taken aboard HMS *Hood* in 1924 when Jellicoe was an
Admiral of the Fleet.
(*Schmidt, Herman John, 1/1-001418-G. Alexander Turnbull Library*)

Armament was contracted separately. Jellicoe's department again treated
both ships as a set, ordering twenty-two Mk X/45-calibre 12in guns,
including six spares, along with thirty-six 4in guns, four of which were
spares, for a combined total of £249,550.[120] This order was split, 'half each'
between Armstrong Whitworth's Elswick works in Newcastle, and the plant
of Vickers, Sons and Maxim.[121] To put that in perspective, at the time

Armstrong Whitworth were also building the Mk XI 12in/50-calibre guns for *Hercules* and, simultaneously, guns for the two 13.5in ships *Lion* and *Monarch*.[122] Some of the equipment, such as obturator nozzles and mounting brackets, was common to all these weapons and – though individually itemised by ship name on the accounts, including *New Zealand* – was charged back to the Admiralty as a job lot.[123]

The heavy guns and mountings were also tendered as a single order for both ships, again split between Armstrong Whitworth and Vickers on the basis that each company would provide a complete ship-set. These were among the most complex pieces of precision heavy engineering of the period, massive structures that extended from the armoured gun house at weather deck level deep into the hull. Each was designed to mount, turn, and individually elevate two 12in guns, all at a speed sufficient to track moving targets against the roll of the ship. The system included machinery able to safely move shells weighing almost half a ton, along with the propellant required to fire them, from the magazines and shell rooms up to the handling room below the gun house, then to the breeches. Into this complex network of cables, caged elevators and flash-tight doors was woven electrical cabling, voice tubes, brass hydraulic pressure lines and myriad other apparatus. Armoured components included the gun house and the barbette protecting the turntable and equipment beneath it. Major itemised components on the Admiralty shopping list included turntables, training gear, slides, pumping engines, pressure pipes, shell room machinery, transporting gear, brackets, shield structure, shield armour, a spare mount, and spare 'front' armour for the gun houses.[124]

The scale, complexity and precision required of the engineering meant that the mountings were expensive. The contract totalled £207,593 per ship from Armstrong Whitworth's Elswick plant and £207,536 from Vickers.[125] That did not include delivery or final assembly – 'erection' – costs, which were left as a variable, depending on where the ships were fitted out. Nor did it include the £1,120 that Armstrong Whitworth charged Vickers for supplying 'drawings, jigs, and gauges'.[126]

Any of these were enormous sums by the ordinary family standards of the day. At the time basic foods such as a 4lb loaf of bread could be had for 5 pence; cheese 7 pence a pound; and tea – imported from India – 18 pence a pound.[127] The average weekly wage of the period in Britain, earned typically over a fifty-five-hour working week, varied between 28 and 33 shillings.[128] The shipbuilding industry, with its skilled workers, nonetheless ran towards the top of the wage rates. At a time when the clothing industry typically paid its workers around £37 a year, annual wages in shipyards and associated industries averaged around £95 12s.[129]

In the end the four main-battery mountings and gun houses for *New Zealand* were fabricated at Elswick,[130] along with one of the three reserve 12in guns; the other two reserve 12in weapons designated for the ship came from Vickers.[131] The guns actually mounted in the ship came from both manufacturers: Elswick made the two guns in A-turret, serial numbers 380 (left gun) and 383 (right gun); and the two guns in Q-turret, serial numbers 382 (left gun) and 381 (right gun). Vickers made the two guns in P-turret, serial numbers 374 (left gun) and 385 (right gun); and the two in X-turret, serial numbers 383 (left gun) and 370 (right gun).[132]

Although Ward made it clear he did not want to get involved in the intimate details,[133] the charge to New Zealand meant this was exactly what happened. The concept of 'systems' procurement and accounting had yet to emerge, so despite tendering the big-ticket items, the Admiralty retained hands-on authorisation when it came to individual components or variations. The outcome was a paper trail in which Sir Charles Inigo Thomas, Permanent Secretary to the Admiralty, passed on builder charges – often item by item – to Hall-Jones. He in turn had to pass them on to Ward's office for authorisation. Nobody in the New Zealand High Commissioner's office in London, or back in Wellington, had the expertise to understand the technicalities, and they had to rely on Admiralty advice.[134] Itemised variations included items such as 'two additional small Bollards on Forecastle Deck', for £31,[135] 'gun metal circuit boxes',[136] and even 'a certain Drawing required in connection with the gun mountings'. The Admiralty passed this last on for payment: £1 12s 6d.[137]

As a result, the final cost of the gift was not clear to Ward's administration beyond the estimated £1.8 million. Nor did it take long for the Admiralty to start detailing construction in ways that bumped the price. Jellicoe's department had a list of suppliers who were routinely invited to submit competitive tenders, and as early as 1 April, Thomas told Hall-Jones they had selected Babcock & Wilcox boilers. These, Thomas explained, were 'best adapted to the requirements of the Armoured Vessel'.[138] That was doubtless true: but as Hall-Jones discovered, the decision was going to add £21,000.[139]

How New Zealand paid for this is a story of itself, usually reduced to the trope that it required a loan that was not fully paid off until 1944–45, twenty-odd years after the ship was scrapped.[140] The imagery is tied up with the idea of the gift being a foolish and unaffordable knee-jerk reaction to a brief crisis. However, it is not strictly true.

Governments of the day seldom paid for large capital works out of cash flow, and most had a heavy debt burden. In Britain, for instance, public debt stood at 30 per cent of gross domestic product (GDP) by the 1909–10 financial year. New Zealand was little different. Loans raised by the dominion for public works in that financial year alone – the year before any borrowing began for the ship – totalled £2,091,090. New Zealand's net total public debt on 31 March 1910, mostly raised on the financial markets in London and Australia, stood at £73,387,420.[141] Business that kept Ward in New Zealand during June 1909, stalling his departure for the Imperial Conference, included a decision to borrow more than £1.25 million to fund further capital works. The calculation was not the purchase price of a capital item, but whether state cash flows could support interest and repayment schedules on loans.

Was the loan unaffordable on those terms? In one of his secret quarterly reports to the Colonial Office during 1909, Plunket reported that the 'question of the strain on our finances' did not 'seem to trouble either Parliament or the Press'.[142] Nor did it. The cost of a ship was dwarfed by the public works projects already in hand, and New Zealand's general position was good by the early years of the twentieth century. The economy was growing after rebalancing in the 1880s, when many small industries emerged and where export income was bolstered by refrigerated dairy and meat exports. Although GDP figures were not formally collected in New Zealand until the 1971–72 fiscal year – requiring economists to estimate earlier values – other figures for the first decade of the twentieth century show that the economy was in good shape. Part of this prosperity flowed from the fact that government was pouring borrowed money into massive public works projects.[143] Most were railway lines, designed to give the internal economy a means to operate efficiently. Significant money was also borrowed to support local bodies, including harbour boards, who were running their own development schemes. Much of the spending – notably wages – then flowed back into the economy.

The cost of a major warship was not exceptional when set against such projects, something that becomes clear if we put her in the context of government borrowing over the same period. The ship was offered in the 1909–10 financial year, the first costs were incurred in the 1910–11 financial year, and the last major sums were paid in 1912–13.[144] The money raised to pay for the ship totalled about 11.8 per cent of the growth in public debt between 1909–10 and 1912–13; and about 1.89 per cent of net *total* public debt to that point.[145] The fact that 88.2 per cent of the growth in New Zealand's public debt between fiscal years 1909–10 and 1912–13 was for works other than the warship gives due proportion to Ward's offer.

What these numbers do not reveal is that the affordability of that debt –

including the battlecruiser – dramatically improved during the same period, thanks to strong state income growth. In the 1909–10 financial year, before anything had been borrowed for *New Zealand*, some 26.66 per cent of New Zealand's government revenue went into debt servicing and repayment. Those costs rose from £2,458,452 in the 1910–11 financial year to £2,717,013 at the end of the 1912–13 year, an increase of £258,261, of which *New Zealand* accounted for about 12 per cent. This was somewhat less than Allen's 1913 estimate to the House.[146] Put another way, the debt servicing cost attributable to *New Zealand* amounted to an additional 0.66 per cent call on total government revenue as it stood in 1909–10. However – and this is the kicker – those revenues then increased by 21.33 per cent to the end of 1912–13, massively outstripping the added battlecruiser cost.[147] Indeed, as a result of state income growth, total national debt servicing costs dropped from 26.66 per cent of government expenditure at the end of the 1909–1910 financial year to 24.51 per cent at the end of 1912–13 – and this in spite of ongoing borrowing.[148]

The final part of the 'unaffordable extravagance' mythology – the fact that money borrowed for the ship was not 'repaid' until 1944–45, also has to be given due place. A quarter-century or more was typical for government

Borrowing for major New Zealand public works, notably railway, dwarfed the cost of the ship. This is the Taonui Viaduct on the Main Trunk Line, early in the twentieth century. (*William Archer Price, 1/2-000200-G. Alexander Turnbull Library*)

loan cycles of the day. In 1944–45 some £58.2 million of First World War debt remained on New Zealand's government books.[149] That gives the 'battle-cruiser debt' place. But the story was far more complex than the usual summary implies. The Naval Defence Act 1909 authorised loans of up to £2 million for the ship and created a 'sinking fund' to repay them – an account, held by the Public Trust Office, into which money was paid from cash flows, building a cash balance to repay any associated loans when they fell due. It was set to accumulate the entire expected cost within seventeen to eighteen years, which was relatively quick by state debt standards. The fact that government shortly changed the way public debt was handled – hijacking the 'sinking fund' cash balance along the way – explains much about the subsequent life of the 'battlecruiser debt', a story we shall pick up in the last chapter.

In any event, funding was never as simple as raising a single loan specifi-cally for the gift and handing the money to Britain. This was partly due to the fact that the British charged the New Zealand government directly as construction went ahead, by item, and the Admiralty were still passing charges on into 1914–15.[150] The process began in late March 1910, when Hall-Jones discovered that £64,750 would be needed before 30 June.[151] He did not have it, and near the beginning of May telegraphed Ward for autho-risation to raise the money by debenture on the London market.[152]

In the end the government covered initial costs via a temporary loan of £459,500, raised under the Naval Defence Act 1909 at 4 per cent interest.[153] In 1912 this was repaid and the figure swallowed in a new £4.5 million loan. This new loan was authorised in part to pay off the temporary loan and fund remaining payments on the ship; but was also intended to consolidate £2,840,500 of other government borrowings.[154] It was initially only a paper entity: it did not exist until it was raised, and government did not do that until it needed the cash – meaning the 'loan' consisted of various stock issues typically offered on the London financial markets, associated back against whatever they were paying for. Administrative costs – which were attributed against the ship for accounting purposes – were paid through the government's Conversion account and their Loans Redemption account.[155]

What this meant was that the 'battlecruiser debt' was in reality a series of ledger entries within a wider programme of government debt management, subject to an accounting trail kept by hand. In August 1913, Minister of Defence James Allen told the House that total capital borrowed by the New Zealand government for the ship was £1,659,500, less than the final cost of £1,701,000.[156] This, he explained, was also less than the original estimate and included all the extras, less refunds. On this basis, some of the costs had been

When Ward made the offer there was already a *New Zealand* in the Royal Navy: a battleship of the *King Edward VII* class, commissioned in 1905. These photos show the battleship at sea, engaging in over-the-stern resupply. Note the high topmasts, product of early wireless (radio), and the extensive stern walk. After much to-and-fro discussion the battleship was renamed *Zealandia*.
(*Archives New Zealand, R1836075-0003 and R1836075-0004*)

covered out of cash flow. However, as it happened, other capital costs were then paid on the ship into the 1913–14 and 1914–15 financial years, with a small last payment late in the war.[157] The final figure, which is sometimes also given as the total cost of the ship, was £1,795,000 – specifically, according to a ledger book summary, £1,795,169 4s 11d.[158]

This, however, was not the actual purchase price of the hardware, because it included the £64,148 cost of raising loans and £32,869 worth of redemption and conversion fees, the latter less just over £40,552 credited in 1916–17.[159] What then was the cost of the actual ship? A post-war tally put expenditure on the hardware, exclusive of fees, at £1,698,152 6s 3d.[160] This included the wartime capital expenditure and – reasonably – can be considered the physical purchase price of the battlecruiser, relentlessly accounted by diligent New Zealand bookkeepers down to that final threepence.[161]

In one sense *New Zealand* – at that finally accounted hardware cost – was a bargain. The *Indefatigables* were among Britain's cheapest capital ships of the late Edwardian period. By comparison, the 13.5in gunned 'battleship-cruiser' *Lion* apparently came in at £1,965,699, not including the cost of remodelling her superstructure post-completion.[162] The contemporary 'super-dreadnought' *Orion* carried a mildly lesser price tag, variously stated in secondary literature but apparently around £1,918,773.[163]

The first steel for the keel of *New Zealand* was formally laid in the Fairfield Shipbuilding and Engineering Ltd yard on the Clyde on 20 June 1910. Work began on *Australia* in the John Brown yard – a little way downstream – six days later. The fact that both ships were under construction drew attention in the Commons. On 29 June McKenna fielded a question about their particulars, which he answered by explaining they were 'generally the same' as *Indefatigable*.[164] So the gift ships made the transition from the abstractions of politics to real hardware.

By the early twentieth century Britain was the shipbuilding hub of the world. It was a national affair, with shipyards from Ireland to Scotland and around England's coasts drawing resources and equipment from a wide industrial base. Some shipyards, including Fairfield, had their own workshops for fabricating major sub-components such as turbines, by license with the designers. However, any element that could not be made on site was brought in, including forged components such as propeller brackets and rudder frames. These were often fabricated by firms such as Halesowen-based Walter Somers & Co., among others.[165] Steel came from a variety of suppliers, many based in the Midlands, such as the Park Gate Iron & Steel Company of Rotherham;[166] or the Steel Company of Scotland, on the north-eastern side of Glasgow.[167] The tools used in the shipyards also drew in national industry, ranging from small lathes made by Drummond Brothers of Guildford and the machine tools of Manchester-based Hulse & Co., to the massive edge planers, shears and plate flatteners of Craig & Donald of Johnstone. Cranes were fabricated for many yards at the Dalmarnock Iron Works of Sir William Arrol & Co.. So too were many of the steel frame buildings on shipyard premises in which components were made, joined by gear such as the Kinnear Patent Steel Rolling Shutters made by Arthur L Gibson & Co., a brand of roller doors designed to close off the enormous openings needed for traversing cranes.[168]

The whole edifice underscored just how integrated the shipbuilding industry was with Britain's domestic economy – financially and geographically – and by its nature highlighted why Britain became so concerned when Germany began taking the same path. Warships merely proxied the wider issues associated with industrial scale and place in world commerce, including the ships that carried it.

The Fairfield yard stood between Govan road and the River Clyde. By 1910 it was a large complex, complete with a brass foundry, sawmill, plating sheds, pipe shops, engine shops, smithies, a joinery shop, moulding loft, frame sheds and drawing offices among other facilities.[169] Ships were allocated one of several construction berths angled to the river, and the keels were laid atop massive wooden blocks. Steel components, fabricated in the workshops to precise dimensions from full-scale patterns prepared in the moulding loft, were brought to the berths and riveted into the structure. These elements were moved into place by cantilever cranes, a contrast with some shipyards where hulls were assembled inside giant steel lattice frameworks supporting moving gantry cranes. Fairfield also used cantilever cranes in its fitting out basin, and a giant 200-ton Arrol-built examplewas commissioned there in 1911.[170] *New Zealand* was one of the first warships to use it.

Constructing the ship was as much art as science. The hull was treated as a single girder when it came to calculating the stresses it would encounter at sea. This needed a certain degree of tension to create rigidity: but any tension outside the design – produced, for instance, by misalignment or minor bend in any of the components – undermined the calculations. The challenge was further complicated by thermal expansion and contraction. All came down to the skill and ability of those making and assembling the components – from those in the moulding lofts who laid out the templates for the components, complete with the marked holes for assembly, to the fabricators and finally the riveters, whose own skills were crucial to the integrity and strength of the final build.

The main issue confronting Ward's government was the paper trail that went with the build. This directly engaged New Zealand officials with one of the world's largest and most complex heavy industries of the day, something with which they were utterly unfamiliar. Accounts went from Fairfield to the Admiralty, from the Admiralty to the New Zealand High Commissioner, and finally to the Minister of Defence in Wellington.

This correspondence reflected the fact that nomenclature had not caught up with technology. Technically, thanks to Fisher, the ship was a 'battleship-cruiser', but neither Admiralty officials nor the companies constructing the ship had a consistent term. Instead the gift ship was variously referred to as the 'Armoured Vessel';[171] the 'Dreadnought cruiser' [sic];[172] the 'Colonial Cruiser';[173] the 'Armoured Cruiser',[174] and variations that included differing uses of capitals. The Admiralty formally changed the type to the two-word term 'Battle Cruiser' on 24 November 1911,[175] and their paperwork switched accordingly – initially with capitals – although New Zealand government correspondence continued to use the older terms for a while.[176] So did the New Zealand public. The two words eventually merged, by common usage over time, into the lower-case neologism 'battlecruiser', though even into the twenty-first century the words were sometimes separate in formal dictionary definitions.[177] Such halting shifts were typical of the way English evolved as language.

The name of the ship also left people from London to Wellington scratching their heads. The obvious moniker, *New Zealand*, was already used by one of the *King Edward VII*-class battleships. One early alternative came from maritime artist W L Wyllie, who ran into a New Zealander in the streets of Portsmouth around the end of April 1910 and ended up discussing 'the new cruiser battleship', along with possible names. As a result he wrote to the High Commissioner in London, suggesting *Arawa*, remarking – with period boldness towards such matters – that: 'There is one advantage in "Arawa", and that is the Bluejacket [sic] would be able to pronounce it.'[178]

Hall-Jones passed Wyllie's letter to Ward, but before it reached New Zealand the Admiralty stepped in: they needed a name.[179] Ward picked *Zealandia* and got Hall-Jones to telegraph it back.[180] However, McKenna had other ideas. The Australian government had used the name of their dominion, and he suggested New Zealand could do the same. The older battleship could be renamed, for which he proposed *Wellington*, 'as this is a name which has been used in the Royal Navy previously, and at the same time the Dominion would retain her double link with the Royal Navy'.[181] Ward suggested *Māori* would be more appropriate.[182] It turned out that this was already in use for a destroyer, and McKenna did not want a double change.[183] Instead he suggested deferring the issue for a year.[184] Meanwhile, the King, George V, approved *New Zealand* for the new ship. The Admiralty continued to order material for both Australian and New Zealand ships as job lots, splitting them between the two vessels.[185] This included long-lead items such as armour, an early cost for which the Admiralty wanted authority to spend £190,000 for *New Zealand* in August. Hall-Jones saw Jellicoe on the 15th and was told 'confidentially' that the armour would be 'as per a recent patent (much superior to the Krupp armour), the Specification of which [sic] had not been made public'.[186]

By this time armour plate was made by processes designed to create steel with a hard but tough surface layer – a blend of two different metallic properties – smoothly trending to softer and more ductile steel through its depth. This ideally meant that the plate did not shatter under a blow, or send pieces of armour broken off the back hurtling through the ship. Meanwhile, the combination of hard surface layer and overall thickness meant the

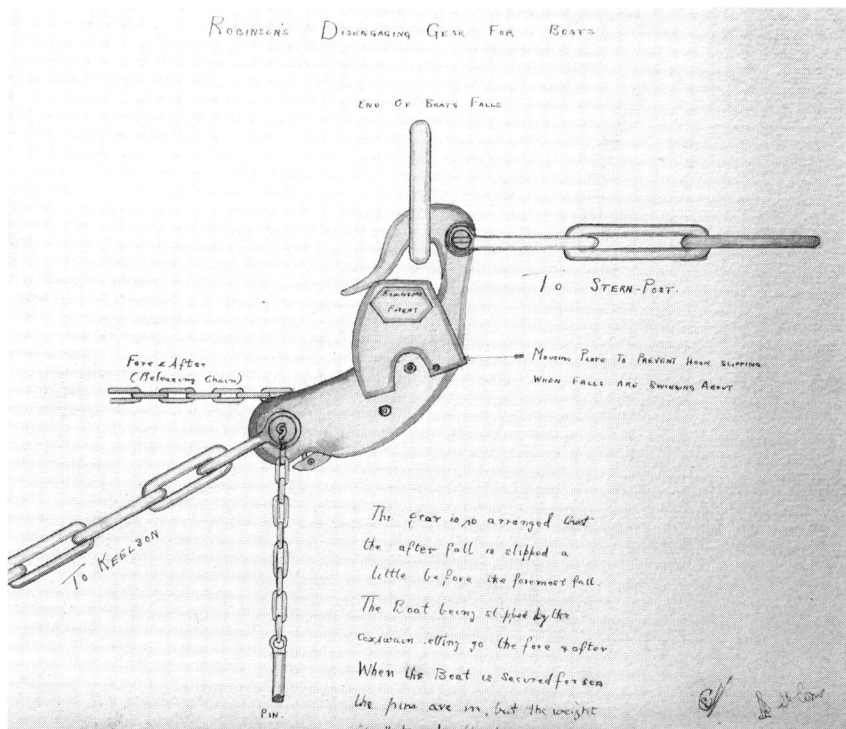

Midshipman Edmund Coore filled his midshipman's diary with diagrams of *New Zealand*'s systems, which he was required to research, underscoring how midshipmen were trained at the time.
(*Detail from qMS-0545, Coore, E G B, fl.1913–1914: Journal, Alexander Turnbull Library*).

armour could not be easily penetrated. This was typically calculated – and tested – against specified sizes of shells arriving at particular angles and velocities. The general chemistry and methods had been variously worked out across the major shipbuilding nations during the late nineteenth century, and by the early twentieth century the science was well enough understood that armour with specified characteristics could be produced for different purposes. Refinements were nonetheless ongoing. The particular process Jellicoe referred to had been devised by Vickers, and was being introduced in 1910.[187]

The common factor between all the armour types of the day was the complexity of their construction. Prospective armour plates were heated, treated with specific surface additives that had to be allowed to react with the steel, often over several weeks, and then cooled in carefully controlled ways. Each piece was given a serial number, and the armour for the two gift battle-cruisers had to take its place in the queue. Such armour was, inevitably, also expensive: and the outcome for New Zealand was that initial account of £190,000. A second bill arrived later for a single plate of armour, No. 8/8834, for £1,574, 12s 6d. This was used for firing trials at Shoeburyness in September 1911.[188]

By January 1911 the Admiralty thought the ship could be launched in late June.[189] Ward was in London that month both to attend the 1911 Imperial Conference and to receive a Baronetcy from the King on the 20th. While in the Imperial capital he resolved the problem of the older battleship name. McKenna had wondered in December about renaming the battleship *Caledonia* to 'keep up the Imperial idea'.[190] Hall-Jones reminded him of the earlier arrangement.[191] They agreed to wait until Ward's arrival in London. At their meeting they decided to rename the older ship *Zealandia*.

HMS *New Zealand* was launched with all pomp and ceremony on 1 July 1911. Movie cameras were set up to capture the moment as some 8,000 people crowded the slipway environs. High-powered guests included Plunket, now retired from his Governorship of New Zealand, while Ward was there with his wife Theresa. It was a moment to wave the patriotic banner. Ward spoke, still hammering his line of a federated empire. The launch, he declared, was 'a proof that the peoples of Great Britain and the Overseas were one in ambition, one in sentiment, and one in kith and kin'. Gracie spoke, calling the ship an 'emphatic token of New Zealand's loyalty and devotion'.[192] There was a brief ceremony led by Reverend Roger Kirkpatrick. Theresa Ward christened the ship with a bottle of New Zealand wine and declared: 'God Protect her! May she never be called upon to engage in battle, but if otherwise I pray that victory may be hers.'[193]

New Zealand at launch day. The launch ceremony – like most major launches – was attended by high-ranking officials with the usual speeches, music, and the inevitable gift for Neptune.
(*Ian Johnston*)

New Zealand directly after launch: two tugs prepare to move her to the fitting out basin.
(*Ian Johnston*)

She then took a casket containing a hatchet from Gracie, cut a line tethering the ship, and the hull began moving into the Clyde, slowly at first but gaining speed, while the drag chains roared. Those ashore, the dignitaries, and the men standing atop her deck waved and cheered as the ship slid into the river.[194] The battlecruiser came to a halt diagonally across the stream, riding high, as she had yet to be fitted with major components. Two tugs awaited to shepherd her into the fitting out basin. There was a reception afterwards for the dignitaries, with more speeches. Plunket declared that the ship was 'not merely a warship', but 'the embodiment of a new epoch in naval history'.[195]

The gift ship was in the water, although far from complete. Hulls were launched at the lowest weights that could be managed, in part to reduce bending stresses as the ship entered the water. Now came the process of fitting out – including adding the main armament along with the superstructure, funnels, and the myriad devices a major warship required by this time. This went ahead from mid-1911 into 1912. But then, before *New Zealand* was commissioned, her fate was overtaken by political gyrations.

Ward's government essentially lost a general election in December 1911; Parliament was deadlocked and the Liberals retained power only through the speaker's casting vote. Ward resigned in March 1912, and his successor Thomas MacKenzie lost a vote of no confidence in May. The Reform party leader William Massey – champion of smallholder farmers – formed a new government. He brought with him a new Minister of Defence, James Allen, and new attitudes to naval matters. These were informed by a shift in New Zealand defence thinking that had begun under Ward's administration, but which was coming to fruition by 1911–12. During this period New Zealand looked closely at its land defence, re-forming its former volunteer units into a small regular army backed by larger territorial forces, with the aim of swiftly forming an expeditionary force if war broke out. It was here, and not at sea, that New Zealand was able to make a contribution to central Imperial defence that was politically acceptable in London. Local naval defence had due place in the overall mix, but what it might comprise, and how it might be achieved, was another matter.

There were also policy changes in Britain. Fisher retired in 1910. He was sixty-nine, still full of vim and departing, in large part, only because of fallout from the Beresford enquiry. In late 1911, McKenna was replaced by a new First Lord of the Admiralty, Winston Churchill. He had been part of the 'small navy' lobby, and in February 1911 – as Chancellor of the Exchequer – tried to get the 1911–12 estimates reduced to four heavy ships. He thought the shortfall could be made good by 'securing' what he called the two 'colonial dreadnoughts'. If both could be stationed 'in the North Sea', he thought he could also get the 1912–13 estimates similarly reduced.[196]

In the event Churchill failed to get the 1911–12 programme cut to four. But then he was appointed First Lord, arriving at the Admiralty on 25 October 1911, with the 1912–13 programme still to be finalised. Churchill was just thirty-six years of age, and seems to have viewed both the Admiralty and Britain's naval policy as his oyster. In theory he was the Admiralty's political head and link to Cabinet, but he began treating serving officers as subordinates, also using the Admiralty's official yacht *Enchantress* as a private transport to take him wherever he needed, in luxury and style, to pursue what he saw as the navy's work. He appointed himself a Private Secretary: Rear Admiral David Beatty, similarly youthful – just forty – and well known in high society. Then Churchill scooped up Fisher, who had gone to live in Italy, building a warm friendship. On Fisher's advice, Churchill arranged for Jellicoe to be made second-in-command of the Home Fleet.[197]

Churchill's vision has been debated by historians, however, his broad motives were clear:[198] he had to keep naval costs constrained against the gyrations of European and world politics. Tensions gained a particular edge with the sharp diplomatic crisis of mid-1911, where Germany used the gunboat *Panther* to assert de facto rights over Morocco, fuelling British fear that Germany intended to build a naval base at Agadir. For a few weeks Europe teetered towards war. All the parties stepped back, but the crisis ratcheted up tensions. Then, in late 1911, Tirpitz began working up a new amendment to his fleet law.

Work continued on *New Zealand* in the fitting out basin at Fairfield and in Armstrong Whitworth's enormous Elswick Ordnance Works on the north bank of the Tyne in Newcastle, where her guns and mountings were being built. This enterprise was another testament to Britain's industrial power of the day; it encompassed more than 40 acres, with plant extending as far west as Scotswood. In many respects the Elswick operation was a self-contained industry, with its own power plants and blast furnaces – three of the latter by 1911 – a brass foundry and eight other steel furnaces. The gun barrel plant included some of the biggest lathes on the planet at the time. The erecting shops, where naval gun mountings rose from pits dug into the ground, were literally cathedrals of industry – vast interior spaces many storeys high, steel frameworks with multi-paned windows and skylighted roofs, illuminating what to the untrained eye was a chaotic mess of machinery, components and equipment.

By late 1911 *New Zealand*'s four heavy mountings, each designed to carry, turn, individually elevate and supply two 12in guns with munitions, had reached the point where it was possible to run 'pit trials': putting the machinery through its paces in the workshop. This was mainly to confirm all was within specification and to calibrate the safety equipment. First off the mark was the midships starboard mounting. The British had been naming their main turrets alphabetically, 'A' forward and 'X' aft, for some years. The advent of all-big-gun warships added letters. This particular mounting for *New Zealand* was labelled 'Q'. On 20 October, Admiralty representatives Lieutenant C V Usborne and Engineering Lieutenant F L Robertson, both from the Admiralty's Department of Naval Ordnance, with others, joined Elswick's representatives and clambered into 'Q' mounting with their notebooks and lists. It had yet to be fitted with sights, sub-calibre gear, air blast gear, air bottles and other equipment, but it was put through its paces. Everything was 'generally in accordance with specifications'.[199]

Trials of the midships port mounting, 'P', followed on 3 November. This was in a different state of completion, still requiring everything from gunsights to percussion firing gear, blast excluders, sub-calibre guns, revolving shell bodies and cordite hoppers among other things. But it was operational enough to be inspected. The forward mounting, 'A', followed on 29 November, and finally the aft mounting, 'X', a month later on 28 December.[200] The inspections helped iron out issues flowing from detail differences between mountings. Each emerged with their own minor differences, all of which had to be individually adjusted. In one instance this came down to the fact that the side sight-setters' positions needed lighting;[201] in another to the way that a voice pipe mouthpiece 'fouls body of operator', which was unique to that mounting.[202] The extent to which these constructions were individual expressions of manufacturing craft – and why their costs were so astronomical in period terms – is clear.

Churchill's spotlight continued to shine on both *New Zealand* and her sister ship *Australia*, which was coming together in the nearby John Brown yard. The First Lord's attention was in no small part driven by Tirpitz's *novelle* of 1912. This passed through the Reichstag on 21 May and increased the legal scale of the German battle fleet to forty-one battleships – classified in Germany as *linienschiffe*: 'line ships' – and eighteen *große kreuzer*: 'large cruisers'. The latter underscored the fact that ship classifications were political devices, not engineering definitions. When the original fleet law was passed in 1898, *große kreuzer* referred to any cruiser over 5,500 tons. As we have seen, the ongoing evolution of the armoured cruiser produced a new type of warship, soon exemplified by the 13.5in-gunned *Lion*, which the British acknowledged by formalising the two-word term 'battle cruiser' in 1911. However, Tirpitz did not introduce a new classification when, after a false start with *Blücher*, Germany began building ships of similar concept. The cost of such vessels rivalled that of battleships, and they carried heavier armour than their British equivalents.[203] But to Germany they were officially still *große kreuzer*. The result was that Tirpitz was able to materially increase the fighting power of the High Seas Fleet.

One of the outcomes of Agadir, with its unsubtle sharpening of the knives, was a move to put the Admiralty itself on a more warlike footing. Until 1912 the offices on Whitehall – the heart of the command-and-control system behind Fisher's fleet distributions – had run on weekday office hours, closing for evenings, weekends and public holidays and leaving only skeleton staff to hand. Now Churchill instituted a standing watch.[204] His motive, he explained to Cabinet in mid-1912, was that Germany's navy might seek fleet action as soon as war was declared.[205] However, Churchill was also determined to constrain the building rate. After the 1909 crisis, annual estimates had settled on four battleships and one battlecruiser, which rate continued into the 1911–12 funding cycle. This last produced four *Iron Duke*-class super-dreadnoughts and their battlecruiser homologue, *Tiger*.[206]

Churchill now looked to slash big ship construction by 20 per cent annually. The reasons have been subject to a good deal of academic debate, including the idea that Churchill, with Fisher's input, cooked up a radical 'strategic' revolution involving battlecruisers, submarines and destroyers. This was suggested as part of the 'revisionist' approach that flowed through the academy in the early twenty-first century, questioning the received truths established fifty or more years earlier by United States historian Arthur Marder. However, while Marder's mid-twentieth century interpretation was a product of his own methodology and time,[207] some of the arguments intended to replace his vision were as clearly expressions of the late twentieth-century academy. This did not mean either position was right by default, or that one discredited the other. It meant, instead, that a historical discussion – necessarily nuanced and framed in shades of grey – needed to continue.

From the perspective of *New Zealand* this debate is perhaps less crucial than the practical steps Churchill took, further underscoring the place of the gift ship in terms of the unfolding naval race. By this time the Admiralty had altered their measure of strength. While the 'two-power standard' was tacitly upheld in the Mediterranean, a different measure was proposed for the North Sea: 60 per cent superiority. Churchill's problem was meeting this new figure while reducing the number of heavy ships being built. Part of the answer came from a further leap in firepower. In February 1911, the Director of Naval Ordnance, Rear Admiral Archibald Moore – who later flew his flag on board *New Zealand* – asked the Ordinance Board to look into larger weapons.[208] The 15in gun that emerged from that process used the 13.5in gun as a conceptual basis; and that gun had been so good that Moore felt able to propose the larger gun for the 1912–13 programme ships.[209]

With that came another opportunity. Fisher had been pressing Churchill to switch construction to battlecruisers.[210] Churchill questioned the scale of battlecruiser armour,[211] but the new 15in gun fired such a heavy shell that eight seemed sufficient for a battleship, freeing weight for propulsion while keeping the rise in displacement – hence cost – within politically acceptable bounds. The upshot was that Churchill was able to persuade the Board to drop the battlecruiser from the 1912–13 programme and order four 'fast battleships', the *Queen Elizabeth* class, with a theoretical speed of 25 knots.[212] To do this within bounds they had to be oil-fuelled, an imported commodity. Churchill persuaded Cabinet to authorise a four-year oil reserve, secured supplies from Persia (Iran), initially via the Anglo-Persian Oil Convention,[213] then obtained a controlling stake in the Anglo-Persian Oil Company.[214] Oil carried multiple advantages – including the crucial point that the ship's ability to sustain top speed was no longer limited by the physical endurance of stokers. The new battleships were not as fast as *New Zealand*, but were dramatically more capable in key military respects. The Fairfield yard was contracted to build one – HMS *Valiant*[215] – even as the gift battlecruiser was completing. The battleship was laid down on 31 January 1913, barely ten weeks after *New Zealand* departed the yard.[216]

The New Zealand gift remained in Churchill's sights. To compensate for numbers, he fell back on his 1911 plan to have *New Zealand* stationed in the North Sea. He also wanted *Australia*, but accepted that the Australian government would not agree. That carried a consequence for New Zealand. In January 1912 Churchill told Lewis Harcourt, the Secretary of State for Dominion Affairs, that because Australia would probably not relinquish the ship, and the subsidy from Australia was about to end, 'we should reduce our force in Australian waters at the earliest possible moment to a minimum'.[217] He then tried to obtain what he called the 'colonial' battlecruisers anyway, arguing to Cabinet that the ships could make a North Sea victory 'complete', but would be useless if they were in the Pacific the day after the Royal Navy was defeated in home waters.[218] Cabinet concurred; but – as Churchill had expected – the idea fell on barren ground in Melbourne. It was a different story in New Zealand. Harcourt passed on the request on 18 April. The Prime Minister, now Thomas MacKenzie, promptly replied that the ship 'should be stationed where Home Government consider her service of the most value'.[219]

This marked the end of the Hong Kong 'fleet unit', and that carried a downside for New Zealand. The new Australian Station – whose 'fleet unit' was funded locally – was defined around the subcontinent, with a dog-leg to incorporate Norfolk Island, but excluded New Zealand.[220] However, the ships Ward had negotiated for local service from the Hong Kong unit did not eventuate. In part this was because Fisher – as First Sea Lord – initially refused to authorise new light cruisers, feeling the type unnecessary in a fleet that had his all-big-gun armoured cruisers. He did not relent until the 1907–08 programme, with the result that the Royal Navy had a shortage. Nothing was available for New Zealand apart from two P-class cruisers, the same type that had formed the Auxiliary Squadron in the 1890s and which were obsolete. However, resolving local naval defence was not a high priority for the government of William Massey that came to power in New Zealand in May 1912. Massey had a range of internal problems, notably industrial unrest and the rise of unionism, which stood at odds with the smallholder farmer community that formed his primary electoral base.

New Zealand continued to fit out through much of 1912. Once again the process underscored the way Britain's shipbuilding industry integrated across

New Zealand, close to completion, in Fairfield's fitting out basin. The hammerhead crane was new at the time.
(*Ian Johnston*)

a wide swathe of the domestic economy, financially and geographically. The Admiralty had a list of competing suppliers from which they obtained tenders for individual items. These included Barr and Stroud range-finders; Chadburn's 'Admiralty Pattern' Ship Telegraphs from Bootle, Lancashire; Greenwood & Batley Ltd steam dynamos and turbine pumps, Keith Fans for 'forced draught and ship ventilation', and more.[221] To this were added the 'patent loud speaking naval telephones' of Alfred Graham & Co., produced in their St Andrew's Works in London; Renold Chains from Manchester, used for turret turning gear and gun rammers, among other naval applications; 'Stone's Patent Hydraulic Underline Ash Expeller' from J Stone, which doubled as a bilge pump; and refrigerating machinery such as the magazine coolers produced by J & E Hall Ltd, based in London.[222]

Equipment was systematically loaded into *New Zealand*. Her watertight bulkheads and double bottom were pressure tested on 12 May and certified.[223] The ship was months away from completion, but already had a small complement of officers and crew. The first officer on deck was the ship's Engineer Commander, Thomas H Turner, who arrived on 19 May 1911, before the ship was launched. There were good reasons for such an early appointment: he had to be 'conversant with the structure of the ship under the engines and boilers, the arrangement of the various valves and cocks, the working of the watertight doors, hatches, sluices and pumps, the system of flooding and ventilating throughout the hull, and with the general construction of the ship'.[224] Watching it come together – and being able to hand that knowledge to his successor – was part of the mix.

Turner was joined after launch by the carpenter, Robert Isitt, who reported for duty on 18 July. The ship's first Commander, Edward Jones – the Executive Officer and initially the most senior officer aboard – arrived for duty in September 1911 while the battlecruiser was in the fitting out basin at Fairfield.[225] The pace accelerated in late 1912. Commander Henry Grace – son of the influential cricketer W G Grace – joined on 15 September, replacing Jones. That month Lieutenant Commander Archibald Anthony Lovett-Cameron joined as torpedo officer.[226] Work continued on the ship as these officers trickled aboard: tasks included docking the ship for inspections and 'swinging' her to recalibrate the compasses, taking into account the weight and location of metal added during the fit out.[227]

New Zealand's first captain took up his duty on 21 September.[228] Lionel Halsey was forty when appointed to command the battlecruiser. Born to an upper-class family in London, he had joined the Royal Navy in 1885, studying in HMS *Britannia*, and was promoted to sub-lieutenant in 1891. He later joined HMS *Powerful* and served ashore during the Boer War, notably during the Battle of Ladysmith. He then served in a number of roles before being promoted captain in June 1905, and was assigned back to *Powerful* as her commanding officer. By this time the cruiser was flagship of the Australasian Squadron, which brought him into New Zealand waters and into contact with many senior officials. Halsey came to *New Zealand* from command of the cruiser *Donegal*.

Sea trials began in October. The battlecruiser was docked for hull inspection on the 8th, then ran a thirty-hour steam test at three-quarter power on the 9th and 10th. This was more important than the maximum speed runs that followed, because it gave the propulsion equipment a workout in realistic operational conditions, producing detailed figures for coal, oil, water and lubricant consumption. However, sprint capability was important for tactical flexibility in battle, and full-power tests were conducted off Polperro on 14 October. Winds were light and variable, sea state between 1 and 2 with a slight swell, and the ship had about 950 tons of fuel aboard. The speed over the eight-hour trial was 25.1 knots average, measured by log – a mechanical device trailed off the stern. It was also measured at 26 knots, precisely, by triangulating bearings from known landmarks. These speeds were achieved with boiler pressures of around 250lb, burning Pennyhyber and Dowlais mixed coal, generating 49,048hp, with an average of 296.687 revolutions per minute (RPM) across the four propeller shafts. These peaked at 308rpm at one point for the port outer propeller shaft.[229] All these were averages across those distances; the ship was capable of more. A sprint across the 'measured mile' produced a mean speed of 25.49 knots deduced by revolutions, 26.3 knots calculated by bearings.[230]

These figures have been variously cited in reference works,[231] but were largely academic from the perspective of ship operations. In *New Zealand*'s case they were

Lionel Halsey (1872–1949), first captain of *New Zealand*. (*W Beattie. Whites Aviation Ltd, WA-10078-G. Alexander Turnbull Library*)

conducted under near-ideal sea conditions with new boilers and the ship freshly out of dock. The main constraint was the relative shallowness of the water off Cornwall.[232] In battle, top speed was always going to be affected by sea state, water depth, coal quality, boiler condition, current displacement and hull fouling among other things. The more crucial constraint was that the ability to maintain maximum available speed was always going to be limited by the physical ability of the stokers and others in the coal supply chain to keep going as the hours went on, an issue that led to a steady increase in stoking crews in wartime. However, the trials showed that no major issues prevented the ship achieving her intended design speed. They also demonstrated that the propulsion plant – which had been intentionally over-designed – could be pushed. None of this was a surprise. Every ship was a unique expression of industrial-age craft with its own small quirks. However, *Indefatigable* was already in service and – despite the minor variations between the designs – had defined the main parameters of that type.

This sprint speed was the figure seized upon by the media. It was unsurprising: the ideal maximum speed of major warships was one of the key statistics sought by a social-military-minded public in their quest for superlatives. The Admiralty described *New Zealand* as having hit '27 knots'.[233] This was duly reflected by Fred Jane, whose *Jane's Fighting Ships* annual of 1914 reported the same figure, but adding that it was achieved on 29,000hp.[234] This last was not as big a lie as offered, essentially in the same breath, for *New Zealand*'s sister ship *Indefatigable*. She was credited with 29.13 knots as 'best recent speed'.[235] As we shall see in the next chapter, this class was, indeed, capable of speeds in excess of design in the right conditions. But – thanks to the draconian physics of fluid dynamics – not by 3 or 4 knots.[236]

New Zealand went on to complete her gun and torpedo trials, then returned to Fairfield's yard. Many officers joined the ship over the next few weeks, including a New Zealander, Lieutenant Alexander David Boyle (1887–1965) – David to his friends.[237] He hailed from Otaio in South Canterbury and became one of about fifty New Zealanders initially serving on the ship. He had joined the navy as a cadet in 1902, initially at officer school aboard *Britannia*, become a midshipman in 1904; and then served aboard *Illustrious*. Later he served under Halsey aboard *Powerful*, then flag of the Australasian Station. He also served aboard *Triumph* and the royal yacht, *Victoria and Albert*, and by mid-1911 was again under Halsey aboard *Donegal*.[238] Now he was assigned to Halsey's command once again. He arrived on 18 November; and while many Kiwis were rotated off as time went on, Boyle remained aboard until well through the First World War.[239]

The ship was nearly ready to be commissioned into the Royal Navy and acceptance inspections began in mid-November. The examination covered virtually every part of the ship from hull and fittings to the rigging, derricks, main engines, auxiliary engines, hydraulic machinery, generating plant, boilers, guns, capstans, anchor gear and stores among other things. We can picture the scene: the Admiralty overseer with his clipboard and pro-forma report sheet, the builders' representatives with their own paperwork, peering into corners under the relatively dim yellow glow of period electric lamps, inspecting every detail of a ship that already had crew aboard and hummed with activity. It was a ship where dockyard hands were still at work, and where the smell of fresh paint inside her hull warred with the older scents of salt, stale cooking oils from the galley – perhaps, at the right time, also the smell of baking bread – all suffused with a slightly sulphurous tang of coal smoke.

It took some days to go through everything, all written on the pro-forma Admiralty report sheet, supplemented by individually typed pages – with carbon copies – listing particular items. The electrical system was signed off on the 16th and Fairfield signed off the ship itself on the 18th. The Admiralty overseer stamped and signed the same report the following day. Only tiny items were amiss, such as the fact that trials to strike the topmast had yet to be carried out.[240] But there was a long list of jobs to be completed, including boiler cleaning, retesting gunsights and 'sundry items' from gun trials, installing steam pressure gauges for the 'air compressing engines' and many other small things. Equipment yet to install included sword lockers. All these things, the report declared, 'may be done before contractors leave'. More crucial remaining work included fitting the Dumaresq tables and plots in A and X barbettes. These electro-mechanical devices were part of the fire-control system.[241]

This did not delay *New Zealand* being formally commissioned into the Royal Navy with a nucleus crew on 19 November, at Govan.[242] It was a significant milestone. More officers joined that day, including Vincent Robinson, a gunner assigned to the ship 'for instructional duties'; and the assistant paymaster, Denzil R Thurstan.[243] So too did some of the essential crew, including thirty-six-year-old Stoker First Class Charles Baulch, twenty-nine-year-old Stoker First Class Ernest Beeney and thirty-seven-year-old Stoker First Class James Poole.[244]

Now came a voyage to Devonport and final docking to coat the bottom, inspect the underwater fittings, and other tests.[245] Final inspections were completed. Some items remained to be fitted, including awnings and 'canvas gear', which Fairfield were going to send south.[246] The full crew came aboard, most of them arriving on 23 November.[247] They included thirty-year-old Able Seaman Oswald Amery, from Rotherham in Yorkshire; Engine Room Artificer 1st Class George Perring, Stoker Petty Officer Thomas Taggart,[248] and others. More men joined over the next few days, among them John Allinson, a Royal Marines private born in 1887 who arrived on 5 December. Most of the ship's band – inevitably, also Royal Marines – arrived on 17 December.[249]

So *New Zealand* entered the Royal Navy, slowly and by degrees. Both the official commissioning on 19 November and the arrival of the nominally full crew on 23 November were in many respects formalities, but they were also symbolic. After all the politics, the debate and the argument, Ward's gift was serving as he had intended. The irony was that in terms of her military statistics she was already obsolescent, underscored by the fact that *Lion*, the first 13.5in-gunned battlecruiser, had been commissioned in June. The point was driven home as *New Zealand* commissioned, when the Federated States of Malaya offered a gift battleship to Britain. This became the fifth unit of the new *Queen Elizabeth* class of fast battleships, *Malaya*. Churchill, meanwhile,

The ship's mascot: a bulldog named Pelorus Jack after a Risso's dolphin that had been meeting ships at French Pass, on the west coast of New Zealand's South Island, since 1888. There were actually two ship's bulldogs of that name: the first fell down the forefunnel in April 1916, but left a 'will' requesting its successor be a proper English 'bull-pup'. The second Pelorus Jack served through Jutland, became frightened of gunfire, and was given to the people of Auckland in October 1919.
(*Torpedo Bay Navy Museum ABT0080*)

began putting pressure on Canada to fund three capital ships.[250] By implication, these were going to be of similar power.

After all the hoopla that went with her offer, the fact that the gift ship was in service spurred remarkably little attention in New Zealand. Her gun and torpedo trials in mid-October 1912 garnered two and a half lines in the *Nelson Evening Mail*.[251] Her formal commissioning on 19 November produced a similar-length report in the *Evening Star*.[252] The *Dominion* gave the same event four lines.[253] Only the *Mataura Ensign* – which described *New Zealand* as a 'fast battleship' on 16 October[254] – offered much column space, mostly recapping the story of the launch.[255] In part this was a function of the fact that immediate news arrived by terse-worded telegraph. However, other issues were dominating the public mind in New Zealand that month, not least of them rising labour tensions that included a lengthy miners' strike. This turned violent in November 1912, with fatalities.

The ship's completion was nonetheless recognised at official level, and government asked the naval artist Lionel Wylie to produce a painting. In an artwork apparently named after the house in which he was living at the time, in Portsmouth, Wylie captured the ship being moved across harbour by tug, under delicate salmon clouds.

By December the crew were aboard and beginning the complex working up process designed to familiarise them with the equipment and train them into a unified whole. *New Zealand* was at sea over New Year 1912–13, caught by a gale that damaged some of the masting. She was back in Portsmouth by the time Midshipman Edmund Coore reported aboard on 15 January 1913. He found the ship 'lying alongside No. 5 wharf in the north yard'.[256] Nine days later the ship was inspected by the Commander in Chief of the Devonport base, Admiral Sir William May. Everything was in order: as Coore put it, May 'expressed his pleasure at the smartness of the ship'.[257]

Where next was already clear. *New Zealand* had joined the First Battlecruiser Squadron on completion – but something bigger was in the offing, a world-spanning cruise that threw her captain, Lionel Halsey, into the public limelight.

CHAPTER 4

HERO OF THE DAY

New Zealand's world tour of 1913 was the first circumnavigation of the globe by any of Britain's new-generation capital ships. The political purpose ran well beyond simply thanking New Zealand for the gift – a role made clear by the fact that the wider itinerary spanned much of the year and embraced an extensive raft of goodwill visits that stretched from Cape Town to Wellington, Auckland to Callao, Rio de Janeiro and finally Halifax. It was pure public relations on a global scale.

The origins of *New Zealand*'s remarkable *wanderjahr* can be traced to Ward's original 1909 arrangement for a visit to New Zealand by the entire China 'fleet unit'.[1] Although that plan disappeared with Churchill's reorganisation, the idea that the battlecruiser alone might still embark on a thank you voyage to New Zealand was cautiously accepted, although it was a hot potato for a while in 1912. While the Admiralty did not wholly buy in to the popular supposition that the fleet had to be ready to defeat a 'bolt from the blue' at any moment, the possibility nonetheless remained of a sudden diplomatic crisis in which war clouds might brew up faster than ships could be recalled. The Agadir crisis, just a few months earlier, gave the argument an immediate justification. So the Admiralty pushed hard to cut the period in New Zealand waters from three to two months. Halsey went in to bat for the New Zealanders. The 'people of the Dominion,' he argued, would 'be very disappointed if we did not go everywhere possible & give as many as possible a chance to see the ship & I feel sure it would be a means of creating a great wave of Imperial loyalty.'[2]

The Admiralty finally allowed ten weeks, promising that 'nothing but the most serious emergency will be allowed to interrupt the arrangements'.[3] However, that has to be set against the fact that the whole venture was scheduled to last nine months – and, in fact, extended a little longer. The actual role of the journey as a public relations exercise at global level – and the Sea Lords' attitude to the popular fear that a momentary loss of 'dreadnought' superiority in local waters would bring automatic nemesis – gains perspective along the way.[4]

In this age of social-militaristic fervour for Empire, local colonial and dominion authorities along the intended route were eager to see the ship;[5] quite apart from the diplomatic benefits of a planned South American leg.

The itinerary was hammered out during the last months of 1912, although aspects were still under discussion after the ship had departed. One initial proposal omitted Australia. Another early plan to go via the Suez Canal, missing out South Africa, was problematic. The Admiralty hydrographer issued instructions in October 1912 to keep the ship light, coupled with a general order that draft in the canal could not exceed 28ft, but this was not considered detailed enough for safety.[6] It was May 1913 before inclining experiments with *Australia* refined the data available for an *Indefatigable*-class hull at specific loadings and trims, and *New Zealand* received her formal certification for the canal.[7] But that was too late for her 1913 world tour, which, in the end, rounded the Cape of Good Hope.

New Zealand remained a key way point, recognised by the Admiralty through such gestures as transferring a New Zealand-born able seaman, R J Greening, from HMS *Hercules* to the battlecruiser so he could visit his home.[8] However, stops were also planned in Portugal, South Africa, Australia, Hawaii, Canada and South America. The context of the latter, given the naval race brewing between Argentina, Brazil and Chile – with the potential both for British industrial profit, and to bring pressure to bear against Germany – was not subtle.

To facilitate her voyage the battlecruiser was temporarily detached from the 1st Battlecruiser Squadron (BCS) on 20 January.[9] The independent command gave Halsey considerable discretion over his ship's movements, and from the Admiralty's perspective meant that correspondence went direct to him, not via the commander in chief of the battlecruiser squadron.[10] Halsey's orders arrived on 4 February with a rider: 'Telegrams are not to be sent from French, Spanish or Portuguese Stations except in case of real necessity, and you are to avoid making the number of H. M. Ship under your command when passing such Stations.'[11]

The fact that the ship was going to tour New Zealand generated a good deal of excitement in the dominion. Massey's government saw the event as a way of shifting attention away from New Zealand's simmering social-industrial troubles. The patriotic card retained its strength, as did the focus on military hardware as symbol of British Imperial power and a symbol of patriotism. Excitement grew during early 1913 as plans for the visit firmed up. Local authorities in coastal towns were eager to have their harbours added to the itinerary, while the mayors and councillors of inland towns clamoured for government support to get their people to the nearest port. The tour swiftly became a political hot potato, followed by arguments over who was going to foot the bill. The New Zealand public wanted to welcome the arrival of their gift to Empire with social events, civic receptions, concerts, sporting matches, public speeches, balls, light displays, fireworks and a whole panoply of other events. All had to be funded, and although subsidising some costs, Massey's government saw much of the burden falling on the local bodies, clubs and groups that had come up with the ideas.

All this planning – along with similar receptions elsewhere along the intended route – relied on the arrival of the star performer. That had its moments. *New Zealand* was due to sail on 30 January to meet an itinerary in which key days had been carefully scheduled, including an intended return to Portsmouth on 15 October. Local authorities along the route were largely planning their own events to this timetable.[12] However, that plan failed before it began. On 13 January, Admiral May was tipped off that the King, George V, wanted to see the ship.[13] The royal visit was fixed for 5 February amidst significant secrecy,[14] delaying the ship's departure until the 6th. The New Zealand High Commissioner, Sir Thomas McKenzie, meanwhile wanted any New Zealanders then in Britain to also have a chance to get on board.[15] After some to-and-fro discussion this was scheduled for the 3rd.[16]

Thomas Mackenzie, New Zealand High Commissioner to the United Kingdom, unveils *New Zealand*'s coat of arms, 3 February 1913. The choice of 'battle honours' is significant: the name had no naval battle honours, but the European 'discoverers' of New Zealand became a substitute, along with the date that Britain established formal sovereignty over New Zealand. The New Zealand government coat of arms – adopted in 1911 – further underscored the message. Morally, the ship was New Zealand's. That these dates and symbols also made the ship an overt expression of colonial power was less obvious at the time.
(*Torpedo Bay Navy Museum ABT0121*)

Royal party with ship's officers and Admiralty officials aboard *New Zealand*, 5 February 1913. Winston Churchill sits to one side of King George V, James Allen – New Zealand's Minister of Defence – on the other.
(*Torpedo Bay Navy Museum ABT 0078*)

For Halsey, busy getting his crew trained and the ship readied for its world-spanning voyage, this was a foretaste of what he knew would be happening, particularly in New Zealand. But it was also a distraction, and it meant that the ship's schedule had to be reorganised, with knock-on effects. He came up with a revised outward schedule that still got them to Lyttelton on the original date of 8 April.[17] That destination was soon revised to an arrival in Wellington on the same day,[18] although Halsey had to be circumspect because social preparations across New Zealand and elsewhere were well under way.

The official visits in Portsmouth ran smoothly, with the ship moored alongside the railway jetty. The ex-patriot New Zealand party came through on the 3rd, with formal speeches; and two days later the monarch arrived. However, George V only stayed about three and a half hours in Devonport altogether, and as soon as he had gone *New Zealand*'s hands began rigging coaling gear. They began coaling at 5.30pm from two lighters, taking on 800 tons.[19] It was a dirty job that drew in much of the crew, and the chill winter's evening did little to offset the sweat of those on deck as the coal was slung aboard and poured down the hatches into the bunkers, where others laboured to distribute it through the spaces. Coal dust, inevitably, got everywhere, a necessary sin in an age when the cleanliness of any warship was still considered a symbol of crew efficiency. The worst of it – as the men well knew – was that the whole routine would have to be repeated before long. And repeated again after that, and so on, for the entire voyage. It could not be avoided. The ship carried a significant supply of fuel oil for spraying into the furnaces, and that could be pumped. But the primary energy to drive her came from coal.

Next morning *New Zealand* cast off at 7.30am and began steaming down harbour at 7 knots, rising to 15 a few minutes later.[20] It was a departure little different from any other she had made from Portsmouth, masking the fact that she was embarking on one of the more interesting cruises yet undertaken by a warship of the era. Those aboard were well aware of the import of the moment, but the excitement was masked by their work. Halsey still needed to bring them up to fighting efficiency, and the exercises continued. On 10 February they practised collision stations, including bringing out the collision mat – a canvas-and-oakum sheet intended to be lowered over a gash in the hull to reduce inflow.[21]

Coore continued his education: he was told to draw pictures of equipment and take the temperatures of the oil tanks, while he also stood watches.[22] By 13 February they were at St Vincent, where the ship took on coal. Coore managed to get ashore to look at the island. The next day was given over to a hockey match against the Western Telegraph Company, but they were away again by the 15th.[23] So the voyage south continued with its crew training and periodic coaling at the far-flung stations the Admiralty had set up for the purpose – many stemming from the 1884 naval panic. Coore, as a young 'middie', had little time to be idle. When they got to Ascension, among other duties, he was required to hand-draw a plan of their anchorage and surrounding landforms in Clarence Bay, with heights marked.[24]

The ship reached Cape Town late on 28 February and moored to Loch Jetty for what Halsey called a 'heavy programme of Entertainments, Sports and Banquets'.[25] The Prime Minister, Louis Botha, had been ambivalent about the visit, turning down an offer by Natal to provide 2,000 tons of coal as a gift for the ship on the basis that South Africa already contributed to the Royal Navy.[26] That same gift, of course, highlighted the fact that social militarism was as strong in South Africa as anywhere else in the Empire, a point further underscored by the crowds who flocked to see the battlecruiser in Cape Town. Their numbers included, by Coore's estimate, around 25,000 children.[27] A total of 58,898 visitors arrived during the time the ship was open to the public – three full and two half-days; along with 1,500 official guests, including the Governor-General, Herbert Gladstone. He was the son of William Gladstone, the Prime Minister whose penurious attitude to naval spending had contributed to the public panics of the 1880s and 1890s. Halsey then invited eighty-seven members of both houses of the South African parliament aboard for the trip to Durban.[28]

All this was classic public relations in an age when military technology symbolised both patriotic sentiment and the power of Empire as a concept, but it also betrayed something more. Despite the increasing sense of self-identity and independence held by Britain's far-flung dominions, their public still looked to Britain for place. In early 1913 *New Zealand* was one of Britain's newest capital ships, symbolising that ideal in a very real and concrete manner. The burden of managing the intersection between public emotion and the reality of the ship fell primarily on Halsey.

New Zealand at Simon's Town.
(*Torpedo Bay Navy Museum ABT0122*)

The South African reception was a mere aperitif for what waited in New Zealand, where the battlecruiser focused a local emotional edifice that entangled self-identity, patriotism and Empire. Plans for the ship's New Zealand tour had been made, remade and reorganised on the back of that status. Amid a fervent explosion of public enthusiasm both at local body and central government level, Massey decided to hand administration over to the Internal Affairs Department and appointed his colleague Francis Henry Dillon Bell to manage the process. Bell – Harry to his friends – was a former Parliamentarian and lawyer who led the Legislative Council and was in many respects Massey's key administrator.[29] At the time he was Acting Minister of Marine, but his appointment to the tour underscored the importance Massey placed on the visit. Politically it was a winner. At a time where labour unrest had already broken into violence, where strikes loomed among the coal miners and waterside workers, Massey needed a public distraction. Massey needed a public distraction. *New Zealand* provided it.

Demand to see the ship prompted large public meetings in many towns, calling on local authorities to act. Bell fielded most of them, and requests continued to pour in after the schedule had been announced, and even after the ship had arrived. Part of the drive came from civic rivalries in this age of town 'boosterism', a curious phenomenon where local identity and status was defined by urban centre. If the ship visited one harbour, then the authorities of nearby harbours felt snubbed, even if their port was too shallow to accommodate the battlecruiser. Meanwhile, mayors of inland towns such as Eltham, in Taranaki, begged extension of the ship's visit to the nearby coastal port of New Plymouth 'to ensure opportunity for country people especially the children' to visit.[30] Other inland mayors worried about crowding: if the people of Ashburton could not visit the ship at Lyttelton, could they do so at Timaru?[31] Schools were eager for children to visit the ship, which Bell resolved by arranging for the Ministry of Education to fund railway tickets.

Bell also commandeered the government steamer *Tutanekai*, a Clyde-built cable ship of some 811 gross tons,[32] to follow *New Zealand* around the country, ferrying the public to the battlecruiser in places where she could not berth. She was not the only ship co-opted to do so, but Bell's decision underscored the complications created by weather. Many New Zealand harbours, including Napier and Gisborne – the two largest on the North Island's east coast – were too shallow for the ship to enter, and Halsey could not risk anchoring in the roadsteads during high seas. The schedule was also time-limited. Bell was reduced to batting off some of the more insistent demands, though always politely. 'The arrangements for [the] journey [of the] battleship [sic] have been made with great care,' he explained in terse telegraphic language to the Chairman of the Whangarei Harbour Board, 'and I fear the day required for [a] visit to Whangarei cannot be spared.'[33]

Bringing the public to the ship was only half the job. Into this was mixed an extensive programme for Halsey and his crew to meet, greet and mingle with as many local officials, clubs and organisations as possible. All was set against period ideas of town boosterism, and the result was a frenzy of action as civic leaders of the harbour towns, in particular, scrabbled to prepare. All wanted to show themselves in the best light – literally in the case of Napier, where the visit became an excuse to fund long-held plans to bring electric lighting both to the town's waterfront parade and its municipal theatre.[34] Elsewhere, dinners with the officers were organised – entry by ticket.[35] Everybody was excited, and nobody in the media drew distinction over the ship's classification, even throwing capitalisation and hyphenation to the winds amidst a heady explosion of naval terms. To journalists she was variously a 'castle of steel',[36] a 'battleship', the 'warship', a 'Super-Dreadnought Battle-Cruiser', a 'super-Dreadnought', or sometimes simply 'our Battle-Cruiser'.[37] Nobody minded: everybody knew the ship to which these words referred, and that was what counted.

All these plans were coming together as *New Zealand* steamed around the world. She made two stops in South Africa after Cape Town. The first, at

New Zealand in Lambton Harbour, Wellington, seen from Mount Victoria. (*Sydney Charles Smith, 1/1-022718-G. Alexander Turnbull Library*)

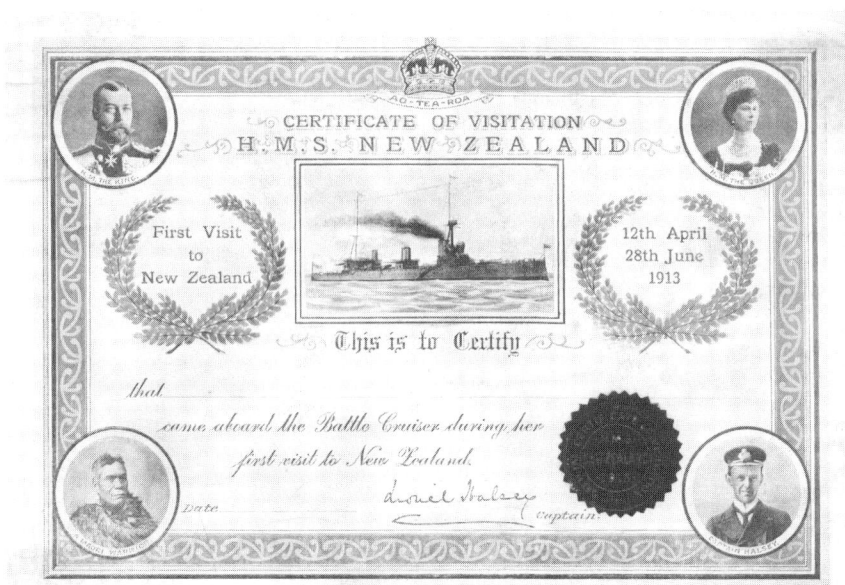

Simon's Town, was largely to put ashore two men with tuberculosis and pick up stores, although some 925 enthusiastic visitors still came aboard.[38] There was a more substantial stay in Durban. The battlecruiser left on 14 February and sailed east across the Indian Ocean for Melbourne, a late change at the request of Australia's Governor. Halsey had originally intended to stop in Hobart to coal.[39] Melbourne was the capital of the Commonwealth of Australia at the time, and Halsey could not dodge the request, forcing a further late change of plan for New Zealand that switched the arrival port from Lyttelton to Wellington. This had an unexpected consequence. Despite having no association with New Zealand's domestic situation, the decision provoked local allegations that the ship was going to support Massey's government against strikers.[40]

The battlecruiser arrived in Wellington on 12 April, where a fleet of small boats gathered to welcome her. The afternoon was taken up by official visits, and the ship was thrown open to the public over the next few days. A flood of New Zealanders poured aboard. Meanwhile, the officers and men were treated like royalty. Events included a three-day sojourn by selected officers to a sheep station near Picton. Others went north to Rotorua, then opening up as a major tourist town. No expense was spared when it came to entertaining the ship's officers and crews. A lunch on 18 April, put on at state expense for officers and government officials in the Wellington Town Hall, began with 'Oysters on shell', soup, fillet of sole; a choice of mayonnaise of chicken or asparagus *en croutes*; poultry – including duckling – and either lamb, sirloin or York ham. Then came trifles, apple pie, liquor jelly, fruit salads, meringues and anchovy straws, with coffee to follow.[41] Such events, inevitably, included formal toasts to King, Governor and Navy.

A total of 98,170 New Zealanders visited the ship during her stay in Wellington.[42] This was nearly 10 per cent of the national population at the time, drawn not just from the capital but the district around. But the reception here was merely the beginning of what – certainly for Halsey – became an emotionally overwhelming round of port visits, all filled with the same riotous enthusiasm. The ship took aboard nearly 1,000 tons of coal on 23 April, which precluded visitors.[43] Next day she sailed from Wellington to the cheers of enormous crowds – so many that Halsey wondered if 'the whole population' had arrived. They crowded the wharves and 'the whole waterside' all the way out to the heads, 'for about 4 miles'.[44] The battlecruiser engaged in brief exercises with the old P-class cruiser *Pyramus,* then turned north for Napier.[45] She arrived off the seaside town early on 25 April to a welcome by seventeen cadets standing on the hill overlooking the small breakwater harbour. A heavy swell was running, but the ship could not enter the harbour in any case and anchored, as planned, in the roadstead.

By 9.45am 1,000 children were on their way to the battlecruiser aboard the *Tutanekai*. They were transferred without incident despite the weather. Napier, already styling itself a resort town, was in party mood. Nobody was at work and the streets thronged with people happy to see the ship in the roadstead. There were parades, performances by brass bands, and – later – dances. Some 300 sailors landed later in the morning, joining a procession led by the Napier Pipe, City and ship's band, which led the sailors to the Drill Hall.

Meanwhile, the mayor, John Vigor-Brown, entertained the officers in the waterfront Masonic Hotel. Sports began on the Marine Parade in early afternoon; the sailors engaged in sprints, leapfrog and a sock race, all before the gaze of around 7,000 enthusiastic spectators. Halsey, meanwhile, was taken on a brief tour of the district, going on to a dinner in the prestigious and exclusive Hawke's Bay Club, whose new rooms on the Marine Parade had not long been open. The sailors attended a stage show at the Municipal Theatre, and there were performances on the Marine Parade. The ship departed next day for Gisborne, but some 16,750 visitors nonetheless got on board her.[46]

New Zealand went on to another riotous reception in Gisborne, then sailed to Auckland for a ten-day stay. None of this interrupted the ship's

N.Z.
H.M.S. NEW ZEALAND

BATTLE CRUISER.

Built by the Fairfield Shipbuilding and Engineering Company,
Govan, Glasgow, to the charge of the Government of New Zealand.

Laid down, June, 1910. Launched, July, 1911.

Commissioned at Devonport by Captain LIONEL HALSEY,
— November 23rd, 1912. —

Length	590 feet
Beam	80 feet
Draught	$30\frac{1}{2}$ feet
Displacement	19,000 tons
Main Armament	8 12-inch B.L. Mk. X 45 calibre Guns
Weight of Broadside	6,800 lbs. = 3 tons
Auxiliary Armament	16 4-inch B.L. Mk. VII 50 calibre Guns
Armour Protection	Belt 12 feet wide, 4 to 6 inches thick

2 Submerged Torpedo Tubes.

8 Twin Searchlights.

Complement 789 Officers and Men.

Turbine Engines, 4 Propellers.

44,000 Horse Power, 31 Boilers.

Speed 27 knots = $31\frac{1}{2}$ miles per hour.

Ship carries 3,200 tons of Coal and 830 tons of Oil fuel.

Cost £2,000,000.

———

Tasman 1642.   **Cook 1769.**
British Colony 1840.

A publicity card handed out during *New Zealand*'s world-spanning voyage, kept as a
memento by Edmund Coore. Some of the numeric details have been rounded.
(*qMS-0545, Coore, E G B, fl.1913–1914: Journal, Alexander Turnbull Library*).

routines as far as Halsey and his officers could help. Coore's routines certainly
varied little; among other tasks, he wrote an essay on the Australian navy.[47]
But the young midshipman had some relief from his training in Auckland,
where he was among the twenty-five officers who landed on 29 April for a
civic reception, arriving at what he called a 'specially decorated landing stage'
to a welcome by boy scouts. There was no privacy; even their transport to the
event took the form of a slow procession in carriages through streets lined
with cheering people. Halsey and his officers reached the town hall and got
a standing welcome from guests inside, including Ward.[48]

This was only the first of a raft of events, including what Coore called a

New Zealand in Auckland, 1913.
(*Lemuel Lyes Collection*)

Foredeck of *New Zealand* while in New Zealand waters during 1913. The ability of the main armament to elevate independently is clearly shown.
(*Lemuel Lyes Collection*)

'very enjoyable' garden party in the grounds of the Governor-General's Auckland residence.[49] Between times, Aucklanders flooded aboard the ship in colossal numbers, including several 'children only' mornings. The fact that particular arrangements had been made for children to see the ship underscores the place Massey and his government saw for the visit. He said as much at the first reception in the Auckland town hall: the ship, he declared, would show the new generation around the Empire the power of Britain and its Empire.[50]

The city was abuzz with excitement. Some boat owners lost no time capitalising on demand to sail out into the Waitemata and look at the ship. 'No crushing, no delay', one advertisement declared of the 'large and powerful launches' offering circuits 'twice around' the ship at 6 shillings a head, a mildly extortionate figure in period money.[51] The only damper on the whole Auckland stay was a run of deserters. One was shortly caught, and the New Zealander who assisted given a hefty fine – £15 – in the police court, with a two-month jail sentence with hard labour if it was not paid. He ended up in jail.[52]

Then it was the South Island's turn. Halsey had asked to have the southern waters prioritised, because of the risk of winter storms. He was declined, and now the itinerary risked disruption if the weather turned foul. He had some leeway if needed.[53] *New Zealand* berthed in Lyttelton on 13 May, drawing enthusiastic crowds from across Canterbury. The first day was 'children only', when around 11,000 came aboard.[54] Over the next few

New Zealand, surrounded by civilian boats. Offering paid sightseeing trips around the ship was a lucrative business for some boat owners during the ten-week tour.
(*Lemuel Lyes Collection*)

Period postcard of *New Zealand*, sold during her 1913 tour of New Zealand.
(*Lemuel Lyes Collection*)

days the officers and crew attended dances, balls, dinners, were taken on tours and – in and around the festivities – the public poured aboard. In the end some 132,365 New Zealanders came aboard during the ship's ten-day stay at Lyttelton,[55] about 13 per cent of the national population.

Halsey was overwhelmed. By his own estimate he had already made at least sixty speeches, but admitted, 'I don't like being the man of the hour at all.'[56] He found endless visitors to the ship stressful. 'Yesterday (Sunday), between 1.30 + 5pm,' he wrote to his mother late in the Auckland visit, 'there were over 19,000 on board – it was simply *awful*.'[57] What worried him particularly was discipline where every crew member was received as a public hero. 'I find it rather hard to control my 800 odd men in a place like this where every soul has gone mad about them and wishes to treat them, however all is well at present, but it means great care, tact and a certain amount of anxiety.'[58]

There was time for exercises off nearby Akaroa with the *Pyramus*; but as Halsey had anticipated, the ship's journey south was marred by rough weather. This forced him to restrict a planned stop in Timaru. The local Women's Branch of the Navy League had sewn a flag to donate to the ship, which was accepted by Lieutenant General Sir Alexander Godley on Halsey's behalf, and only later sent to the ship.[59] By the time they reached Oamaru, a little further south, the seas had settled enough to let them put men ashore to play football. The weather remained rough, and when *New Zealand* steamed up to a planned anchorage off the Otago heads on 31 May she was compelled to wait three days for the seas to settle. Halsey took the time to write to his mother 'Enthusiasm ... seems to increase,' he wrote to his mother 'and it is awfully hard to keep going with all that one has to do.'[60] The ship was too large to enter Otago harbour safely, however, Halsey and some of his men went ashore. From Dunedin he was able to head north by train to officiate at events in Timaru and Oamaru. He hoped this would 'in a small way' compensate for the 'disappointment ... in not having had the ship there'. His duties included unveiling a memorial at Oamaru to the memory of his old friend, Captain Robert Falcon Scott, who had died late the previous year after reaching the South Pole.[61]

This part of the South Island was the home ground of the ship's executive officer, Alexander David Boyle. He was not the only officer with New Zealand connections who drew media attention, Lieutenant Rupert Garsia hailed from Christchurch,[62] as did Penrose Barcroft – Mick to his friends – who was one of the two sub-lieutenants aboard. Of the sixteen midshipmen, one – Hugh Anderson – was also a New Zealander. All this was laid out in the media; here were local scions making good in Britain: the very definition of success in New Zealand at the time. As much attention, though, was given to the fact that two of the 'middies', aged seventeen, were nobility: the Earl of Carlisle and Lord Burgernesh. And the ship had Prince George of Battenberg aboard.[63]

The battlecruiser rounded the South Island, briefly stopping in Milford Sound before making a lightning visit to Westport, then Nelson, Picton and again to Wellington. In the capital she was able to berth at King's Wharf without pilot assistance because she was drawing 28ft at the time and there were 42ft of water at the wharf.[64] From Wellington she steamed up the North Island's west coast to Whanganui. She reached the coastal town early on 16 June, where she was met by *Tutanekai* and a local steamer, *Himitangi*, which had 700 children on board. The town had put on its best for the ship: one storekeeper had even built a sugar model of the battlecruiser for his window display. Halsey received gifts that included game and livestock: five deer, two swans, thirty-two pigeons, a hare and twenty lambs. Then, after a brief display of her searchlights at dusk, the ship steamed north for New Plymouth. Some 20,000 people lined the waterfront there to watch her arrive next morning. Not everybody got on board, but the ship was surrounded by boats with curious onlookers. About half a century earlier the district had been the focus of significant warfare, and Halsey and his officers were driven around the district, 'including the scenes of the fighting … and the graves and memorials of many naval officers and men who had fallen'. Halsey was also invited to formally open the Taranaki Oil Well Ltd refinery, with a ceremonial tap-turning.[65] At Hawera he was given a cannon ball from HMS *Alligator*, a sloop that had bombarded Māori in 1838, one of the less savoury displays of British gunboat diplomacy of the period.[66]

From here the battlecruiser steamed around North Cape and then south to visit Russell, in the Bay of Islands. The ship arrived in rough weather, but Halsey went ashore to a significant reception across the bay at Waitangi. What followed surprised Halsey, as he wrote later to his father:

> My goodness me … you would have laughed, as after about half an hour's dancing … a young Maori woman dashed up and kissed me, much to the amusement of my officers, there being about 20 of them there. It really was most embarrassing as you can imagine, however Battenberg has a worse time of it …[67]

The formal events at Waitangi carried more meaning for Māori than Halsey perhaps realised. This was the place where Māori had signed a treaty of sovereignty in 1840 with a British naval officer, Captain William Hobson, who was acting on behalf of the Crown. And in part for these reasons, but also because of the political status of a visit by prominent warships at the time, Māori saw *New Zealand* as more than just a symbol of patriotism: the battlecruiser was also an expression of Empire. This became one level with which Māori engaged with the ship – something also made clear by the nature of the koha (gifts) given by them to Halsey and his officers.

The issue of the koha deserves further exploration, not least because one of those gifts, coupled with a loan from a Pākehā (colonist), gained lives of their own in the ship's story. *New Zealand* – as entity – was showered with gifts from all sides during her New Zealand tour. Clubs, organisations, local bodies and individuals wanted to provide something, vicariously associating themselves by gesture. Such offerings included a good deal of silverware, which Halsey carefully logged, not least because these things were socially prized, becoming part of the ship's story and officer subculture. Presentations included a stag's head from B M Wilson; two boar's heads; a silver claret jug presented to the officers by the 'residents of Wellington', a silver salver from James Allen, another from the Wellesley Club of Wellington, an ivory hammer, a silver shield from the Canterbury Swimming Association and a

Māori aboard *New Zealand* in 1919. Parties of Māori visiting the ship during her 1913 tour were similar. While many wore European-style dress, some put on more traditional attire in recognition of the formality and solemnity of the occasion.
(*Torpedo Bay Navy Museum 2006.186.239.p29.2*)

Silver box gifted to the wardroom of *New Zealand*, 1913.
(*Torpedo Bay Navy Museum FT1219*)

The piupiu gifted to Captain Lionel Halsey.
(*Torpedo Bay Navy Museum 042 2007.1.1*)

good deal more, including a silk ensign and jack from the 'women of New Zealand', which the ship subsequently flew.[68] Among them were two hei tiki – small carved pendants. These did not come from Māori. One was presented by the Boy Scouts of Wellington on 13 April, the other as a loan by the manager of the Crown Brewery in Christchurch, C J Sloman, on 13 May.[69] Other gifts were made for the benefit of the crew, including 800 2oz tins of 'Capstan Navy Cut' tobacco from the British Empire Trading Company.[70]

Officers also received personal gifts and bouquets – so many of the latter that Halsey thought his own cabin had become a 'conservatory of flowers'. He wrote to his mother listing other gifts presented to him personally, which included 'a most lovely album with a very nice illuminated frontispiece … containing every New Zealand stamp … they have also given me all the N.Z. Stamps [sic] mounted in a frame, and such a nice plate with the inscription inlaid in Greenstone … I am fairly loaded with gifts of all sorts, and have got the most marvellous collection of Maori Rugs [sic] that anyone has I should say.'[71]

One personal gift that Halsey did not mention in that letter was a piupiu. This was a warrior's skirt, made from rolled flax. It looked like a kilt and fulfilled the same military function, enabling the wearer to move quickly through dense undergrowth. During the New Zealand Wars of the 1860s, Māori had been more mobile than British troops by virtue of this approach; and colonial forces soon adopted kilts for the same purpose.[72]

This piupiu remains perhaps the best known of the gifts from Māori, but a good deal of mythology swirls around it, including the supposition that such gifts were patriotic expressions of loyalty, or that they had mystic power. This demands explanation. By the early twentieth century New Zealand considered itself to have the best race relations in the world: Māori and Pākehā (the British colonists) had fought, made up and were now the best of friends. Superficially, as far as the Pākehā of the day were concerned, this vision had a basis in truth. By 1913 Māori had the right to vote, had representation in Parliament, and were closely familiar with Pākehā ways of life; most spoke English fluently, by this stage sometimes as a first language. However, colonial power and embedded racism was as clear in New Zealand as elsewhere at the time. Despite the treaty signed at Waitangi in 1840 that guaranteed significant rights, notably to their own land, Māori had been economically marginalised by 1913 and – although there were exceptions – primarily lived in poor ruralised communities. Much of their land had gone during the nineteenth century, and a good deal of what remained had passed to the government in the years just prior to *New Zealand*'s tour, primarily through the lever of impoverishment.

Through these same years, the largely urbanised Pākehā population – whose rural-dwelling farmers shared the same urban ideals as their city-dwelling brethren – had engaged in wholesale cultural appropriation. By 1913 New Zealand was well into its 'Māoriland' phase, in which the dominant Pākehā population took Māori symbols and words as a sign of Pākehā local identity, a layer atop the overall sense of being British.[73] This appropriated self-image was reflected aboard the battlecruiser, despite it being primarily Royal Navy: the ship's official letterhead paper featured a crown with the word 'Ao-tea-roa', with hyphens, beneath.[74] This word – Aotearoa – was usually translated at the time as 'long white cloud', referring sometimes to the North Island, more often the whole of New Zealand.[75]

What this meant for the visiting battlecruiser was that many gifts of Māori cultural items to the ship – notably both hei tiki – were from Pākehā . It also meant that relatively few Māori visited the ship by comparison with numbers of Pākehā, but those who did were typically rangatira – high-ranking chiefs; or prominent politicians, often arriving in formal parties. An academic study has argued that leading Māori took the opportunity to restate the relationship they expected – but had been denied – with the Crown.[76] This is certainly clear enough from reports of what was said. 'The whole source of our peace is the Treaty of Waitangi,' one chief explained. 'And the strength of the British Navy. Let both live and be strong!'[77] In Whanganui [Wanganui], Halsey was told: 'We are also glad to remember that the promise of … Queen Victoria, in the Treaty of Waitangi, has been fulfilled by her and her illustrious successors.' Delegates urged him to 'tell the King of the loyalty and patriotism of the Māori people'.[78]

All of this was in line with the main Māori relationship strategy of the day, broadly pushed by Apirana Ngata and the Young Māori Party, which attempted to engage with the colony in terms of its own values, enhancing the Māori place within it, preserving Māoritanga (culture) and obtaining redress for prior injustices, many stemming from government dereliction of the Treaty.[79] It was not the only strategy: another Māori focus from the late nineteenth century involved seeking legal redress through Britain, notably the Privy Council, again on the basis of the Treaty. All strategies, however, looked to engage at the highest level. And the battlecruiser was by far the most prominent symbol of Empire seen in New Zealand for some time. It became, therefore, a vehicle for again reminding Britain of its Treaty obligations, which Māori did not consider had been fulfilled.[80]

One of the problems with the origin of the piupiu is that its donor was never recorded, an issue complicated by the fact that Halsey received a number of what he called 'mats' at different times; for example, a gift of a 'mat' made by Rotorua Maori in Auckland on 26 June 1913, where the period report states it was placed on Halsey's shoulders without comment.[81] One story is that 'the' piupiu was given to him on 7 May by Rangitīaria Dennan ('Guide Rangi') in Rotorua,[82]another that it came from a Te Arawa chief of the same district. There has also been suggestion it came from Ngāi Tahu.[83] History, of course, is always a discussion: and in this regard perhaps the most compelling origin story of the piupiu is that Halsey received it in Wellington, late in the morning of 21 April, from a delegation of twenty-five leading Māori.[84]

Visitors to the ship in Wellington on that day included Tūreiti Te Heuheu Tūkino, one of the key chiefs of Ngati Tuwharetoa.[85] The moment was political, and not just because the group included Māori members of Parliament. Several gave speeches in te reo Māori.[86] Coore imagined that this was because they could not speak English. In fact, almost all Māori spoke English fluently – not least because they had been openly punished for using their own language in prior decades. Key members of the visiting party were politicians and leading Māori, who spoke English fluently and routinely. Using te reo Māori during a formal kōrero (talk/discussion) aboard the battlecruiser was intentional, rendering the moment symbolic and politically charged, and this purpose is consistent with what was apparently said.[87] The speeches that day were not closely recorded, but Coore jotted down repeated references to Queen Victoria.[88] At the time her name was usually used when the Treaty of Waitangi was being obliquely invoked, a reference that underscores the wider political meaning of the visit to Māori.

Afterwards, the guests presented Halsey and other officers with a range of personal gifts. Halsey's included a piupiu along with a tewhatewha – a long-handled and bladed fighting staff with similar function to a battleaxe, but requiring a different technique for use in battle. He also received two robes, two tangiwai (teardrop-shaped pendants),[89] korowai (cloaks woven of flax) and what Halsey regarded as a floor mat.[90] The term 'mat', at the time, was used by both the British and by New Zealand Pākehā to refer to any material Māori made of flax or other fabric, including clothing. Specifically who of the group gave Halsey the piupiu is not clear from period accounts. Halsey himself attributed it to Te Heuheu, who he recorded had also given him a 'mat' and a kawakawa rewa, an ornament made of pounamu (greenstone). The *Evening Post*, however, carried a detailed report of the visit and reported the piupiu being given by the Member of Parliament Taare Rakatauhake Parata, on behalf of Mana Hiniona.[91] What all the accounts agree on is that no hei tiki was given that day.[92]

Mythology has also swirled around what was said when the piupiu was presented, usually to the effect that Halsey was told it would protect the ship if he wore it in battle. One variant suggests that predictions were made that the ship would not be damaged. However, although Boyle told the story forty years later,[93] and it is repeated in secondary material as if true, there is no evidence in accounts of the day that anything of the sort was uttered during the Wellington visit. Potentially the tale – recorded later – conflated other visits by high-ranking Māori, where comments regarding the ship's anticipated fortunes were made.

Either way, the idea that Māori literally believed these gifts would bestow protection – as the legend suggests – needs examining. It fitted the period stereotype of indigenous people shrouded in 'primitive' beliefs, but this was simply not true for Māori. Despite rural segregation and impoverishment as a people, Māori were intimately familiar with Pākehā society of the day – and, by the early twentieth century, had been for generations, engaging the colonists in sophisticated ways framed by a close understanding of British values and systems. Māori also had a pragmatic world view, noted by the first British to spend time in New Zealand, because it closely matched the British approach. This did not exclude spirituality, but it meant that practical realities were accepted and understood for what they were. This included military matters.

In this regard, Māori had held an excellent practical understanding of industrial-age warfare and its technologies since the early nineteenth century, when chiefs such as Hongi Hika deliberately obtained key field techniques from the British – both offensive and defensive – then adapted them to New Zealand conditions of the day.[94] We can test the issue of the piupiu being offered as a magical protective device by asking why a tewhatewha, given on the same day as the piupiu, was not offered as a device for ensuring the ship's armament would always strike. No such comment was made. Nor was the piupiu traditionally seen by Māori as a magical garment; it was a practical item of clothing worn by combatants in the field. This last was likely its primary meaning as a gift to Halsey; the ship was personified by its captain – another concept British and Māori shared closely. Period reports make clear Halsey was told the piupiu was to be worn during battle. This was the correct function of the garment, which remark Halsey took to mean he should do so when the ship was in action.

In this context the idea that wearing it in battle would *protect* the ship presents as a lower-deck legend, framed by hearsay reports of what was told to Halsey, potentially by conflating remarks Māori made across multiple visits to the ship. Indeed, there is some evidence that the belief did not actually arise until after Halsey wore the piupiu during the First Battle of Heligoland.[95] It was an interpretation fuelled by the derogatory period stereotype of indigenous people as primitive and superstitious. The fact that the 'protection' belief was attributed to two unrelated gifts – one of them not from Māori at all, but a loan from a Christchurch brewer – makes the point clear.[96]

For Māori, the more crucial import of the koha (gifts) related to the political function of the visit to the ship, which symbolised Māori engagement with Pākehā society on the one hand; and offered, at the same time, a mechanism by which the unfulfilled promise of that engagement – symbolised by the Treaty of Waitangi – could be highlighted in an age of embedded racism by colonial authorities. This is underscored by the fact that both the likely donors of the piupiu, as one example, were politically active. Parata was an MP and member of the Liberal party and Te Heuheu, at the time, lived locally in Lyall Bay, a suburb of Wellington.

Halsey missed the local political symbolism, but was embarrassed by the value of what was pressed upon him that day, writing to his father to confess that 'the Maori chiefs are flooding me with curios, and one has given me a Kiwi mat, which I am told could be got for hundreds of pounds ... I feel much more like a king than a poor naval officer'.[97] Although the piupiu was his personally, Halsey left it with the ship when John Green took command in mid-1915. He subsequently bequeathed the garment to his daughter Ruth, whose own will donated it to New Zealand. The piupiu – by its history an item of significant cultural value and importance to New Zealand – was received by the Royal New Zealand Navy Museum at Torpedo Bay in 2005.[98]

From the Bay of Islands the battlecruiser sailed south to Auckland for a week, in part to coal and reorganise the ship's stores. Halsey attended events and gave speeches, then hosted a ball on board ship. And then the hectic ten-week whirl was over. By the time *New Zealand* left Auckland for Suva at 3pm on 28 June, some 376,114 New Zealanders had been aboard, more than a third of the entire population.[99] By estimate, another 125,000 or thereabouts had been able to see her from the quayside or boats that had circled the ship – in total around a full half-million, one in every two New Zealanders. This was from a population where not everybody could get to the ship, and which in any case included babes in arms, the elderly, infirm; even the disinterested. Social militarism, at personal level, was not for all, despite its intensity as a general social phenomenon of the day.

The fact that over a third of a million visitors were counted aboard from a nation whose population stood at around 1 million, coupled with the intense spotlight focused on Halsey and his officers, took its toll. As the ship steamed quietly north to Fiji, Halsey wrote to his mother: 'I really am relieved to get a spell, as things were at appalling high pressure the whole time and never seemed to ease down.'[100] He was, by place, the man in the spotlight – but by nature very much the reluctant hero of the day. And he was not alone in such sentiment; it had been an extraordinary ten weeks in which even ordinary sailors had been feted by the New Zealand public. However, this was not the end of the festivities. When *New Zealand* steamed out of Auckland on 28 June 1913 she was only halfway through her world public relations tour. The battlecruiser reached Suva on 1 July, then after five days in Fiji steamed north for Honolulu, which she reached on the 12th. Here the ship took on 1,930 tons of coal and 280 tons of oil.[101] By the 23rd they were at

Esquimalt, the British base on Canada's west coast, and spent a week in Vancouver before steaming south for California and then Panama, reached on 29 August.[102]

What followed was more crucial, from the British perspective, than the New Zealand tour. There were many diplomatic benefits to showing the flag in the Americas, and by April the Admiralty was under pressure to add Mexico to the list. The Mexican revolution was in full swing, but the Commander in Charge of the West Coast of America station urged a visit on the basis that the United States Navy already had a high profile.[103] This produced plans for a stop in Mazatlán, where Halsey met Brigadier General Reynaldo Diaz and was warned not to let his crew outside the town. Some 600 locals went on board to look at the ship.[104] *New Zealand* then sailed south to Acapulco in fine weather and increasing heat. Halsey kept a watchful eye on the environmental conditions, concluding the ship was 'well ventilated in the living spaces'.[105]

From Acapulco they sailed to Panama, then south to Peru, where the ship arrived at Callao on 8 September.[106] Over the next two months the battle-cruiser journeyed around the South American coast, visiting Valparaíso, Punta Arenas, Montevideo and Rio de Janeiro.[107] This was virtually as long as the ship had spent in New Zealand, and once again the politics were overt. Chile was an important British trading partner, not least because Chilean nitrates were essential to the munitions industry. Furthermore, Argentina, Brazil and Chile – the 'ABC' states – had been locked in a growing naval race of their own for some years. As in Europe, national power was proxied by naval strength, which led to all three ordering their own dreadnoughts despite the load these put on their economies. British industries were profiting from the effort, but were in competition with yards in Germany and the United States. There was also the fact that – if war broke out – Britain wanted to be able to purchase any ships under construction without diplomatic incident: and the potential for major South American naval vessels to join the British in the North Sea could not be ignored.

All this added up, and although British relations with Chile in particular were already strong, Halsey knew his ship was there to leave a trail of general goodwill towards Britain among various South American nations that were themselves at odds. Over this was layered the fact that the ship's tour was an obvious display of British influence, standing against similar visits from other nations, including the United States. This was something the British consul in Callao in Peru, for one, thought important.[108]

The bulk of the Chilean fleet was at Valparaíso, saluting *New Zealand* with light shows and flag displays. Halsey reported that they were 'most hospitably entertained' by the Chileans and 'the greatest good feeling was shown by our hosts'. The Chilean ships saluted her with twenty-one guns from all vessels, illuminating all ships that night. The city was in festival mood, celebrating independence. When *New Zealand* left on 23 September, the Chilean warships fired rockets in salute while the crews cheered.[109]

British naval forces in the area came under Rear Admiral Christopher Cradock, and included the new light cruiser *Glasgow*, which was off the south-western coast of South America at the time. *New Zealand* made contact with *Glasgow* on 29 September, just after leaving Punta Arenas. The battle-cruiser reached Montevideo – spelt Monte Video in Halsey's reports – on 3 October,[110] then went on to Rio de Janeiro.[111]

From South America the battlecruiser sailed to Trinidad, where there were problems obtaining coal and oil;[112] then – on Cradock's orders – to Dominica so Halsey could officiate alongside Cradock at a court martial for a stoker who had assaulted another. The rear admiral arrived aboard his flagship HMS *Suffolk*, where the court martial was held; and next day *New Zealand* went on to Jamaica, arriving at Kingston on 7 November.[113] She spent the next few days in the Caribbean, visiting Grenada and finally Barbados. Depth restrictions here – which required Halsey to keep draft less than 30ft – meant she could not fully coal for the journey back to England,[114] so she sailed north to Halifax in late November to top up. This produced an opportunity for a brief formal visit by officers to Ottawa.

New Zealand returned to Portsmouth on 6 December and re-joined the battlecruiser squadron. She was shortly docked for refit. It had been the longest single voyage made by a dreadnought-era capital ship to that time, some 45,320 miles. To achieve it, the battlecruiser had burned more than her own displacement in coal – some 31,833 tons in total – all of which had been moved by the muscle power of the crew.[115] The public relations aspect had been a howling success. A total of 500,151 people had boarded the ship worldwide, more than two-thirds of them New Zealanders.[116]

All that had marred the journey was a small but steady drizzle of desertions throughout, to the point where at one stage Halsey had to signal the Admiralty to send out thirteen more stokers.[117] There was universal acclaim for Halsey's conduct and that of his crew through the voyage. The Admiralty certainly recognised Halsey's part;[118] he was eventually knighted for his work. The public relations benefit of the voyage left a lasting impression on the Admiralty, and the expedition became a direct precursor for the next major initiative of this type, a world tour by the Special Service Squadron of 1924.

Back in New Zealand the excitement and hoopla of *New Zealand*'s visit faded quickly. Local papers reported on her reception across the Pacific,[119] but there were arguments over where the costs of entertaining her crew throughout New Zealand should fall. Some local authorities had spent significant sums, but received little support even from nearby local bodies, exemplified by the Auckland experience where the city council had planned to spend about £1,000, but as late as 24 April had obtained only £146 3s towards their costs from neighbouring local authorities, whose people were going to benefit from the spending.[120] Initial government planning made it clear that anything local bodies did was at their own financial risk, but the issue became politicised and in the end central government passed legislation retroactively guaranteeing council costs. Meanwhile, the separate and deeper-set issue of industrial unease reared its head to the point where watersiders' strikes were backed by popular sentiment, and Massey authorised 'special constables' – a makeshift militia, in lieu of the army – to enforce control in the major centres.[121] The battlecruiser, in short, had been a public distraction for a while, but no more.

The ship's tour of New Zealand came just as the policy debates that had provoked her into being entered their final act. The problem for officials in Wellington remained local naval defence, which had been snatched away by Churchill's precipitate cancellation of the China fleet unit and the ships meant to be stationed in New Zealand waters. Late in 1912 the government sent the Minister of Defence, James Allen, to London to discuss local protection, throwing a political cloud over *New Zealand*'s pending world tour. The Admiralty were aware of the delicacy: when Halsey was given independent command in January 1913, the Military Branch – part of the Admiralty's secretariat and in charge of matters political – quietly advised him to 'be careful in the manner in which he referred to the question of a New Zealand naval policy'.[122]

By this time Canada had a Conservative government under Robert Borden, who offered to pay for three dreadnoughts for Britain, conditional on having greater voice in Imperial affairs and on the ships later becoming the nucleus of a Pacific force. This appeared to be Ward's policy on steroids, but was not. It lacked a federal aspect, and the end game Borden had in mind was a Canadian naval force. By this time Australia's fleet unit was operational, and Massey was being criticised in the media for lacking a defence policy. The *New Zealand Times* even went so far as to claim that New Zealand, alone among the nations, was groping blind.[123] Allen blamed Ward, writing later that he did not think Ward had any idea of naval policy at all.[124]

However, when Allen arrived in London, he had only a vague plan to offer by which New Zealand would establish its own naval force. This got

James Allen (1855–1942), New Zealand's Minister of Defence 1912–1920.
(*S P Andrew, 1/1-013396-G. Alexander Turnbull Library*)

the same chilly reception that had greeted the Australian fleet ideas a decade or so earlier, not helped by the dislike Allen and Churchill took to each other. In 1929 Allen wrote that 'from the first it was evident that the First Lord held opinions as to the attitude New Zealand should adopt which differed from mine'.[125] Churchill felt that Allen, for his part, was 'full of very foolish and retrogressive ideas'.[126] Surviving records reveal that, although the language remained diplomatic, there was a good deal of tension.[127] One meeting was so fraught that Harcourt secretly sent the minutes to the Governor, back in Wellington.[128] The Admiralty, for their part, felt obliged to urgently telegraph Halsey – by this time in Melbourne – again warning that 'future naval policy of New Zealand' was 'still under discussion in London' – and Halsey 'should be careful to avoid such subject as far as possible'.[129]

By the time he left London, Allen had agreed – against his intent – that the annual subsidy would be used to pay for manning two old cruisers stationed in New Zealand waters.[130] The Admiralty offered to send a third such cruiser, but this was rejected; and Churchill finally wrote to Allen at the end of August 1913 to advise that Britain did not have any fast cruisers to spare. In any case, 'no military need exists at present for vessels of this speed. There are apparently no foreign cruisers of an equal type which require to be met within thousands of miles of New Zealand. If there were, we should immediately match them by similar vessels.'[131]

Massey then asked the Admiralty whether they might consider sending two *Bristol*-class cruisers, but was told that if New Zealand wanted such ships they would have to buy them. Two would cost £700,000.[132] This was not surprising; the request came amidst a political argument in London over the 1914–15 estimates. These looked likely to top £50 million for the first time in the history of the Royal Navy, and by late 1913 Churchill was under intense pressure to find ways of reducing costs. Pandering to a New Zealand request that he had already dismissed a few months earlier was not on the agenda. Massey's government was left with little option. At the end of October 1913, Massey announced his intention to have one *Bristol*-class cruiser built for local service. It would be manned by New Zealanders, but control would pass to Britain if war broke out. 'I have no doubt,' he told the House, 'that the Imperial authorities are, in their judgement, doing the best possible in the interests of the Empire as a whole, but the New Zealand government think a commencement should be made to improve the naval position in the South Pacific.'[133]

This has been interpreted as evidence of a policy to provide New Zealand with at least a token naval element.[134] However, although Allen wanted such a force, there is no evidence that Massey agreed.[135] His aim in purchasing the cruiser was less to emulate the Australians as to resolve the practical issue created by Churchill's decision to get rid of the China station fleet unit. In the end the cruiser was not ordered, and the only addition to the ancient gunboat *Torch* and the two P-class cruisers already in local waters was the obsolete cruiser *Philomel*, veteran of the thirty-eight-minute war against Zanzibar in 1898. She reached New Zealand in early 1914 under Captain P H Hall-Thompson,[136] effectively symbolising the failure of Ward's gift as a device for both federalising defence and securing local protection along the way.

CHAPTER 5

FIRST WORLD WAR

> A cruiser of the *Breslau* class recommenced firing, but we did not care a farthing for, straight ahead of us in lordly procession, like elephants walking through a pack of dogs, came HMS *Lion*, HMS *Queen Mary*, HMS *Invincible* and HMS *New Zealand*, great, grim and uncouth, as if they were some antediluvian monsters.[1]

With the luxury of hindsight it is easy to talk about the 'golden summer' of 1914, a romantic image around which to wrap a last, glorious expression of the 'old order' with its monarchies, stratified wealth, high society and conceits, before Europe crashed into war of a scale never before seen in the history of the world. This notion of partying even as war clouds brewed was almost literally true, as events turned out, for *New Zealand* – but wider historical reality was a little different. Certainly the weather did not match nostalgic memory: in London, at least, the summer of 1914 was hot but also somewhat damp.[2] More crucially, nobody imagined that a European war might break out. Britain's larger problem that year was internal. Prime Minister H H Asquith's controversial Government of Ireland Bill – the so-called 'Home Rule Bill' – went before the House for the third time in May, with its implicit potential to trigger civil war in Ireland and downstream dislocation across the Empire.

New Zealand was still part of the First Battlecruiser Squadron and, as the summer unfolded, embarked on a journey to Kronstadt, the deep-water harbour near the Russian capital of St Petersburg. It was her second goodwill venture in a year, this time in company with the 13.5in-gunned battlecruisers *Lion*, *Princess Royal* and *Queen Mary*, and supporting vessels. The journey carried a political complication. Russia had been making overtures to Britain about military ties for some years. These culminated in a February 1914 proposal by the Tsar, Nicholas II, for a naval agreement. Britain rejected it; the Russians persisted, and finally in May the Foreign Office agreed to discuss matters. This was passed to Germany via their spy in the Russian embassy in London. The story got into the *Berliner Tageblatt*, and from there back to the British media.[3] On 11 June, Edward Grey denied that discussions were taking place. Beatty's four battlecruisers and their escorting cruisers left for Kronstadt just two days later.

The diplomatic implication was awkward, but the goodwill visit gained political deniability because the British despatched the Second Battle Squadron to Kiel. This was at the invitation of the *Kaiserliche Marine*, marking the week-long sailing regatta that had been held annually in the Baltic port since the early 1880s. The events of 23–30 June were particularly significant for Germany because they also marked the formal opening of new and larger locks on the Kiel Canal, the artificial waterway linking Germany's Baltic harbour with the North Sea. It became clear that there was a good deal of camaraderie at personal level between Britain's sailors and the Kaiser's.[4] *Kapitan* Adolf von Trotha, serving aboard SMS *Kaiser*, said as much to Jellicoe on 6 July: 'The visit of the English squadron during the "Kieler-Woche" was a special and great pleasure for us and we hope heartily that our English comrades have had a nice stay here.'[5]

For Coore, *New Zealand*'s journey into the Baltic lent new interest to his duties as a midshipman. By 14 June they had the Danish coast in sight, 'low and sandy with very few towns'; and next day they entered the Great Belt, passing into the Baltic through a narrow channel with difficult navigation. Coore noticed windmills ashore.[6] They were met in the Gulf of Riga by a squadron of Russian cruisers led by the armoured cruiser *Rurik* – British-built, completed in 1908 as one of the more powerful examples of her type. The battlecruisers were piloted into Kronstadt harbour and moored. Coore was required to take bearings on local landmarks after *New Zealand* was fastened to her buoy, remarking in his work book that there was a 'consider-able Russian fleet here of 7 battleships and 5 cruisers'.[7]

The British were received with open arms by the Russians. Officers of both navies dined in each other's wardrooms, there were social events ashore, and at one point the officers and crew of *Queen Mary* reciprocated by hosting what Coore called a 'small dance'. A little later he was able to watch a concert and 'Russian ballet' ashore. The warmth of the reception impressed him. 'Everywhere ashore great enthusiasm prevails between the Russians & ourselves.'[8] The highlight came near the end of their stay; a formal visit to the ship by the Tsar. *New Zealand* was 'dressed' by the forenoon of the 27th, in time for the arrival of the Imperial yacht with Tsar Nicholas II and the Tsarina, Alexandra Feodorovna, formerly Princess Alix of Hesse. The Tsar arrived in the uniform of a British admiral. The Russian royal party sailed under the stern of *New Zealand*, and boarded *Lion* to a thirty-one-gun salute by the squadron. After lunch the royal party boarded *New Zealand*, where the officers shook hands with the Tsar.

All this was prelude to the formal dance scheduled for that evening – the 'party of the century' by which Beatty intended to impress the Russian royals, showing them just what the Royal Navy could do when it came to high society. The deck of *New Zealand* was tagged as the dance floor. Coore recalled how the ships were rigged:

> Directly the yacht had left we slipped from our buoys & made fast alongside the port side of the *Lion*. All hands were then employed rigging the quarter deck & amidships deck for the dance. The quarter deck had the red and white bunting awnings spread & the amidship [sic] deck was decorated in blue & white, the band being forward of Q turret. The cloak rooms & supper rooms were in *Lion*. A dais was rigged in the *Lion* overlooking the ballroom, for the principal guests.[9]

Guests included several New Zealanders living in St Petersburg, including Harold and Aubrey Williams. They were, reputedly, not married – potentially scandalous, although their status was not spoken of in other than hushed tones. Aubrey Williams described the ship as 'beautifully decorated'.[10] Coore's account of the party is remarkably coy: we learn only that the ball began at 10pm, finished about 4am the following morning, and that it was marked aboard *New Zealand* by an 'exhibition of the Maori dances', which Coore recalled 'amused the guests'.[11] This was a haka, taught to the crew by Māori during the visit to New Zealand.[12] Aubrey Williams reported, later, that it was 'danced by 20 of the crew' which was 'a decided novelty to the Russians and had to be repeated'.[13] There were also 'many inquiries as to Maori customs and as to the meanings of the names 'Cook', 'Tasman' and 'Ao-te-aroa [sic], inscribed on the turrets [sic]'.[14]

In short, the ball was, by all accounts, a success, but there was little sleep for the crew. As soon as the dance was over they began re-rigging the ship for normal duties. At 8am on 28 June *New Zealand* cast off from *Lion* and returned to her buoy.

That day – 28 June – was the last full day of the visit. Coore and some of the other officers spent most of the afternoon

New Zealand's haka party in action. While from a twenty-first century perspective this group – with its make-up – presents as symbolic of cultural appropriation and the embedded racism of the early twentieth century, at the time the group were viewed as a further connection with New Zealand. (*Torpedo Bay Navy Museum ABT0179*)

118

This ball, held aboard *New Zealand* in Bombay in 1919, captures something of the feel of the grand reception at Kronstadt five years earlier.
(*Torpedo Bay Navy Museum 2006.186.239.p7.1*)

at sports events put on by British ex-patriots living in the Russian city. When he got back to the battlecruiser he found that a new navigating officer was aboard, 'to take the place of Commander Jones who is sick'.[15] He made no comment about the events in Sarajevo that day, where Archduke Franz Ferdinand – heir to the Austro-Hungarian throne – and his wife Sophie had been assassinated at 11.30am local time by nineteen-year-old Gavrilo Princip. If the news reached the ship at all that afternoon, it seems the incident was not considered worthy of remark. This is not surprising. Nobody knew their future, and just then the assassination – though important in Austria-Hungary – was not a major incident.

Next day the squadron left Kronstadt, heading back to Britain. *New Zealand* was due to become part of the Mediterranean fleet, decommissioning on 30 August,[16] before being recommissioned and taking up her new role in September as flagship of Rear Admiral Archibald Moore. Before then, however, she was scheduled to be part of the first full mobilisation of the entire Home Fleet, including reserve forces. This was the major fleet event of the year and had its origins in Churchill's late-1913 arguments with Cabinet over the scale of the 1914–15 estimates. In a gesture to meet ongoing demands for cuts he replaced the annual fleet exercises with a cheaper option:

a test mobilisation of the reserve fleet, brief sea exercises, and display of the combined force at Spithead.[17] This was scheduled for July 1914.

By this time the forces in home waters were arranged in three major formations: the First Fleet of the fully commissioned dreadnoughts and supporting warships; the Second Fleet, with older but effective vessels carrying nucleus crews, intended to be swiftly brought up to full fighting efficiency; and the Third Fleet of obsolescent vessels, which were brought into service on mobilisation by reservists. To bring the Second and Third fleets up to full complement was an administrative challenge, closing down the shore establishments and drawing on up to 20,000 civilians who had signed up for the Royal Naval Volunteer Reserve.

Full-commission ships such as *New Zealand* were integral to the mix. The battlecruiser was back at Portland by 7 July, where she coaled. By this time the Balkan crisis was brewing: government in Vienna intended to use the assassination as a pretext for dismantling Serbia as an independent state and were pressuring the Serbians. Russia backed Serbia while Germany backed Austria-Hungary – a mix that potentially drew in the Triple Alliance. But despite Germany's so-called 'blank cheque' promise to support Austria-Hungary, the chance of the major powers going to war seemed low in early July. Indeed, the Kaiser departed on his annual holiday aboard his yacht *Hohenzollern*, in part to signal that all was generally well.[18]

All this was of less import aboard *New Zealand* than the exercises, which included three-quarter charge firing practise against a target towed by *Queen Mary*.[19] On 6 July *New Zealand* followed the rest of the battlecruisers to the Solent and the anchorage off Spithead, between Portsmouth and the Isle of Wight, where the First Fleet assembled under Admiral Sir George Callaghan, flying his flag in the new super-dreadnought *Iron Duke*. *New Zealand* anchored behind *Princess Royal* on the southern side of the channel, about a mile north-east of Ryde, with the dreadnought *Hercules* directly to port. Coore watched the Second Fleet follow the battlecruisers in, led by the *Lord Nelson*, although he had little time to sightsee; his officer training never stopped, and he was required to produce a map of the anchorage, with ships named in position.[20]

Next day the Third Fleet arrived, and with that the entire force Britain had in home waters was drawn up in five great columns, flanked by smaller ships and with rows of seaplanes at moorings off Haslar. Coore was told to produce a sketch plan of the anchored fleet. Along the way he captured the history of the Royal Navy; many of the names he wrote harked back to the Nelsonic age and beyond: *Temeraire, Neptune, Conqueror, Leviathan, Orion, Agamemnon, Minotaur, Dreadnought, Bellerophon, Colossus, Achilles, Swiftsure,*

Thunderer, *Ocean*, *Vanguard*, *Glory* and *Revenge* among others. *Revenge* was the oldest battleship in the navy, last survivor of the eight authorised by the Naval Defence Act 1889. She had been a gunnery training ship until May 1913 and was tagged for scrapping – but in July 1914 was still moored in the waters adjacent to Ryde.[21] Coore added her to his diagram.

The next few days were filled with ceremony. The battlecruiser squadron hired the steamer *Queen* to ferry dignitaries to the ships. The King was late arriving on the 19th, but finally turned up to a twenty-one-gun salute, while the seaplanes made demonstration flights. That evening Coore watched a 'very fine searchlight display'.[22] Next day, a Sunday, the First Sea Lord, Prince Louis of Battenberg, arrived aboard *New Zealand*. He 'attended Church on the quarter-deck & went round the ship, after which he lunched with the Captain'.[23] Battenberg's son George was, of course, aboard. Next day *New Zealand* and other ships of the fleet sailed to exercises in the Channel.

The crisis in Europe gained intensity in the last week of July. It has sometimes been portrayed as having but one outcome thanks to iron-clad alliance systems and mobilisation timetables. Henry Kissinger summed the view up in 2014: once the crisis began, war was 'structurally unavoidable'.[24] To an extent this was true. Period war plans by the major European powers, particularly Germany, relied on interlocking mobilisation and movement, planned with attention to railway capacity. In the German case this was

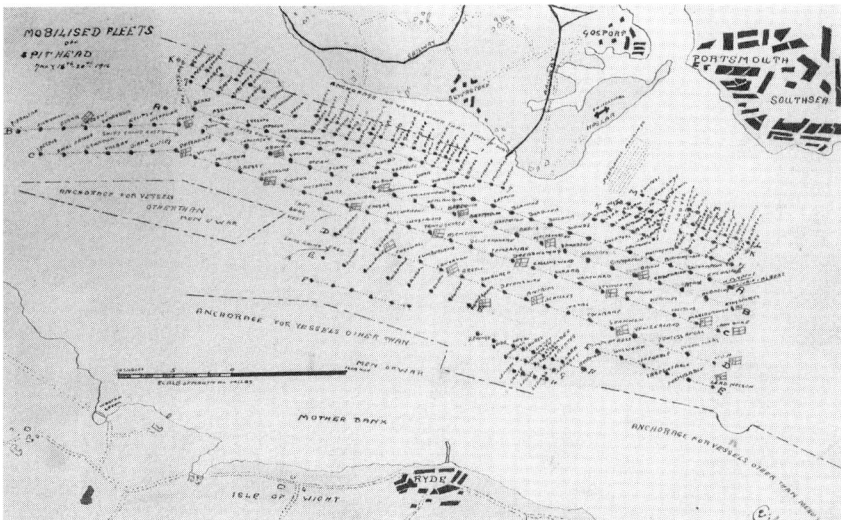

Edmund Coore's sketch plan of the fleet at anchor off Spithead.
(*Detail from qMS-0545, Coore, E G B, fl.1913–1914: Journal, Alexander Turnbull Library*)

designed to serve *Generaloberst* Helmuth von Moltke's version of the 'Schlieffen Plan', dealing with a two-front war by knocking out France in six weeks, then exploiting the power of railway to transfer Germany's armies east to confront Russia. The scheduling could not be altered without lengthy re-planning. So – the argument goes – Europe moved, step by mechanistic step on the back of mobilisation and railway schedules, into war.

In fact, such a vision understates human agency. The mobilisations that began from 29 July could have been stopped. Indeed, Tsar Nicholas II cancelled Russia's general mobilisation, but the order was reversed by the foreign minister, Sergei Dmitryevich Sazonov. Why did nobody step back? The 'revisionist' argument paints a picture of European tensions ratcheted upwards for a generation by an ambitious and 'Reich-minded' Germany, given power by a general mindset of public social militarism and Imperial rivalries. Those deeper issues, indeed, had provoked the Anglo-German naval race and – as we have seen – the very existence of *New Zealand*. By this argument, the villains during the July crisis were key government voices in Germany.

The historical point is that we know what the First World War became, but while warnings of land deadlock had been bandied about in British army circles by 1914,[25] the period vision of war as a swift and politically rewarding experience was seductive. This was understood at the time: the British Foreign Secretary, Edward Grey, felt that 'neither the Emperor nor Bethmann-Hollweg nor Jagow planned or desired war', but that military authority, particularly, was in favour of it.[26] In short, to those at the time, Europe crashed into war not as a result of diplomacy whose hands were controlled by mobilisation timetables, but because it offered opportunity to unleash what Churchill called the 'vials of wrath'.[27] Just as influential government and military voices in Germany saw the crisis as a way of achieving hegemony, similar voices in Russia and France saw it as a way of curbing those same ambitions.

Britain was under no direct obligation to join, but even as the debate played out in Whitehall, the fact that – by coincidence – the navy was fully mobilised was not something to throw away. Churchill took credit for halting the dispersal, although the decision was actually made by the First Sea Lord, Prince Louis of Battenberg.[28] The news reached *New Zealand* on 27 July, when Boyle heard that 'all third fleet ships were remaining mobilised'.[29] Orders came to coal to war stowage.[30] That was not immediately possible for *New Zealand*, and Boyle went ashore to play golf.[31] Next day, Tuesday, 28 July, they took aboard 1,000 tons of coal along with other stores.[32] Boyle recalled there was 'still no news about sailing or of our future movements'.[33] Some off-duty crew were given night leave. But the political drama was moving: Churchill and Battenberg, worried about leaving Britain exposed if the First Fleet was sent to war station at Scapa Flow via the Irish Sea, decided to send it instead through the Straits of Dover at night on the 29th, using darkness to cover the movement and foil any surprise torpedo boat attack. To do this they had to sail by 7am on the 29th.[34] The order reached the fleet around 10pm on 28 July.

Aboard *New Zealand* this meant only one thing: all leave was cancelled, and the ship's corporals went ashore to help police round up the men.[35] The battlecruiser was not the only ship doing so. Some men from the fleet were still outstanding by 6am, by which time *New Zealand* had steam for 20 knots. Parties were sent to 'pipe' the recall in the streets of Weymouth and Portland, blowing boatswain's whistles in the 'general call' code, a rising and falling pitch, to alert any sailors still in the boarding houses and the prostitutes' rooms. So the European drama echoed into the streets of a British town: Boyle recalled that the 'piping caused quite a sensation and woke up Weymouth, who cheered the men as they left'.[36]

In the end all but eleven of *New Zealand*'s crew were aboard when the battlecruiser squadron left the Solent, forming up at the head of the First Fleet with the light cruisers. Their destination was not disclosed, even to the crew. Coore presumed this a precautionary move as 'very little was known' about the European crisis. Still, they were not taking chances: all guns were loaded and 'the ship was prepared for action'.[37] The Admiralty had two reasons for secrecy, both related to risk management. One was a fear, later outlined by Churchill, that a surprise German torpedo boat attack might open the war.[38] The other was that a move by the fleet to its war station sent a diplomatic message that the Admiralty felt inappropriate just then.[39]

That day Russia and Germany began mobilising. Edward Grey, writing later, recalled little of the drama that followed in Westminster during the first three days of August – days of 'almost continuous Cabinets and of immense strain'.[40] Britain was not obligated to join Europe's war, but the issues were complex, and the 1839 commitment to support Belgium – later identified as the pivotal issue – but one factor. Another was the need to stand by France and the arrangement by which the bulk of the French fleet was in the Mediterranean. That put the onus on Britain to deny the Channel and France's northern coast to the German fleet.[41]

Halsey, Boyle, Coore and the others aboard *New Zealand* were not privy to the diplomacy, but they knew war was likely upon them. The fleet passed Dover at night with guns manned. All day during the 30th they steamed into the North Sea, 'destination unknown but generally supposed to be Scapa

Flow in the Orkneys'.[42] During the day news arrived from the Admiralty: relations were 'very strained'.[43] Boyle was optimistic though cynical. 'Personally I feel all the time there will be no war ... I am probably quite wrong.'[44]

New Zealand's main armament was kept loaded and the forward 4in gun crews closed up. During the afternoon the light cruiser *Boadicea* chased a 'suspicious vessel' that, rumour had it, was the German battlecruiser *Von der Tann*.[45] Of course it was not, but the mood in the fleet was tense. The crew were told their destination that day, and the fleet reached Scapa Flow around 5pm on the 31st. Boyle found the anchorage 'full of colliers' and watched as the battlecruiser 'passed destroyers at the entrance on patrol duty'. He did not think the flow was particularly secure, 'there are 5 ways of getting in but still there are not many places that will hold a fleet this size ...'[46]

New Zealand began coaling at 1.30am on 1 August, taking on 500 tons from the collier *Francis Duncan* while rain poured from the night sky.[47] Preparations for war continued after daylight, and during the late afternoon dog watches, parties hurled all spare spars and wood overboard, 'as well as the pinnace, 3rd cutter and 1st whaler'.[48] That day censorship was imposed across the fleet. Boyle grumbled that he was no longer allowed to mention the name of his ship.[49] Next day, a Sunday, he watched a destroyer arrive with broken bows after a collision. 'Everybody is looking a little worried about the show but of course they try not to show it.'[50] For Coore it was the 'usual Sunday routine', but after church service Halsey addressed the crew and told them he thought war inevitable.[51]

There was still no news aboard the battlecruiser by 3 August, but that day word came that Vice-Admiral John Jellicoe had been promoted admiral and made commander in chief; and that Rear Admiral David Beatty was promoted acting vice-admiral. All this reflected long-standing behind-the-scenes plans in the Admiralty. Fisher had been lobbying Churchill for Jellicoe's promotion if war broke out since 1911. 'Everything revolved around Jellicoe!'[52] Churchill listened: Jellicoe had been tipped to be fleet commander if war broke out – and had been given sealed orders to that effect as the crisis unfolded.[53] It was a slap for Callaghan, one Jellicoe felt deeply, but Churchill made clear it was an Admiralty decision.[54]

Late that day the battlecruisers went to sea in support of the light cruisers, 'looking for a supposed German transport'.[55] They were still at sea the next day, 4 August, in what Boyle called 'beautiful clear weather',[56] when news came that Britain had issued an ultimatum to Germany.[57] *New Zealand* was still at sea when the ultimatum expired at 11pm, and suddenly the ship was at war.

It was a moment of frisson. The drama of the past few days – the potential for surprise torpedo attack in the straits, the rumours of German ships here or there – pursued with due zeal but a nagging sense that it was just pretend – became real. Yet by contrast with the views of later generations, the likelihood of fighting was not viewed with dread. The anxiety of the unknown – of injury, loss, or drowning – was there, but so too was a sense of destiny, of Imperial honour, of doing duty, and of earning a social elevation and status that could be obtained in no other way. In these last days of the old world, social-militarist ideals of glory and duty stood as strong aboard *New Zealand* as they did aboard the rest of the Royal Navy and among Britain's far-flung military, all now gathering up for its greatest challenge since the days of Napoleon. The mood aboard the gift battlecruiser on the night of 4–5 August 1914 was resolute. 'Spent night at guns,' Boyle wrote, 'as we will do all the war.'[58] It was not an idle remark. Nobody knew how long the war might last, but there was a general supposition that it would be short. Halsey soon telegraphed the New Zealand High Commissioner: 'Please convey the following message to New Zealand. "All on board *New Zealand* will endeavour to uphold the honour of the Dominion."'[59]

The popular notion of a short war was joined by the idea that the German fleet would immediately issue forth for a showdown. This was so widely believed by the public around the Empire that by 6 August rumours were swirling in Wellington that a major naval battle had already taken place, with loss of fourteen German and six British vessels, including *New Zealand*.[60] Flags on the yardarms of HMS *Philomel* in Devonport, Auckland, were mistaken for being flown at half-mast, giving apparent credibility to the talk.[61] The media dismissed it as rubbish – news 'which has manifestly not been scrutinised by any censor'.[62] It was not the first time that false information had swept a population, nor the last. Nor was it tolerated. 'Any canard-monger who is caught,' the *Evening Post* declared, 'is promised a lesson to last for life.'[63]

This popular vision was not entirely shared in the Admiralty. While some voices within the fleet also believed an early showdown likely – in part, as James Goldrick has argued, because pre-war exercises were usually geared to that end[64] – the Royal Navy also had a more practical and significantly longer-term strategy in mind. Although a specific Trade Division was not set up in the War Staff until 1914,[65] naval warfare had always been about suppressing enemy sea-borne trade while securing British maritime routes. British policy did not shy away from fleet action if opportunity presented, but was also focused around longer-term blockade of enemy sea lanes, simulta-neously preventing German ships from trading on the high seas and bottling up German naval forces, both to prevent them blockading the British and to protect Britain itself from invasion.

The Admiralty's problem was how this might be done. The main German North Sea bases – officially the North Sea Naval Station – were on the south side of the Heligoland Bight, in part behind the chain of islands that were all that remained of a range of hills submerged by water at the end of the last glaciation. These bases, from west to east, were at Emden, in the Ems river bight; Wilhelmshaven in the Jade river bight, which also held the main dock facilities; and Bremerhaven, at the mouth of the Weser. An air station was set up at Cuxhaven, slightly to the north. The primary base was Wilhelmshaven. The waters were shallow and the river systems made heavy ship navigation from Wilhelmshaven subject to tides. However, it was the only place Germany had. Local waters were protected by minefields and by fortifications at Wesermünde, Wilhelmshaven and on Heligoland, a small island in the gulf, backed by harbour defence forces that included older light cruisers and submarines.

From the British perspective the relative concentration of German bases, here and in the Baltic, made blockade deceptively easy. Up until 1911–12 plans involved an age-of-sail style 'close blockade', suitably updated for modern technology, but conceptually something that Nelson, Collingwood or Rodney would have recognised. This required British destroyer and light ship flotillas to enter German waters and suppress their German opposite numbers, simultaneously blocking any merchant trade. That in turn would enable the battle fleet to operate with relative impunity nearby, able to engage the High Seas Fleet if it emerged. There was talk of seizing key islands in the Frisian chain, such as Borkum, to support the effort.

The problem was that torpedo, submarine and mine technology rendered all this impractical, and Callaghan received orders cancelling the approach in April 1912. Churchill's Admiralty War Staff then tackled the problem, initially proposing an 'intermediate' arrangement involving a line of ships across the middle of the North Sea. Exactly what was intended has been subject to historical debate. However, by the end of 1912 this 'intermediate blockade' had been replaced by a new idea: distant blockade. That idea has also been subject to academic discussion, including whether it was fully introduced then or in July 1914, how the idea evolved, and how all could be reconciled with Jellicoe's Grand Fleet Battle Orders. Historical proposals have run from the mid-twentieth century 'orthodoxy' proposed by Arthur Marder – a product of its time and his methodology – to late-twentieth century 'revisionism' and the early twenty-first century view of David G Morgan-Owen,[66] which might, reasonably, be called 'post-revisionist'.

The fact that the understanding of history is an ongoing discussion does not reduce the point that when war broke out, the Admiralty responded by implementing 'distant blockade'. This approach used light forces to block both exits of the North Sea to German trade, backed by a battle fleet stationed at Scapa Flow, near the largest opening in the north. The forces securing the southern exit – and the vital supply line to the British Expeditionary Force in France – were protected by the fact that the main British fleet could cut off the retreat of any German force sailing to attack them. This same system, backed by judiciously laid minefields, also protected Britain from invasion. And this, in turn, fundamentally shaped *New Zealand*'s First World War.

As we have seen, British arrangements for the blockade were in place by the time war broke out. The First Fleet, supported by part of the Second, became the Grand Fleet, based at Scapa Flow. The remainder of the Second Fleet and all of the Third – still at Portland – became the Channel Fleet, officially from 8 August. Lighter forces under Commodore Reginald Tyrwhitt were positioned at Harwich, covering south-east England. All, however, rested on Jellicoe's Grand Fleet retaining its superiority. The immediate problem in August 1914 was that – as Boyle noticed – Scapa Flow was not yet ready to act as a main fleet anchorage. Nor was there consensus within the Admiralty over the frequency of the fleet 'sweeps', reintroduced as doctrine as recently as July 1914. Jellicoe was opposed to over-aggressive forays.[67] Amidst all this there was also the prospect that the Germans might yet sashay forth from Wilhelmshaven for a grand showdown.

The strategy did not require an intrusion into German home waters to maintain the blockade, secure Britain's coasts, and retain command of the Channel. And yet, as we saw in the first pages of this book, just three and a half weeks after war broke out, *New Zealand* and the battlecruiser squadron went racing into German home waters. Why? In part it was due to Churchill's pugnacity, which found an ally in Commodores Tyrwhitt and Roger Keyes, commanding destroyer and submarine forces at Harwich. Although close blockade had been abandoned, British submarines of the 8th Flotilla poked into German home waters around Heligoland, in part to block any German sally into the Channel while the British Expeditionary Force was being transferred to France. By the third week of August these submarines had discovered that the Germans daily sent light forces into the Heligoland Bight, partly to shepherd U-boats out for patrols into the North Sea, partly to foil any British effort to mine the waters.[68]

Keyes promptly proposed an attack, and that found fertile ground with Tyrwhitt and Churchill. Forces committed included Tyrwhitt's brand new flagship *Arethusa*, a fast light cruiser; and the sixteen destroyers of his 3rd Flotilla; along with the 1st Flotilla led by the cruiser *Fearless*, with eleven of its sixteen destroyers.[69] Other light ships were supporting Keyes' submarines. With suitable timing it would be possible to tackle the German light forces in a lightning raid before any heavy ships could be deployed in support. The Germans were known to be deploying their forces in an arc west of Heligoland; an outer ring of destroyers backed by an inner ring of minesweepers. Light cruisers, primarily from local harbour defence forces, were positioned near the island. The British plan called for a push into the bight towards Heligoland, followed by a sweep west, mopping up any German forces on the way.

The Admiralty scheduled the raid for 28 August. However, the Admiralty's Chief of Staff, Vice-Admiral Doveton Sturdee, refused to allow either the battlecruisers or the Grand Fleet to support, but did permit 'Cruiser Force K' –*New Zealand* and the older battlecruiser *Invincible*, then at the Humber under Rear Admiral Gordon Moore – to sail to the Heligoland Bight as support. The fact that battlecruisers were being committed to support a raid on enemy home waters was interesting. Beatty had made just such a proposal on assuming command of the force in March 1913.[70] It also echoed Admiralty concepts by which the battlecruisers might become a heavy punch to support lighter forces on deep patrols into the North Sea.[71] And it meant that *New Zealand* had an early chance to see action.

By this time the raid had gained a dimension. On 24 August the British Expeditionary Force encountered the enormous German First Army at Mons and were forced to retreat. Two days later – as Tyrwhitt left Harwich – a second engagement at Le Cateau did not halt the German advance. This opened up concerns that the northern French ports – and with them the BEF's supply line back to Britain – might be in danger.[72] The navy decided to land reinforcements at Ostend on 26–28 August. Keyes' raid into the Heligoland Bight, coincidentally, meant that German naval forces that might have interfered were going to be busy.[73] Jellicoe was advised of the intent to occupy Ostend and of the Heligoland raid in a single message on the 26th, for which he offered to take the Grand Fleet to sea in support.[74] He was refused permission to close in,[75] but allowed to despatch Beatty with *Lion*, *Princess Royal* and *Queen Mary*, supported by Commodore William Goodenough's First Light Cruiser Squadron. Tyrwhitt had already departed Harwich when this decision was made, and remained unaware of these reinforcements for some time.

The weather on the morning of 28 August was fine, the coastal region misty, with the result that the raid devolved into a succession of pursuits and brief engagements between often isolated forces.[76] Command and control issues flowed from the lack of visibility, affecting both sides, compounded for the British when Tyrwhitt's flagship ended up in a brief but violent duel with the German light cruiser *Stettin*, under Karl Nerger.[77] A sense of the confusion was revealed aboard *New Zealand* around 9.30am when a message from Keyes to Tyrwhitt was intercepted: 'Have our light cruisers come to this area?' Halsey passed the message on to Beatty.[78] Tyrwhitt was silent just then: *Arethusa* lost her wireless and searchlights, and until the wireless was repaired around 9.45am, Tyrwhitt could only control his force with flags and semaphore. The poor visibility then made it difficult for him to assess the scale of forces he faced, and the intended sweep west was delayed. To add spice to the mix, Tyrwhitt was now aware of Beatty and Goodenough's forces, but Keyes – aboard the destroyer *Lurcher* – was not.[79]

Aboard *New Zealand* there was a sense of excitement, but nothing to do. Boyle – commanding X-turret – recalled that Moore's force found Beatty's around 5am, and at 8.15am they received a message that the destroyers were being engaged. Then Keyes' message arrived. Other than that there was no news.[80] They ran back and forth at 24 knots waiting on developments. There was brief alarm at 9.45am when another urgent signal arrived from Keyes, directed at *Invincible*; he was being chased by four cruisers and leading them towards Moore's force. This was recorded as '9.05' aboard *New Zealand*, whose record appears to have been about forty minutes out.[81] Tyrwhitt also intercepted the message and asked Goodenough to support. But then, as the mists lifted slightly, Keyes discovered the pursuing ships were actually Goodenough's cruisers.[82] This was his first inkling that anybody other than Force K was in support, and the outcome had been that Goodenough was sent to chase himself. A staff monograph, afterwards, opined that Keyes' signals 'added a distinct element of excitement to the operation'.[83]

There was more excitement aboard *New Zealand* around 10.15am, when *Invincible* opened fire on a suspected German submarine. It was then thought to be attacking *New Zealand*, and Halsey responded with 4in fire from the forward mountings. Boyle shortly thought he saw the boat surface on the port quarter and got what he called a 'clear view'. He 'got X-turret trained on her but she dipped before I could fire'.[84]

The battles west of Heligoland continued as scattered German light forces arrived. Visibility was patchy, made worse by the funnel smoke of several dozen vessels surging around at high speed. By this time the Commander in Chief, Admiral Friedrich von Ingenohl, was aware something was up, authorising Hipper to send the two available battlecruisers, *Moltke* and *Von der Tann*, out in support. They got steam up but were unable to cross the outer Jade bar until noon, when the tide had risen.[85]

Around 10.46am, *Arethusa* ran into the light cruiser *Strassburg* and was again damaged, at which point *Fearless* and most of a destroyer flotilla arrived, forcing the German vessel to retreat. Another German vessel appeared out of the mists. This was the light cruiser *Coln*, but in the poor visibility she presented to the British as a larger vessel, likely a *Roon*-class armoured cruiser. Tyrwhitt – with his own flagship's speed reduced – now called Beatty for support.[86] This signal was received aboard *Lion* at 11.25am, followed three minutes later by a second call for help, then a third from the destroyer leader. *Coln* disappeared again into the mists after a few salvoes had been exchanged, but *Strassburg* now returned to view and reopened fire.[87]

Beatty briefly queried his flag captain, Ernle Chatfield; he was reluctant to lose a battlecruiser, and the dangers of mines, submarines and the chance of German heavy vessels – invisible in the mists – were manifest.[88] But based on Tyrwhitt's reports he felt that Goodenough's cruisers alone – already split into two groups – were insufficient, and he judged that Hipper would not yet have had time to sail.[89] So he lost little time, surging into the bight, supported by four destroyers and with Goodenough's cruisers nearby. Speed was essential, and at 11.45am he called for 27 knots. Both *New Zealand* and *Invincible* began to lag – *Invincible* more so than *New Zealand*.[90] As we saw in the first pages of the book, the men in the stokeholds were working like Trojans, building the fires to push the battlecruiser through the water as quickly as her displacement, hull condition and water depth allowed.

Visibility was down to around 6,000yd, creating the risk of suddenly coming across enemy forces within torpedo range. The battlecruisers shortly found part of Tyrwhitt's 1st Flotilla, which joined the advance. Boyle recalled that they 'heard heavy firing ahead [and] went in at full speed'.[91] This led the force to *Arethusa* and part of the 3rd Flotilla, which were being engaged by two German light cruisers, *Coln* and *Stettin*, and in trouble. Beatty, it seemed, had arrived literally in the nick of time – and for all the uncertainties of the morning, was certainly needed.[92]

The situation from *New Zealand* remained murky. Boyle 'could distinctly see shells falling amongst the destroyers, and the light cruisers firing as fast as they could at something but couldn't see what'. Shortly they passed a wrecked German cruiser, 'She was in a frightful state two out of three of her funnels were lying flat and both masts gone, well down in the bows and burning. It didn't look as if there could be many people aboard alive. We passed fairly close to her and went on at full speed in chase of other cruisers.'[93] Boyle could not identify the ship: in fact she was the *Mainz*, which had engaged Goodenough's cruisers and part of the destroyer force.[94]

Around 12.50pm *Lion* opened fire, but nobody on *New Zealand* could see the target – 'the smoke was so thick you could see nothing'.[95] *Princess Royal* and *Queen Mary* then opened fire – again on targets invisible aboard *New Zealand*. Finally, gun flashes became visible through the mists to port, and A-turret opened fire on them. There was a sense of excitement aboard. Boyle's right-hand gun layer, Petty Officer Harrington, hurled his cap and began 'cursing loudly'. The upperworks of a cruiser then became visible through the smoke and mist, which New Zealand engaged as she passed. Boyle recalled the moment his turret engaged: 'As she grew aft all turrets commenced, mine in the stern last, and then all I could see was the mast heads and occasionally the bow and stern the rest of her was enveloped in black smoke from bursting shells. She was only 4,000yd off.'[96]

New Zealand fired at this target for about twenty minutes, by Boyle's account 'getting off 82 common shell at her, until her guns were silenced'. There was a cheer when the last gun fell quiet. However, Boyle's turret, aft, was hampered by bad visibility, initially missing salvoes because the target could not be seen. Then the left-hand cage jammed, preventing the left gun firing until it was cleared. As a result they fired only 14 rounds by Boyle's account.[97] 'When the smoke cleared,' Boyle wrote later, 'you could see all her funnels down and masts gone and she was burning amidships.'[98]

By this time *Lion* had moved on to another target that loomed out of the mist ahead, the old cruiser *Ariadne*. She too was reduced to a wreck.[99] At 1.10pm, however – with *Arethusa* relieved and the immediate threat averted – Beatty signalled the retreat. Galloping into the rescue was one thing: lurking on a misty battlefield in enemy home waters quite another. There was concern aboard *New Zealand* about German mines or torpedo attack. Halsey himself thought he saw two mines near the ship.[100] And there was the risk of German heavy forces arriving. So the battlecruisers swung about and began heading for the North Sea.

Coln was still afloat, and they came across her. Boyle watched what was going on:

Destroyers were sent to try and rescue some of her crew but when they attempted to get near her they thought she fired a shot so they came back and the *Lion* opened fire again. After five rounds her bow went down and stern into the air and she sank like a stone. The destroyers then went off to see if they could pick up anybody, we don't yet know if they were successful or not.[101]

Boyle had nothing but admiration for the German sailors, many of whom had been best friends with the British at Kiel just eight weeks earlier: 'It was a very inglorious victory considering our superiority and I think the Germans very, very gallant fellows ... I trust some of them were saved.'[102] Around 6pm the *Invincible* and *New Zealand* parted from the 1st BCS and 'fell in with two of our submarines E4 and 5 who had several German prisoners onboard, including 1 Lieut. [sic] rescued from a destroyer'. They 'spent the night steaming up and down the N[orth] sea doing nothing and saw nothing'.[103]

The battle had been a confused affair, in large part due to visibility problems flowing from mist and funnel smoke, but there had been major administrative failures, notably the Admiralty's failure to ensure that Tyrwhitt and Keyes were informed of Beatty and Goodenough's presence. Into that came the patchy fog, eventually compounded by funnel smoke, where even commanding officers had struggled to get a clear picture. Fears of mine and submarine gave shape to passing shadows. Only much later, when German accounts were available, was a fuller impression possible.[104]

Spirits aboard *New Zealand* were high afterwards: they had taken part in the first real battle of the war. The Kaiser's moustache had been tweaked, operations off Ostend had been secured, and what one sailor aboard *New Zealand* called 'some good ships and some unfortunate men' had been sent to the bottom.[105] Later, a photograph of the battlecruiser at speed in the bight, taken from an escorting destroyer, was used for the ship's 1914 Christmas card.[106] Halsey had worn the piupiu and tiki over his uniform during the battle, at the request of the crew, and shortly cabled the High Commission: 'Please inform the women of New Zealand that their ensign flew on board during the Battle of Heligoland.'[107] This was a reference to the ensign given him in 1913.

The battle certainly made a splash in New Zealand. 'The might of Britain', the *Sun* declared on 4 September, adding – with complete disregard for technical classification – 'Battleships at Heligoland'.[108] The gift battle-cruiser drew fresh attention: cinemas advertised newsreel footage of 'life on board HMS *New Zealand*', some of it taken in New Zealand the year before, along with clips of her being launched.[109] Other reports were gloriously praiseworthy: 'Great naval victory. *New Zealand* engaged. Fearlessness of our destroyers before German fleet', the *Feilding Star* declared in what, for the day, were banner headlines, going on to admire the 'brilliancy and daring of the British naval raiders at Heligoland' in which 'every cruiser' had been 'disposed of'.[110] Only a few voices dissented. 'Everyone in New Zealand is, of course, gratified to learnt that the battleship [sic] presented some years ago by this country to the Motherland has taken part in the naval action which has been attended with success ... This, however, is no reason whatever for attempting to make party capital out of a policy which is the subject of considerable difference of opinion in New Zealand.'[111]

All the hoopla and cheering masked the darker issues that emerged – all of which were kept from the public. One was the damage done to the British ships by the blast of their own guns. Aboard *New Zealand* there was a good deal of destruction in the 'officers' cabins and messes'.[112] Another problem was visibility, which made tactical control difficult and amplified problems with fire control. Ranges dropped to as little as 4,000yd, but as Boyle remarked afterwards, it had still taken five battlecruisers about twenty minutes to sink a single German light cruiser. German build quality and damage-control procedures were one reason, but the main problem was that very few of the shells hit. All *New Zealand*'s were 'overs', as Boyle wryly observed. 'I suppose the whole squadron fired about 350 rounds of common shell from 13.5" and 12" guns.'[113] This was atrocious – not least because fire control was a *raison d'etre* for the all-big-gun concept. And yet, on that misty day in August 1914, the battlecruisers had struggled to hit at relatively short ranges.

The indifference of British naval gunnery during the early part of the First World War, particularly, has been subjected to academic debate to the point where one proposal has been that the heavy naval gun, in general, failed as a weapon during that conflict.[114] While this might be debatable, the historical question must be why such a conclusion is plausible; and the fact remains that heavy naval gun performance in the First World War was not good, when set again the precision with which land-based artillery could fire. Part of the issue was the relative novelty of the technologies. Gunnery had not been a huge issue in Napoleonic times, but the advent of industrial-age weaponry expanded the range, creating problems that got worse as technology developed. The firing ship was going to be rolling, pitching and potentially turning, all the while trying to hit a target that was also manoeuvring, and not necessarily on a parallel course. Variables included target size, speed, heading relative to the firing ship, and the rate at which the range was changing. At longer ranges, these issues were important because of the rise in flight time: a gunner had to aim where the enemy ship would be in a minute or so – not where it was when the guns fired. But even if these could be identified there remained the issue of solving the equations by hand.

By 1914 the process of fire control began with data from a coincidence rangefinder, typically mounted high for best horizon. These devices had first been introduced in the early 1890s and were a tube with a lens at each end, mounted at 90 degrees to the length of the tube. Pentaprisms transferred both images to an eyepiece in the middle – two eyepieces, in the case of Barr and Stroud units – where they appeared as the top and bottom half of the image.

The operator then altered the angle of the pentaprisms to bring the images together – hence the term 'coincidence'. When the image halves were aligned, the range could be read from a display.[115]

The instrument worked on the basis of triangulation. Because the length of one side was known – the baseline of the rangefinder – the ability to discover ranges depended on determining the angle of the other two sides, via the degree to which the pentaprisms had to be turned. This swiftly hit the limits of mechanical precision. While the Barr and Stroud FA3 model of 1903 was considered accurate to 8,000yd, the Admiralty wanted better results and requested tenders in 1904. Barr and Stroud produced a 9ft baseline system that the Admiralty purchased in bulk at £325 a unit.[116] Barr and Stroud soon became entangled in competition with Vickers, and by 1914 some of the newest ships were receiving 15ft baseline systems. *New Zealand*, however, had 9ft units. These included an Argo rangefinder – an extra atop the original contracts, with a fitting cost of £115.[117]

However, knowing the range at any moment was only part of the fire-control calculation: range was always going to change as the ships moved, because they were unlikely to be on parallel courses, and calculating the rate of change was surprisingly complex. One of the first devices to tackle that problem was the Dumaresq, a mechanical calculator invented by John Dumaresq in 1902, built by Elliott Brothers, and in service by 1906. This calculated rate-of-change-of-range and the necessary deflection – the angle to which the guns had to be pointed to ensure the shells reached a target that moved during the flight time. These were issued to ships in multiples and, as time went on, in progressively improved models. *New Zealand* originally had one in the working space underneath each gun house. The problem was that target speed and course could only be calculated indirectly.[118] The invention of the inclinometer towards the end of the First World War solved the issue, but that was too late for the major battles.[119]

Various other devices emerged over the same period. Equipment included the Vickers Clock, a spring-powered mechanical device developed by Percy Scott and Vickers' engineers that presented range as a clock face, with moving hands, to show range and the rate of change. One was ideally needed for each turret, and the Admiralty ordered 246 of them in 1906.[120]

Getting the information to the guns was another issue. The answer was the Transmitting Station, a central position to which the fire-control obser-vations were passed from the rangefinders and spotters. By 1914 this was achieved largely by Graham Navyphones, or the Graham Telaupad system – the name given to headphones and a hands-free microphone that enabled quick communication to any part of the ship that had been wired appropriately. Fire-control solutions were then passed to the gun layers in each turret, in some cases by electro-mechanical systems that provided follow-the-pointer instructions.

Two transmitting stations were typically set up aboard each ship, and by outbreak of war the stations were also becoming the centre for calculating 'fire-control solutions', aided by purpose-designed calculators known as 'fire-control tables'. There were two competing types by 1914. The one primarily picked by the navy was the Dreyer table, developed by naval officer Frederic Dreyer and Elliott Brothers' engineer Keith Elphinstone. It was a mechanical computer, complete with bicycle chain drive, incorporated a Dumaresq, and produced answers in near real time, plotting results on paper. The device was not perfect: manual plots had to be added to the automatic plot, and the system tended to lag during a fast-moving battle, requiring manual resetting.[121] However, it was a significant step forward.

A competing device was designed by Arthur Pollen and built by the Argo Company.[122] The usual historical view has been that Pollen's invention was superior, but that politics resulted in the Dreyer system being ordered from Elliott Brothers and more widely adopted in the fleet. This, allegedly,

Midshipman's workbooks were more than just diaries: they were also places where 'schoolwork' was kept, often as large fold-out drawings tipped between the bound pages. This is Edmund Coore's block diagram of *New Zealand*'s fire-control system, as it stood in late 1914.
(*Detail from qMS-0545, Coore, E G B, fl.1913–1914: Journal, Alexander Turnbull Library*)

explained some of the abysmal shooting of the battlecruisers, except *Queen Mary*, which had the Argo system. This view flowed from opinion of the day and was established as orthodoxy in the 1980s. Of course, the study of history is a discussion, and this was subject to debate in academic journals, being further questioned in 2001 when a PhD thesis proposed a different interpretation, with implications for the Battle of Jutland.[123]

Fire-control equipment, in short, was in a state of evolution during the period. *New Zealand*, certainly, experienced the issue: her gear was modified even while she was under construction, atop the original contracts and at the expense of the New Zealand government.[124]

All this counted for nothing if the guns could not be pointed in the required direction, and this was no small challenge at the turn of the twentieth century. Earlier mountings struggled to follow fast-moving targets or compensate for ship roll. In 1905 Jellicoe, as Director of Naval Ordinance, tackled the problem.[125] The B.VIII design 12in mountings that emerged from Jellicoe's initiative first went to sea on *Dreadnought*, which became the first British battleship theoretically able to constantly track a target with all main guns, using hydraulics controlled by hand wheels. It took time to perfect: early tests showed that *Dreadnought*'s guns could not change elevation at a rate able to compensate for rolling.[126] Further design improvements followed. *New Zealand* had the modified B.VIII* mounting, delineated with an asterisk.[127]

Another challenge was getting all turrets firing at the same target in co-ordinated salvoes. The idea of 'director' fire control from a central position had been around for years by the early twentieth century, but never fully implemented. A director system fitted to HMS *Africa* in 1907 was able to transmit elevation data but not bearing information. A prototype that could do both was fitted to HMS *Neptune* in 1911, followed by an improved model fitted to HMS *Thunderer*. Firing tests in 1912, versus HMS *Orion* – which lacked the system – made clear that director firing was the way forward.

New Zealand was part of a second batch of seventeen ships scheduled to be fitted with director control, but was still waiting for both it and a Dreyer table by the outbreak of war. Among other fire-control gear, she had Barr and Stroud 9ft rangefinders, Dumaresqs, Vickers range clocks, and Vickers follow-the-pointer sights for the main armament. The Vickers sights were automatic, moving on camshafts to show gun layers the elevation; but they were delicate – maintenance instructions warned users to be careful: 'As the accuracy of the sights depends entirely on the truth of the cam surface, every endeavour must be taken not to injure the surface in any way.'[128] However, the battlecruiser did not have the Evershed transmitter that gave bearing data to the main guns and, thanks to priority being given to newer vessels, did not receive one until after the Battle of Jutland.[129] As a result, she had only a Barr and Stroud Mk II receiver to tell turret commanders where the target was.

Lack of both director control and the full Dreyer system does not explain *New Zealand*'s atrocious shooting at Heligoland. Mist and bad lighting played a part, however, another reason was that the jury was still out over the best way to apply the answers produced by the fire-control gadgetry, and how best to fire ranging shots with which to supplement the instruments with direct observation. All these issues had been subject to ongoing pre-war debate among naval officers, into which was infused argument over the equipment. By 1911–13 a system involving rate plotting – the rate at which the range changed – was being introduced. This was pioneered by the Second Battle Squadron, and was thought to be a way of overcoming some of the inaccuracies of the equipment.[130] The best approach to ranging shots, meanwhile, continued to be subject to experimentation. The solution later considered optimal – firing two quick salvoes in groups of four guns, getting the second away while the first was still in the air – was not introduced until September 1916.[131]

The First Battle of Heligoland was only the first of a relatively quick-fire series of activities in which *New Zealand* was involved during the first months of the war, including supporting a raid on the airship bases at Cuxhaven. Although the First World War is usually remembered as a time of largely static trench systems on the Western Front and an impasse at sea where the major fleets variously sat idle in harbour or engaged in endless 'sweeps' of the North Sea, no such future was envisaged in late 1914. The ground war in the west was a fast-moving affair running very much in Germany's favour. A surprise German victory at Tannenberg in late August had averted the risk from the east, compensating for delays incurred by the 'Miracle of the Marne' that stalled von Kluck's armies outside Paris but then led to the 'race to the Channel' as the Germans surged north to try and outflank the British and French forces. There were concerns in Whitehall that Germany – on top of these commitments – was simultaneously capable of deploying a 250,000-strong invasion force against Britain. All this threw weight on the Royal Navy maintaining its superiority at sea, and there was a good deal of action – some of it in hope of bringing the High Seas Fleet to battle.

For *New Zealand* the first months of the war were dominated by sorties with Force K and the 1st BCS, primarily from Invergordon, on rumour of German patrols.[132] The British battlecruisers sailed as far as the Norwegian coast, inevitably seeing nothing, often amidst heavy seas. A floating dock had been brought up from Portsmouth to support the forces now stationed at Invergordon, and late on 25 October *New Zealand* entered it for routine maintenance, delayed briefly because the ship had a 'slight list to port' that had to be corrected. When the dock was pumped out the next day it was discovered that three of the propellers 'appear to have hit something'. Drama erupted just after noon; there were reports of German submarines 'coming up harbour'. Despite being in dock, *New Zealand*'s 4in guns were manned. Around 12.40, the other battlecruisers opened fire on a suspicious wake. It was a ridiculous moment that underscored the nervousness of the fleet at the time; as Coore remarked afterwards, the water was only 3ft deep at that point. However, 'a haystack was set on fire & a shell passing through the roof of a cottage, bruised a baby's legs'.[133]

The ship's hull was cleaned and fresh anti-fouling paint applied, New Zealand's crew went ashore on route marches, spent time on leave, and entertained themselves with sports matches against local teams. There was more drama on 30 October when warning came of a Zeppelin attack. The battlecruiser was still in dock, and the crew hastened to man the 4in guns and what Coore called the 'anti-aerial 3-pounder' – actually a Hotchkiss 6pdr.

New Zealand's propellers and rudder while in dock. This particular picture was taken at Cockatoo Island, Sydney, in 1919; but the experience of docking was similar on every occasion – enabling essential inspection and cleaning, among other tasks.
(*Torpedo Bay Navy Museum 2006.186.239.p24.1*)

Another picture of *New Zealand* in dock at Cockatoo Island. The dock is being refilled, but the ship is not yet buoyant and timber baulks are still in place. The process, again, was the same every time the ship was docked.
(*Torpedo Bay Navy Museum 2006.186.239.p24.2*)

These weapons were not effective against Zeppelins and, afterwards, a heavier gun was ordered. 'We are having an anti-aerial 3in gun mounted on top of P turret,' Coore reported.[134] This was not installed until March 1915.

Meanwhile, another whirlwind was tearing through the Admiralty. The First Sea Lord, Prince Louis of Battenberg, resigned amidst public outcry over his German ancestry. After a brisk debate with the King, Churchill brought Fisher back on 29 October. The old admiral was seventy-three but had lost none of his energy, and he arrived to a succession of dramatic moments. There had been ongoing alarms in Scapa Flow, which led to Jellicoe temporarily withdrawing the Grand Fleet to Lough Swilly in Ireland. One outcome of that was the loss of the super-dreadnought *Audacious* to a mine on 28 October.[135] Then, on 3 November, a German battlecruiser force bombarded Great Yarmouth. *New Zealand*, at Invergordon, was ordered to sea with the rest of the squadron, but all were recalled later in the day.

The bad news kept coming: reports arrived on 4 November of a British naval defeat four days earlier, off the coast of Chile at the hands of the German East Asiatic Squadron. Fisher – in part cajoled by Churchill – responded decisively, despatching *Invincible* and *Inflexible* with supporting ships to South American waters and ordering the 13.5in-gunned *Princess*

Royal to the Caribbean in case von Spee tried to reach the Atlantic through the Panama Canal. *Invincible*, at that moment, was flagship of Cruiser Force K, under Moore. He transferred his flag to *New Zealand*.[136] Fisher's decision to send *Princess Royal* prompted a spat with Jellicoe, who protested the loss of such a powerful unit – not least because she burned twice the coal of *New Zealand*, his own choice for the job.[137]

Jellicoe had good reason to be concerned. By November 1914 British dreadnought superiority in North Sea waters was marginal, and several of the newer ships were not fully worked up. There were problems with condenser leaks in some of the 13.5in-gunned dreadnoughts, and other ships were away for docking. The fact that the brand new battlecruiser *Tiger* was ordered to join was small compensation; Jellicoe protested that she was not mechanically fit and had yet to be worked up. Fisher finally conceded that Jellicoe was right, but all he could do was transfer *Indomitable* from the Mediterranean to support Beatty.

What followed was largely driven by German initiatives. The Kaiser had forbidden the High Seas Fleet to risk itself, however, he allowed the First Scouting Group of Rear Admiral Franz Hipper greater leeway. This was the German equivalent of Beatty's: a battlecruiser squadron, occasionally supplemented by the slower *Blücher*, a large armoured cruiser with a dozen 8.2in guns. Von Ingenohl began developing plans to trap part of the Grand Fleet and whittle it down to parity. This involved using Hipper's battlecruisers to attack British coastal towns and draw out the British battlecruiser force and supporting units, allowing Hipper to lead them into the jaws of the High Seas Fleet, which would be loitering in the central North Sea.

What the Germans did not know was that the British could read their naval signals. Several German codes were in operation, and one fell into Australian hands after their naval forces captured a German merchantman on 11 August, although it was 9 September before the authorities in Melbourne realised it. Then copies of the main German naval code, *Signalbuch der Kaiserlichen Marine* (SKM), were captured by the Russians from the cruiser *Magdeburg* on 26 August. One copy was taken to England and handed to the Admiralty, underscoring the excellent relations between the two navies, for they were not allies.[138] A further German code was captured in December. Handling this information fell to a new Admiralty branch set up under Sir Alfred Ewing. They were issued an office known as Room 40, which became the name of the intelligence effort. It took time to get everything up to speed, nearly producing disaster in December when Hipper prepared a further major raid: a plan for early-morning attacks on Scarborough, Whitby and Hartlepool.

As a result of Room 40, the Admiralty were partially forewarned, although nobody knew where the raid would strike. Tyrwhitt was ordered to get under way before daylight on the 15th, while Keyes' submarines were sent to patrol off Terschelling. Jellicoe was ordered to send the Second Battle Squadron – six super-dreadnoughts under Vice-Admiral Sir George Warrender – to support Beatty's four battlecruisers, which included *New Zealand*. Beatty, then stationed at Cromarty, received orders to sail late on 14 December and rendezvous with Warrender. They would then sail for the middle of the North Sea, south of Dogger Bank – a good position to intercept the Germans irrespective of which town they struck.

Jellicoe was unhappy about splitting the Grand Fleet. However, the Admiralty judged that the entire High Seas Fleet was not likely to sail. In fact, Jellicoe's concerns were on the money. Von Ingenohl sailed for a point south of the Dogger Bank with fourteen dreadnoughts, eight pre-dread-noughts and supporting light forces including fifty-four destroyers. By the early hours of 16 December, Beatty and Warrender's forces were not far from the High Seas Fleet. Around 5.15am, Beatty's destroyer screen – east of the capital ships – ran into the destroyer screen of von Ingenohl's force. A brief skirmish led von Ingenohl to conclude that his destroyers had run into the screen of a larger force – which was true – but to his mind it was the Grand Fleet. He had stretched the Kaiser's instruction by poking this far into the North Sea, and at 5.30am ordered the High Seas Fleet home.[139]

Von Ingenohl's caution meant that Beatty and Warrender's forces, including *New Zealand*, narrowly escaped being caught by a superior force. The close call provoked due hand-wringing afterwards. Churchill, later, insisted the British could have used their superior speed to make good an escape,[140] but such a claim took no account of the fact that Beatty and Warrender might have accepted engagement, or the fact that the Second Battle Squadron was only marginally faster than the High Seas Fleet, or of the risk of torpedo attack from the German light forces. A Royal Marine aboard *Orion*, reflecting on the incident years later, felt that the British would have given a good account of themselves, but the outcome was obvious.[141]

Unaware of the near-miss, Beatty and Warrender continued to search for Hipper. The day was initially clear, and a report from the destroyer *Shark* that the armoured cruiser *Roon* had been sighted reached Warrender around 7.30am, who assumed Beatty would go in pursuit. Beatty never received it, and a repeat from *New Zealand* was delayed about 30 minutes.[142] *New Zealand* was closest to the point notified by *Shark*, so Beatty sent her in pursuit at 24 knots. Just then the clear winter's morning gave way to mist that, as Coore put it, made visibility from *New Zealand* 'very small'.[143] Then news came that Scarborough was being bombarded, and the British force steered in that direction amidst what Coore described as thick fog.[144] The priority now became intercepting Hipper on the way back.

Around 11.30am, in deteriorating weather – and after various efforts by the British to locate the Germans – Goodenough's cruisers ran into Hipper's screen. Coore, aboard *New Zealand*, heard the sound of firing and 'saw flashes of gunfire on port bow', but then it stopped.[145] Goodenough had apparently mistaken an order by Beatty for one directed to his own command, and abandoned the contact. Around 1pm, reports came of German forces to the south, and Beatty's battlecruisers briefly went in pursuit. Although nominally slower than the larger 13.5in ships, *New Zealand* – just six weeks out of dock – was able to keep up: Coore reported that the ship made 12,000hp over design.[146] However, there was no sign of their quarry. A little later, Room 40 reported that the High Seas Fleet was near Heligoland. They were on their return journey, but to the Admiralty it looked like they might be coming out. Jellicoe put to sea, concentrating the Grand Fleet and sweeping south. By then, von Ingenohl was back in harbour.

The whole affair had been something of a fiasco: the Germans had attacked civilian targets and the Royal Navy had been unable to either stop or catch them. Beatty was furious with Goodenough for botching the opportunity to bring the German battlecruisers to action, proposing to have him sacked and replaced by Halsey.[147] It said much for Halsey's status; his star had risen sharply with *New Zealand*'s 1913 world tour. In the end Goodenough kept his job. The problem, however, highlighted the way the service tradition of direct obedience stood against the need to take the initiative. Efforts to address it had been percolating through the navy for a generation or so, but had never gained much ground. The raid also played out against a backdrop of a stalling land war. By December the so-called 'race to the Channel' had ended with both sides digging in for winter.

Action continued at sea, where the focus turned to the Dogger Bank. Hipper felt that British trawlers fishing the shoals might be reporting German movements, and in January 1915 wondered about using his battle-cruisers to raid them and British light forces patrolling the area. Hipper anticipated early February, when *Von der Tann* was expected back from dock, but a good weather forecast prompted him to approach von Ingenohl on 23 January and ask him to order the effort for the next day. Von Ingenohl could not offer support because one of his battle squadrons was on its way to train in the Baltic. Hipper nonetheless took the risk and sailed with just three battlecruisers – *Seydlitz*, the new 12in-gunned *Derfflinger*, and *Moltke*, joined once again by *Blücher*. The latter's practical maximum sea speed of

23–24 knots limited the tactical flexibility of the force, which otherwise had a typical sea speed, in formation, of about 25–26 knots.[148] However, as Robert Massie has observed, it was not perhaps the rash decision it seemed: *Blücher*'s twelve 21cm guns had a high rate of fire and a range of up to 20,900yd.[149] With their supporting light ships, they departed the Jade at 5.45pm on 23 January, aiming to sweep Dogger Bank early the following morning, sink any British light forces, and return to Germany late that day.

The Admiralty became aware of these plans around noon on 23 January thanks to Room 40 decrypts,[150] preparing a trap with Beatty's battlecruisers, Goodenough's cruiser force and Tyrwhitt's light ships, backed by the Third Battle Squadron of pre-dreadnoughts to catch Hipper if he veered north. The Grand Fleet was ordered to sea in case the High Seas Fleet sailed. Fisher – in bed with a cold in his apartment in Admiralty Arch – approved the plan. And, as Churchill later remarked, the stage was set for the first clash of modern heavy warships in history.[151]

By this time Beatty's battlecruisers and the pre-dreadnought squadron were temporarily at Rosyth in the Firth of Forth. The force had been reorganised: *New Zealand*, as Moore's flagship, led the Second Battlecruiser Squadron, which stood at two ships. The Germans had not sailed on an optimal day for their force, but nor did Beatty. *Queen Mary* had just gone into dock and some of the crews were ashore on leave. Orders to raise steam for 20 knots at thirty minutes' notice reached *New Zealand* at 2.15pm, plunging the ship into a frenzy.[152] Then a problem arose. Prince Louis of Battenberg was aboard, visiting his son. Both Moore and Halsey suggested he should stay, but Prince Louis – diplomatically – declined. One historian has speculated that had he remained, he might have been able to influence the officers in the subsequent battle.[153] However, one cannot speculate on the 'what ifs'. Sea battles, particularly, carry many variables: and the fact was that Prince Louis departed.

It was winter. Goodenough's cruisers left in darkness at 6.10pm and the battlecruisers sailed at 6.26 by *New Zealand*'s log.[154] These times need qualification: absolute and co-ordinated time was problematic aboard these warships. *New Zealand*'s wireless record of the next day, for instance, was out by some minutes, depending on what it is matched against. Other times, recorded by Boyle in his diary, varied again. This was typical: most ships' time-keeping varied by a few minutes.[155]

The battlecruisers *Lion*, *Tiger*, *Princess Royal*, *New Zealand* and *Indomitable* ploughed on at 18 knots, hoping to reach a point to the east of the Germans and so cut them off from their base. Beatty made contact with Tyrwhitt's force at 6.30am on the 24th, then swept into the Dogger Bank area looking for Hipper.[156] *New Zealand* went to action stations at 6.55am,[157] and just ten minutes later, one of Tyrwhitt's cruisers, *Aurora* – leading the 1st Destroyer Flotilla – sighted a three-funnelled cruiser and four smaller warships to the east. In the pre-dawn darkness there was a moment of confusion: it might have been British. Captain Wilmot Nicholson ordered a challenge by searchlight. The response came in the form of a single letter flashed from the ship – and gunfire.[158] It was *Kolberg* with four torpedo boats. A brief gun duel followed; and Beatty – slightly to the north – turned to intercept.

The tableau emerged as the light grew. *Kolberg* reported the engagement with light British forces to Hipper, who was steaming from the south-east. Then, around 7.30am, Goodenough spotted the Harwich force to the south and turned to pursue German forces to the south-east. A few minutes later the German battlecruisers became visible from *Aurora*, steering north. From Beatty's perspective this meant he was narrowly on course to get between the Germans and their base. About the same time, however, Hipper received a report from *Stralsund* to the effect that eight British heavy units were approaching. At 7.45am he ordered a turn-about, signalling his light forces to hasten south-west. Back at Wilhelmshaven, von Ingenohl ordered his only available battle squadron to raise steam and put to sea, though they were hours away from being able to offer support.[159]

As a result of Hipper's turn, the battle became a stern chase, but the day was clear, it was early, and they were still well distant from Heligoland. Beatty kept calling for more speed: 25 knots at 8.12am and, four minutes later, 26 knots.[160] The problem aboard *New Zealand* was Beatty's demand: 26 knots was *New Zealand*'s maximum sea speed. Then, at 8.34am, Beatty called for 27 knots. Aboard *New Zealand*, young stokers such as Patrick Murphy, William Newcombe, Albert Norris, James O'Connor, Ernest Carter, Patrick Casey, James Pithie, Tom Reed and William Snailham – among over 290 others – bent their backs to the task.[161] By 8.40am, *New Zealand* had achieved that speed – an astonishing feat that relied as much on the muscle power of the stokers as the over-design built into the propulsion plant.[162] Just two minutes later Beatty called for 28 knots. Despite the best efforts of their sweating stokers, shovelling coal endlessly into the maws of the furnaces, *New Zealand* and *Indomitable* began to fall back – *Indomitable* the more so. After a while *Princess Royal* – which had not been docked in months – also began to lag, but Beatty did not slacken the pace, and at 8.52am *Lion* began a succession of ranging shots on *Blücher* at the prodigious range of 20,000yd. They fell short. Then Beatty ordered 29 knots – an aspirational order designed to urge his ships to ultimate effort. At 9am *Tiger* also opened fire.

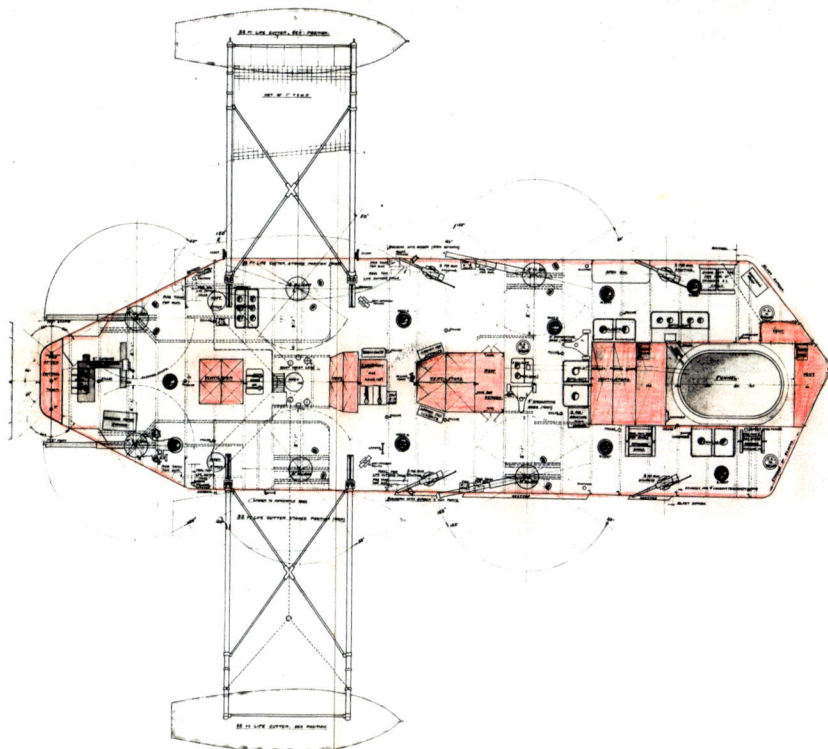

Above: The aft flying deck plan of *New Zealand*, from the Fairfield builders' drawings, showing the 'sea' position of the ship's cutters.
(*Detail from builder plan, flying deck, Papers-3925-1-1_1_mm, Alexander Turnbull Library*)

Right: The midships flying deck plan of *New Zealand*, from the Fairfield builders' drawings. Note the provision for stowing coaling gear.
(*Detail from builder plan, flying deck, Papers-3925-1-1_1_mm, Alexander Turnbull Library*)

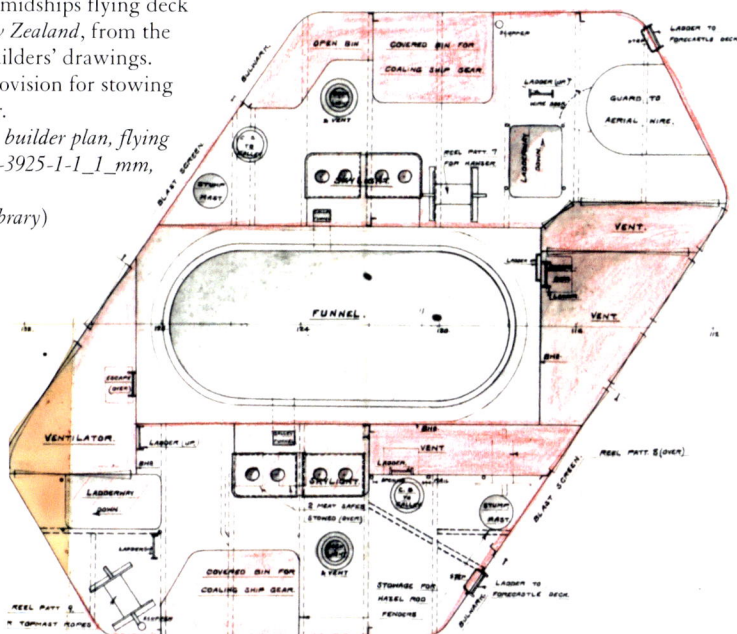

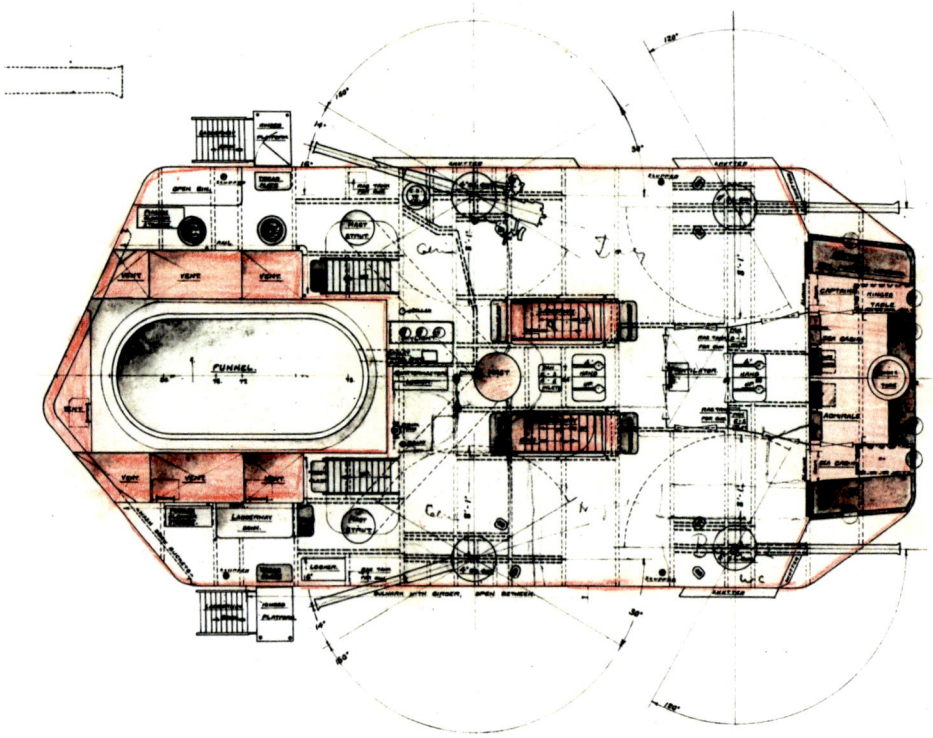

Above: The forward flying deck plan of *New Zealand*, from the Fairfield builders' drawings. Noteworthy elements include the relatively compact sea cabins for captain and admiral, along with arcs of fire for the 4in guns.
(*Detail from builder plan, flying deck, Papers-3925-1-1_1_mm, Alexander Turnbull Library*)

Below: The boat deck of *New Zealand*, from the Fairfield builders' drawings.
(*Detail from builder plan, boat deck, Papers-3925-1-1_1_mm, Alexander Turnbull Library*)

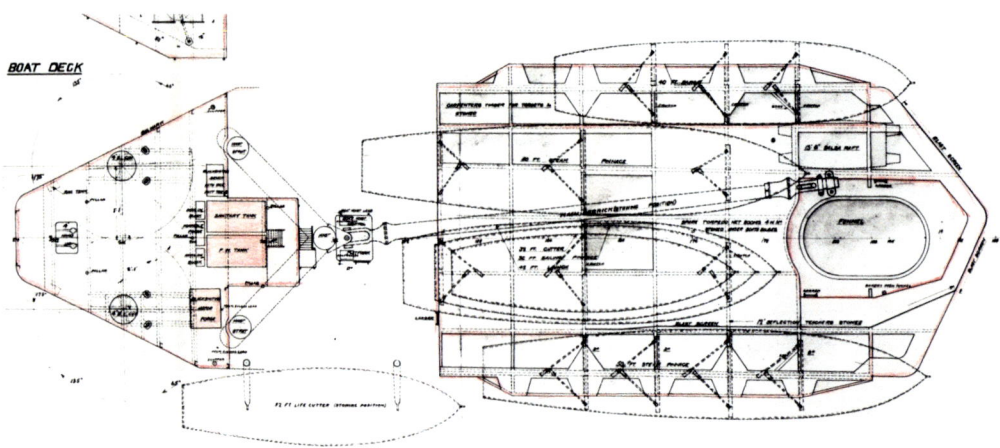

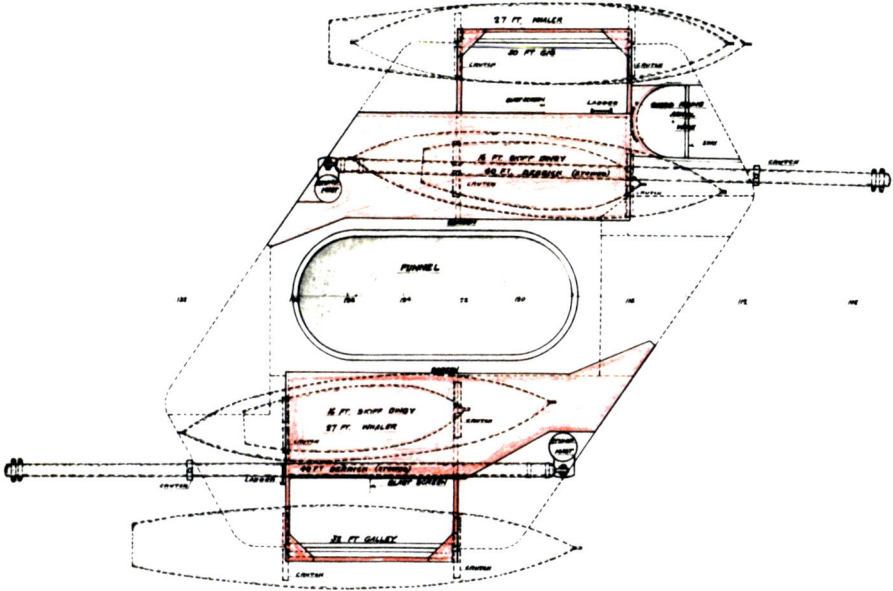

Above: The midships boat stowage of *New Zealand*, from the Fairfield builders' drawings. (*Detail from builder plan, boat deck, Papers-3925-1-1_1_mm, Alexander Turnbull Library*)

Below: *New Zealand*'s signal deck: detail from her builders' plans. The size of the signal house is salutary. Searchlights were an integral part of the system. (*Detail from builder plan, boat deck, Papers-3925-1-1_1_mm, Alexander Turnbull Library*)

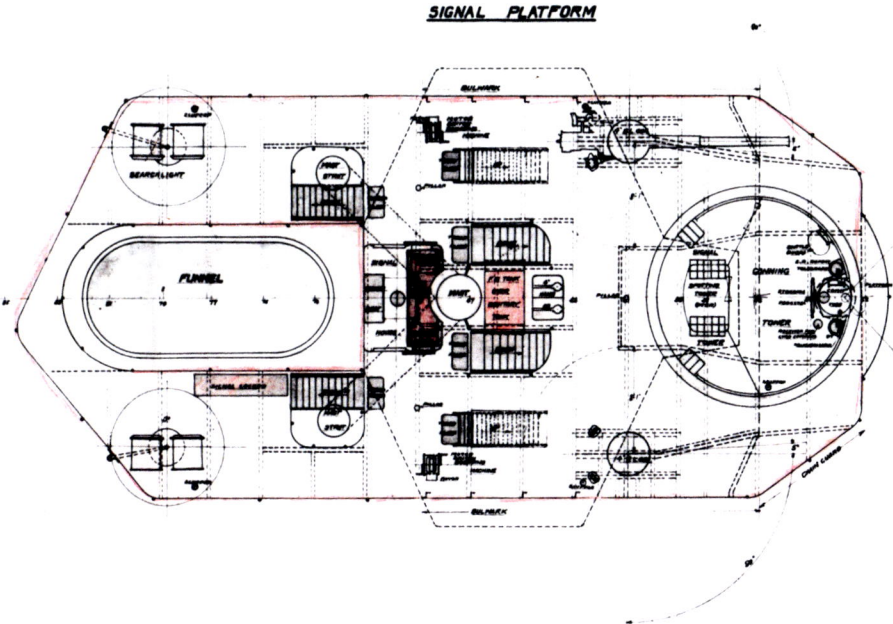

The battlecruiser *New Zealand* at the Battle of Jutland, depicted
by the marine artist Ian Marshall. *(Estate of Ian Marshall)*

I. H. M.

Above: A number of the officers aboard *New Zealand*, including the fire-control officer, Arthur Smith, were artists. Others included Chief Petty Officer Edward ('Eddie') Fitzgerald, who produced this view of what he saw from the conning tower at 12.40pm, during the Battle of Heligoland Bight. (*Torpedo Bay Navy Museum 047 2007.1.3*)

Below: Edward Fitzgerald was in the conning tower of HMS New Zealand when Queen Mary blew up. This is his painting of the stern, slewed around and sinking, as New Zealand passed. (*Torpedo Bay Navy Museum, 2007.1.5*)

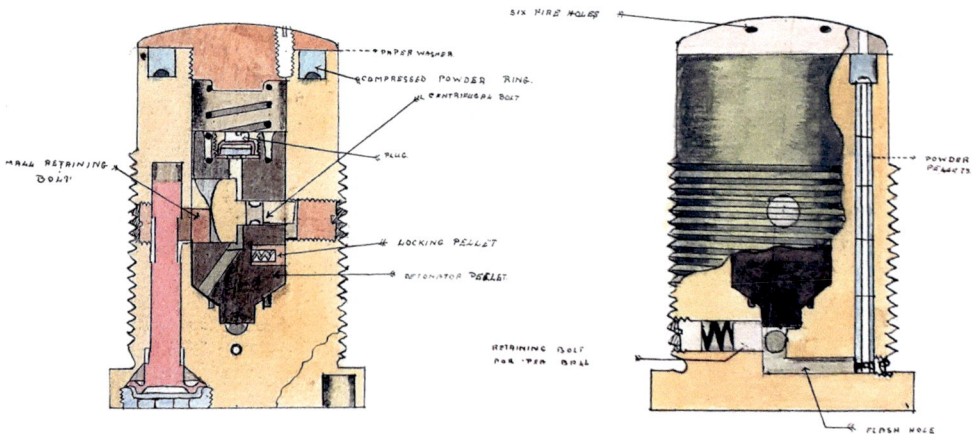

BRIDGE

Builders' plans of *New Zealand*'s bridge and compass platform. It was in these open-air locations with their wide view, and not in the armoured conning tower, that senior officers tended to gather during battle. (*Detail from builder plan, boat deck, Papers-3925-1-1_1_mm, Alexander Turnbull Library*)

Above: Edward Fitzgerald's dramatic painting of the Battle of Dogger Bank at '11 am'.
HMS *Lion* is listing and sheering off to starboard.
(*Torpedo Bay Navy Museum 2007.1.4 – Dogger Bank*)

Below: Damage to *New Zealand*'s X-turret barbette glacis and adjacent deck.
(*Torpedo Bay Navy Museum 2006.743.6.11*)

So began the Battle of Dogger Bank, the world's first engagement between all-big-gun warships. By chance it also engaged the classic imagery of social-militarist Britain: the battlecruisers – the cavalry of the fleet – galloping in pursuit of a fleeing enemy, led from the front by their heroic commander who, naturally, was well out ahead. David Boyle, commanding *New Zealand*'s X-turret, could only see the 'masts and funnels' of Hipper's ships, but felt conditions were otherwise excellent. 'It was a perfect clear day very little wind and all of them was [sic] in exactly the right direction for us. In fact the position of the fight was ideal.'[163]

We can imagine the scene aboard *New Zealand*: Halsey with Sloman's hei tiki around his neck and the piupiu atop his uniform, the officers variously standing on the bridge with its cramped chart houses behind, or in the conning tower peering through vision slots that roared with the half-gale of their passage, professional officers who were excited and anxious and eager all at once. In the conning tower, Chief Petty Officer Edward Fitzgerald stood, again taking in the scene. Ratings stood on the compass platform above, bracing themselves against the wind and waiting by the signal halyards, searchlights and the two semaphore positions, peering forwards at the three 13.5in battlecruisers racing ahead under great plumes of coal smoke, the smoke of Hipper's force visible beyond. The main decks were soused with spray as the ship surged through the water at close on 27 knots, drenching those in the gun houses, among them Prince George of Battenberg. He was peering through his spotting hood and almost blinded by wind-driven spray that rendered his rangefinder useless and got into his clothes.[164]

As always, most of those aboard *New Zealand* could not see out. Below decks the stokers were again enduring endless labour, sweating and cursing in the heat as the trimmers brought trolley-loads of coal from the bunkers, sometimes urged on by one of the seven chief stokers, men such as forty-four-year-old Michael Griffith, thirty-six-year-old Robert Lane, or thirty-eight-year-old John Murphy.[165] The chiefs' attentions were otherwise largely given over to the pressure gauges and the Chadburn engine order telegraphs. Their efforts paid off: the ship achieved 320 revolutions and developed an estimated 65,250hp – well over her design maximum – for an indicated speed of 27 knots.[166] In the gun houses, magazines and munitions trunks the men waited anxiously. For now, though, gunners such as Owen Whitmarsh, James Taylor or Vincent Robinson could only wait;[167] the ship was falling behind the 'splendid cats' and the range even to *Blücher* was too great.

By 9am the range logged in *New Zealand* to *Blücher* was 19,900yd.[168] Over the next half hour the British line drew closer to the German, approaching at a slight angle to allow all guns to bear and to avoid any mines dropped in the German wake. *Lion* – the foremost and nearest British ship – was hit several times. Beatty ordered Tyrwhitt's forces into station ahead 'at utmost speed' to foil a possible German torpedo boat attack. By 9.30am shells from the 13.5in ships were falling around the German battlecruisers, and three minutes later Beatty ordered general engagement by 'opposite numbers'. This did not go well. Because *Indomitable* was now well back, the battle theoretically was four-on-four with *New Zealand* engaging *Blücher*. What actually happened was that *Tiger*'s commander, Henry Pelly, assumed that at 5:4, *Tiger* would engage *Seydlitz* along with *Lion*. This left *Moltke* unengaged and able to concentrate on *Lion*. Worse, *Tiger*'s gunnery officer, Evan Bruce-Gardyne – the 13th Laird of Middleton – then mistook *Lion*'s shell splashes for *Tiger*'s.[169]

At this stage *New Zealand* was not closely engaged. Around 9.27am, by *New Zealand*'s log, a shell landed some 500yd distant.[170] Boyle saw it fall, followed by several others '1000 yards short of us' and others 'around the ships ahead'.[171] He was fascinated. 'They nearly all burst on hitting the water, sending out black smoke and flame. None of these seemed very big. The noise of these shells bursting and the guns firing was getting a bit thick.'[172] At 9.33am – 9.40am according to Boyle's account – Beatty signalled a general engagement. *New Zealand* was some 18,100yd from *Blücher* and opened fire 'at our maximum range'. This made rapid fire impractical: 'our guns kept getting down to the stops'.[173] *New Zealand* continued to slowly pot away at *Blücher* for the next forty minutes. Meanwhile, the battle between the 'splendid cats' and Hipper's three battlecruisers continued, apparently in Beatty's favour after a hit by *Lion* knocked out both *Seydlitz*'s after turrets, sending flames roaring high above the ship. But *Lion* also began to suffer from the concentrated fire of the German vessels.

After about an hour several things happened in quick succession. Around 10.30am, *New Zealand* scored a significant hit on *Blücher*, striking a horizontal ammunition trunk beneath the armoured deck. This was used to transport munitions for the two forward wing turrets, and to house key voice pipes and cabling, and at that moment it contained thirty-five cartridges. The result was catastrophic: all internal communications – including those for fire control and engine commands were lost, and the steam pipes from the forward boilers were severed.[174] A few minutes later *Blücher* swung to port, slowing and on fire, but still shooting at *New Zealand*; shells fell around the battlecruiser at 10.42am, by the ship's timing. Around the same time – 10.39am by *New Zealand*'s log, 10.30 according to Boyle – observers aboard the battlecruiser saw *Lion* listing and hauling out of line.[175] And then a succession of new flag signals rose to the halyards of Beatty's crippled flagship, picked up by spotters tasked with reading them at distance, squinting against the icy half-gale and the smoke of the forward guns periodically fouling their position.

At 10.47am, by *Lion*'s timing, Beatty signalled by flag that his forces should 'close the enemy as rapidly as possible consistent with keeping all guns bearing'. This was missed by some ships. Then further hits on *Lion* resulted in a complete power failure.[176] A few minutes later, at 10.54, Beatty himself thought he saw a periscope to starboard and ordered his entire force to turn away eight points.[177] By this time *Lion* was able to make only 15 knots and had around 3,000 tons of water aboard, giving her a 10 degree list to port, with no electricity and A-turret out of action.[178] Once the submarine scare was over Beatty wanted to get the ships back on to the pursuit, but the loss of power and most of the signal halyards made it difficult. At the suggestion of his Flag Commander, Reginald Plunkett, and his Flag Lieutenant, Ralph Seymour, he finally made several signals intended to instruct his captains to continue the chase: 'Compass B – course NE' and 'AF'. These were intended to cause the battlecruisers to pursue Hipper on a course that kept them clear of potential torpedo boat attack and any mines dropped by the fleeing Germans.

There were three problems. The first, as Goldrick has pointed out, is that there were other options in the signal book: Beatty had been poorly advised by Plunkett and Seymour.[179] The second was that nobody outside *Lion's* bridge knew why Beatty ordered the earlier eight-point turn. The third was that the first message was still flying when the second was raised, and had not yet been hauled down, which was the sign to execute it. This meant that those who saw it read the two messages together as 'attack the rear of the enemy bearing north-east'. Beatty then wanted to hoist the Nelsonic 'engage the enemy more closely', but it had been replaced in the 1906 Signal Book by 'keep nearer the enemy'.[180] This was raised, but not correctly received by most of the ships.[181]

Moore, aboard *New Zealand*, was certainly puzzled. The turn to port had not been explained. Now the signals seemed to be pointing to something other than Hipper's main force.[182] As a result, the entire squadron focused on the crippled armoured cruiser. By 11.40am, according to *New Zealand*'s log, *Blücher* was 'badly on fire fore and aft, fore turrets blazing'.[183] Boyle recalled that the range had dropped to about 5,600yd.[184] About this time it appeared to the British that *Blücher* had struck her colours and was sinking, so Tyrwhitt sent light ships in to rescue survivors, and at 12.02pm Moore signalled 'cease fire'.[185] By this time *Blücher* appeared a 'regular shambles' to observers aboard *New Zealand*, 'guns were pointing in all directions. The fore-turret was burning fiercely, and the whole ship was in flames practically fore and aft ... All hands alive were on the after deck and some were jumping overboard.'[186]

Moore realised command had fallen to him. Hipper's battlecruisers were some 12 miles distant to the south-east, obviously fleeing, while his own force was just 80 miles from Heligoland. The helter-skelter pursuit had spanned around 100 miles of the North Sea. He decided to steam west to support the crippled *Lion*. *Blücher*, meanwhile, rolled over and sank. Efforts by the British destroyers to rescue survivors were hampered by the arrival of the Zeppelin A64 and a German seaplane. They had been on patrol further north, responded to a message Hipper had sent for help, and now began dropping bombs. Goodenough ordered the British ships to clear the area. Beatty, who had jumped across to a destroyer and gone in pursuit of his battlecruisers, hoisted his flag aboard *Princess Royal* around 12.20pm and ordered a sixteen-point turn, but it was too late. Hipper's forces were approaching the horizon, and there was not time to catch him before he reached the safety of home waters.

In the quiet after the battle, Boyle had time to write his diary, and at 5.30pm a short evening service was held aboard *New Zealand* on the cable deck. Next day flags were lowered to half-mast and the ship's company sent to Divisions to recognise the funeral aboard *Tiger* of five men killed during the battle.[187]

German media afterwards insisted that *New Zealand* had been sunk.[188] In fact, she had not even been hit, something the crew put down to Halsey's decision to wear the hei tiki and piupiu. She had also fired a significant number of shells: 12 rounds of common 12in and 139 rounds of high explosive,[189] divided unevenly between the turrets: 31 rounds by A-turret, 33 by P-turret, 28 by Q-turret and 47 by X-turret.[190] Apart from the final engagement, when the range had dropped, the only confirmed longer-range hit *New Zealand* made was the one on *Blücher*'s ammunition trunk at around 10.30am.

The loss of *Blücher* was trumpeted in papers across the Empire as due revenge for the German bombardment of civilians,[191] masking the fact that the battlecruisers had got away. The New Zealand High Commissioner, Thomas Mackenzie, telegraphed his congratulations to Halsey as soon as news came of *New Zealand*'s part. Halsey responded promptly: 'The flag is ready to hoist again.'[192] A few days later he telegraphed: 'All aboard are proud of having represented the Dominion, and receiving its appreciation.'[193] Beatty recognised the efforts by the stokers and engine room crews. Halsey forwarded names, and Beatty singled out Chief Engine Room Artificer 2nd

Class William Dand, Chief Stoker John James and Stoker Petty Officer John Sims for mention in his despatch on the battle.[194]

Admiralty opinion differed: a much greater victory had, perhaps, been to hand. Fisher was furious that Moore had not continued the pursuit, sending a note to Beatty prefixed with his usual 'burn' instruction, demanding: 'WHAT POSSIBLE EXPLANATION IS THERE?'[195] A little later, Pelly took the brunt of his anger. The general interpretation, then and later, was that Britain threw away an opportunity through a combination of signalling mishap and the weight of tradition. There is, however, a coda. By the time the force turned back only *Tiger* and *Princess Royal* were still in the pursuit. *Lion* was disabled, *New Zealand* some distance back, and *Indomitable* effectively so far behind as to be out of the race. Historical 'what ifs' are fraught with danger, but a 2017 statistical analysis of First World War-era naval gunfire, utilising approximate Bayesian computation (ABC), concluded that there was a high probability Britain would have lost a ship had the pursuit continued.[196]

There were lessons about hardware. It was clear that armour did not have to be penetrated in order to fail: plates on *Lion* had been driven inwards by failure of the backing structure after 12in hits from *Derfflinger*, causing flooding. Another discovery was that battles could take place at unprecedented distances: the 13.5in ships had opened fire at a range outside the limit of their fire-control accuracy. But perhaps the key issue was the quantity of ammunition thrown at the Germans for only minimal result, other than during the final engagement against *Blücher*. *Lion*, for instance, expended 243 rounds of 13.5in armour-piercing shells during the chase.[197] In that time, aside from those on *Blücher*, the entire force had scored perhaps three hits.

One answer to the problem was to increase the rate of fire. That carried problems. One of the techniques used to keep displacement – hence cost – under control during the naval race had been to reduce on-board munitions stowage, typically to 80 rounds per heavy gun. Fisher felt this was sufficient: ships no longer spent months at sea. However, by the time war broke out there were questions as to whether ships had enough even for one engagement. The answer was to store shells outside the shell rooms and pack the magazines with more cordite. In a sense it seemed not too great a risk: shells were steel, and the chance of the fuse being triggered or the bursting charge detonating after a hit nearby seemed low. In other ways it was foolhardy. The risks had been highlighted when the battleship *Bulwark* blew up in the Medway on 26 November 1914 with the loss of 738 men. The court of enquiry found that munitions, including thirty old cordite charges, had been stored in corridors between the magazines. Overheating due to the proximity of an engine room bulkhead likely set off a faulty shell, or ignited the cordite.[198] A few days later, HMS *Kent* was nearly lost to ammunition fire during the Battle of the Falkland Islands.[199]

Cordite was the main villain in this mix: it was volatile, became unstable as it aged, and was carried aboard every warship in significant quantities. It had been developed as a gun propellant in the late 1880s by Sir James Dewar and the Manchester-based German chemist W Kellner.[200] It was produced in rods of approximately ⅓in diameter, packaged in silk bags with a black-powder igniter, and usually stored in cases. By 1914 the composition had been modified to reduce bore erosion, but this did not alter the primary properties. However, the need to increase both quantity aboard and rate of supply to the guns intruded. The answer involved locking open the flash-tight magazine doors and defeating the safety interlocks designed to block a direct path from the gun house to the magazines and shell rooms. Storage case lids were left open and charges sometimes removed for quick loading into the hoists, despite the risk of the gunpowder igniter trickling out of the silk and creating a fire hazard on the magazine floors.[201] All this increased the rate of shooting, but meant there was a high risk that fire in the gun house or handling room could spread into the magazines.[202] It was also done in contravention of Admiralty requirements, reiterated after the near loss of *Kent*.[203]

Into this fed an increasingly cavalier approach to safety. Cordite was man-ufactured in numbered batches and monitored for quality as it aged, meaning the stocks aboard ship had to be managed carefully. However, when Alexander Grant joined *Lion* as chief gunner in June 1915 he found the ship had thirty-four 'lots' of cordite aboard instead of the usual fifteen.[204] It was so chaotically stored it was impossible to engage in normal procedures by which a whole batch was removed if one sample failed a test. He was told not to 'make a noise', but saw the captain, Ernle Chatfield, anyway; and the ship's stock of cordite was replaced. The other problem Grant found was in magazine practices. Men were entering the spaces in hobnailed boots, sometimes with cigarettes behind their ears and matches in their pockets. The cigarettes were unlit, but it contravened pre-war regulations. Grant gained Chatfield's support in reforming *Lion*'s magazine procedures.[205] The rest of the fleet, however, remained vulnerable in various ways.

The battlecruisers became a separate formation a few weeks after the Battle of Dogger Bank. This administrative shift came about in part because of an earlier debate within the Admiralty over whether the German raids were better handled by stationing a few heavy ships further south. Churchill did not want to divide the battlecruisers. Jellicoe objected altogether, wanting the battlecruisers at Cromarty so they could concentrate swiftly with the

Grand Fleet.[206] Fisher had his own ideas, telling Beatty that Jellicoe 'might as well be at Timbuctoo [sic]' while he stayed in Scapa Flow – that Jellicoe should be at Rosyth and Beatty's own force in the Humber.[207] The issue of deployment was still under discussion a few days before the Battle of Dogger Bank, and resolved in the subsequent fortnight. Jellicoe stayed at Scapa, but Beatty's battlecruisers, with a significant number of supporting cruisers and destroyers, were ordered to Rosyth, the major dockyard and naval base on the northern side of the Firth of Forth. From 11 February the force became formally known as the Battlecruiser Fleet, though still subsidiary to Jellicoe.

The new location was more salubrious for *New Zealand*'s crew than the desolate and wind-swept Orkneys. The dockyard itself was new; it had been authorised in 1903, construction had begun in 1909, and the nearby town of Rosyth was established the same year as a modern garden city to house dockyard workers. In 1915 the docks were still under construction: it was March 1916 before the first was ready. The whole complex was not far from Edinburgh. Downsides included the fact that the base lacked firing practice facilities and was upstream of Arrol's enormous rail bridge – a problem if the Germans found a way to damage the bridge sufficiently to temporarily block the channel. One of the key reasons for the move south was that it put the battlecruisers in a better position to intercept further German raids. However, the fact that Fisher called the new force a 'fleet' underscored the role he saw for his 'New Testament' ships. He resigned – spectacularly – from the Admiralty in mid-May after clashing with Churchill, ending a career that had lasted more than sixty years.[208]

All nine British battlecruisers were eventually based at Rosyth, a concentration made possible by the fact that German forces outside the North Sea were largely mopped up.[209] The fleet was soon joined by the tenth ship, *Australia*, which became flagship of the Second Battlecruiser Squadron, flying the flag of Rear Admiral William Pakenham.

By this time it was clear that the war was not going to end quickly, which brought new issues. As James Goldrick has pointed out, 1914 brought surprises for the Royal Navy, mostly flowing from the fact that fleet action seemed elusive; but the reality of a longer war provoked change in everything from the leave given sailors through to ensuring good entertainments ashore. Shipboard routines were amended: watch-keeping practices were reviewed in light of the fact that even off-duty men seldom gained sufficient rest. Another issue provoked by a longer-term struggle was manpower – in part because wartime steaming demanded more stokers than peacetime complements allowed. This issue also highlighted the fact that the relentless 'sweeps' burned coal in prodigious quantities – all of which had to be manhandled.[210] One of the answers involved disbanding the Royal Naval Division – a land force Churchill had organised – to retrieve the stokers serving with it.

New Zealand was based at Rosyth for the rest of the conflict, her war a pattern of endless but largely fruitless 'sweeps', variously supporting the light ships that enforced the blockade, or in response to news of a German foray. These brief periods at sea were punctuated by periods of idleness in harbour. None of this had been anticipated before the war. There is no particular need to outline these events in every detail, other than to note that they became a numbing routine that took its toll on morale. Crew came and went. In June 1915 a new captain was appointed: John Frederick Ernest Green – 'Jimmy', to his friends, a career officer who arrived from the armoured cruiser HMS *Natal*.

So *New Zealand*'s war played out, her presence in the North Sea – ironically, and despite the gyrations of pre-war politics – bringing Ward's concept of strengthening the Empire at its centre to fruition. And the ship was upheld, back in New Zealand, as a symbol of the dominion's contribution. There was one major exception to the endless routines of patrol and idleness: the Battle of Jutland, the only collision of the main fleets of the war. This came suddenly at the end of May 1916, and *New Zealand* was in the thick of it.

CHAPTER 6

JUTLAND

It was miles more exciting than the other shows and we had a pretty
hot time as we had to take on not only their battlecruisers, but about a
dozen of their leading battleships and in addition to that they had a
most terrific advantage of light …
Sub-Lieutenant Mick Barcroft to Bell Irving, 15 June 1916.[1]

The Battle of Jutland was the only clash of the great fleets in the First World
War, a hectic afternoon and evening on 31 May–1 June 1916 whose human
impact for both nations is still remembered by families who lost loved ones in
the battle. As Peter Hart and Nigel Steel have pointed out, it produced
casualties for the Royal Navy of similar scale to those of an army 'push' on the
Western Front, a point often forgotten by history.[2] The majority of the 6,784
British officers and men killed during the battle were aboard the three
battlecruisers and two armoured cruisers sunk with the loss of virtually all
hands.[3]

New Zealand was nearly not in the battle at all, after an incident on
21 April. Pakenham's squadron sailed from Rosyth at 4am that day to
support a cruiser and destroyer sweep into the Kattegat, enforcing the
blockade. Soon afterwards word came that the High Seas Fleet was sailing.
Beatty took the rest of the battlecruiser fleet to sea and rendezvoused with
Pakenham. Jellicoe, meanwhile, put to sea with the Grand Fleet. By mid-
afternoon the battlecruisers were north-west of Horns Reef and steaming in
line abreast. At 3.35pm Beatty ordered the ships to begin zig-zagging. Just then
they entered a bank of fog. *Australia* was sailing with a cruiser to port, and
swung to starboard while keeping a watch for *New Zealand*, which had been
in that direction. Visibility was so poor, however, that when the two vessels
spotted each other at 3.42pm they had no room to manoeuvre and struck a
glancing blow. *Australia* came off second best, her side torn open from frames
59 to 78 by the armour plates protecting *New Zealand*'s side abaft P-turret,
while *New Zealand*'s port outer propeller tore into *Australia*'s hull below Q-
turret. This damaged the propeller and left *New Zealand* briefly uncontrol-
lable. As a result, she swung across *Australia*'s bows and was rammed.[4]

To collide twice in three minutes was embarrassing. But here, close to
enemy waters, it was potentially lethal. *Australia* came to a stop to let damage

control parties stem incoming water, but *New Zealand* was able to keep moving. Both ships returned to Rosyth without further incident, where *New Zealand* was docked for repairs. *Australia*, however, had to be sent first to Newcastle, then Devonport. Both ships were out of action for around five weeks. The incident had a curious sequel when it finally surfaced back in New Zealand: reports that *New Zealand* had rammed *Australia* were dismissed on the basis that the collision had been the other way around.[5] Trans-Tasman rivalries died hard.

Both battlecruisers were still in dock on 24 April when word came that the High Seas Fleet was coming out. Jellicoe – who had just returned to Scapa – put the Grand Fleet to sea once again. Next morning the German battlecruisers appeared off Lowestoft, bombarding both that town and Yarmouth. This was unusual by this stage in the war. Von Ingenohl had resigned in February 1915, essentially as fallout from the Battle of Dogger Bank. His successor, Hugo von Pohl, prioritised unrestricted submarine warfare, a direct way of attacking British commerce, and under his command both the High Seas Fleet and the First Scouting Group were significantly less active than before. By early 1916, Britain had also overcome its early war issues. Some thirty-one dreadnoughts and super-dreadnoughts were in service or working up, in addition to the ten battlecruisers.[6] As usual, not all were available at any given instant, but the relative balance was heavily in the British favour.

The renewed activity by the Germans was largely down to the new commander of the High Seas Fleet, *Vizeadmiral* Reinhard Scheer, whose approach had found favour at government level. The Lowestoft raid, indeed, was simply the beginning of a series of significant fleet movements, of which the sortie that led to Jutland was the second. The renewal of German fleet activity, however, again raised the question of where to best locate British ships to intercept a raiding force. The Lowestoft raid was a case in point: Tyrwhitt made contact and tried to divert the German forces, buying time until Beatty could arrive, but once again the Germans slipped the net.[7] Argument over the adequacy of armour in the older battlecruisers flared again among fleet officers in wake of the debacle: Pakenham openly pointed out that six had 'little armour protection'.[8] Jellicoe finally agreed to reinforce Beatty with the Fifth Battle Squadron under Rear Admiral Hugh Evan-Thomas. This was the fleet's 'fast wing', made up of the *Queen Elizabeth*-class battleships ordered in the 1912–13 programme and the Malayan gift ship of the same type. They were slower than the battlecruisers, but had excellent protection and armament. Meanwhile, Vice-Admiral Jerram's powerful Second Battle Squadron of 13.5in-gunned super-dreadnoughts with supporting light forces were sent to Cromarty. Separately, the issues with the battlecruisers' gunnery were resolved when – during a conference on 12 May – Beatty agreed to send his ships north, squadron by squadron, to Scapa where practice facilities were available. The Third Battlecruiser Squadron, the three oldest battlecruisers under Rear Admiral Horace Hood, sailed on 22 May.[9]

New Zealand returned to Beatty's force on 30 May, some days ahead of her sister ship; and in absence of *Australia* became Pakenham's flagship. She had a fair number of new crew aboard, among them thirty-five-year-old Able Seaman Timothy McCarthy, who had joined on 27 April while the ship was still under repair; thirty-seven-year-old Stoker Archibald McCallum, Ordinary Signalman Sidney Mocket, and others, who had arrived a little earlier.[10] By this time *Queen Elizabeth* had gone into dock, but the remainder of Beatty's force was available to sail: *Lion*, *Princess Royal*, *Queen Mary*, *Tiger*, *New Zealand* and *Indefatigable*, with their fourteen supporting light cruisers – two of them destroyer leaders – and eighteen destroyers. They were joined by Evan-Thomas's battleships *Barham*, *Valiant*, *Warspite* and *Malaya* and his supporting force of a light cruiser – as destroyer leader – and nine destroyers. The battlecruiser force included a small seaplane carrier, *Engadine*. Naval aviation was in its infancy, and the ship had to stop to launch and recover its aircraft, but there were high hopes for aerial reconnaissance.

Scheer intended to follow the Lowestoft raid with a further foray, but was hampered by the fact that *Seydlitz* had struck a mine and repairs were going to take some time. Hipper was also absent on sick leave. Then, on 25 April, the German government buckled to United States pressure to end unrestricted U-boat warfare. This meant that a number of submarines became available. Scheer now planned to bombard Sunderland, drawing Beatty out of nearby Rosyth and ambushing the battlecruiser fleet, with the help of U-boats. The plan relied on clear and calm weather, mainly so that Zeppelins could foray further north and give advance warning of a sortie by the Grand Fleet. It was scheduled for 17 May, when *Seydlitz* was due to re-join after repairs. However, problems with condensers in some of the High Seas Fleet battleships prompted Scheer to defer the scheme to the 23rd. By then he had sixteen submarines available, supplemented by others from the Flanders Flotilla, which enabled him to expand the submarine traps to include the Harwich force and Grand Fleet.

Scheer despatched them on the 17th. However, late on the 22nd he discovered *Seydlitz* was not ready. The clock was ticking: the U-boats could not remain on station beyond 31 May. In the end *Seydlitz* did not re-join the fleet until 29 May, by which time the weather had deteriorated and prevented the intended Zeppelin reconnaissance. Scheer then switched to his alternative plan, a foray north up the Danish coast with the First Scouting Group leading the way. He issued the orders on the afternoon of the 30th, and the German battlecruisers left harbour in the pre-dawn hours of 31 May. The High Seas Fleet followed as light began to grow in the sky. Sixteen dreadnoughts were available that day, shortly joined by six pre-dreadnoughts of the Second Battle Squadron under *Konteradmiral* Franz Mauve, although their lower speed restricted the tactical flexibility of the fleet.

The British knew something was up: Scheer's orders to his U-boats had been intercepted by Room 40. The message of 30 May was also received by the British, and although not fully decrypted, indicated that something was about to happen the next day. At 5.16pm the Admiralty signalled both Beatty and Jellicoe to sortie, ordering them east of the Long Forties. *New Zealand* was due to coal next morning and the crew had rigged coaling gear ready for an early start: now they stowed it and prepared for sea.[11] The battlecruiser cast off from her mooring buoy at 7pm, and half an hour later those on deck watched three minesweepers head to sea, clearing the way for the fleet. *New Zealand* finally weighed anchor at 9.45.[12] Evan-Thomas followed forty minutes later. Jellicoe, meanwhile, had already left Scapa Flow at 9.30 and Jerram had put to sea from Cromarty at 10pm.[13]

What these arrangements implied was that both fleets were likely to reach the same general area at about the same time. Jellicoe ordered Beatty to a point 100 miles north-west of Horns Reef and 65 miles south of the Grand Fleet by 2pm on 31 May. If Beatty found nothing, he was to steam north to rendezvous with Jellicoe.[14]

At this stage the British were expecting the German battlecruisers, but were unclear about the High Seas Fleet. During the morning of 31 May the Director of the Operations Division at the Admiralty, Captain Thomas Jackson, asked Room 40 staff where directional wireless had located the call sign of *Frederich der Große* – Scheer's flagship. He was told it was in the Jade. This was consistent with information that the Zeppelin reconnaissance had not flown. Jellicoe, received it around 12.48pm, reasonably supposing that the High Seas Fleet was not at sea. Jackson, however, had merely asked a question without giving his reasons, and been given a literally correct answer. It was not informative. In fact, Scheer routinely transferred his flagship's radio call sign to a shore station when leaving harbour, a deliberate subterfuge designed to mislead the British – and Room 40 staff were aware of the fact.[15] But Jackson, whose relationship with them was at best dysfunctional, never asked.

Daily routines continued aboard the battlecruiser fleet as the ships steamed to position. It was pay day, and if battle was not joined the men had the prospect of an easy afternoon of 'make and mend'. This was when they were meant to catch up on such matters as repairing their uniforms, maintaining their kit and so forth, but it was effectively time to themselves.

By about 2pm that afternoon Beatty's force was at the expected position, still in cruising formation with the battlecruisers in two columns, flanked at some distance by the light cruisers as advanced scouts. Evan-Thomas's four battleships and their supporting destroyers were some 5 miles behind. The seas were relatively calm, the winds light and sky cloudy but not overcast. There was no sign of an enemy. This sweep had, it seemed, been no different to the many that had preceded it. At 2.10pm Beatty signalled the turn north. However, the cruiser *Galatea*, north-east of *Lion*, initially missed reading the signal, and then her own lookouts saw a ship to the east, blowing off steam. Captain Edwyn Sinclair decided to hold course. The ship was the *N. J. Fjord*. Beyond, lookouts on *Galatea* shortly saw destroyers and then two light cruisers. At about 2.25pm, according to Beatty,[16] Sinclair signalled their presence and a few minutes later *Galatea* and the light cruiser *Phaeton* opened fire on the German vessels, the cruisers *Frankfurt*, *Pillau* and two destroyers.[17]

At 2.45pm, according to the official record, Beatty ordered *Engadine* to launch a reconnaissance flight.[18] They hoisted out Aircraft 39. The pilot, Flight Lieutenant F J Rutland, and an observer was able to identify four German light cruisers during a brief flight where cloud kept their altitude low, coming under heavy anti-aircraft fire as they approached.[19] Soon afterwards they found the German battlecruisers, but were forced down by a broken fuel pipe and, although recovered by *Engadine*, unable to report.[20] The unfolding drama, meanwhile, prompted Jellicoe to call for 18 knots at 2.55pm, and two minutes later order all ships to 'raise steam for full speed with all despatch'.[21] Hood, steaming a little south of Jellicoe's formation, had already ordered his own ships to do so fifteen minutes earlier, soon after *Galatea*'s report came in.[22] At 3pm, Jellicoe ordered the Grand Fleet to action stations.[23] Hood began steaming south, increasing to 22 knots at 3.15, intending to support Beatty.[24] He was formally ordered to do so by Jellicoe around 4pm.[25]

Beatty turned south-east and increased to 22 knots at around 3.32pm, with the aim of cutting any German forces off from their base. However, Beatty's flag signal to turn was missed aboard *Barham* – in part due to not being repeated by *Tiger* using a lamp. Evan-Thomas saw the battlecruisers turn but – in the absence of an order – continued to steam north. He remained at a loss to know why Beatty had not signalled by searchlight. By the time Beatty did so and the battleships had turned, Evan-Thomas's four battleships were 10 miles behind Beatty's force and out of support range.[26] Beatty's speed of 22 knots – close to the Fifth Battle Squadron's practical maximum sea speed that day of a little under 24 knots[27] – also made it difficult for them to close the gap.[28]

Beatty continued to steam south-east. Hipper, meanwhile, had turned west and by about 3.20pm sighted the smoke plumes of Beatty's heavy ships. According to the combined British signal log, the German battlecruisers were sighted from *New Zealand* at roughly the same time. She was the first of Beatty's heavy ships to do so.[29] Beatty ordered the battlecruiser fleet to action stations at about 3.27pm. The bugle call came just as men across the force were sitting down to tea. Aboard *New Zealand*, the gunnery officer, twenty-eight-year-old Lieutenant Commander Arthur Douglas Wales Smith,[30] recalled that some officers ran from the wardroom to the deck 'to have a look around', but the 'general attitude was one of scepticism'.[31] After so many false alarms and raised hopes the possibility of action this time seemed remote. Boyle recalled that the report was met with the cry 'what awful rot', and everybody 'went on eating'.[32] But five minutes later the bugles blew for action stations. Boyle hastened to his cabin 'to get a life-saving waistcoat and glasses' before heading to X-turret, 'the faithful one at the stern that I have had ever since it was built'.[33] Meanwhile, the carpenters began readying timbers to shore up bulkheads, or for other duties as needed.[34]

At about 3.30pm, Beatty changed course to approach Hipper, increasing speed to 25 knots,[35] though he had to slow a few minutes later to allow the Second Battlecruiser Squadron to join the rear of his battle line. By this time Evan-Thomas was around 7½ miles behind. Beatty was subsequently criticised for his decision to charge without concentrating his ships: it cut his firepower by about half for the time it took the Fifth Battle Squadron to get within range. It is possible Beatty was determined to begin the engagement quickly after the Dogger Bank experience, and he had, after all, six battle-cruisers to Hipper's five. However, his failure to concentrate his force smacked of command error. He elided the issue in his despatch to Jellicoe.[36]

Nobody knew how the battle might play out. 'Action stations,' seventeen-year-old Boy First Class James Eames wrote nervously aboard *New Zealand*, 'everything ready for action, will we win? Will we come through alright? What's going to happen?'[37] The senior officers gathered on the upper bridge – outside and above the conning tower: Rear Admiral William Pakenham and his flag lieutenant, joined by Green, who according to one account – but not from a direct eyewitness on the upper bridge – was wearing the piupiu over his uniform and the hei tiki around his neck.[38] Other accounts suggest he was too portly to wear the piupiu comfortably,[39] but touched it during the battle, where it hung in the conning tower; and that the hit the ship received during the battle was considered by some of the sailors to be a consequence of his not wearing it.[40]

Smith climbed to his action station on the foretop, feeling as if events were unreal:

> It was still hard to realise that a battle was actually commencing. I had great difficulty in convincing myself that the Huns were in sight at last, it was so like battle exercise the way in which we and the Germans turned up on to more or less parallel courses and waited for the range to close sufficiently before letting fly at each other … Everyone seemed cool enough … in the control position, all sitting quietly with their instruments waiting for the fight to commence.[41]

Such sentiments: the feeling of being at exercise, of coolly focusing on the equipment and the job at hand to the exclusion of the outside world, were of themselves likely part of a defence mechanism. It was one shared with soldiers on the Western Front, and with combatants across the whole conflict of that era; and it was entirely understandable. Boyle, too now at his action station in X-turret, felt as if it were a 'dummy run'.[42] The moment did not become real until he 'looked through my slit in the armour' and saw the German ships. 'The sort of feeling one gets when one goes to the dentist to have a tooth out comes over you,' he wrote later. 'Nobody can truthfully say they enjoy these things. I know I do not.'[43]

The conning tower was crammed: among others it held the Navigating Officer, Commander Kenelm Everard Lane Creighton;[44] the Torpedo Officer, Lieutenant Commander Archibald Lovett-Cameron; the Assistant Navigating Officer; the Admiral's Secretary; Chief Petty Officer Edward Fitzgerald; the Chief Quartermaster and 'several seaman ratings tending the voice pipes'.[45] Below decks, as always, the stokers and trimmers laboured to keep the furnaces roaring. The gunners and magazine hands were ready, the surgeon prepared, mess tables given over as makeshift sick bays if needed; and aloft the signallers waited by the flag lockers and searchlights.

One of the issues when reconstructing *New Zealand*'s part in the battle is that the times noted by different log keepers within a single ship often varied. This was acknowledged in *New Zealand*'s range log, which was qualified as 'rough GMT'.[46] One analyst has suggested that times in that log are five to six minutes fast.[47] Nearly two weeks after the battle, Green produced a chronology that, he insisted, was 'absolutely reliable, as they come from

3 different sources'; but still repeated some of the figures from the range log.[48] Green's combined log, however, still varied from that of other ships.[49] The problem was true for every ship in the battle – all of which also varied from each other. This became an issue, later, for analysts trying to piece together the combined signal log, which was eventually published in 1920.[50]

Lion opened fire on the leading German ship, *Lutzow*, at about 3.48pm, joined shortly by the other three 13.5in ships. This began what was later dubbed the 'run to the south'. The Germans were on an approximately parallel course to the east, steaming in line ahead: *Lutzow*, *Derfflinger*, *Seydlitz*, *Moltke* and *Von der Tann*. At odds of 6:5, the British line was meant to fire at 'opposite numbers' with a two-ship concentration on the lead German vessel. Once again this was not followed precisely. *New Zealand* did so correctly – indeed, had been 'ranging on 4th ship from right' – *Moltke* – since about 3.45. But she could not engage until 3.57pm by her own log, 3.51 by other accounts,[51] when the indicated range fell to 18,100yd.[52] At that point Smith opened fire with Common Pointed Capped (CPC) shell.[53] From that moment until what, by the range log, was 8.39pm, nearly five hours later,[54] *New Zealand* fired more shells than any other capital ship in the battle, and did so despite a 30ft crack in the right-hand barrel of the Elswick-made 12in gun in Q-turret, serial number 381. That gun still blasted out 54 shots without failing.[55]

Shooting was nonetheless difficult. As Mick Barcroft remarked later, 'their ships had a thick bank of fog behind them so that they hardly showed up at all'.[56] *New Zealand*'s first salvo went far over – the initial range, it seemed, was a radical over-estimate, albeit one shared with other ships in the fleet.[57] Within two minutes Smith had dropped that estimate to just 15,800yd.[58] *Moltke* was also being targeted by *Tiger*, but neither British ship scored hits during these initial minutes. The Germans, however, began taking their toll. A few minutes after 4pm, according to Creighton, there was a commotion in *New Zealand*'s conning tower:

We had only been in action a few minutes, when the Admiral's Secretary came across to where the Torpedo Officer [Lovett-Cameron] was stationed in the conning tower and drew his attention to the *Indefatigable*. He crossed at once to the starboard side and laid his glasses on her. She had been hit aft, apparently by the mainmast, and a good deal of smoke was coming from the superstructure aft, but there were no flames visible. He thought it was only her boom boats burning.[59]

Indefatigable – the next astern – should not have been visible from Creighton's position, but it seemed that 'her steering gear was damaged', because she 'did not follow round in our wake, but held on until she was about 500 yards on our starboard quarter, in full view from the conning tower'.[60] Pakenham, on the upper bridge, thought 'two or three shots' had simultaneously struck around the 'outer edge of upper deck in line with after turret', causing a 'small explosion'. He then watched the battlecruiser fail to follow the turn, 'sinking by the stern'.[61] Down in the aft torpedo control station, Midshipman William Carne – who had turned eighteen just six days earlier[62] – watched the scene unfold and lifted his camera, taking a picture of *Indefatigable* abreast his own ship, apparently submerged by the stern to the second funnel and rolling to starboard.[63]

Indefatigable was clearly sinking, but she did not slip quietly beneath the waves. The description of her final minute has sometimes been attributed to Lovett-Cameron,[64] but is part of Creighton's lengthy account:

> Whilst he [Lovett-Cameron] was still looking at her through his glasses she [*Indefatigable*] was hit by two shells, one on the foc'sle and one on the fore turret. Both shells appeared to explode on impact. Then there was an interval of about 30 seconds, during which there was absolutely no sign of flame or fire or smoke, except the little actually formed by the burst of the two shells … At the end of the interval … the ship completely blew up, commencing apparently from for'ard. The main explosion started with sheets of flame, followed immediately by a dense, dark smoke, which obscured the ship from view. All sorts of stuff was blown high into the air, a 50-foot steam picket boat, for example, being blown up about 200 feet, apparently intact though upside down.[65]

Pakenham, in his official despatch, thought that the ship listed heavily to port *after* this explosion.[66] Such are the ambiguities of memory. Marine archaeo-logical work, later, confirmed that the ship's fore section had been destroyed, giving weight to Creighton's account.[67]

For those aboard *New Zealand* the loss of *Indefatigable* and her crew of 1,119 was a shock. Nobody, just then, knew if any aboard had survived,[68] although Boyle saw 'one raft with two men hanging on to it'.[69] And the obvious question was whether *New Zealand* would be next. Up in the spotting top, Smith was focused on *Moltke* and missed the drama, but he heard the assistant paymaster 'who was keeping a record of the action immediately behind me' say '*Indefatigable* – hit'. Smith later recalled, wryly, that 'he was going to say "sunk", but thought it might rattle the control party'.[70] However, there was no time to mourn. Green ordered a shift of target to the next astern, *Von der Tann*. Later Smith wrote that they straddled *Von der Tann* 'at once', which he thought 'accounts for our own immunity from damage'. He continued:

> [The] Huns [were] firing very rapidly and the pitch of our salvoes was often difficult to see owing to the enemy ship being obscured by our own cordite smoke. I saw a few of our projectiles hit, but am certain that, as a rule, hits cannot be seen and the straddle is the Control Officer's only guide.[71]

In fact, *New Zealand* scored no hits during this time.[72] The incoming German shells, however, were clearly visible from Smith's spotting position:

> We could see the German projectiles in flight, as dots getting larger, till they pitched short or whizzed past us. Their riccos were so easily visible that we could see the colour the shell were painted (yellow with a black tip or band near the nose). The riccos made a quaint booming sound rather like the howitzer shell at the Dardanelles.[73]

Just a few minutes had passed since the ships opened fire, and as Creighton recalled, 'our attention was entirely absorbed in the very fierce battle that was now progressing'. His own focus was 'keeping station on our next ahead' as the ships snaked through the water, altering course to throw off the German shells.[74] For a few minutes *New Zealand*'s battle became a classic ship-to-ship duel: Smith continued to target *Von der Tann*. His opposite number on *Von der Tann*, *Korvettenkapitan* Erich Mahrholz, was targeting *New Zealand*.

Quite suddenly, Smith saw 'splashes other than those due to the fire of *New Zealand*' rising around the German ship.[75] The Fifth Battle Squadron had arrived. Barcroft, later, remarked that they were 'jolly glad to see them' as 'things were getting a bit warm'.[76] Evan-Thomas had managed it by cutting corners and pressing his ships to their best sea speed,[77] helped by the fact that the German ships were down to a little over 20 knots. At about 4.08pm *Barham* opened fire on *Von der Tann* at a range of 19,000yd.[78] Within a few minutes all four super-dreadnoughts were in action, engaging first *Von der Tann* and then *Moltke*, both of which were forced to manoeuvre to avoid the fire. *Von der Tann* nonetheless lost her fore and after turrets; and then one of the two midships turrets jammed, leaving Mahrholz with just two 11in guns in one turret 'which only shot now and then'.[79] Aboard *New Zealand*,

Creighton, still with his focus on the charts and station keeping, got the impression that German fire had become 'quite wild'.[80]

Smith had been firing since about 4pm at indicated ranges from 18,100 down to 10,800yd. Some of the shots, variously at *Moltke* or *Von der Tann*, were over. None had struck home. Smith saw hits on *Von der Tann* around 4.22,[81] implicitly from his ship. In fact none were: German accounts make clear only three hits were scored on *Von der Tann* during the 'run to the south', one from *Barham* at about 4.09 and two from *Tiger*, the first at about 4.20 and the second at 4.23.[82] Given the timing discrepancies, it is likely the hits Smith saw were from *Tiger*. About then, however, Smith lost sight of *Von der Tann* in the mist – possibly a result of the latter's violent manoeuvres – and shifted to *Moltke*.

Von der Tann continued to target *New Zealand*, and four minutes later an 11in shell from one of *Von der Tann*'s two remaining guns slammed into the port side of X-turret barbette 'about 1 foot above the deck', blowing a hole 'about 2 feet in diameter' in the 9in armour and penetrating the tongue of the 'towing slip which was secured around the turret'.[83] This unwelcome gift from Mahrholz – one of 55 shells the German battlecruiser had aimed at *New Zealand*[84] – apparently burst on the deck. The explosion blew a hole in the teak planking and the steel beneath, damaging bag racks on the mess deck below. A splinter shattered a grindstone in the engineers' workshop.[85]

It could have been much worse. As matters stood the blast slammed everybody inside the gun house, particularly those in the spotting hoods:

Damage to HMS New Zealand's X-turret barbette glacis and adjacent deck.
(Torpedo Bay Navy Museum, 2006.743.6.11)

Boyle later told Smith he 'thought he was dead', but 'found he was not' and 'was carrying on'.[86] The blast was felt in the working chamber below. The gun house filled with yellow fumes and the men scrambled for their respirators, but found they could breathe anyway.[87] They continued firing, but according to the ship's records only managed 2 further rounds before the turret would not train.[88] Boyle found 'a thin man' to help inspect the rollers – a necessity to squeeze into the spaces:

> ... after perspiring freely partly from fright and partly from exertion we found a shell had hit the armour that protects the roller path and a large bit had been knocked on the roller. We moved this and some splinter that had got in between the rollers ... Alas she would not move and [we] decided to be brave and proceeded outside the turret and see if there was anything stopping her outside but there was nothing. Another inspection of the rollers was necessary. I ... found bits of shell in the rollers and removed them and to our joy the turret went around.[89]

This process took about twenty-five minutes. Smith was unaware his ship was temporarily down to six guns until Boyle called him during a lull in the battle, a little later, to report that 'his turret had been hit by a very large "brick"'.[90]

The two forces continued to steam south. From the German perspective an isolated part of the British fleet had been found, and now Hipper was leading them to the High Seas Fleet. From Beatty's perspective – where, thanks to Jackson's obstinance, nobody knew the High Seas Fleet was at sea – the battle was a chance to finish Dogger Bank. But then the afternoon – already tragic with the loss of *Indefatigable* – took an even darker turn. Aboard *New Zealand*, Creighton was focused on the navigation, but just six minutes after the hit on X-turret, looked ahead and:

> ... suddenly saw a salvo hit *Queen Mary* on her port side. A small cloud of what looked like coal-dust came out from where she was hit, but nothing more until several moments later, when a terrific yellow flame with a heavy and very dense mass of black smoke showed ahead, and the *Queen Mary* herself was no longer visible. The *Tiger* was steaming at 24 knots only 500 yards astern of *Queen Mary*, and hauled sharply out of the line to port and disappeared in this dense mass of smoke. We hauled out to starboard, and ... passed her about 50 yards on our port beam, by which time the smoke had blown fairly clear, revealing the

stern from the after funnel aft afloat, and the propellers still revolving, but the for'ard part had already gone under. There was no sign of fire or of cordite flame, and men were crawling out of the top of the after turret and up the after hatchway.[91]

Fitzgerald captured the moment in a painting, an image of mind with ships over-large, the stern section of *Queen Mary* spun around and rolling to port, spewing fire from the base of X-turret. Exactly what happened to produce this horrifying tableau has since been subject to discussion.[92] The most likely scenario, based on marine archaeological work and subsequent analysis, is that B-magazine detonated, triggering a slow deflagration in Q-magazine that was visually masked by burning coal and fuel oil, resulting in structural failure and break-up forward.[93] The aft section then slewed as it sank.

The point for our story is the impression that *Queen Mary*'s sudden destruction left aboard *New Zealand*. The loss of *Indefatigable*, twenty minutes or so earlier, had been on the disengaged side and – though horrifying – somehow remote. But *Queen Mary* had blown up in the ship's path. Creighton watched the spectacle from the conning tower:

When we were abreast and only about 150 yards away from her, this after portion rolled over and, as it did so, blew up. The most noticeable thing was the masses and masses of paper which were blown into the air as this after portion exploded. Great masses of iron were thrown into the air, and things were falling into the sea round us. There was still up in the air, and I suppose at least 100 or 200 feet high, a boat which may have been a dinghy or pinnace, still intact but upside down as I could see the thwarts. Before we had quite passed, *Queen Mary* completely disappeared.[94]

Everybody noticed the paper. Smith, in the spotting top, saw:

… the stern of a ship projecting about 70 feet out of the water, with the propellers revolving slowly … clouds of white paper were blowing out of the after hatch, and on her stern I read 'Queen Mary'. She passed us about 100 yards on our port beam, and a moment later there was a blinding flash, a dull heavy roar, which ceased as suddenly as it had begun, followed by a few seconds' silence, and then the patter of falling debris. All that was left of the 'Queen Mary' was a great mushroom-shaped cloud of smoke about 600 to 800 feet high, which temporarily obscured our view of the enemy.[95]

Eames reported the same: 'what a sight what was once our best firing ship is now in pieces, her after deck is floating by, two men are crawling along on their hands and knees. Paper is flying about her after deck turns over and explode. Every soul onboard must be blown to pieces.'[96] Boyle, too, saw the stern coming 'past us sticking right up in the air', and as it passed 'went up with an appalling explosion'.[97] Everybody agreed about that explosion, including survivors from *Queen Mary*, who recalled a 'big smash' as they swam away.[98] Debris rattled down across *New Zealand*, including a ring bolt that was later found on deck.

The scene that unfolded to watchers aboard *New Zealand* has never been fully explained. The paper was thought to be rolls of Dreyer table plotting paper known to be stored near the after hatch,[99] likely propelled by escaping air as the stern filled. However, the reports of a final explosion remain intriguing.[100] Marine archaeological work in 2006 showed that X-magazine had not detonated.[101] Precisely what happened is therefore unclear. Perhaps only isolated charges exploded, but does this explain the small boat descending from '100 or 200' feet? Given that it took *New Zealand* up to ninety seconds to traverse the 1,000-plus yards to the sinking stern,[102] it seems unlikely this was from the earlier detonation. In 2015, marine archaeologists found a propeller from one of *Queen Mary*'s larger boats, not stored aft, near

Ring-bolt from HMS *Queen Mary*, collected from the deck of *New Zealand* where it had fallen, and preserved in the collection of the Torpedo Bay Navy Museum.
(*Torpedo Bay Navy Museum GBI0005*)

the stern section; but that may not have been related to Creighton's observation of a descending boat.[103] Archaeological work was hampered by the fact that the wreck was in poor condition by the turn of the twenty-first century. Time and subsequent damage, including from Second World War depth-charging and encounters with anchors, had taken due toll, and identifying specific 1916-era damage was challenging.[104]

All these unknowns underscore the fact that available information, even when it includes empirical data, cannot answer every question we ask of history. That point is true of warships sunk by violent explosion. However, the human reality – which was what counted in the moment to the horrified watchers aboard *New Zealand* – was that a modern battlecruiser with 1,284 men on board had gone down in just a couple of minutes. Many of those aboard, watchers aboard *New Zealand* knew, were likely still alive inside the wreck, trapped with no way of escape. Nobody, just then, knew who had survived – if any – and the dead likely included friends such as Midshipman T A M Robertson, a New Zealand-born sailor who had been aboard the gift battlecruiser during her 1913 world cruise, before his transfer to *Queen Mary*.[105] Later, Creighton insisted that the 'spirits of our men were splendid' – that despite 'the fact that they had all plainly seen *Queen Mary* blow up, the idea of defeat did not seem to enter their heads'.[106] Not everybody shared his opinion in the moment. Boyle – who had also watched *Indefatigable* sink – 'began to wonder when our turn to go ballooning was coming'.[107] Eames – youthful, excited and frightened – scribbled: 'Only four of use [sic] left, (things are looking shakey [sic]), against the whole Hun Fleet.'[108]

There was still a battle to fight. *New Zealand* returned to the line behind *Tiger* and continued to fire for the next fifteen minutes or so at *Moltke*, at indicated ranges of between 16,400 and 17,350yd, again without scoring any hits.[109]

About the same time that *Queen Mary* blew up, a destroyer battle erupted between the two lines. At 4.15, Beatty had signalled his destroyers to attack Hipper's ships: Hipper responded by sending his own destroyers to counter-attack. This resulted, after about fifteen minutes, in a fierce melee that left two British destroyers crippled and stopped, but not before an attack was prosecuted on Hipper's line and *Seydlitz* torpedoed. *Kapitän* Moritz von Egidy kept her in line, at speed, for the moment. But the ferocity of the destroyer battle told: Beatty recalled his ships at 4.45.[110]

All this time the light cruisers attached to Beatty's force had been pushing south, and had managed to reach a position ahead of the battlecruisers. Visibility was patchy, but around 4.35pm Goodenough, aboard his flagship *Southampton*, saw a line of smoke to the south-east that swiftly resolved into cruisers – and then, beyond, a line of heavy ships. It was Scheer, steaming north to spring the trap on Beatty. At 4.38pm, according to the published signal logs, Goodenough sent an urgent message, simultaneously with an alert by *Champion*.[111] Now the tables were reversed: Beatty's task became leading the High Seas Fleet to Jellicoe.

At 4.40pm Beatty signalled a sixteen-point turn to starboard in succession, by flag,[112] but it took some minutes for the battlecruisers to reverse course. The High Seas Fleet became visible off *New Zealand*'s port bow at 4.44pm by her record, one minute before they executed the turn.[113] They were the last ship in line and by Green's later claim came under fire from Scheer's approaching dreadnoughts, but could not fire back 'owing to being unable to get enough elevation on'. The range was estimated to be around 19,000yd.[114] German accounts suggest *New Zealand* was targeted only by *Moltke* at this time, at long range.[115]

About then the Fifth Battle Squadron flashed past *New Zealand*, still steaming south.[116] It turned out that Beatty's signal – which had been raised only for one minute – had been missed aboard *Barham*, and Beatty did not realise the point until 4.48pm, when *Barham* passed *Lion* in the opposite direction. He made the turn signal again, but Seymour did not lower it until 4.54, and Evan-Thomas was waiting on that instruction to execute. As a result, the four battleships turned within range of the High Seas Fleet. Although one analysis suggests they were only under fire at that moment by Hipper's battlecruisers,[117] they were targeted by Scheer's dreadnoughts as they steamed away.

So ended the 'run to the south', the first phase of the battle and the one in which *New Zealand* and her crew experienced the most dramatic and intense action of the whole encounter. It had lasted a little under an hour, and it had not gone well for the British. Part of the issue was gunnery. Between 3.48pm and 4.54, British heavy guns had scored just seventeen hits on the German battlecruisers, none of them by *New Zealand*.[118] The Germans, however, had scored forty-four hits on the British heavy ships, including fourteen on *Tiger*, and had sunk two.[119] While *Tiger*'s experience again made clear that British ships – like the German – were well-built, the loss of *Indefatigable* and *Queen Mary* was worrisome. Something had clearly gone wrong.

There had also been a command failure. Beatty had rushed headlong into the fight, leaving his most powerful ships behind and making it difficult for Evan-Thomas to assist. To the extent that this helped him get between the Germans and their base it was explicable, but he had then thrown away the range advantage of his 13.5in guns by waiting until his 12in ships were also in range before opening fire. By this time the 13.5in gunned ships had largely been back-fitted with prisms and sighting strips that enabled the guns to be sighted out to the full 20-degree elevation of their mountings.[120] By contrast with Dogger Bank, Beatty could have taken full advantage of what his weapons could do, but he did not. Analyst Nathan Ott has suggested that range over-estimation was not the deciding factor, [121] and the motive was simply to pursue a medium-range battle, in line with British doctrine of the day.[122] That may have been so, but Beatty nonetheless threw away an opportunity.

The second phase of the battle – the 'run to the north' – was less eventful aboard *New Zealand*. Hipper's battlecruisers also turned and continued to engage both Beatty's four surviving ships and the lead ships of the Fifth Battle Squadron, but at significant distance. By 4.42pm, according to *New Zealand*'s range log, the 'enemy were out of range' at an indicated distance of 18,850yd. Around 4.58, according to that log, Creighton thought the range had dropped to 18,000yd, and the ship again opened fire with sights set 'to the longest range at which it would bear'.[123] But a few minutes later it was clear the Germans were out of range, and the guns fell silent.

Although Beatty was fleeing north, not on a course for any British base, Scheer now ordered a chase. His own fleet began to spread out as the faster dreadnoughts surged ahead, notably the four new *König* class of the Third Battle Squadron, under *Konteradmiral* Paul Behncke, each with ten 12in guns. Evan-Thomas had great difficulty opening the range; *Barham*'s maximum sea speed at this point, it seems, was 23.8 knots.[124] The severity of the situation was emphasised by Evan-Thomas's call for 25 knots – unattainable, but indicative of need.[125] Smith watched them from *New Zealand*, thinking the squadron a 'wonderful sight ploughing along in a boil of enemy splashes and firing as evenly and regularly as at practise shoots'.[126]

Hipper shortly slowed, in part to allow Scheer's force to catch up, in part to give respite to his own crews, especially the stokers. This allowed Beatty's force to draw ahead and to the west; the German battlecruisers disappeared into the mists, and for about half an hour or so there was a lull. It was a moment to draw breath: *Lion* with smoke still billowing from a fire aft and the marks of battle along her hull, Q-turret pointing askew; *Princess Royal* battered; *Tiger* battered but still steaming full speed, and *New Zealand* – all guns available, scarcely damaged, her crew readying for the next bout. Despite calls for speed that pushed to her limits, she had kept up, helped by the fact that she had gone to sea without coaling and was running below war displacement, but also a testament to the endurance of her stokers and the over-design of her propulsion plant. All the while, the thunder of the Fifth Battle Squadron's guns – some 8,000yd or so behind *New Zealand* – rolled through the late afternoon air.

What Beatty knew – and which Hipper and Scheer did not – was that Jellicoe was not far away. There was some uncertainty as to precise positions, but one of Beatty's priorities became ensuring that Hipper and his supporting forces, including *Konteradmiral* Friedrich Boedicker's Second Scouting Group of four light cruisers, did not report the approaching Grand Fleet until it was too late for Scheer to escape. After a while Beatty therefore signalled that action would be renewed, turning his four surviving battle-cruisers and their supporting forces north-east, across the expected track of the Grand Fleet. Now the light favoured the British: the westering sun illuminated the Germans as they appeared from the mist, and at the same time dazzled the German gun layers.

By around 5.30pm, Hipper's forces were intermittently visible from *New Zealand*, but otherwise all that Pakenham, Green, Creighton, Smith and the others with a view could see of the enemy was the flash of guns through the haze, as Scheer's leading battleships engaged the Fifth Battle Squadron, itself visible to the south-west. This masked the fact that multiple forces were approaching a relatively small area, mostly invisible to each other in the patchy mists. Hipper was steaming generally north but was to the east of Beatty's force, with Boedicker's Second Scouting Group about 5 miles to the north-east beyond that. Still further to the north-east, unknown to either, was Rear Admiral Horace Hood's Third Battlecruiser Squadron: *Invincible*, *Inflexible* and *Indomitable*, with two escorting cruisers and four destroyers.

Hood had been steaming south in the hope of providing support. Due to positional errors in *Lion*, Hood's squadron was arriving well to the east of Beatty's flagship, but this put them in direct line with Hipper's advanced scouts. Around 5.35pm, HMS *Chester*, one of Hood's two cruisers, spotted Boedicker's four cruisers. *Chester* was badly damaged by a rain of incoming shells. Hood then took his three battlecruisers into the fray, damaging *Pillau* and *Frankfurt* and stopping *Wiesbaden*. Hipper sent his torpedo boats ahead to intervene. A further melee between the supporting forces followed, pitting Hood's one remaining light cruiser and four destroyers against thirty-one of Hipper's torpedo boats.

Beatty's ships, meanwhile, swung eastwards and began engaging Hipper. At 5.42pm, according to *New Zealand*'s official despatch, gun flashes were observed from Hipper's ships. At 5.47 – by the range log – *New Zealand* opened fire on the second ship from the left, all that was visible through the mists, at a range of 17,200yd.[127] The timing on the range log appears to have been a little fast, but in any case shooting was intermittent 'owing to mist and smoke', and *New Zealand* scored no hits. Still, Barcroft for one felt they had 'hotted up the Huns a good bit'.[128] Then, at 5.56pm by Green's chronology, watchers on *New Zealand* saw grey shapes loom into view through the mists to the north-west, 'line after line of great grey hulls', all 'in perfect line and perfect order'.[129] Jellicoe had arrived.

By this time Jellicoe was deeply uneasy; none of his commanders had reported exactly where the Germans were and visibility was poor.[130] He had to deploy the fleet from cruising formation – six columns – into a single line, and wanted to do so in a way that would allow him to 'cross the German T'. This would bring the broadside of his entire battle line to bear on the leading German ships, while the Germans could reply only with their forward guns, and where most of their ships would be masking others. To achieve this Jellicoe had to both know where the enemy was, and get the timing right. Make a mistake and he risked being savaged during deployment, or finding the guns of his own fleet half-masked.[131] At 5.55pm, according to the timing in the published official despatches, Jellicoe signalled *Marlborough*, leading the western column: 'What can you see?' *Marlborough*'s commander, Captain George Ross, reported that *Lion* was in sight.[132] Five minutes later Beatty's flagship and three surviving consorts became visible from the bridge of *Iron Duke*. Because of navigational differences between the flagships, Beatty was 11 miles from his expected position and arrived from an unexpected direction, compounding Jellicoe's problem.[133] Jellicoe promptly signalled Beatty by searchlight: 'Where is the enemy fleet?'[134]

Beatty did not know and could reply only that Hipper was bearing south-west. Curiously, aboard *New Zealand*, Smith could see Scheer's leading dreadnoughts and, at 6.06pm according to his gunnery log – again, apparently a little fast – opened fire on 'the leading battleship' at an estimated 16,000yd, firing three salvoes without observing hits.[135] Meanwhile, Jellicoe repeated the query to Beatty,[136] who did not reply until 6.10 when the leading ships of the High Seas Fleet became visible from *Lion*.[137] His message reached Jellicoe four minutes later. According to Dreyer, Jellicoe pondered the problem for about twenty seconds, then ordered the fleet to deploy on the port wing, south-east by south.[138] This formed a battle line a little further north than otherwise – delaying opening fire by a few minutes – but meant that the entire fleet was crossing the German 'T' and steaming to put itself between Scheer and his base. It also put the super-dreadnoughts of Vice-Admiral Cecil Burney's Second Battle Squadron in the van. With this manoeuvre, Jellicoe gained tactical mastery of the field. Post-war analysis of the alternatives showed he made the right decision,[139] and it is an indication of Jellicoe's ability that he made that choice under pressure, despite being let down by his scouts.

As the fleet deployed, a succession of quick-fire events brought fresh drama and tragedy. Jellicoe's arrival meant that a large number of ships were manoeuvring in a relatively small space. Beatty was pushing across the bows of the Grand Fleet's columns to get to his position at the head. His own ships were still heavily engaged: at 6.19pm, by Smith's range record, *New Zealand* fired on the 'left-hand' battleship at an indicated range of 17,000yd.[140] Shells were falling all around: as he wrote later, 'Lord knows why we weren't hit, the sea seemed to be covered with falling shell.'[141]

There was little room between Beatty's line and Jellicoe's, as it deployed, for the screening cruisers and destroyers; the smaller ships had to manoeuvre, often violently, to avoid collisions in a space later dubbed 'Windy Corner'.[142] Worse, Jellicoe had to reduce speed to 14 knots to give Beatty clearance, causing his ships to bunch up. Some, such as *Marlborough*, could see the Germans and opened fire, but for a few minutes the focus was on assembling the line.

Rear Admiral Robert Arbuthnot's four armoured cruisers, part of Jellicoe's advanced screen, entered this frenzy with dramatic effect when Arbuthnot spotted the crippled *Wiesbaden* to the east. Without hesitation he turned his flagship *Defence* and stormed across the chaotic battlefield to attack this new target. In the confusion of ships dodging ships he was followed only by *Warrior*, and the first outcome was a near-collision with *Lion*. The second was deadly. The two armoured cruisers began engaging *Wiesbaden*, but then came under heavy fire from *Lutzow* and *Seydlitz*, along with the dreadnoughts *König*, *Grosser Kurfürst*, *Markgraf*, *Kronprinz*, *Kaiser* and *Kaiserin*.[143] At 6.20pm *Defence* was hit, rolled to the blow, was struck again forwards and then exploded in sheets of fire along her length.[144] She sank quickly. Eyewitness impressions were confirmed in the early twenty-first century by marine archaeological work, showing that the forward magazines had detonated and the wing-mounted 7.5in guns – mounted in turrets along her sides – had suffered deflagration explosions.[145] By the official record there were no survivors.[146] *Warrior* turned away, badly damaged by a barrage from *Grosser Kurfürst*, *Kronprinz*, *Kaiser* and the secondary battery of *Markgraf*.[147]

Meanwhile, Evan-Thomas's four super-dreadnoughts were approaching Jellicoe's starboard wing from the south. He had steamed a different course from Beatty to join the Grand Fleet at its van. Navigational differences meant he arrived too far west, so he turned to join the rear of the line, manoeuvring to allow space for *Marlborough*'s column. *Warspite*'s helm then jammed and the battleship swung towards the Germans, coming under heavy fire at a range of just 8,000yd. The jam was not cleared by the time she completed the circle, giving Captain Edward Philpotts no option but to keep turning. By this time the crippled *Warrior* was approaching, but by chance *Warspite* steamed around her, drawing the German fire. Many German dreadnoughts joined in, including Scheer's flagship *Frederich der Große*.[148] *Warspite* survived the barrage – underscoring the quality of her design and construction – but her speed was reduced to 16 knots and Evan-Thomas ordered her home.

The High Seas Fleet continued to push north. About 6.20pm, watchers aboard Behncke's flagship *König* saw the Grand Fleet emerge from the mist across the northern horizon, deploying for battle. And then, with what Smith – aboard *New Zealand* – described as a 'roar which seemed to shake the world', Jellicoe's dreadnoughts opened fire.[149] So the first fleet action began. Within five minutes Behncke's squadron was under heavy barrage. *Iron Duke* herself opened fire at about 6.30, loosing nine salvoes at *König* and scoring seven hits.[150] The British were hampered by smoke drifting across the battlefield, much of it from the armoured cruisers and battlecruisers; gun layers often had to fire at targets that came in and out of sight. A number of the British dreadnoughts targeted *Wiesbaden*, which lay motionless between the two fleets.[151]

By this time Hood's three battlecruisers had seen Beatty's ships and were about 4,000yd ahead of them, but at about 6.20pm – just as the drama with *Defence* played out a little to the west – they were spotted by Hipper's battle-cruisers. A sharp engagement followed in which the previous week's gunnery practice paid off for the British: *Invincible* began hitting *Lutzow*. But then, at 6.33 according to *Indomitable*'s commander Francis Kennedy, *Invincible* was straddled with at least one hit aft. One minute later, 'a salvo or one shot appeared to hit her about "Q" turret and she immediately blew up.'[152] *Inflexible* and then *Indomitable* sheered to port; and by the time they swept by, *Invincible* had sunk.[153] But she did not entirely disappear. The explosion had blown her in two, and – because the water at that point was relatively shallow – the fore and aft sections were 'standing upright about 70 feet out of the water'.[154] Marine archaeological work later confirmed that P- and Q-magazines had detonated.[155] There were only five survivors.[156] *New Zealand* steamed past the wreck six minutes later;[157] Smith, in the spotting top, saw a 'solitary figure on a Carley float … poling along to assist someone else in the water'.[158] Beatty shortly ordered Kennedy – now senior officer in the Third Battlecruiser Squadron – to form up astern.[159]

By this time the view from *New Zealand* was partially obscured by mists and smoke. The battlecruisers were a little to the south-east of Jellicoe's developing battle line, with Hipper's ships visible off *New Zealand*'s starboard bow and the High Seas Fleet emerging off the starboard quarter. Green later reported that they fired 'continuously as mist and smoke allowed',[160] engaging *Derfflinger* at between 9,700yd and 10,300yd over a six-minute period,[161] by Smith's reckoning between 6.21½ and 6.27½.[162] Eames, excited, described it in hyperbolic terms: 'We turn our fire on an enemy Battle Ship [sic], she blows up shells are flying.'[163] *Derfflinger* was also being engaged by *Indomitable* at this point. The German ship recorded three hits, none of which seem to have come from *New Zealand*.[164] Just after 6.27pm, according to Smith's range record, fire was checked; there were no targets visible, and although Green's despatch indicates fire was not checked until 6.41,[165] *New Zealand* did not fire again for some time, either way.

Scheer's flagship, *Frederich der Große*, was in the middle of the German line, and it took him some minutes to receive enough information to work out what was happening. His priority became extricating his fleet, but he had planned for such an eventuality: an emergency battle turn, simultaneously reversing track by 180 degrees and reversing the order of steaming. This had to be accomplished by the ships at the head of the line while under heavy fire, but they managed it and by about 6.45pm the High Seas Fleet was steaming away. From the British perspective, they simply disappeared into the mist.

Jellicoe ordered the Grand Fleet to turn south-east and – a little later – due south, securing a position between the Germans and their base. About this time *Marlborough* was hit by a torpedo, possibly fired from *Wiesbaden*, but retained her place in the line. The battlecruisers – now ahead of the Grand Fleet – turned south-east at about 6.30pm, steaming at 26 knots. *New Zealand* had no difficulty keeping up.[166] The fact that she had left Rosyth light on coal likely assisted, but much again was down to the ongoing efforts of her stokers.

Soon afterwards something peculiar happened. At 6.45, according to Green's chronology, they began circling 'gradually to starboard'. They were still circling at 6.59 when *Inflexible* and *Indomitable* arrived astern and joined the line, and according to Green's chronology the course did not stabilise south until 7.10.[167] The cause was not discovered until later: a gyrocompass failure aboard *Lion* caused Beatty to lead the squadron in a circle. Oddly, within a week Beatty insisted it had not happened, first pressing *Lion*'s navigator, Commander Arthur Strutt, over the matter, then getting Lieutenant William Chalmers to edit *Lion*'s records. Strutt later consulted Creighton, who confirmed that *New Zealand* had also made the thirty-two-point turn.[168] It showed up clearly in the navigation tracks, including *New Zealand*'s,[169] and was published as a full circle in a chart of the Second Battlecruiser Squadron's movements, sent to the New Zealand government.[170] However, Beatty had his own public charts changed to an s-turn,[171] and apparently continued to lie about the issue into the early 1920s.[172]

By the time *Lion* was circling, Scheer had ordered a further 180 degree turn, followed by a second advance to the east, led by his damaged battle-cruisers. He never fully explained his motives. In his post-war memoir he suggested it was 'too early for a nocturnal move', and he was reluctant to let Jellicoe 'decide when he would elect to meet us next morning'. A return to battle, he proposed, would 'surprise the enemy', 'upset his plans for the rest of the day', and 'if the blow fell heavily … facilitate … breaking loose at night'.[173] Later he gave other reasons, including supporting the *Wiesbaden*.[174] Scheer did indeed order several destroyers to try and rescue *Wiesbaden*'s crew at 7pm,[175] but the more compelling interpretation of the fleet manoeuvre is that Scheer – who did not know precisely where Jellicoe was – hoped he might be able to get past the rear of the British battle line. That was certainly how it appeared later to Churchill.[176]

The actual result was that Jellicoe's battle line – now fully deployed – crossed Scheer's 'T' for the second time in three-quarters of an hour. The German battlecruisers and leading dreadnoughts were promptly engaged by twenty-five of the British dreadnoughts.[177] Within minutes *König*, *Grosser Kurfurst*, *Markgraf*, *Kaiser*, *Von der Tann*, *Seydlitz*, *Derfflinger* and *Heligoland* were hit by everything from 12 to 15in shells. *Derfflinger* alone was targeted by *King George V*, *Benbow*, *Superb*, *Bellerophon* and *Temeraire*.[178] The British shifted target as German ships appeared and disappeared: *Iron Duke*, for example, first engaged a 'hostile battleship' at 7.15pm, but just five minutes later switched to a 'battle cruiser of the "Lutzow" type'.[179] The German line began to crumple amidst a forest of shell splashes. Scheer ordered another emergency battle turn at 7.12pm, but he needed to relieve the pressure before the head of his line was unable to manoeuvre. So he ordered his battlecruisers to charge the British line and ram it, heedless of the consequences.[180]

The so-called 'death ride' of the German battlecruisers remains one of the most heroic actions that day: a drive towards the Grand Fleet by ships already battered by three and a half hours of intense combat. The order to ram was hyperbolic: the purpose was to draw fire, made clear by the associated wireless order.[181] *Kapitän zur See* Johannes Hartog of *Derfflinger* – temporarily leading the force – obeyed, knowing he was likely leading them to their deaths. It put them, as *Derfflinger*'s gunnery officer, Commander Georg von Hase, remarked later, '*in absoluten wurstkessel*'[182] – a figure of speech whose literal translation, 'absolutely in the sausage boiler', was a fair description of what followed. A storm of shells fell on and around the German battlecruisers as they advanced, smashing equipment, ripping the structure of the ships apart, and killing men. *Derfflinger* took fourteen hits, the battered *Lutzow* another five.[183] But the ploy worked: the dreadnoughts of the High Seas Fleet, once again, turned away and disappeared into the mists. It was not easy. The ships had bunched; some dreadnoughts turned early, stopped, even reversed engines. But they began moving west, and at 7.23pm, Scheer ordered his destroyers to launch torpedo attacks, covering the withdrawal of the battleships and extricating the battlecruisers.[184]

Jellicoe 'held on until the last moment' and then ordered a turn-away in the face of the destroyer attack.[185] This was standard doctrine designed to open the range and reduce the rate at which the torpedoes overtook the ships, all while simultaneously presenting smaller targets.[186] He was later criticised – notably by Churchill – for not turning towards and keeping the Germans in sight,[187] but we have to remember that he stood between the Germans and their base and had every reasonable expectation of remaining so. This meant that action in the last hour of daylight was less critical than maintaining his fleet intact and being in a position to renew action on his own terms next day. This gives context to criticism revolving around the post-fact notion that he had thrown away a 'last chance' to maintain the engagement. The turn-away worked. German torpedoes began pouring into the British line at around 7.30pm – twenty-one in all – forcing the dreadnoughts to manoeuvre sharply. Some passed close: *Hercules*, for instance, came within 40yd of a torpedo, but none of the German weapons found a mark.[188] Later, Reginald Bacon estimated that several ships had been saved by the turn-away.[189] However, it also meant the Grand Fleet lost touch with Scheer. Jellicoe turned south, then began angling west.

New Zealand never fired during the second fleet action; the battlecruisers were about 6 miles south of *Iron Duke* and too far away, and by now the sun was setting. At this latitude and season the night was going to be short, and Jellicoe was in a good position to renew the action when daylight returned. One act, however, remained to be played out before dark, in which *New Zealand* played a key part. Beatty could not see the enemy, but at 7.47pm – by the official signal log – asked Jellicoe to send him Jerram's Second Battle Squadron, with which he intended to cut off the Germans.[190] Jellicoe received the signal at 7.54 and, assuming Beatty was in contact with Scheer, despatched the force.[191] Jerram could not find Beatty in the twilight; but Beatty, meanwhile, sent his scouting cruisers ahead and turned his own force to the south-west. As a result of these manoeuvres, Beatty's ships found Hipper's First Scouting Group to the west a little after 8pm, near Mauve's six pre-dreadnoughts. As it happened, Scheer's dreadnoughts were about 2 miles further west again, but not visible through the dusk and haze. There were just four ships in the German battlecruiser line, which was led by *Derfflinger*:

Lutzow had been detached: Hipper was aboard a destroyer, looking for a new flagship. By this time he had found that only *Moltke* was in any condition to sustain battle, and even she had about 1,000 tons of water aboard.

Beatty's force opened fire just after sunset at around 8.20pm, interrupting Hipper's effort to board *Moltke* and resume command.[192] *New Zealand's* range log, apparently running a little fast, recorded the first salvo at 8.24, against the '3rd ship from right' at an estimated 11,500yd.[193] Green later thought Smith had opened fire at 8.21.[194] The target was *Seydlitz*, down by the bows due to flooding from the torpedo hit hours earlier, and with severe shell damage. It was another moment of drama. Smith recalled that the fourth salvo 'hit with a dull red flare which showed up splendidly in the dusk', so he called for rapid fire 'and the enemy hauled out of line listing heavily and on fire'.[195] Barcroft watched it happen, his excitement lending a certain colour to memory. A fortnight later he wrote to a friend that:

> Light was very bad for both sides now and we fairly shook them. It only lasted about a quarter of an hour, but during this period they never put a hit on any of our squadron while we were simply pelting them. We got about twelve direct hits on our opposite number who caught fire and was a sheet of flame and smoke from end to end, and when it cleared away she had disappeared, sunk we hope, but he may have got away into the fog.[196]

In fact, *New Zealand* engaged at ranges down to 9,100yd and scored three hits on *Seydlitz*. German reports indicate the first hit, at 8.28pm,[197] struck the roof of the after turret and put the shell hoists out of action. The second, two minutes later, hit the 12in armoured belt and burst outside it – but broke the plate, knocking out a chunk of armour. The third hit did much the same at the joint between lower and upper armoured belts. Both hits subsequently resulted in flooding.[198] *Seydlitz* also received two hits from *Princess Royal* that damaged the upperworks forward.

Green reported later that *Seydlitz* was 'in a sinking condition' when she hauled out of line.[199] To some extent this was an effort to extend the results his ship had achieved, but it was also reasonable; the German battlecruiser was down by the head. However, she was not gone. A few more minutes of fire might well have sunk her, but she was saved by the arrival of the German pre-dreadnoughts. Mauve had seen the plight of his colleagues, swung his squadron to cover the retreat of the battlecruisers, and was promptly engaged by *Tiger*, *Princess Royal* and *New Zealand*. Smith first targeted *Schleswig-Holstein*, hitting her within a minute with a 12in shell that disabled one 6.7in gun and ignited exposed cartridges. Three men were killed and nine wounded.[200] Smith then switched to the *Schlesien*,[201] scoring near-misses at ranges estimated to be around 10,700yd. But the light was fading. By 8.38pm – on Smith's timing – it was too dark to see the fall of shot, and he checked fire a minute later.[202] The four hits made during these brief encounters were the only confirmed ones *New Zealand* made during the battle.

At about 8.41pm, three minutes after *New Zealand*'s guns fell silent, the ship shook to a sudden blow. Eames thought it was 'something like a large mine field blowing up'.[203] Green thought they had struck something underwater, but there were no reports of damage. Then lookouts noticed 'what appeared to be a burst of air under water about 50yd on starboard beam'.[204] A similar underwater blow was also felt by the other battlecruisers at about the same time, possibly at precisely the same time given the differences between their logs, though this cannot be empirically determined.

The incident was never explained. The battle had taken the ships in a circle: according to *New Zealand*'s track, they were at most around 6,000yd south-east of the area where *Queen Mary* had gone down four hours earlier.[205] This track was not precise, they may have been closer, and it is possible that buoyant detritus from the wreck, or other debris from the 'run to the south', was floating around. However, that does not explain the fact that each ship in the squadron registered a single significant underwater shock at what could have been the same moment. One possibility is that something on *Queen Mary*'s wreck settled or collapsed; the 'burst of air' seen to starboard of *New Zealand* was what might be expected of an underwater air pocket being released. Perhaps the battlecruisers had reached the wreck site just as a bulkhead collapsed. There was also potential for isolated munitions to explode a little while after sinking.[206] The engagement with the German battlecruisers had just ended, and it is plausible that the concussion of near-miss shells bursting in the water had been sufficient to affect something on the edge of collapse aboard the wreck, a little way off. Ultimately, of course, we can never know.

As the twilight turned into the short northern night, Jellicoe decided not to press the engagement: he knew the Grand Fleet was not geared for night action.[207] However, he had every expectation that battle would be renewed in the morning. The only risk was that Scheer might slip the net, but Jellicoe already blocked his shortest route home, via Horns Reef. That left the other swept passages, a little further west, which Jellicoe judged Scheer would take.[208] At 9.01pm, by the combined signals record, Jellicoe ordered the Grand Fleet back to cruising formation and set course south,[209] intending to be in a position to intercept the High Seas Fleet after dawn on 1 June. He hedged his bets by ordering fifty-one of his destroyers to take position 5 miles behind the Grand Fleet, where they would see and report on any effort by Scheer to reach Horns Reef.[210]

The battlecruisers were well ahead of the main fleet, but nerves remained on edge. Aboard *New Zealand* the risk of destroyer attack made it a difficult night. Boyle was tired, but refused to leave his station and spent a 'deadly night staring into darkness expecting to be attacked any moment by their destroyers'. By 2.30am he felt he could 'not really see anything with fatigue', so he 'routed out Baker my midshipman and lay down on the bare iron deck of the turret and in one moment was fast asleep'.[211]

The German destroyer attacks never came, but few expected what Scheer actually did. His practical options by sunset on 31 May were either to push past the Grand Fleet at night and risk losses, or be annihilated in the morning. And nights were short at that latitude and time of year. At 9.14pm he ordered a course for the swept channel leading to Horns Reef at 16 knots. This put the two fleets again on a converging course, but Jellicoe's forces were moving at 17. As a result, the Grand Fleet drew ahead, and Scheer was able to brush past the rear through the night, skirmishing with Jellicoe's destroyers as he did so. There is some suggestion that Scheer knew where they were as a result of German intelligence decrypts of Jellicoe's signals.[212] The British destroyer commanders and their crews fought back, but nobody reported back to Jellicoe that the High Seas Fleet was barging through.

This failure by Jellicoe's commanders was compounded by Jackson's staff, back in the Admiralty buildings. Room 40 had been deciphering Scheer's signals, and at 9.55pm, by the signals record, the Admiralty informed Jellicoe that three destroyer flotillas had been ordered to attack the Grand Fleet at night.[213] Just over half an hour later they advised that Scheer was returning to base, 'course was SSE ¾ E, speed 16 knots'.[214] This was decrypted aboard *Iron Duke* about five minutes past midnight, and Jellicoe had it about ten minutes later.[215] Why did he not act? It is difficult to say. However, Jellicoe had already been misled by Admiralty intelligence about Scheer's movements, and it had possibly lost credibility for him. He might have had more confidence had he been sent even one of the corroborating messages decoded by Room 40, including the request for airship reconnaissance off Horns Reef – a dead give-away when combined with the course and speed information.[216] However, he was not. This was a failure by the Operations Division, further compounding the failure of Jellicoe's own commanders to report what was happening. When the sound and flash of battle became evident astern of the fleet, Jellicoe supposed these were the expected German torpedo boat attacks, met by his own destroyers.

Mist cloaked the sea around the British forces as light grew around 2.45am. Visibility was down to '3 or 4 miles' – and Jellicoe ordered the fleet into line ahead, ready for battle.[217] But then a message arrived from the Admiralty, giving the German position a little earlier at around 40 miles east of the Grand Fleet.[218] They were too far away to intercept before reaching the swept channel through the minefields. All that remained was mopping up, including searching for *Lutzow*.[219] The British sailed north through a battlefield littered with oil slicks, floating debris, and what Eames, aboard *New Zealand*, called 'hundreds, aye thousands, of dead. Friend and foe alike, some clinging together, others in small boats'. His words betrayed his emotions, otherwise he felt only relief. 'We have come through the Biggest Naval Action [sic] ever known. Thank God.'[220]

The battlecruisers returned to Rosyth mid-morning on 2 June. *New Zealand* dropped anchor at 9.55am to the cheers of people ashore. About fifty minutes later the collier *Fernhill* came alongside and they began taking on coal – a back-breaking 1,178 tons of it. When that was done they began munitioning the ship, another labour-intensive task that brought aboard 480 12in shells and did not finish until 3.30am the following morning.[221] That tally underscored the intensity of the engagement off Jutland. In four and a half hours the battlecruiser had fired 100 shells from A-turret, 129 from P, 105 from Q and 96 from X – this last despite that turret being out of action for the last phase of the 'run to the south'.[222] This total of 430, by the ship's own accounting, differs from figures given elsewhere;[223] but any of the various figures suffices to show that *New Zealand* fired more heavy shells than any other ship during the battle. Damage was minimal: apart from the hit on X-turret barbette the ship had only been struck by splinters from near-misses. The ensign staff was damaged by one splinter, the No. 2 picket boat holed in three places, and the No. 3 cutter damaged in the bows. It was also discovered that a shell had narrowly missed the foremast, passing through the silk jack.[224] The crew were in no doubt as to why. 'Our luck has been the most extraordinary thing that has ever happened,' Barcroft wrote later to a friend, 'and everybody puts it down to the charms etc which we were given by the Maoris [sic].'[225]

Nobody aboard was killed, although the ship suffered vicarious casualties. Other than Robertson, the former crew member lost aboard *Queen Mary*, there was Midshipman A H Barlow, who had been aboard *New Zealand* during her 1913 world tour but by the time of Jutland was serving aboard *Black Prince*.[226] This armoured cruiser was lost in the first minutes of 1 June when – looking for the Grand Fleet in the darkness – she ran into the High Seas Fleet and was raked by battleship fire at short range.[227]

After the battle, the chunk of armour blown off X-turret glacis was retrieved and became something of a trophy. The officer with his hand on the chunk is David Boyle.
(*Torpedo Bay Navy Museum ABT0141*)

Officers and crew of *New Zealand*'s X-turret, after the battle, with the ship's mascot, Pelorus Jack (II).
(*Torpedo Bay Navy Museum 2006.743.6.3.2*)

It did not take long for accolades to arrive from New Zealand. Although the notion that battle was glorious had been blown out of the social mindset by this time, thanks to Gallipoli and the tragedies of the Western Front,[228] the battlecruiser had come through Jutland with minimal human cost – and remained a powerful symbol of patriotic sentiment. Massey telegraphed Green, via Mackenzie, as soon as the news broke:

> The whole Dominion is thrilled with pride at the conspicuous bravery and gallantry displayed by her officers and men. We rejoyce that *New Zealand* was in the battle and played a magnificent part … Convey to all on board our salutations and best wishes.[229]

Green – like Halsey – made clear that he considered the battlecruiser was morally New Zealand's: 'We are all proud to belong to New Zealand's ship, and to have had the opportunity of upholding the honour of the Dominion.'[230] These words were widely reported.[231] Other telegrams arrived from communities and groups across New Zealand, such as the Canterbury Branch of the Navy League. Green, again, presented his command as morally New Zealand's. 'We are proud to belong to your ship.'[232] Green later had the damaged piece of the ensign staff cut out and sent to the New Zealand government as a memento. It was initially displayed in London, then sent to New Zealand, where it arrived at the end of November. The Minister of Defence, Frederick Jones, decided to have it exhibited around the country.[233] A week later the New Zealand War Contingent Association in London decided to strike a medal 'as a Christmas present to the officers and men of *New Zealand* in commemoration of the Jutland battle'.[234] Mackenzie arranged for around £125 worth of gifts, including tobacco, to be sent to the battlecruiser as a Christmas present from the government of New Zealand.[235]

Debate over the battle quickly erupted in Britain,[236] a discussion that has continued among historians since.[237] Most of it runs outside the scope of this book, but it is worth noting that much of the argument of the day pivoted on events judged against the expectation that Jellicoe was meant to deliver a 'second Trafalgar'. The point that his command was a risk-management exercise relative to maintaining sea superiority was seldom raised in a debate that became polarised around polemic elevation of either Beatty or Jellicoe as the hero.[238] Either way, the popular historical trope by which Jutland was 'tactically' won by Germany and 'strategically' by Britain is given place by the fact that, while Beatty erred during the 'run to the south', Jellicoe generally made the right decisions. He deployed his fleet to gain control of the field, then maintained it. Much of the criticism levelled at Jellicoe over his conduct during the two brief fleet encounters missed the point that he had that control and reasonably anticipated maintaining it into the next morning – let down in that matter, as we have seen, by his own commanders and by his own cynicism towards Room 40. As matters stood he forced the Germans from the field of battle, twice, and British naval superiority was untouched – reasonably rendering Jutland a British victory by both tactical and strategic measure.

For some aboard *New Zealand* the aftermath fell rather flat. 'We have had a job of work at last which was rather a change for us,' Barcroft wrote afterwards, 'but now everything seems to have quietened up again and I don't suppose the Huns will pop out again for some time yet.'[239] Smith was more upbeat. 'I expect we shall have another scrap directly the fleets are repaired. The Huns are getting desperate and must do something to impress the neutrals and try and raise the blockade.'[240]

As it happened, Smith was right. Scheer had been driven from the field, but he had lost none of his pugnacity, and although some ships were still under repair, sortied on 18 August, again trying to trap part of the British fleet while ambushing the rest with U-boats. *New Zealand*, with five other battlecruisers, put to sea in response. Beatty was once again aboard *Lion*, temporarily reduced to a 6-gun vessel, as Q-turret was still under repair at Armstrong Whitworth's Elswick works. Thanks in part to reconnaissance failure by both sides on the 19th, there was no encounter. Amidst the possible dangers of U-boats and mines the Admiralty wondered about keeping the Grand Fleet out of the southern North Sea. However, this third major sortie by the High Seas Fleet that year was also its last. In early October, after debate at naval and government level, the Germans decided to renew unrestricted submarine warfare. For the British fleets it did not reduce the endless pattern of fruitless sweeps punctuated by time at anchor – the price, in effect, of being the dominant power in the North Sea.

The Battle of Jutland brought other consequences for *New Zealand*. The battle had again highlighted the atrocious shooting of the battlecruisers. They had blown off an enormous quantity of ammunition for little result: *New Zealand*'s confirmed hit rate was less than 1 per cent. Secondary sources often state that she fired 420 shells, but her own tally was 430. Of these, only four were confirmed hits.[241] Part of the reason was that she had been engaging, at times, close to maximum range; and with the guns on or near their elevation stops their ability to correct for the roll of the ship was hampered. But not all fighting had been at long range, and the other battlecruisers had fared little better. Historically, the shooting of the entire battlecruiser fleet at Jutland was so bad that a 2004 analysis of heavy gun performance intentionally omitted their results from the data set as statistical outliers.[242]

Many issues with equipment and procedures had been revealed by the battle, and Jellicoe set up committees within the fleet to consider them.[243] However, for the Royal Navy the crucial question was why three battlecruisers and an armoured cruiser had blown up after only a few hits. Was there, as Beatty wondered during the battle, indeed 'something wrong with our bloody ships',[244] or had something else been to blame? There were lessons to learn, and this had a direct outcome for *New Zealand*.

Initial thinking reflected earlier criticism of battlecruiser armour, which had been an issue before the war and remained a hot topic into early 1916.[245] In his initial despatch on the battle, written in the first weeks of June, Jellicoe put the losses down to the 'indifferent armour protection of our battlecruisers, particularly as regards turret armour and deck plating'.[246] However, the Director of Naval Construction, Eustace Tennyson d'Eyncourt, sent two constructors – Stanley Goodall and Stephen Payne – to examine the damaged battlecruisers. They concluded that the problem was the relaxation of munitions handling protocols, creating a path for flash to pass from turret to magazine.[247] This pointed the finger at officers who had variously endorsed or turned a blind eye to the practice, and Beatty soon began insisting that the problem had been plunging fire penetrating the decks and reaching the magazines.[248] It was impossible to prove him wrong empirically, because the lost ships could not be examined. The fact that the surviving vessels showed few signs of deck hits undermined the argument but could not wholly dislodge it.[249] After all, the surviving ships might have been preserved for the very reason that they had *not* suffered such hits. Nobody could absolutely prove otherwise.

The main problem was that Beatty's reaction muddied the waters, reducing the argument to *either* armour failure, *or* munitions procedures. In fact, the issue was more complex than that. As Jellicoe later pointed out, the problem with flash still required the armour to fail somewhere, in order for a shell to burst where the resulting flash could ignite the cordite.[250] The fact that warships were complex systems likely to fail in complex ways – requiring, in turn, complex explanations for outcomes – was made clear when Beatty sent a memorandum to the Admiralty requesting that a committee look into everything from the position of magazines, their protection, turret armour, flash doors, charge igniters, protecting charges by metal cases, and a raft of other matters.[251] He also wanted the safety of nose fuses in high-explosive shells investigated. There was good evidence that shells did not sympathetically detonate even in a magazine explosion, but Beatty was worried that a fire – with a rise in temperature – might ignite the bursters in the high-explosive lyddite rounds.[252] This had been identified as a potential cause of *Bulwark*'s loss nearly two years earlier.[253]

In the context of the cordite handling debate, Beatty's request looked like a disingenuous 'bait and switch' ploy, but the points were reasonable, and as a senior seagoing officer he could not be ignored. The debate went on between Jellicoe, Beatty and senior Admiralty officials – including the Third Sea Lord and Controller, Rear Admiral Sir Frederick Tudor Tudor –[254] for much of the rest of 1916. Some of it survives today as correspondence that, by nature, can capture only a shadow of the issue – missing, for instance, the committee work within the fleet and any personal discussions that went on between officials at each end of the chain.[255]

What was clear was that something had to be done about munitions handling protocols, and this became the first of Jellicoe's five post-battle priorities.[256] It required more than a simple return to pre-war systems, a point discovered when *Lion* was examined after the battle. Her magazine doors had been closed half an hour before the cartridges in the gun house ignited, and the magazine was flooded. However – despite freely venting through the broken roof of the turret – back pressure in the ammunition trunk had still buckled the magazine doors. This led investigators to conclude that the magazines would have exploded had they not been flooded. That issue had to be addressed; and one of the outcomes was a series of physical improvements across the fleet. Reinforced magazine doors, fireproof 'fearnaught' screens and enhanced flash protection in the munitions trunks were developed and eventually added. It was, however, well into 1917 before the systems had been developed and tested.[257]

It was also clear that armour had potential to fail without being penetrated directly, as the damage to the 9in plate on *New Zealand*'s X-turret glacis showed. Elsewhere, armour had failed at joints between the plates. These issues had already become evident after Dogger Bank, where the Director of Naval Ordnance concluded that belt armour needed better supporting structures and keyed joints.[258] Jutland drove the lesson home.

Irrespective of all these matters was the long-standing concern that armour that was effective against 11 or 12in weapons was not going to be adequate against the 15in guns the Germans were thought to be introducing. At Jutland, even 11in shells had penetrated 6in armour.[259] The risk for older-design capital ships such as *New Zealand*, however, was more due to the design of their protective systems, particularly at longer ranges. The issue was given emphasis by the fact that British armour-piercing shells had been found inadequate, prompting design changes that dramatically improved their performance.

The debate that followed was shaped by argument over whether a plunging hit risked penetrating deck armour and sending red-hot splinters ripping through bulkheads into the magazines. This had not happened to surviving ships at Jutland, other than *Barham*, where a 12in shell splinter had penetrated the crown of a 6in magazine.[260] D'Eyncourt was reluctant to further up-armour new ships because it would bump up displacement and cost without enhancing the offensive capacity, although he did concede that battlecruiser turret protection should match that of the battleships.[261] This was, in effect, accepting Jellicoe's point that the flash problem still required armour to fail somewhere along the way.[262]

However, d'Eyncourt felt the risk of deck penetration in the existing fleet could be alleviated by adding thin internal armour to protect the magazine crowns from splinters. This was possible without major reconstruction, or overloading ships that – typically – were already leaning against displacement and stability limits thanks to wartime additions. All capital ships, not just the battlecruisers, were subsequently examined and modified as needed,[263] making clear that for the Admiralty – as usual in such matters – risk assessment was not based on arbitrary ship classification, but on the engineering particulars of any given vessel.[264] One of the outcomes for *New Zealand* was that, in November 1916, she was taken into dockyard hands to have 1in armour plate added to areas of the main deck: enough forwards to cover A-magazine and the 4in magazine; amidships covering Q and P magazine; and aft, around X-magazine. It was extended vertically by 3ft 6in around the magazine trunks and escape shafts. Then in June 1917 – during another refit – 1in plate was added over the boiler rooms, on the lower deck 'at the bottom of Inner and Outer Upper Coal bunkers'.[265]

The ship also received the benefit of the fire-control enhancements that came out of another of Jellicoe's post-battle committees.[266] Together, the post-Jutland modifications significantly improved *New Zealand*'s fighting power. However, it was never put to the test: after the change of policy in late 1916 the High Seas Fleet did not again venture forth. In November 1917, *New Zealand* was part of a covering force during the Second Battle of Heligoland Bight, but not called to action. The shots that Smith aimed at *Schlesien* during that long twilight of 31 May 1916 were, as events panned out, the last that *New Zealand* ever fired at an enemy.

CHAPTER 7

THE LAST VOYAGE

After Jutland, *New Zealand*'s First World War returned to drudgery. Crew came and went, as did officers. Green left in October 1917, temporarily replaced as captain by Edward Kennedy before a new captain, Richard Webb, came aboard. The battlecruiser covered mine-laying operations during 1918, sailed with her consorts to patrol the North Sea, and lay idle in harbour. Occasionally New Zealand soldiers, on leave from the Western Front, arrived to visit.[1] By the time the war ended the ship's commander was Leonard Donaldson. Amidst this relentless routine, only two of the crew saw any serious action: Able Seamen William Lodswick and Harold Eves, who joined the daring raid on Zeebrugge in April 1918.[2]

The armistice of 11 November 1918 came relatively quickly, on the back of a Communist uprising in the High Seas Fleet and the effective collapse of the German government. It was not a peace treaty – fighting could renew if Germany failed to meet the terms – but by any practical measure the war was over. *New Zealand* had steamed 84,458 miles since August 1914 and had burned 97,034 tons of coal.[3]

The armistice included terms that required Germany to surrender its submarines and best warships, which would be interned in British waters. The list included six battlecruisers, nine dreadnoughts, seven light cruisers and forty-nine torpedo boats. In the end only five battlecruisers sailed: the sixth, *Mackensen*, was on the list but – it turned out – had never been completed. Arrangements took some days to finalise, given spice by the possibility that the mutinous crews might not obey an order to sail. However, they did; and on the misty morning of 21 November the entire Grand Fleet assembled in two columns off Rosyth, the left hand led by the Second Battlecruiser Squadron and *Australia*. *New Zealand* followed directly behind.

The Grand Fleet of late 1918 was a massively more effective and powerful force than Jellicoe had led at Jutland, and not just because it now included a US Navy squadron. Many post-Jutland improvements had been implemented. Another of Jellicoe's committees, led by Dreyer, had produced new-style armour-piercing shells, vastly more effective than prior designs.[4] The ships were at action stations and shells ready in the cages, but the guns were not loaded. So the crews waited for the Germans. Then through the mists loomed the brand new light cruiser *Cardiff*, towing a kite balloon and piloting the German column, which was led by their battlecruisers: *Seydlitz*, *Moltke*, *Hindenberg*, *Derfflinger* and *Von der Tann*. It was the first time anybody aboard *New Zealand* had seen them since Jutland. By about 1pm the German force was anchored in the Firth of Forth, surrounded by guard ships that included the Second Battlecruiser Squadron. Men went aboard the German vessels to inspect them for compliance with the surrender conditions: *New Zealand*'s ship was the 'Iron Dog', *Derfflinger*.[5] They found the crew sullen and mutinous, the ship dirty.[6]

Where next was clear for much of the immense naval force with which Britain ended the First World War. The so-called 'Great War' had cost Britain more than £3.25 billion – an astronomical sum for the period, raised by loans and the decision to step back from the 'gold standard'. The 12in-gunned dreadnoughts and battlecruisers were obsolete and not needed in a world where Germany had ceased to be a significant naval power. Some, such as *Bellerophon*, were reduced by early 1919 to training roles. The majority were simply decommissioned and put into reserve – a status where their most probable future, with luck, was occasional employment as tenders or in support duties, eventually followed by scrapping.

New Zealand had a more active role. In December she sailed for Norway to pick up Queen Maud and Prince Olav.[7] Afterwards she was taken into dockyard hands for modifications to fit her out for special duties: a second globe-spanning voyage, in part to make a thank you visit to New Zealand, but more particularly as Admiral Sir John Jellicoe's personal transport, taking him on a significant tour of four major dominions to provide advice on future naval policy. This issue had been bubbling away since the Imperial War Conference of early 1917, when a resolution had been passed asking the Admiralty to look into post-war naval arrangements. This did not have great priority; but in May 1918 the Admiralty produced a memorandum essentially calling for a single, centrally controlled navy. That did not go down well with the dominions. It was the old pre-war issue once again, and the outcome was an arrangement by which a representative would tour the dominions once the war ended and advise accordingly.

Jellicoe was tapped for the job in November 1918. The politics were overt: he had been made First Sea Lord in November 1916 but was dismissed in December 1917, essentially after falling out with the government over the issues caused by the renewal of unrestricted U-boat warfare.[8] Now, with war's end, he was in effect being bundled out of sight, sorting out the naval needs of India, Australia, New Zealand and Canada in the new world order. It got Jellicoe out of England and away from Whitehall and the Admiralty at a time when the navy was still coming to grips with the realities of post-war funding. It also took him away from the controversies brewing over his wartime performance, including Jutland. What the voyage did *not* do was transport him to New Zealand to take up the post of Governor-General: that, as we will see, came a little later.

It took some weeks to prepare *New Zealand* for the voyage. Some of her 4in guns were unshipped, and cabins built adjacent to her forward super-structure to house Jellicoe and provide working space for his staff of eight, which included Dreyer. The ship was refitted with peacetime trim for the first time since 1914, when most of it had been thrown overboard into Scapa Flow. She was commissioned on 11 February 1919 with a virtually new crew and commander, Captain Oliver Leggett. The crew came primarily from the naval barracks at Devonport and included a young Irishman, Frederick Kelso, twenty-four years of age and a leading signalman.[9] Four New Zealanders were aboard, including Boyle – now a lieutenant commander; Surgeon Lieutenant George Macintosh; Sub-Lieutenant M S Thomas; and a midshipman, eighteen-year-old Derek Perry.[10] Perry hailed from Hawke's Bay and was grandson of the prominent colonial-age pastoralist G P Donnelly.[11]

New Zealand's second world-spanning voyage began when she left Portsmouth in foul weather on 21 February, which only got worse as they entered the Bay of Biscay. Around 1.30am the following day Jellicoe turned up on the bridge as the ship plunged through heavy seas. It turned out he had been washed out of his cabin by water pouring through holes left by the dockyard and never filled.[12] Three days later they reached Gibraltar, where Jellicoe made the first of his official visits. This underscored the fact that, by contrast with *New Zealand*'s first cir-cumnavigation of the globe, this journey was not wholly about public relations: the ship was also transport, office and

Admiral of the Fleet Sir John Jellicoe aboard *New Zealand* in 1919.
(*Torpedo Bay Navy Museum APC0069*)

home to enable Jellicoe to complete his mission. Public relations events and official engagements – often featuring Jellicoe as the hero of Jutland and a senior representative of the Royal Navy – were on the agenda, but promotion of ship and Empire was relatively muted by comparison with the triumphant displays of seven years earlier. By 1919 the soldiers were coming home – often broken and maimed. Europe was weary of war, and an influenza pandemic had torn around the globe, killing as it went. It was still raging in 1919, prompting many social events on *New Zealand*'s itinerary to be cancelled.[13]

The ship now had its Suez Canal certificate,[14] and from Gibraltar steamed through the Mediterranean to Port Said. Here the battlecruiser took aboard nearly 2,000 tons of coal with local help. Kelso watched local labourers, male and female alike, carrying anything up to 60lb of coal each, on their heads, in baskets, before dumping it down the chutes.[15] Next day the battlecruiser left for the canal, finding it still fortified, with military camps and 'large quantities of war material' clearly visible.[16] After a brief stop at Suez, they entered the Red Sea, steaming south under canvas awnings to 'ward off the sun'. A canvas pool was rigged on the upper deck – used by Jellicoe as well as the crew.[17] The heat did not prevent the usual Sunday Division – an inspection – requiring the crew to wear their blue serge jumpers.

By 14 March they were off Bombay, where Jellicoe began his official

Coaling lighters alongside *New Zealand* at Port Said.
(*Torpedo Bay Navy Museum 2006.186.239.p4.1*)

New Zealand passing through the Suez Canal.
(*Torpedo Bay Navy Museum 2006.186.239.p4.2*)

work. The ship was opened to visitors on the 16th, a Sunday: Kelso watched several 'English girls' arrive in a small boat and sing 'many popular songs'.[18] The city was a panoply of colour, smell and activity – and a political hotbed. War emergency regulations had been extended, provoking strikes and – then – Mahatma Gandhi's non-co-operation effort. *New Zealand*, meanwhile, took on 1,740 tons of coal, and around 300 local labourers were hired to repaint her. She emerged on 22 March with a new light grey paint scheme. The ship hosted a dance on the 25th and four days later the ship sailed for Karachi, an impromptu visit organised during their stay at Mumbai. This was tinged with tragedy: one of the sailors, twenty-four-year-old A B Rennie, fell off a balcony ashore and was killed.

Before they returned to Bombay, a cypher message arrived advising that Jellicoe was promoted Admiral of the Fleet. There was a scurry to lower his admiral's flag and raise the Union Jack to the masthead – the official flag of that rank. Jellicoe continued his work with Indian authorities while the crew of New Zealand went sightseeing and attended entertainments arranged by the YMCA, but that was cancelled on 11 April after what Kelso called 'some trouble on shore'.[19] Landing parties were organised and the ship's boats readied to take them ashore, but they were not required.

The ship left for Colombo on 1 May, arriving two days later and taking

Boxing match aboard *New Zealand* while in Indian waters.
(*Torpedo Bay Navy Museum 2006.186.239.p11.2*)

on 1,800 tons of coal and 700 tons of oil.[20] They crossed the equator at midnight on 7 May – with the required visit, next day, from 'King Neptune' and his 'Queen' who, it turned out, wanted to honour Jellicoe as commander of the victorious fleet, and the ship for her part in the war. The day underscored the way the ship had become Jellicoe's home, and the immense personal respect held for him among officers and crew.

By 9 May the battlecruiser was approaching Keeling Island in heavy swells. This had been the site of a classic ship-to-ship battle in 1914, when HMAS *Sydney* – one of the escorts of the first Australia–New Zealand troop convoy of the war – had defeated SMS *Emden*. The wreck of the *Emden* was still ashore on the island, and Leggett diverted the ship so everybody could have a good look. They reached Albany on the 15th, beginning an Australian tour that took in Perth, Adelaide, Melbourne, Hobart and Sydney. The pandemic cast a shadow over events, curtailing a number of social activities, but the mood was relieved on 19 July when peace was finally reached with Germany, after lengthy negotiations in Versailles. While Jellicoe went about the task of reporting on Australia's future naval needs, *New Zealand* exercised with elements of the RAN, including *Australia*. As the visit came to a close on 6 August the ship was docked in the Cockatoo Island facility at Sydney – filling it, as Kelso noted, to capacity.[21] Her bottom was scraped and painted. She was refloated two days later, coaled, and spent a final week in Sydney before sailing for New Zealand.

'King Neptune' and his 'Queen' meet Admiral of the Fleet Sir John Jellicoe, 8 May 1919.
(*Torpedo Bay Navy Museum 2006.186.239.p12.3*)

The 1919 visit to New Zealand produced another rush of postcards such as this.
(*Lemuel Lyes Collection*)

New Zealand reached Wellington early on 20 August. She was welcomed by boys from Scots College, standing by a bonfire making semaphore signals: 'Hurrah for Jellicoe, welcome to New Zealand from Boys of Scots College, Wellington.'[22] The battlecruiser could not berth immediately; the pandemic raged in New Zealand, too, and authorities had to complete a medical inspection.[23] In other ways what followed was a repeat of 1913: Jellicoe went ashore at 10.10am, followed over an hour later by men from the ship who marched through Wellington streets to the cheers of assembled crowds. As in 1913, New Zealanders also flocked to board her. The ship was opened to visitors that afternoon, receiving 9,870 in a few hours – a visit marred only when two boys lost fingers when a 4in gun breech snapped shut after they had managed to prise it open. More New Zealanders flocked aboard over the next few days – by 24 August around 50,000 all told.[24] It was, in many respects, a repeat of 1913. Jellicoe was a particular focus of attention and had a visitors' book opened for any who came to see him personally.[25] His guests in Wellington included J B Harcourt, local chairman of the Navy League.

The ship went on to Lyttelton, arriving early on 1 September to threatening weather that turned to 'wind and snow'.[26] Winter, it seemed, had yet to recede. Next morning dawned clear and fine, the hills capped with

New Zealand arriving at Lyttelton, 1 September 1919.
(*Torpedo Bay Navy Museum 2006.186.239.p26.2*)

New Zealand at Lyttelton, 2 September 1919 after an unusual snowfall that left the decks icy. The lighter-grey paintwork applied in India is clearly evident, and the cabin built as an office for Jellicoe is clearly visible adjacent to the starboard superstructure. (*Photographer unknown, 1/2-072638-G. Alexander Turnbull Library*)

snow, and it was then that a local photographer snapped what has become one of the enduring and classic images of the battlecruiser, moored to the wharf at Lyttelton with snow-capped hills behind. Kelso found the ship dangerous to walk on – the upper deck was 'sheathed with ice', and crew got to work chipping it off. Later the men went on leave into Christchurch and amused themselves 'snowballing in Cathedral square'.[27]

The ship arrived at Picton on 13 September, spending time in Queen Charlotte Sound before returning to Wellington two days later. Then the battlecruiser sailed north, skirting past Napier without stopping and reaching Auckland on 22 September. Local authorities again feted the crew and sports clubs hosted matches. There were more gifts, and many telegrams of congratulations sent to the ship, her commander and crew. Pre-war fantasies of glory may well have been blown out of New Zealanders, but the ship remained a symbol of the dominion's part in the war, a tangible expression of its contribution, and a symbol of victory. Morally, as Jellicoe recognised in many of the forty-odd receptions he attended during the six-week visit, the ship was New Zealand's. Still, the public joy at her presence was not quite that of 1913. The mood had changed. By mid-1919 the country was filling with returning soldiers, many of them maimed or suffering the effects of their wounds. The global influenza pandemic had then swept the country – two lethal waves of it since mid-1918 – and the excitement and symbolism of seeing the ship was set against the slightly flat sense of victory achieved only at tragic cost.[28]

Jellicoe worked diligently throughout the visit.[29] He borrowed papers from the Minister of Defence, Naval Adviser and other officials, and he consulted Massey, Ward and Allen.[30] However, he was hampered by being out of London: debate was ongoing in Whitehall and Admiralty over the future fleet, to which he was not privy, but which was obviously going to affect his proposals. When he asked for details of upcoming building programmes in June 1919 he was told that they relied on 'negotiations for limitations of armaments', and that current construction was 'confined … to completion of ships in an advanced stage'.[31] Nobody in the Admiralty seemed very interested in his work – underscoring the point that dominion issues were a low priority for an Admiralty struggling to organise the post-war navy in an environment of rapid cost-cutting. It also reinforced the implication that Jellicoe had been sent on the mission largely to get him out of the way. 'Lord Jellicoe's report is very comprehensive,' one official minuted, 'and as far as D.O.D.(f) is concerned it is difficult to see how time is to be found to study it.'[32] The detail and outcomes of Jellicoe's mission fall outside the scope of this book, other than a proposal to repay the cost of *New Zealand*;[33] but many of his recommendations – certainly as far as New Zealand was concerned – were eventually adopted, in essence if not in detail.[34]

New Zealand left the dominion that had brought her into being for the last time on 3 October. Heavy rain threw a damper over the farewell ceremonies, but did not reduce the scale of the crowds who turned up at the quayside. Nor did the wet deter many of the crew, who went ashore to see the festivities. There were poi dances, a haka, and a responding haka by the ship's own party. A 'man standing in a cart' called for three cheers for the ship; the ship's company cheered back. And then a bugle sounded, recalling the men. With – as Kelso put it – the 'rain falling merrily, with a sea of umbrellas all round',[35] the ship moved away from the wharf stern-first, turned, and began steaming across the Waitemata. One Royal Marine missed the sailing, caught a motorboat and was brought aboard before the ship left harbour.

So *New Zealand* left the country whose people considered her their own, passing quickly out of sight into the grey mists.

The ship sailed initially for Suva, but the next main destination was Canada, final focus of Jellicoe's four-dominion mission. Afterwards the ship passed through the Panama Canal, spent time in Jamaica – and engaged in a full-calibre main battery practice – before visiting Cuba and Trinidad in January 1920. Here there was a further tragedy: Regulating Petty Officer Thorn fell off a wharf and drowned. A planned visit to Tristan da Cunha was cancelled, and the battlecruiser made course for England. *New Zealand* returned to Portsmouth early on 3 February, where HMS *Victory* fired the

HMS *New Zealand* in 1919, the cabin built to accommodate Jellicoe and his staff clearly visible adjacent to the forward superstructure. [Credit details to be added]

19-gun salute due an arriving Admiral of the Fleet. After almost a year away, Jellicoe had come home. Lady Jellicoe and their children came aboard *New Zealand* by boat, and by 10.30am the ship was moored to the same wharf that they had left close on a year earlier. *New Zealand*'s last voyage was over.

Next morning Jellicoe, 'visibly affected as he spoke', addressed the officers and crew, giving 'praise and advice'. Kelso saw that 'Lady Jellicoe too was on the verge of tears', and the Jellicoes were not alone: 'many others' were 'obviously emotionally affected and sad'.[36] It was a poignant moment. Jellicoe – the popular, kind, sharply intelligent and always thoughtful officer who had become Admiral of the Fleet – had been aboard virtually a year, and the battlecruiser had been his home. His career had been entwined with this ship since her conception – since the time when, as Controller, he had organised her construction. And this voyage marked the end of his naval career. He had already accepted the post of Governor-General of New Zealand, sailing there later in 1920 aboard the *Corinthic*.[37] But that was another life, yet to play out. So he spoke, poignantly and emotionally, to the men of the battlecruiser. At sunset, his flag was hoisted down for the last time.[38]

Next day *New Zealand* sailed for Devonport, anchoring around 10.15pm in Plymouth Sound. Early on 6 February, with help from a tug, she entered harbour and was secured to the No. 6 Buoy in the Hamoaze. She did not pay off immediately: arrangements had been made to send most of the crew on six weeks' leave. The ship, meanwhile, remained under the charge of Boyle, with a skeleton crew of 250.[39] It was, in many respects, the direct reverse of the way the battlecruiser had entered service less than a decade earlier.

New Zealand was decommissioned on 15 March 1920. It was a solemn moment and, the departing officers and crew knew, likely the end of her seagoing career. The 12in-gunned capital ships were obsolete and among the first to be demobilised into reserve. *New Zealand* escaped for a time purely because she was selected for special duties. The fate of these ships was, however, clear. While reserve status was not a swift path to the scrapyard, the post-war environment was new. By early 1919 the Treasury – which held the government's purse strings and was responsible for providing Cabinet with advice on fiscal policy – wanted significant military cuts, and in July the Chancellor of the Exchequer, Austin Chamberlain, urged Cabinet to slash the Royal Navy to fifteen commissioned capital ships, with more cuts to follow in 1920. This helped frame a mood of constraint, given teeth by the Committee on National Expenditure under Sir Auckland Geddes, which recommended a 'Ten Year Rule' that required the military to plan on not having to fight a major war for another decade. Lloyd George ordered a halt to new capital ship construction, and the naval estimates for 1920 were cut from £170 million to £60 million.

By the time *New Zealand* followed the other 12in ships into the reserves in early 1920, this environment had given shape to their likely fate. They were obsolete. Under the 'ten year' rule there was little practical chance of their serving again, and their path to the disposal list seemed clear. The only question was timing. On 8 June, *New Zealand* was recommissioned with a reserve crew as tender to HMS *Hercules*,[40] but that did not alter her status. Winston Churchill said as much in February 1921 when – as Secretary of State for the Colonies – he approached the New Zealand government over disposal of gunnery prize funds donated to the ship by the people of Timaru and Christchurch, on the basis that the battlecruiser 'most probably will not again be permanently in commission'.[41] This practical reality, months before disarmament negotiations in Washington were even proposed, gives context to the fact that *New Zealand* was scrapped in accord with the Five Power Treaty – informally known by the metonym 'Washington Treaty' – of 1922.[42]

The Five Power Treaty provided the international framework for post-war naval power balances, halting a new naval arms race between the United States, Japan and Britain and instead defining fixed strength ratios between the major powers. Technically, that treaty was indeed *New Zealand*'s death warrant: she was on a list of agreed disposals, reducing the Royal Navy to parity with the United States Navy. However, by any practical measure the treaty simply gave specific timing to the fate already awaiting Britain's 12in-gunned capital ships. Some, indeed, had gone before the treaty was signed – *Hercules*, *Bellerophon*, *St Vincent* and *Temeraire*, for example, were put on the disposal list in 1921 and negotiations begun with scrappers, ahead of any agreement to meet in Washington.[43] The only major exception was that *Australia*, which had returned to the Royal Australian Navy, remained in full commission for a while. But in late 1920 she was partially demanned, no longer seen as relevant or affordable in the post-war world, and given a role as a training ship. *Australia* was formally decommissioned in December 1921 – again, ahead of the treaty that listed her for scrapping.

None of this was surprising against the way post-war international relations and economics were generally shaking down against the backdrop of the First World War, with its enormous social, political and economic impact. The naval side was part of the mix. In this regard, although relations between Britain and the United States were good – and the association between both navies excellent – Congress had authorised a massive naval build-up in 1916, directed at Japan but also challenging the Royal Navy's superiority.[44] This became a sticking point in early 1919 when British and United States delegates met in Paris to discuss a peace treaty with Germany.[45] It also triggered a new naval race with Japan. However, this came amidst a general world mood for disarmament, a British drive to cut costs, and the fact that a new arms race was largely unaffordable. The United States government showed little appetite to extend their 1916 plan, particularly as the US economy crashed into depression in 1920–21. That brought a 17 per cent drop in gross domestic product over fourteen months.[46]

Early in 1921, incoming US President Warren Harding – elected on a platform of fiscal cuts[47] – proposed an international disarmament conference. The idea fell on fertile ground, and what followed in Washington, from November that year, produced multiple treaties that shaped the early interwar power balances. These included a Four Power Treaty replacing the Anglo-Japanese alliance, a Five Power Treaty on naval arms limitation, and a Nine Power Treaty that pledged independence for China. The naval treaty was signed by Britain, the United States, France, Italy, Japan – and, separately, Britain's self-governing dominions, New Zealand, Australia, Canada and South Africa.[48] It ended the new naval arms race, imposed a battleship building 'holiday', and defined naval strengths according to a formula that listed scrapping dates for the next twenty years, dividing them into 'pre-' and 'post-Jutland' categories. A total of twenty-one of Britain's 'pre-Jutland' ships were listed in Section II of the treaty for immediate scrapping, including all the 12in dreadnoughts and battlecruisers.[49] As we have seen, that was essentially a formality.

News that the gift ship would be disposed of broke across New Zealand after the treaty was concluded in early 1922. A correspondent of the *Auckland Star*, Dunbar Johnston, wondered whether memorabilia might be taken from the ship.[50] This had its sequel in late March when the Minister of Defence, Robert Heaton Rhodes, formally asked Allen – now High Commissioner in London – to let the Admiralty know that 'articles of interest' might be taken before the ship was disposed of.[51] He was not the only one to think of it. John Green – now a rear admiral[52] – shortly wrote to Allen, pointing out there was 'every prospect of *New Zealand* not being employed again', and listing various mementoes that could be removed – 'scrolls put in various parts of the upper-deck superstructure ... a handsome carved shield over the Quarter Deck ... together with a piece of armour that was punched out of X-turret at Jutland'.[53]

Other voices chimed in. New Zealand's delegate to the conference in Washington, Sir John Salmond, thought her disposal should be made an 'occasion of an appropriate ceremony', conveyed with 'dignity and honour'.[54] That was not for the New Zealand government to decide, but Rhodes got the ball rolling on the memorabilia. The Prime Minister, William Massey, was particularly interested in the ship's flags, which 'had been actually used during the war' and could therefore 'serve a most useful purpose in connection with lectures to school children'.[55] By April there was brisk argument as to distribution of mementoes. The Dominion Museum was thought to be too full.[56] The Auckland War Museum applied for its 'fair share'.[57] Jellicoe – now Governor-General – was privately approached over the hei tiki that Sloman had lent to the ship in 1913, writing to Rhodes to remind him not to overlook it.[5]

The navy shortly stepped into the mix. By 1922 the essence of Jellicoe's proposal for New Zealand's naval defence had been implemented, creating the New Zealand Naval Division. In June, the commander of this force, Commodore A H Hotham, wrote requesting some of the military gear aboard the battlecruiser – including a 50ft picket boat, a 42ft motor launch with stores and spares, and a laundry 'complete for instalment in a naval base'.[59] The Public Works Department were offered the ship's dynamos.[60] However, the Chief Engineer, Frederick Furkert, did not think they were likely to be useful.[61]

The upshot was a shopping list of trophies, furniture, woodwork and equipment that was stripped from the ship and crated for shipment to New Zealand. It featured some material from the old pre-dreadnought *Zealandia* and included gunnery shields, a boomerang, two greenstone mere (clubs), silver cups, two hei tiki – one on loan from Sloman – a silver tea service, silver salvers and more. The first batch was assembled in seven crates at the Royal Navy barracks, Devonport, by August 1922. Other equipment included some of the ship's searchlights, a steering wheel, and 4in QF guns with associated gear and rangefinders.[62]

Allen arranged for the ship's former captains to receive furniture from the captain's cabin. He also obtained furniture for the High Commission, including the wardroom buffet.[63] This, however, was then requested in New Zealand, eventually spurring a debate over who was going to pay for the shipping. A motor-launch and five crates of 'laundry equipment' were, later, assembled at Rosyth – where the ship was being scrapped – awaiting shipment.[64] Everything began arriving in New Zealand in late 1923, although some items had been mis-packed and not everything could be found.[65] One of the biggest problems was the buffet, which arrived in four cases. It turned out that nobody actually wanted it. In the end this enormous piece of furniture was delivered to New Zealand's Parliamentary restaurant, Bellamy's, on the basis that it was both 'ornamental and useful'.[66]

West end of the wharf at Rosyth with *New Zealand* being dismantled for scrap, 1923. The bows of HMS *Agincourt* intrude at the bottom of the frame.
(*Archives New Zealand R1836075-0020*)

New Zealand being dismantled, *Agincourt* adjacent with *Princess Royal* – still largely intact – beyond. The quantity of steel and other material pulled from the ships is clear from the detritus on the quayside, which includes – intact – the cabin built for Jellicoe in 1919. (*Archives New Zealand R1836075-0024*)

The 80-ton scrap shears used during the demolition process, able to cut plate up to 2in thick. (*Archives New Zealand R1836075-0026*)

Britain's warship disposal programme provoked a good deal of interest among businessmen hoping to profit from sale of scrap steel. They included A Wallace Cowan, who negotiated to buy *New Zealand*, *Princess Royal* and *Agincourt*. The details of how and where they would be scrapped emerged from his discussions. The Rosyth naval base was being reduced, and the Admiralty wanted to find work for dock hands who were otherwise unemployed. Cowan and his fellow shareholders thought the site excellent because 'first-class' berths were available. Cowan decided to call his enterprise the Rosyth Shipbreaking Company, setting up his friend F S Bell as managing director. The formal transfer came late in the process: *New Zealand* changed hands on 19 December 1922, ten years and one month after first commissioning. By this time the three ships had already been delivered to Rosyth and were moored 'alongside a wharf on the South side of the Wet Basin in the Naval Dockyard'.[67] The Admiralty passed the sale proceeds, some £20,000, to the New Zealand government.[68]

Cowan's company shortly began work, initially running the effort from offices aboard one of the ships. A little later they cut the admiral's accommo-

New Zealand's stern section at the 'beach berth' for final cutting up, 3 July 1924.
(*Archives New Zealand R1836075-0037*)

Forward section of *New Zealand*'s hull, beached above low tide level, 3 July 1924.
(*Archives New Zealand R1836075-0034*)

The end: last metal at the beach berth, 30 September 1924.
(*Archives New Zealand R1836075-0043*)

dation from *Agincourt*, lifting the structure ashore as a site office. The heavy guns from the three ships were cut up with oxy-acetylene torches, boilers and engines lifted out with the help of a 30-ton hammerhead crane: and so the three ships were steadily dismantled, piece by piece. According to the scrappers, the process produced around 40,000 tons of steel and about 10,000 tons of armour plate – the latter, apparently, difficult to sell.[69] One surprise discovery was 3,000 tons of coal remaining in the bunkers, which was lifted out and sold. Technically, the three ships had to be broken up within eighteen months of the Treaty being signed, and time ran short. In the end *Agincourt* was cut in half, symbolically marking her 'destruction' for legal purposes.[70]

New Zealand's end came when the remains of her hull were beached above the low-tide mark and cut up. The last pieces were lifted from the mud in September 1924. Soon afterwards the company sent the New Zealand government a photo album documenting the process.[71] In December, Cowan gave an ink stand and cigar boxes made of teak from the battlecruiser to Massey and Allen in what journalists called a 'somewhat pathetic' ceremony at New Zealand House in London – a term that, at the time, referred to emotional overtones or pathos. A third cigar box was sent to Ward, back in

New Zealand.[72] Cowan, meanwhile, used teak from the ship to make a floor for his own home.[73]

All that remained to deal with were the artefacts removed from the ship, some loose ends to tie up over prizes funds that the Admiralty had returned to the New Zealand government in 1921 – and the debt on the ledger books. The prizes funds were an administrative problem. One had been inherited from the 1905 battleship, explicitly on terms that required it to be passed only to any warship named *New Zealand*. No new ship had been built, and it was still extant in 1937, creating an auditing headache.[74]

That left the debt on the government ledger. One of the received truths about *New Zealand* is that the loan for the ship far outlasted her service life and was not paid off until 1944–45, underscoring the idea that she was an extravagance. This timing has been repeated even in New Zealand government histories, but it is not entirely true.[75] As we have seen, there was nothing unusual about the fact that the New Zealand government paid for *New Zealand* with borrowed capital. Nor was the expected span of repayment long; if anything, Ward's government set up systems for relatively quick redemption by government debt standards. However, as events panned out, zeroing the 'battlecruiser' ledger balance on the state accounts was essentially shaped by the way the New Zealand government changed its policies after the expense of the First World War – a figure that dwarfed the cost of the battlecruiser.

The first repayment system for the battlecruiser was the 'sinking fund' administered by the Public Trust Office, designed to accumulate payments from annual cash flows with which to repay the equivalent cost of the ship relatively quickly by government debt standards. This worked as intended for a while. In 1913 Allen told the Parliament that the fund, which was growing at about £50,000 per annum, plus interest, 'will be sufficient to repay the loan in about seventeen years'.[76] However, that soon changed. In the early twentieth century, New Zealand's public debt was largely made up of money raised on the commercial markets, usually in the form of debenture issues. The First World War provoked a dislocating quantity of debt atop earlier sums, and in 1922, the New Zealand government arranged for a little over £27 million of public debt to be converted to a loan from the British government, paid off in six-monthly instalments. This was known as the Imperial Funded Debt.

By this time the 'sinking fund' credit balance was £963,131 short of the sum required to cancel the battlecruiser's book debt. This shortfall was added by ledger entry, still as a 'Naval Defence Act Account' – sometimes simply 'Naval Defence Account' in the annual disclosures – to the new 'Imperial Funded Debt' ledger. That left a balance of £832,035 on the original 'Naval

Defence Account' ledger against the ship, while the 'sinking fund' continued to accumulate at £71,807 per annum, plus compound interest.[77] The battlecruiser debt, in short, had been split in two by an accounting decision, one part subject to a different repayment arrangement.

That caused issues in 1924 when the Admiralty passed on £20,000 raised on sale of the ship for scrap. The government initially wanted to use the windfall to part-pay loans for electrical reticulation. This was stopped by the Controller and Auditor-General, George Campbell, who thought it should be set against the 'naval defence loans included in the [Imperial] Funded Debt'.[78] The money accordingly went to the Public Debt Redemption fund held by the Public Trust Office.[79] By this time the credit balance of the 'sinking fund' stood well above the remaining figure in the original Naval Defence ledger, so Campbell suggested the surplus should be paid to the Imperial Funded Debt along with the scrap money, reducing the battlecruiser line entry in that account. In the end some £180,000 was transferred into the Public Debt Redemption Fund from the 'sinking fund', plus the scrapping price.[80]

The accounting arrangements changed again when the remaining battlecruiser 'sinking fund' cash balance was swept up in the Repayment of Public Debt Act 1925 and – standing at £876,379 19s 5d on 31 March 1926 – merged with the Public Debt Redemption Fund, but without being set off against either part of the Naval Defence ledger debt.[81] Government, in short, had hijacked the money. This new approach was designed to let the New Zealand government redeem older debt when it could and offer new stock at more favourable terms. It completely disconnected the loans attributed to the ship from the original system intended to repay them. As an official pointed out in 1929, there was now no special fund to repay the three consolidated stock loans against which the residual Naval Defence debt – meaning the part not transferred to the 'Imperial Funded Debt' – had been raised.[82] The first of these was due in November 1929; the last, some £442,170, due on 1 February 1963.[83] However, the point was moot: the combination of the Imperial loan and the 1925 Act meant that the ship's two ledger debts and the accumulating cash account intended to pay them had been absorbed into a new government debt programme.

This had its own problems. The Great Depression hit New Zealand's government finances hard.[84] While the country did not – quite – default on sovereign debt, repayments were problematic, and in October 1936 government handed the task of managing national debt to the Reserve Bank of New Zealand.[85] One result of the situation was that nothing was deemed paid from the two ledger debts attributed to *New Zealand*. The 'Funded

Debt' ledger entry stood at £577,446 11s 5d in 1931–32, largely thanks to the sums deducted from it in 1924, and was shown as due in 1945.[86] This remained unchanged at the end of the 1942–43 financial year.[87] The part of the debt accounted via the Repayment of the Public Debt Act 1925 was also not deemed paid and stood at £812,209 0s 11d the same year.[88]

However, government made a significant change in the 1943–44 financial year, largely in response to a pre-war balance of payments crisis. A new economic stabilisation programme began actively restructuring state debt and redomiciling it in Wellington. Essentially, this system arbitrarily wrote off entries in the debt ledger as a variety of financial instruments were repaid. On the basis of early repayment of various securities, a total of £858,902 5s 5d was deemed repaid from the Naval Defence Account at the end of the 1943–44 financial year, along with capital figures on the ledger for other and unrelated debts.[89] A final £530,753 16s 0d was cancelled in the 1944–45 year, again joining other unrelated debts, on the basis of early repayments of securities due between January 1945 and April 1963.[90]

The naval sums, with due allowance for accounting adjustments, were the figures attributable to the battlecruiser. From a strict bookkeeping perspective, then, the ship was indeed 'repaid' in 1944–45, but it was wholly an accounting exercise, reflecting another change in government policy towards New Zealand's public debt. The historically meaningful point is the comment in a 1929 audit report that, if the original 'sinking fund' had not been 'disturbed', it would have accumulated enough by 1930–31 to cover the £1,795,169 4s 11d attributed to the battlecruiser.[91] This makes it clear that the ledger duration of the 'battlecruiser debt' after that time was a function of shifting government debt management policies, not a shortfall relative to the battlecruiser.

There is a final point: inflation. Compound inflation absorbed much of the debt by devaluing the real worth of the money across the period the debt was held.[92] The £1,389,666 1s 5d cancelled in the 1943–44 and 1944–45 financial years had broadly been incurred between 1910 and 1913. Discounting the shilling and five pence, that had the buying power of £2,642,868 in the first quarter of 1945, but only the actual ledger balance needed to be paid.[93] Put another way, at the end of financial year 1930–31 – the date when the original repayment scheme would have come to fruition – the £1,795,169 book entry assigned to the ship was equivalent to £2,735,923 in inflation-adjusted terms.[94] Time and the effects of inflation, in short, reduced the battlecruiser's capital cost to New Zealand over the period. The interesting point is that the bulk of that inflation occurred between 1913 and 1931. During the Great Depression, prices deflated, peaking at 12 per cent in

1932.[95] This effectively *increased* the debt, and price levels had not returned to pre-1931 values by 1945.[96] The mid-1920s decisions to alter the original repayment system, in the longer term, cost money. And that is without considering the interest paid on the various government debt instruments over the period, which was running typically at between 3 and 4 per cent.

Some of the ship's hardware survived. Four 4in guns had been requested to bolster New Zealand's coast defences,[97] and two later became fixtures outside the Auckland War Memorial Museum. Sloman's hei tiki was returned to the Canterbury Museum in 1932.[98] The buffet was eventually disposed of by Bellamy's and, after mouldering in the Parliamentary basement, was eventually returned to the navy and restored. The auxiliary steering wheel was donated by the breakers to the 'New Zealand Sheepowners Acknowledgement of Debt to British Seamen' fund in 1924, along with an engine telegraph.[99] The wheel was displayed for a while by the Wellington Maritime Museum, then transferred to Te Papa Tongarewa, the Museum of New Zealand.[100] The piece of armour knocked from X-turret glacis at Jutland became a significant exhibit in the Royal New Zealand Navy museum at Torpedo Bay, Devonport, along with other artefacts from the ship. These eventually included the piupiu, which Halsey lent to New Zealand for the 1940 centennial exhibition, but which passed into his daughter's hands on his death in 1949. She bequeathed it to New Zealand on

New Zealand's wardroom buffet, as restored.
(*Torpedo Bay Navy Museum SFB001*)

The HMS *New Zealand* display at the Royal New Zealand Navy's Torpedo Bay Navy Museum.
(*Torpedo Bay Navy Museum SFB001*)

her death in 2002, and it was received by the Royal New Zealand Navy in 2005, becoming an exhibit at their Torpedo Bay Museum.[101]

Joseph Ward's bold scheme to reinforce the Empire at its heart, inspire followership, and so command Imperial policy at the expense of Australia, failed politically at the first hurdle. However, even his gift – framed as a simple symbol of Imperial sentiment – had lasted only a little over fourteen years, from the first steel cut at the Fairfield yard through to the last slash of the scrapper's gas axe. This same period spanned the effective end of social militarism as a deep-set cultural phenomenon, certainly in New Zealand. After 1918 Britain was still idealised as 'home', but the experience of war entered the mix. The near-religious adulation accorded military hardware, mainly through its entanglement with national identity, quietly faded. There was still enthusiasm for such things, underscored by the reception given the Royal Navy's Special Service Squadron when it toured New Zealand in 1924. This was another no-holds-barred public relations effort, essentially the successor to *New Zealand*'s world cruise of 1913. But the First World War cast the event in subtly different light. Citizen armies drawn from a socially significant proportion of the population had faced the horrors of industrial-era warfare with its 'whizz-bangs', snipers, artillery, machine guns, wire, gas and relentless death. They returned home changed by the experience. Patriotic fervour still flowed, and New Zealanders again flocked to see and board the ship in huge numbers, but there could be no return to the glory days of pre-war innocence.[102]

It is easy, looking back, to judge *New Zealand* as an extravagance; an unaffordable gift offered in the heat of a moment by an impetuous politician. This vision has certainly driven some of the assertions surrounding her story, contributing to a significant array of misunderstanding and, at times, outright myths surrounding the vessel. In a sense this array of shibboleths is neither surprising nor alarming, and unpicking the mythologies underscores the way the study of history so often works, as a discussion. One of the purposes of this book has been to provide the political and economic side in significantly more detail, shedding light on *New Zealand*'s historical foundation and giving social context to the gesture.

At heart, *New Zealand* stood at the intersection of many forces swirling about Britain's globe-spanning Empire in the first years of the twentieth century. In these respects she was an expression of the social ideals of the day, given power by the depth to which those ideals were held at the time, particularly in New Zealand. This was no overnight flash: as we saw in the first chapter, the phenomenon of social militarism – evolving as it went – can be traced back well before Ward's gift. By the turn of the twentieth century it was entwined with self-identity. New Zealand shared this thinking with the rest of Empire, but when this was mixed with the ideation of Britain as 'home', a concept that had emerged in New Zealand on the back of a flood of new British colonists from the 1870s, it gained power. Without that social dimension, Ward's response to Australian talk – his act of gifting Britain a ship without discussion or calling Parliament – would never have been possible. Ward simply could not have taken the political risk.

The idea of the gift stood at the intersection of other forces. The dissonance of defence perception between Britain and her two Australasian dominions – coupled with further differences between Australia and New Zealand – was always going to provoke differing policies. The New Zealand Liberal party vision of federated defence, held alone among all of Britain's children, was uniquely suited to the concept of a gift ship. In this purpose, Ward's gift – as expressed by New Zealand – differed from the idea of ship gifts expressed at the same time in Australia, where the act was more purely patriotic. But it was in the Australian sense that it was received by the Empire at large, and Ward's idea failed to initiate his federal policy. The irony was that in the gyrations that followed between 1909 and 1914, New Zealand's gift ended up being stationed where Ward had wanted it.

Ultimately the story of *New Zealand* is one of people: Ward, Fisher, Churchill, Allen, Halsey, Green, Smith, Boyle, Coore and many others. For the people of New Zealand, the ship was always morally 'theirs', irrespective of the fact that she was part of the Royal Navy. This social reality was recognised and understood by *New Zealand*'s successive captains. The ship had significant meaning for those who served on her; it was their home. Officers such as Boyle, whose life aboard the ship broadly matched her service career – certainly saw it as more than just steel. The crew were often not just colleagues but also friends and, in the way usual to such communities, sometimes considered family. Their memories of their time aboard outlasted the ship; and so this gift to Empire passed into history.

Selected Engineering Particulars[1]

These details from *New Zealand*'s Captain's Ship's Book vary from the statistics given in secondary literature in minor particulars, and include results of inclining experiments. Figures are original Imperial measures from source, including mixed decimal points and fractions. At this time, normal operational displacement with particular weights of coal, munitions, feed water and crew stores was called 'load'. The concept of 'standard displacement' was a product of 1921–22 negotiations relative to the Five Power Treaty in Washington.

Weights

Design displacement:	18,800 tons
Seagoing displacement, load draft:	18,500 tons
Seagoing displacement, deep load:	22,070 tons
Metacentric height at mean draft of 24' 3½" with boilers full to working height and all water, provisions, and part-crew	2.96'
Weight to increase draught by 1 inch at load draught	75.0 tons
Longitudinal centre of buoyancy relative to Bulkhead 118 at displacement 22,845 tons (distance from bulkhead)	28.61'
Moment (load to change trim by 1 inch at load draft)	2420 tons
Weight of auxiliary machinery	219.3 tons

Dimensions

Length between perpendiculars	555 ft
Length overall	590 ft
Longitudinal hogging at 458 ft	1¼"
Beam	79' 10"
Transverse hogging at 71' 3"	Nil
Deep load draft forward	29' 4"
Deep load draft aft	30' 4"
Load draft forward	24' 9"
Load draft aft	27' 2"

Propulsion and fuel

Coal carried at load draft	1000 tons
Design shaft horsepower at authorised natural forced draft	44,000
Speed at authorised natural forced draft	25.8 knots
Propeller maximum design rpm	275
Trial speed, Polperro measured mile (via bearings), 14 October 1912	26.3 knots
Maximum propeller rpm on trial (port outboard)	308

Auxiliary equipment

Projectors [searchlights]	8

Pumps (all electric centrifugal except 10-ton)

Boatswain's store	30 ton
Forward capstan compartment	30 ton
Pump room (frames 44–50)	30 ton
Pump room (frames 218–229)	30 ton
After capstan compartment	50 ton
Steering flat	30 ton
Main deck forward	10 ton
Main deck aft (2)	10 ton

Main armament

Main armament:	8–12in Mk X BL/45=calibre
Mountings (mark)	BVIII*
A-turret guns (on completion, L-R)	Elswick #380 and #383
Q-turret guns (on completion, L-R)	Elswick #382 and #381
P-turret guns (on completion, L-R)	Vickers #375 and #385
X-turret guns (on completion, L-R)	Vickers #383 and #370

LOAN AND PURCHASE COSTS[1]

TABLE 1

**Loans accounted against the cost of HMS *New Zealand*
(pounds-shillings-pence)**

Financial year	Borrowing attributed to cost of ship*	Loans raised to cover cost of raising loan	Loans raised to cover expenses of redeeming and converting loans
1910–11	1,120,250-0-0	–	5,930-0-0
1911–12	279,752-10-1	47,821-13-11	–
1912–13	283,500-5-2	13,872-16-0	–
1913–14	15,000-0-0	–	8,670-0-0
1914–15	2,100-0-0	–	8,636-13-6
1915–16	–	–	50,184-4-3
1916–17	–	–	LESS 40,552-18-0
TOTAL	**1,700,602-15-3**	**61,698-9-11**	**32,867-19-9**

*ie: the ship component within the wider borrowing programme.

TABLE 2

Costs attributed to HMS *New Zealand*
(pounds-shillings-pence)

Financial year	Expenditure under the Naval Defence Act 1909 (actual cost of hardware)	Cost of raising loans (added to capital)*	Cost of loan redemptions (not added to capital)
1910–11	489,289-0-0	431-3-9	5,930-0-0
1911–12	605,711-0-0	48,030-9-0	–
1912–13	525,000-0-0	13,878-16-2	–
1913–14	69,034-14-6	1,782-1-0	8,670-0-0
1914–15	9,000-0-0	26-9-0	8,636-13-6
1915–16	–	–	50,184-4-3
1916–17	–	–	LESS 40,552-18-0
1917–18	117-11-9	–	–
TOTAL	**1,698,152-6-3**	**61,148-18-11**	**32,867-19-9**
	Totals		
		Capital expenditure	1,698,152-6-3
		Cost of raising loans	64,148-18-11
		Cost of redemptions	32,867-19-9
		TOTAL	**1,795,169-4-11**

*Actual expenditures differ from loans raised to cover this cost.

BIBLIOGRAPHY

Alexander Turnbull Library (WTu)

EPH-B-State-1900/1949, 'Luncheon: the captain and officers of HMS *New Zealand* given by the government of New Zealand'.

fMS-195, *New Zealand* (ship), Captain's Ship's Book.

Micro MS Coll 05, ADM 116/1285, 1286, Case 177/1, Voyage of HMS *New Zealand* to New Zealand and other Dominions and Colonies 1912–13.

Micro MS-99 Halsey, Sir Lionel 1872–1949, personal papers 1905–1923 (Australian Joint Copying Project M1179; Hertfordshire County Record Office, Hertford, England).

Micro-MS-Coll-05-5905, United Kingdom, Admiralty: records relating to the Pacific, 1714–1910 (collection), Naval missions – Lord Jellicoe to Australia and New Zealand (Cases 1099/1, 1099/4, 1099/5, 732) (ADM 116/ 1831, 1834, 1835, 1871A).

MS-Papers-0283, Barcroft, Mick, Papers.

MS-Papers-5210-142, Series 3, Sir Francis Henry Dillon Bell – Political Correspondence and Papers.

MS-Papers-8464-05, Leece, George, 1865–1901, Papers.

qMS-0545, Coore, E G B, fl.1913–1914: Journal.

Archives New Zealand (ANZ)

R11741448 ADAV 16028 A5 141/23/48 Naval Defence Sinking Fund Account 1921–1938.

R1836075 ABFK W3947 3/ The Rosyth Shipbreaking Co. Ltd, album.

R19162149 ACHK 16603 G48 5 / F/4 G48 'Admiral Fanshawe – Vulnerability of Australia and New Zealand', Confidential Enclosure.

R19162214 ACHK 16603 G48 20 /N/17 G48 Naval policy – (a) Conferences between Admiralty and New Zealand Minister of Defence in 1913 – (b) CID Papers concerning representation of Dominions on the Committee of Imperial Defence (R19162214) 1913–1913.

R19162326 ACHK 16604 G49 10 / 16i Plate 8a G49, 'Maps etc accompanying volume: British – Plan of Battle sent by Vice-Admiral Commanding Battle Cruiser Fleet to Commander-in-Chief – 17 July 1916'.

R19162327 ACHK 16604 G49 10 /16j Plate 9a, 'Maps etc accompanying volume: British - Second Battle Cruiser Squadron, 2pm, 31 May 1916 to 4am, 1 June 1916 – Track'.

R19162355 ACHK 16604 G49 17/34 G49 (a) Defence Scheme of New

Zealand, 1906 (Copy No. 5) – (b) Defence Scheme of New Zealand, 1908 [with attached correspondence dated 1913].

R21463719 AAYT 8490 N1 18 /1/34 N1, 'Accounts – Naval Benevolent Fund, New Zealand – HMS New Zealand prizes fund – General – Correspondence'.

R21464062 AAYT 8490 N1 85 /6/1/11 N1 'HM Ships – Administrative and general – *Bristol* class cruisers, etc. 1906–1914'.

R21467044 AAYT 8490 N1 680/22/5 Missions – Lord Jellicoe's visit to New Zealand, 1919.

R21467087 AAYT 8490 N1 691/22/6/9 N1 'Naval Board and policy – Naval defence – Policy and agreement – New Zealand prior 1914, 1905–1914'.

R21464096 C363 197 N1 92/6/9, 'Ships and repairs: HMS "New Zealand"– general'.

R22319678 ADBQ 16145 ALLEN1 8 / Naval Defence – General, Un-numbered file.

R22430265 AAYS 8638 AD1 760 /17/69, 'Shipping – HMS "New Zealand" (ship) – Correspondence re-1911–1927'.

R24501777 ACHK 16558 G2 16 /1909/311'5 April 1909 Subject: Colonial Conference, 1907 – Correspondence relating to and action taken on Resolutions of Conference'.

R24501803 ACHK 16558 G2 17/1909/696, 'Imperial Defence Conference. Papers for publication and copies of confidential proceedings'.

R24751781 AD1 565 D1909/2929, 'New Zealand offer of dreadnoughts – resolution of thanks by Chamber of Commerce, London'.

R3485891, ACGO 8394, IA71 1/1913/1661, Boxes 1–5, 'Visit of HMS "New Zealand" (ship) – Correspondence concerning the building and equipping of the ship'.

CO 209/270 Governor's secret quarterly reports.

Canterbury Museum
Folder 698, 199/75, Diary of Captain (Lt Commander) A D Boyle.

Appendices to the Journal of the House of Representatives (AJHR)
1900, Session 1, A-03a, 'Federation of Fiji with New Zealand'.

1909, Session I, A-04, Despatches regarding the Imperial Conference and the dreadnought offer.

1909, Session II, A-4a 'Naval and Military Defence of the Empire; conference with representatives of the self-governing Dominions on the, 1909'.

1909, Session I, A-5, 'Imperial Naval Conference (proceedings of informal meeting of members of the House of Representatives on the question of the representation of New Zealand at the').

1912, Session II, A-4, 'Imperial Conference 1911 (papers paid before the, dealing with naval and military defence', Schedule B.

1912, Session II, B-18H, 'Prospectus of the £4,500,000 loan'.

1913, Session I, B-06, 'Financial statement (in Committee of Supply 6th August 1913) by the Minister of Finance, The Hon. James Allen'.

1926, Session I, B-08, 'The Naval Defence Act Sinking Fund, statement of securities in which the fund is invested'.

1932, Session I-II, B-01, Part 3, 'Public accounts for the financial year 1931–1932, Part 3'.

1943, Session I, B-01, Part 2, 'Public accounts for the financial year 1942–43, Part 2'.

1944, Session I, B-02, 'Repayment of the public debt: report and accounts of the public debt commission for the year ended 31st March 1944'.

1945, Session I, B-02, 'Repayment of the public debt: report and accounts of the public debt commission for the year ended 31st March 1945'.

General Assembly Library (GA)

CD 3523 'Minutes of the Proceedings of the Colonial Conference, 1907'.

CD 3524 'Papers Laid before the Imperial Conference, 1907'.

CD 4325 'Correspondence relating to the naval defence of Australia and New Zealand'.

CD 4948 'Conference with the Representatives of the self-governing Dominions on the Naval and Military Defence of the Empire, 1909'.

CD 5135 'Report of the Dominions Department of the Colonial Office'.

Command Paper 256 (1909) 'Report of the Sub-Committee of the Committee of Imperial Defence Appointed to Inquire into Certain Questions of Naval Policy raised by Lord Charles Beresford'.

New Zealand Parliamentary Debates (NZPD)

1908, Vol. 143.
1909, Vol. 146.
1909, Vol. 148.
1945, Vol. 269.

New Zealand Statutes

Naval Defence Act 1909 (9 Edw VII 1909, No. 9).

New Zealand Yearbooks

New Zealand Yearbook 1913
New Zealand Yearbook 1926
New Zealand Yearbook 1945

Newspapers
Auckland Star
Evening Mail
Evening Post
Evening Star
Feilding Star
Greymouth Evening Star
London Gazette
Lyttelton Times
Manawatu Times
Marlborough Express
Mataura Ensign
Nelson Evening Mail
New Zealand Herald
New Zealand Times
Otago Daily Times
Otago Witness
Pall Mall Gazette
Pelorus Guardian and Miners' Advocate
Poverty Bay Herald
Rangiteiki Advocate and Manawatu Argus
Sheffield Independent
Star [Christchurch]
Stratford Evening Post
Sun [Christchurch]
Sydney Morning Herald
The Age
The Edinburgh Gazette
The Press
The Scotsman
Timaru Herald
Tuapeka Times
Wairarapa Age
Wanganui Chronicle
Wanganui Herald
West Coast Times
Yorkshire Post and Leeds Intelligencer

Published primary sources
—— Gunnery Drill Book for His Majesty's Fleet, Book I. 1913.
—— *Navy List*, H M Stationery Office, London, January 1921.

—— *The Monthly Naval List*, H M Stationery Office, London, May 1914.

Battle of Jutland, 30th May to 1st June 1916, Official Despatches, HMSO, London, 1920.

Churchill, R S, (ed), *W S Churchill Companion Vol. III*, William Heinemann, London, 1969.

Corbett, Julian, *History of the Great War: Naval Operations, Vol. 1*, Longmans, Green & Co., London, 1920.

Fawcett, H W and G W W Hooper, *The Fighting at Jutland* (abridged edition), Macmillan & Co., London, 1921.

Gooch G P and Harold Temperley (eds), *British Documents on the Origins of the War 1898–1914, Vol. VI, Anglo-German tension*, H M Stationery Office, London, 1930; Johnson Reprint Corporation, London.

Greenwood, G and C Grimshad (eds), *Documents on Australian International Affairs*, 1901–1918, Thomas Nelson (Australia) Ltd, Melbourne, 1977.

Handcock, W D and David Charles Douglas (eds*), English Historical Documents 1974–1914*, Routledge, London, 1977.

Kelso, Frederick (ed. John Dunmore), *The Last Voyage of HMS New Zealand*, New Zealand Books, Palmerston North, 1972.

Kemp, P K (ed), *The Fisher Papers*, Vol. I, Navy Records Society, London, 1960.

Kemp, P K (ed), *The Fisher Papers*, Vol. II, Navy Records Society, London, 1964.

Lambert, Nicholas (ed), *Australia's Naval Inheritance*, Royal Australian Navy Maritime Studies Programme, Department of Defence (Navy), Canberra, 1998.

Marder, Arthur (ed), *Fear God and Dread Nought: The Correspondence of Admiral of the Fleet Lord Fisher of Kilverstone*, Vol. II, Jonathan Cape, London, 1956.

Naval Staff Monographs (Historical), Fleet Issue, Monograph 11, 'The Battle of Heligoland Bight, August 28th, 1914', Naval Staff Training and Staff Duties Division, July 1921.

Naval Staff Monographs (Historical), Fleet Issue, Monograph 13, 'Summary of the Operations of the Grand Fleet, August 1914 to November 1916', Training and Staff Duties Division, February 1921.

Naval Staff Monographs, Fleet Issue, Monograph 12, 'The action of Dogger Bank, January 24th, 1915', Naval Staff Training and Staff Duties Division, July 1921.

Patterson, A Temple*, The Jellicoe Papers*, Navy Records Society, London, 1966.

Tracy, Nicholas (ed), *The Collective Naval Defence of Empire 1900–1940*, Routledge for Navy Records Society, New York, 2019.

Theses

Black, Nicholas Duncan, 'The Admiralty War Staff and its influence on the conduct of the naval war between 1914 and 1918', PhD thesis, University College, London, 2005.

Briggs, M, 'The too vast orb: the Admiralty and Australian naval defence 1881–1913', PhD thesis, University of Tasmania 1991.

Brooks, John, 'Fire Control for British Dreadnoughts – Choices of Technology and Supply', PhD thesis, Department of War Studies, King's College, London, 2001.

Campbell, Todd Christopher, 'Financing the Royal Navy 1905–1914: sound finance in the Dreadnought era', MA thesis, University of British Columbia, 1994.

Humphreys, Edward William, 'Some aspects of the federal political career of Andrew Fisher', MA thesis, University of Melbourne, 2005.

Lindgren, Scott M, 'The genesis of a cruiser navy: British first-class cruiser development 1884–1909', PhD thesis, University of Salford, 2013.

Morgan, Henry S, Jr, 'The Fisher Revolution: reforms in the Royal Navy 1890–1910, early naval management in action', Master of Science thesis, United States Naval Postgraduate School, 1964.

Ott, Nathan, 'Battlecruisers at Jutland: A comparative analysis of British and German warship design and its impact on the naval war', Senior Honors Thesis, Ohio State University, July 2010.

Peeks, Ryan Alexander, '"The Cavalry of the Fleet", organisation, doctrine and battlecruisers in the United States and the United Kingdom, 1904–1922, PhD thesis, University of North Carolina, Chapel Hill, 2015.

Romano, Gail, 'A searchlight on New Zealand: what the visit of an Imperial Battlecruiser tells us about the country in 1913', MA thesis, Massey University, Palmerston North, 2019.

Street, Kathryn, 'The Colonial Reinvention of the Hei Tiki: Pounamu, Knowledge and Empire, 1860s–1940s, Victoria University of Wellington, MA thesis, 2017.

Weir, T G, 'New Zealand's Naval Policy 1909–14', MA Thesis, Canterbury, 1973.

Books, articles and academic papers

– *Chronicles of the NZEF.*

– *Onward, HMS New Zealand* [no publication data given: brochure 1919].

Asquith, H H, *The Genesis of the War*, London, 1923.

Bacon, Admiral Sir Reginald, *The Jutland Scandal*, Hutchison, London, revised edition, 1925.

Barclay, A R, 'The Premier and his troubles', S Lister, Printer, Dunedin, 1909.

Bell, Christopher M., 'On Standards and Scholarship: A response to Nicholas Lambert', *War in History*, Vol. 20, No. 3, 2013.

Bell, Christopher M, 'Sir John Fisher's naval revolution reconsidered: Winston Churchill at the Admiralty, 1911–1914', War in History, Vol. 18, No. 3, 2011.

Blum, Alan ,'A history of tobacco trading cards', in Karen Slama (ed), *Tobacco and Health*, Plenum Press, New York, 1995.

Broadberry, S and C Burhop, 'Real Wages and Labor Productivity in Britain and Germany: a Unified Approach to the International Comparison of Living Standards', 2010, http://dx.doi.org/10.1017/S0022050710000331

Broadberry, Stephen and Carsten Burhop, 'Real wages and labour productivity in Britain and Germany 1871–1938: a unified approach to the international comparison of living standards', University of Warwick, 2009.

Brooks, John, 'Dreadnought: Blunder or Stroke of Genius?', *War in History*, Vol. 14, No. 2 (April 2007).

Brown, David K, 'British Warship Design Methods 1860–1905', *Warship International*, Vol. Vol. 32, No. 1 (1995).

Brown, David K, 'HMS *Invincible*: the explosion at Jutland and its relevance to HMS *Hood*', *Warship International*, Vol. 40, No. 4, 2003.

Brown, David K, and Iain McCallum, 'Ammunition explosions in World War I: a re-examination of the evidence', *Warship International*, Vol. 38, No. 1, 2001.

Burt, R A, *British Battleships 1889–1904*, Seaforth, Barnsley, 1988.

Burt, R A, *British Battleships of World War One*, Seaforth, Barnsley, 2012.

Buxton, Ian and Ian Johnston, *The Battleship Builders: Constructing and Arming British Capital Ships*, Seaforth, Barnsley, 2013.

Campbell, John, *Jutland: an analysis of the fighting*, Lyons Press, New York, 1998.

Chesneau, Roger and Eugene M Kolesnik, *Conway's All The World's Warships 1860–1905*, Conway Maritime Press, London, 1979.

Churchill, R S, *W S Churchill Vol. II: The Young Statesman, 1901–14*, William Heinemann, London, 1967.

Churchill, Winston, , *The World Crisis 1911–1918*, abridged one-volume edition, Four Square, London, 1960.

Collins, Michael, 'The Banking Crisis of 1878', *Economic History Review*, 2nd Series, Vol. XLII, No. 4.

Corbett, Julian, *History of the Great War: Naval Operations, Vol. 1*, Longmans, Green & Co., London, 1920.

Crawford, John and Ellen Ellis, *To Fight for the Empire: An Illustrated History of New Zealand and the South African War, 1899–1902*, Reed,

Auckland, 1999.

Dunley, Richard, 'Sir John Fisher and the policy of strategic deterrence, 1904–1908', War in History, Vol. 22, No. 2, April 2015.

Ejstrud, Bo, 'A near miss: heavy gun efficiency at Jutland', *Warship International*, Vol. 41, No. 2, 2004.

Fisher, Admiral of the Fleet Sir John, *Records*, Hodder & Stoughton, London, 1919.

Friedman, Norman, *Naval Weapons of World War One*, Seaforth, Barnsley, 2011.

Friedman, Norman, *The British Battleship 1906–1946*, Seaforth, Barnsley, 2015.

Friedman, Norman, 'How promise turned to disappointment', *Naval History Magazine*, Vol. 30, No. 4, August 2016.

Friedman, Norman, *British Battleships of the Victorian Era*, Seaforth, Barnsley, 2018.

Gartner, Ken Te Huingarau, 'Te Heuheu T kino V, T reiti', in https://teara.govt.nz/en/biographies/3t13/te-heuheu-tukino-v-tureiti

Goldrick, James, 'The problems of modern naval history', *The Great Circle* Vol. 18, No. 1, pp 48–58, Australian Association for Maritime History, 1996

Goldrick, James, 'Coal and the advent of the First World War at sea', *War in History*, Vol. 2, No. 3, 2014.

Goldrick, James, 'The Impact of War: matching expectation with reality in the Royal Navy in the first months of the Great War at sea', *War in History*, Vol. 14, No. 1.

Goldrick, James, *Before Jutland: The Naval War in Northern European Waters*, Naval Institute Press, Annapolis, 2015.

Grey, George (Viscount Grey of Fallodon), *Twenty Five Years, Vol. II: 1892–1916*, Frederick A Stokes, New York, 1925.

Grove, Eric, 'The battleship *Dreadnought*: technological, economic and strategic contexts', in Robert J Blyth, Andrew Lambert and Jan Ruger (eds), *The Dreadnought and the Edwardian Age*, National Maritime Museum, Surrey, 2011.

Haggie, Paul 'The Royal Navy and War Planning in the Fisher Era', *Journal of Contemporary History*, Vol. 8 No. 3, July 1973.

Hankey, Maurice, *The Supreme Command*, Vol. I, Allen & Unwin, London, 1961.

Hough, Richard, *Admiral of the Fleet: The life of John Fisher*, Macmillan, New York, 1969.

Jane, Fred T (ed), *Jane's Fighting Ships 1914*, Sampson Low Marston, London, 1914; David & Charles reprint, 1968.

Jellicoe, Admiral Viscount Jellicoe of Scapa, *The Grand Fleet 1914–16: its creation, development and work*, Cassell & Company, London, 1919.

Jellicoe, Nicholas, *Jutland: the unfinished battle*, Seaforth, Barnsley, 2016.

Kennedy, Paul, 'Dogger Bank: Clash of the Battle Cruisers' Bernard Fitzsimons (ed), *Warships and Sea Battles of the First World War*, Ure Smith, Sydney, 1973.

Lambert, Nicholas, 'On Standards: a reply to Christopher Bell', *War in History*, Vol. 19, No. 2, 2012.

Lambert, Nicholas A, 'Righting the scholarship: the battle-cruiser in history and historiography', *The Historical Journal*, Vol. 58 No. 1, March 2015.

Laterbach, Albert T, 'Militarism in the Western World: A comparative study', *Journal of the History of Ideas*, Vol. 5, No. 4, October 1944.

Leggett, Don, 'Spectacle and witnessing: constructing readings of Charles Parsons' marine turbine', *Technology and Culture*, Vol. 52, No. 2, April 2011.

Loughmann, R A, *Life of Sir Joseph Ward*, Dunedin, 1928.

MacKay, Neill, Chris Price and Jamie Wood, 'Dogger Bank: Weighing the Fog of War', *Significance*, Royal Statistical Society, June 2017.

Mackay, Ruddock F, *Fisher of Kilverstone*, Clarendon Press, Oxford, 1973.

Mackay, Ruddock, 'The Admiralty, the German Navy, and the re-distribution of the British fleet 1904–05', *Mariner's Mirror* Vol. 56 No. 3, August 1970.

Mangan, J A, '"Muscular, Militaristic and Manly": the British middle-class hero as moral messenger', *The International Journal of the History of Sport*, Vol. 13, No. 1, 1996.

Mangan, J A, 'Duty unto death: English masculinity and militarism in the age of new imperialism', *The International Journal of the History of Sport*, Vol. 12, No. 2, 1995.

Marder, Arthur, *From the Dreadnought to Scapa Flow*, Vol. I., Oxford University Press, London, 1961.

Marder, Arthur, *The Anatomy of British Sea Power*, Frank Cass, London, 1940.

Massie, Robert K, *Dreadnought: Britain, Germany and the Coming of the Great War*, Random House, New York, 1991.

Massie, Robert K, *Castles of Steel*, Pimlico, London, 2005.

McBride, William M, 'Nineteenth century American warships: the pursuit of exceptionalist design', in Don Leggett and Richard Dunn (eds), *Re-inventing the Ship: Science, Technology and the Maritime World, 1800–1918*, Routledge, London, 2012.

McCartney, Innes, *Jutland 1916: the archaeology of a naval battlefield*, Conway, London, 2016.

McKenzie, Clutha (ed), 'The History of HMS *New Zealand*', Navy League, Wellington, 1919.

Milhollen, Hirst, 'Roger Fenton, Photographer of the Crimean War', *Quarterly Journal of Current Acquisitions*, Vol. 3, No. 4, August 1946, Library of Congress.

Morgan-Owen, David G Morgan-Owen, 'An "intermediate blockade"? British North Sea Strategy 1912–1914', *War in History*, Vol. 22, No. 4, 2015.

Morris, Jan, *Fisher's Face*, Penguin, London, 1995.

Padfield, Peter, *The Great Naval Race: Anglo-German naval rivalry 1900–1914*, Hart-Davis, London, 1974.

Parkinson, Roger, *Dreadnought: the ship that changed the world*, I B Tauris, 2015.

Partridge, Michael, *Gladstone*, Routledge, London, 2003.

Pemberton, W Baring, *Battles of the Crimean War*, Pan, London, 1968.

Porter, Frances, 'Scholefield, Guy Hardy', https://teara.govt.nz/en/biographies/4s12/scholefield-guy-hardy

Reddell, Michael and Cath Sleeman, 'Some perspectives on past recessions', Reserve Bank of New Zealand *Bulletin*, Vol. 71, No. 2, June 2008.

Reddell, Michael, 'The New Zealand Debt Conversion Act 1933: a case study in coercive domestic public debt restructuring', Reserve Bank of New Zealand *Bulletin*, Vol. 75, No. 1, March 2012.

Redford, Duncan and Philip D Grove, *The Royal Navy: A history since 1900*, I B Taurus/National Museum, New York, 2014.

Reinhardt, Carsten and Anthony S Travis, *Heinrich Caro and the Creation of Modern Chemical Industry*, Springer Science + Business Media Dordrecht, 2000.

Reitzel, William, 'Mahan on Use of the Sea' from B. Mitchell-Simpson III (ed), *Wars, Strategy and Maritime Power*, Rutger's University Press, New Brunswick, New Jersey, 1977.

Robinson, Murray, 'Battle of Jutland centenary: HMS *New Zealand*', *Sea Breezes*, 25 April 2016.

Roskill, S W, 'The dismissal of Admiral Jellicoe', *Journal of Contemporary History*, Vol. 1, No. 4, 1966.

Rubin, Louis D, Jr, 'The continuing argument over Jutland', *The Virginia Quarterly Review*, Vol. 77, No. 4, Autumn 2001.

Scheer, Reinhard, *Germany's High Seas Fleet in the World War*, Cassell & Co., London, 1920.

Schliehauf, William, 'A concentrated effort: Royal Navy gunnery exercises at the end of the Great War', *Warship International*, Vol. 35, No. 2, 1998.

Schmalenbach, Paul, 'SMS *Blucher*', *Warship International*, No. 2, June 30, 1971.

Seligman, Matthew S, 'A great American scholar of the Royal Navy? The disputed legacy of Arthur Marder revisited', *The International History Review*, Vol. 38, No. 5, 2016.

Seligman, Matthew, 'Intelligence information and the 1909 Naval Scare: the Secret Foundations of a Public Panic', *War in History*, Vol. 17, No. 1, 2010.

Shannon, Richard, *Gladstone , Vol. II, 1865–1898*, University of North Carolina Press, Chapel Hill, 1999.

Sinclair, Keith, *A History of New Zealand*, Pelican, London, 1959, Revised Edition, 1969.

Smith, Paul, 'Ruling the waves: government, the service and the cost of naval supremacy 1885–99' in Paul Smith (ed), *Government and Armed Forces in Britain, 1856–1990*, Hambledon Press, London, 1996.

Sprout, Margaret Tuttle 'Mahan, Evangelist of Sea Power' in E M Earle (ed) *Makers of Modern Strategy,* Princeton University Press, Princeton, 1971.

Staff, Gary, *Skagerrak: the Battle of Jutland through German eyes*, Pen and Sword Maritime, Barnsley, 2016.

Steel, Nigel and Peter Hart, *Jutland 1916: Death in the Grey Wastes*, Cassell, London, 2004.

Stern, Robert, *The Battleship Holiday*, Seaforth, Barnsley, 2017.

Sturton, Ian, (ed), *Conway's All The World's Battleships 1906 to the present*, Conway Maritime Press, London, 1987.

Sumida, Jon Tetsuro, 'Expectation, Adaptation and Resignation: British battle fleet tactical planning, August 1914– April 1916', *Naval War College Review*, Vol. 60, No. 3, 2007.

Taylor, Carlisle, *Life of Admiral Mahan*, John Murray, London, 1920.

Tikkanen, Henrikki, 'Favouritism is the secret of efficiency!' Admiral Sir John Fisher as the First Sea Lord, 1904–1910, *Management and Organisational History*, March 2016.

Trainor, Luke, *British Imperialism and Australian Nationalism: Manipulation, Conflict and compromise in the late nineteenth century*, Cambridge University Press, 1994.

Warren, Kenneth, *Steel, Ships and Men: Cammell Laird, 1824–1993*, Liverpool University Press, Liverpool, 1998.

Wodehouse, John, ed. Angus Hawkins and John Powell, *The Journal of John Wodehouse, First Early of Kimberley, 1862–1902*, Camden Fifth Series, Vol. 9, Royal Historical Society, University College, London, 1997.

Wood, F L W, 'Why did New Zealand not join the Australian Commonwealth in 1900–01?' *New Zealand Journal of History*, Vol. 2,

No. 2, October 1968.

Woodward, David, 'Heligoland: the first sea battle' in Bernard Fitzsimons (ed), *Warships and Sea Battles of the First World War*, Ure Smith, Sydney, 1973.

Wright, Matthew, *Blue Water Kiwis*, Reed, Auckland, 2001.

Wright, Matthew, and Graham Howard, 'The Reserve Bank Inflation Calculator', Reserve Bank of New Zealand *Bulletin*, Vol. 66, No. 4, December 2003.

Wright, Matthew, 'The policy origins of the Reserve Bank of New Zealand', Reserve Bank of New Zealand *Bulletin*, Vol. 69, No. 3, September 2006.

Wright, Matthew, *Two Peoples, One Land*, Reed, Auckland, 2006.

Wright, Matthew, 'Mordacious years: socio-economic aspects and outcomes of New Zealand's experience in the Great Depression', Reserve Bank of New Zealand *Bulletin*, Vol. 72, No. 3, September 2009.

Wright, Matthew, *Convicts: New Zealand's Hidden Criminal Past*, Penguin, Auckland, 2010.

Wright, Matthew, *Guns and Utu*, Penguin, Auckland, 2011.

Wright, Matthew, *Illustrated History of New Zealand*, David Bateman, Auckland, 2012.

Wright, Matthew, *The New Zealand Experience at Gallipoli and the Western Front*, Oratia Books, Auckland, 2017.

Wright, Matthew, *The History of Hawke's Bay*, Intruder Books, Wellington, 2019 (second edition).

Wright, Matthew, *Waitangi: A Living Treaty*, Bateman Books, Auckland, 2019.

Wynd, Michael, 'HMS *New Zealand* in World War I', in Andrew Forbes (ed), *The War At Sea, proceedings of the King-Hall Naval History Conference 2013*, Sea Power Centre, Canberra

Websites

http://adb.anu.edu.au/biography
http://dreadnoughtproject.org
http://navymuseum.co.nz
www.clydeships.co.uk
www.london-weather.eu
www.navweaps.com
www.nzlii.org/nz/legis/hist_act/nda19099ev1909n9194
www.theriddleofthesands.com
https://discovery.nationalarchives.gov.uk
https://knowledgebank.org.nz

https://mises.org
https://navymuseum.co.nz
https://teara.govt.nz/en/biographies
www.businessinsider.com.au
www.canterburymuseum.com
www.gracesguide.co.uk
www.jutlandcrewlists.org
www.loc.gov/law
www.merriam-webster.com/dictionary
www.naval-encyclopedia.com
www.naval-history.net
www.navyhistory.org.au
www.northeastmedals.co.uk
www3.stats.govt.nz

About the author

Matthew Wright is a New Zealand writer with over 35 years hands-on professional experience as a published author and in publishing. He has qualifications in writing, music and anthropology, and holds multiple post-graduate degrees in history. He is a Fellow of the Royal Historical Society at University College, London.

His published work includes over 600 articles, academic papers and reviews, and over 60 books on topics that include biography, engineering, military and social history. These include a best-selling general history of New Zealand and two critically acclaimed biographies of Lieutenant-General Sir Bernard Freyberg. He has been published by Penguin Random House, Bateman Books and Oratia Books.

Visit Matthew Wright online at www.matthewwright.net

NOTES

Introduction

1   AJHR 1909, 1909 Session I, A-04, Despatches regarding the Imperial Conference and the dreadnought offer, Despatch from the Rt. Hon The Prime Minister, Wellington, to His Excellency the Governor, Woodville, 22 March 1909.

2   See e.g. Ian Sturton (ed), *Conway's All The World's Battleships 1906 to the present*, Conway Maritime Press, London, 1987, p. 59; repeated as if true, including on social media, see, e.g. 'Drachinifel' HMS *New Zealand* – Guide 201, accessed 18 October 2020.

3   For example, Norman Friedman, *The British Battleship 1906–1946*, Seaforth, Barnsley, 2015, p. 105, claimed that the 1909 Imperial Conference (wrongly called 'Colonial' in this account) was followed by the Australian decision to buy a battlecruiser and that New Zealand then followed suit. This sequence was precisely backwards.

4   See, e.g. https://teara.govt.nz/en/artwork/34120/hms-new-zealand, accessed 30 March 2021.

5   See, e.g. http://navymuseum.co.nz/hms-new-zealand-piupiu, accessed 12 April 2020.

6   Richard Hough, *Admiral of the Fleet: The life of John Fisher*, Macmillan, New York, 1969, p. 26, 180: Ruddock F Mackay, *Fisher of Kilverstone*, Clarendon Press, Oxford 1973, p. 513.

7   James Goldrick, 'The problems of modern naval history', *The Great Circle*, Vol. 18, No. 1, pp. 48–58, Australian Association for Maritime History, 1996.

8   Canterbury Museum, Folder 698, 199/75, Diary of Captain (Lt Commander) A D Boyle, 28 August 1914.

9   For discussion see Chapters 5 and 6.

10 As example, *Battle of Jutland*, 30th May to 1st June 1916, Official Despatches, HMSO, London, 1920, see, e.g. pp. 5, 7 etc.

Chapter 1. The Prussia of the Pacific

1   Beatty had been knighted on 22 June: *The Edinburgh Gazette*, 23 June 1914, p. 717.

2   www.dreadnoughtproject.org/tfs/index.php/H.M.S._New_Zealand_at_the_Battle_of_Heligoland_Bight, accessed 1 May 2020.

3   David Woodward, 'Heligoland: the first sea battle' in Bernard Fitzsimons (ed), *Warships and Sea Battles of the First World War*, Ure Smith, Sydney, 1973, p. 24. German ships were penned up behind the outer Jade bar until at least noon, due to tide; but the British apparently did not know this.

4   Robert K Massie, *Castles of Steel*, Pimlico, London, 2005, pp. 93–94.

5   See, e.g. *The Scotsman*, 28 August 1914; *Sheffield Independent*, 28 August 1914, *Yorkshire Post and Leeds Intelligencer*, 26 August 1914, *Evening Mail*, 28 August 1914, etc.

6   The 12in Mk X weapons of *New Zealand* and *Invincible* typically fired 850lb shells; the Mk V 13.5in of *Lion* and *Princess Royal* fired 1,250lb shells; the Mk V 13.5in of *Queen Mary* 1,400lb shells. For summaries see www.navweaps.com/Weapons/WNBR_Main.php, accessed 30 March 2021.

7   These were 1905 figures, see S Broadberry and C Burhop, 'Real Wages and Labor Productivity in Britain and Germany: a Unified Approach to the International

Comparison of Living Standards', 2010, http://dx.doi.org/10.1017/S0022050710000331, pp. 405, 408.

8   Murray Robinson, 'Battle of Jutland centenary: HMS New Zealand', *Sea Breezes*, 25 April 2016, www.seabreezes.co.im/index.php/features/ships/2111-battle-of-jutland-centenaryhms-new-zealand, accessed 10 February 2020. This was not the director control system installed later, see R A Burt, *British Battleships of World War One*, Seaforth, Barnsley, 2012, p. 13.

9   Wtu qMS-0545, Coore, E G B, fl.1913–1914: Journal: particularly interpolated water-colours.

10   The 'Gunnery Drill Book for His Majesty's Fleet. Book I. 1913' indicates forty-nine men were involved; Robinson indicates forty-four.

11   Gun statistics noted in www.navweaps.com/Weapons/WNBR_12-45_mk10.php, accessed 10 February 2020.

12   'A Battleship's Engine Rooms', *The Press*, 17 April 1913.

13   www.dreadnoughtproject.org/tfs/index.php/H.M.S._New_Zealand_at_the_Battle_of_Heligoland_Bight, accessed 1 May 2020; see also Wtu qMS-0545, Coore, E G B, fl.1913–1914: Journal, 28 August 1914.

14   Coore, E G B, fl.1913–1914: Journal, 28 August 1914, see workbook.

15   Wtu fMS-195, *New Zealand* (ship), Captain's Ship's Book gives rpm values.

16   Burt, *British Battleships of World War One*, p. 112, notes trials speed of 26.3 knots; but see also the Captain's Ship's Book.

17   Burt, *British Battleships of World War One*, p. 109.

18   Wtu qMS-0545, Coore, E G B, fl.1913–1914: Journal, information card, appended in January 1913 entries.

19   'A Battleship's Engine Rooms', *The Press*, 17 April 1913.

20   For description see http://dreadnoughtproject.org/tfs/index.php/Kilroy_Stoking_Indicator, accessed 10 February 2020.

21   www.jutlandcrewlists.org/new-zealand, accessed 6 June 2020.

22   Ibid.

23   Ibid.

24   https://discovery.nationalarchives.gov.uk/details/r/D6746074, accessed 6 June 2020.

25   James Goldrick, 'Coal and the advent of the First World War at sea', *War in History*, Vol. 2, No. 3, 2014, p. 328.

26   'A Battleship's Engine Rooms', *The Press*, 17 April 1913.

27   Goldrick, 'Coal and the advent of the First World War at sea', p. 329.

28   'A Battleship's Engine Rooms', *The Press*, 17 April 1913.

29   Murray Robinson, 'Battle of Jutland centenary: HMS New Zealand', *Sea Breezes*, 25 April 2016, www.seabreezes.co.im/index.php/features/ships/2111-battle-of-jutland-centenaryhms-new-zealand accessed 10 February 2020.

30   Burt, *British Battleships of World War One*, pp. 109, 112.

31   Depth in the Heligoland Bight averaged 51m (around 154ft).

32   qMS-0545, Coore, E G B, fl.1913–1914: Journal, 28 August 1914.

33   www.dreadnoughtproject.org/tfs/index.php/H.M.S._New_Zealand_at_the_Battle_of_Heligoland_Bight

34   qMS-0545, Coore, E G B, fl.1913–1914: Journal, 28 August 1914.

35   www.dreadnoughtproject.org/tfs/index.php/H.M.S._New_Zealand_at_the_Battle_of_Heligoland_Bight, accessed 8 February 2020. The Royal Navy had not adopted the twenty-four-hour clock at this time.

36 www.dreadnoughtproject.org/tfs/index.php/H.M.S._New_Zealand_at_the_Battle_of_Heligoland_Bight, accessed 8 February 2020.

37 Matthew Wright, *The New Zealand Experience at Gallipoli and the Western Front*, Oratia Books, Auckland, 2017, pp. 32–34.

38 Ibid., pp. 92–95, 178–180.

39 Useful early summary of the phenomenon is in Albert T Lauterbach, 'Militarism in the Western World: A comparative study', *Journal of the History of Ideas*, Vol. 5, No. 4, October 1944, esp. pp. 458–460.

40 Niall Ferguson, *Empire: how Britain made the modern world*, Penguin, London, 2004, pp. 222–240.

41 Via Roger Fenton's work, see Hirst Milhollen, 'Roger Fenton, Photographer of the Crimean War', *Quarterly Journal of Current Acquisitions*, Vol. 3, No. 4, August 1946, Library of Congress.

42 For discussion see, e.g. J A Mangan, '"Muscular, Militaristic and Manly": the British middle-class hero as moral messenger', *The International Journal of the History of Sport*, Vol. 13, No. 1, 1996.

43 W Baring Pemberton, *Battles of the Crimean War*, Pan, London, 1968, pp. 100–108.

44 Cited in James Morris *Pax Britannica*, Faber and Faber, London, 1968, p. 118.

45 www.theriddleofthesands.com/by-jingo-macdermotts-war-song-1878-g-w-hunt, accessed 12 February 2020.

46 Morris, *Pax Britannica*, p. 404.

47 Alan Blum 'A history of tobacco trading cards', in Karen Slama (ed), *Tobacco and Health*, Plenum Press, New York, 1995, p. 923.

48 www.nam.ac.uk/explore/garnet-wolseley, accessed 20 April 2020. There has been debate as to whether Wolseley was the specific target.

49 Morris *Pax Britannica*, p. 404.

50 J A Mangan, 'Duty unto death: English masculinity and militarism in the age of new imperialism', *The International Journal of the History of Sport*, Vol. 12, No. 2, 1995.

51 Byron Farwell, *Queen Victoria's Little Wars*, Allen Lane, London, 1973, pp. 253–294.

52 See, e.g. Niall Ferguson, *Empire: how Britain made the modern world*, Penguin, London, 2004, pp. 222–240.

53 Ibid., p. 222.

54 Norman Friedman, *British Battleships of the Victorian Era*, Seaforth, Barnsley, 2018, pp. 180, 222–223.

55 Ibid., pp. 137–38, 184, 190–191 is illustrative.

56 Paul Smith, 'Ruling the waves: government, the service and the cost of naval supremacy 1885–99' in Paul Smith (ed), *Government and Armed Forces in Britain, 1856–1990*, Hambledon Press, London, 1996, p. 24.

57 See, e.g. *Pall Mall Gazette*, 26 September 1884, 21 October 1884.

58 John Wodehouse, ed. Angus Hawkins and John Powell, *The Journal of John Wodehouse, First Earl of Kimberley, 1862–1902*, Camden Fifth Series, Vol. 9, Royal Historical Society, University College, London, 1997, p. 350.

59 Smith, p. 24.

60 Michael Collins, 'The Banking Crisis of 1878', *Economic History Review*, 2nd Series, Vol. XLII, No. 4, pp. 504–527.

61 Arthur Marder, *The Anatomy of British Sea Power*, Frank Cass, London, 1940, p. 106, quoting Lord George Hamilton, First Sea Lord.

62 Friedman, *British Battleships of the Victorian Era*, p. 250.

63   Michael Partridge, *Gladstone*, Routledge, London, 2003, p. 231.

64   Richard Shannon, *Gladstone , Vol. II, 1865–1898*, University of North Carolina Press, Chapel Hill, 1999, p. 552.

65   See www.dreadnoughtproject.org/tfs/index.php/John_Poyntz_Spencer,_Fifth_ Earl_Spencer, accessed July 2020.

66   See, e.g. Partridge, pp. 230–231.

67   Ibid., p. 231.

68   Ibid., p. 233.

69   Matthew Wright, *Illustrated History of New Zealand*, David Bateman, Auckland, 2012, pp. 61–71.

70   Ibid., p. 102.

71   Ibid., pp. 177–178.

72   Ibid., pp. 225–228.

73   Matthew Wright, *Blue Water Kiwis*, Reed, Auckland, 2001, pp. 11–12.

74   *New Zealand Statutes 1887*, 51 Vict, pp. 129–31.

75   *New Zealand Parliamentary Debates* (NZPD), 1909 Vol. 148, p. 809.

76   Some in Fiji petitioned for it, see *AJHR* 1900 Session 1, A-3g,'Federation of Fiji with New Zealand'.

77   Matthew Wright, *Blue Water Kiwis*, Reed, Auckland, 2001, p. 19.

78   Farwell, pp. 339–353.

79   John Crawford and Ellen Ellis, *To Fight for the Empire: An Illustrated History of New Zealand and the South African War, 1899–1902*, Reed, Auckland, 1999, p. 14.

80   Wtu MS-Papers-8464-05, Leece, George, 1865–1901, Papers, George Leece to his mother, 24 September 1900.

81   Luke Trainor, *British Imperialism and Australian Nationalism: Manipulation, Conflict and compromise in the late nineteenth century*, Cambridge University Press, 1994, pp. 9–11.

82   F L W Wood, 'Why did New Zealand not join the Australian Commonwealth in 1900–1901', *New Zealand Journal of History* Vol. 2, No. 2, October 1968, pp. 115–129.

83   Argued by ibid., p. 127.

Chapter 2: An Impetuous Offer?

1   ANZ, Allen Papers, 'Naval Defence – General'. Un-numbered file, letter 12 February 1914, Allen to Australian Minister of Defence.

2   Neville Meaney *The Search for Security in the Pacific*, Vol. 1, Sydney University Press, Sydney, 1976, p. 177.

3   This was the interpretation of T G Weir 'New Zealand's Naval Policy, 1909–14', Unpub. MA thesis, Univ. Canterbury, 1973.

4   For New Zealand's interwar naval defence policies see Wright, *Blue Water Kiwis*, pp. 66–71.

5   See www.jutlandcrewlists.org/new-zealand, accessed 26 August 2020.

6   Andrew Roberts, *Salisbury: Victorian Titan*, Phoenix, 2000, p. 629.

7   These were, in order, seven *Royal Sovereigns*, one *Hood*, nine *Majestics*, six *Canopus'*; eight *Formidable*s in three batches with slight differences between each; six *Duncan*s; and eight *King Edward VII*s. Fred. T Jane (ed), *Jane's Fighting Ships 1914*, Sampson Low Marston, London, 1914; David & Charles reprint 1968, pp. 47–54.

8   Two *Centurions*, one *Renown* and two *Triumphs*; see, e.g. ibid., p. 48.

9   Ibid., pp. 55–62. Not including the *Defence* class of the 1904–05 programme.

10   See, e.g. James Morris, *Pax Britannica*, Faber & Faber, London, 1968, pp. 425–426;

Byron Farwell, *Queen Victoria's Little Wars*, Allen Lane, London, 1973, pp. 12, 21–22, 136–37, 342–43.

11 Noted in, e.g. John Brooks, 'Dreadnought: Blunder or Stroke of Genius?', *War in History*, Vol. 14, No. 2 (April 2007), pp. 157–178.

12 H H Asquith, *The Genesis of the War*, London, 1923, p. 112.

13 Jan Morris, *Fisher's Face*, Penguin, London, 1995, p. 125.

14 Mackay, p. 513.

15 For analysis see Henrikki Tikkanen, 'Favouritism is the secret of efficiency!' Admiral Sir John Fisher as the First Sea Lord, 1904–1910, *Management and Organisational History*, March 2016.

16 For discussion see Henry S Morgan, Jr, 'The Fisher Revolution: reforms in the Royal Navy 1890–1910, early naval management in action', Master of Science thesis, United States Naval Postgraduate School 1964, esp. pp 49–50, 93.

17 P K Kemp (ed), *The Fisher Papers*, Vol. I, Navy Records Society, London, 1960, p. 19.

18 His first day in the office was actually 20 October, see Ruddock F Mackay, *Fisher of Kilverstone*, Clarendon Press, Oxford 1973, pp. 313, 315.

19 Duncan Redford and Philip D Grove, *The Royal Navy: A history since 1900*, I B Taurus/National Museum, New York, 2014, pp. 10–12.

20 Mackay, p. 312.

21 See, e.g. Jan Morris, *Fisher's Face*, pp. 123–125.

22 Maurice Hankey, *The Supreme Command*, Vol. I, Allen & Unwin, London, 1961, p. 24.

23 Redford and Grove, p. 13.

24 Mackay, p. 315.

25 Marder, *The Anatomy of British Sea Power*, p. 68. For further analysis, see Margaret Tuttle Sprout 'Mahan, Evangelist of Sea Power' in E M Earle (ed) *Makers of Modern Strategy*, Princeton University Press, Princeton, 1971, pp. 415–445; William Reitzel 'Mahan on Use of the Sea' from B Mitchell-Simpson III (ed), *Wars, Strategy and Maritime Power*, Rutger's University Press, New Brunswick, New Jersey, 1977, pp. 95–107; and for biographical details see e.g. Carlisle Taylor, *Life of Admiral Mahan*, John Murray, London, 1920.

26 Kemp (ed), *Fisher Papers*, Vol. I, pp. 160–61.

27 Redford and Grove, pp. 16–17.

28 Hankey, Vol. I, p. 27.

29 Mackay, p. 315.

30 Ibid., p. 316.

31 Hankey, Vol. I, p. 38.

32 Kemp (ed), *Fisher Papers*, Vol. I, p. 81.

33 Ibid., p. 17.

34 Ibid., p. 159.

35 P K Kemp (ed), *The Fisher Papers*, Vol. II, Navy Records Society, London, 1964, p. 81. Fisher's italics.

36 Richard Dunley, 'Sir John Fisher and the policy of strategic deterrence, 1904–1908', War in History, Vol. 22, No. 2, April 2015, pp. 155–173, esp. p. 157.

37 Arthur Marder (ed), *Fear God and Dread Nought: The Correspondence of Admiral of the Fleet Lord Fisher of Kilverstone*, Vol. II, Jonathan Cape, London, 1956, p. 85.

38 For discussion see Ruddock Mackay 'The Admiralty, the German Navy, and the re-distribution of the British fleet 1904–05', *Mariner's Mirror* Vol. 56 No. 3, August 1970, pp. 341–46.

39   Correspondence in Marder (ed), *Fear God and Dread Nought*, Vol. II, pp. 318–464.

40   Paul Haggie 'The Royal Navy and War Planning in the Fisher Era', *Journal of Contemporary History*, Vol. 8 No. 3, July 1973, pp. 113–131. p. 130.

41   For example, David K Brown, 'British Warship Design Methods 1860–1905', *Warship International*
      Vol. 32, No. 1 (1995), pp. 59–82; R A Burt, *British Battleships 1889–1904*, Seaforth, Barnsley, 1988; Roger Chesneau and Eugene M Kolesnik, *Conway's All The World's Warships 1860–1905*, Conway Maritime Press, London, 1979.

42   See, e.g. Brooks, 'Dreadnought: Blunder or Stroke of Genius?'

43   Fisher was aware of it, see Brooks, 'Dreadnought: blunder, or stroke of genius?', p. 169.

44   Noted in ibid., p. 165.

45   Scott M Lindgren, 'The genesis of a cruiser navy: British first-class cruiser development 1884–1909', PhD Thesis, University of Salford, 2013, p. 276.

46   www.gracesguide.co.uk/Albert_John_Durston, accessed 26 July 2020; see also Brooks, p. 163.

47   Don Leggett, 'Spectacle and witnessing: constructing readings of Charles Parsons' marine turbine', *Technology and Culture*, Vol. 52, No. 2, April 2011, pp. 305–306.

48   *Auckland Star*, 28 June 1907.

49   See, e.g. *Star* [Christchurch], 4 October 1904.

50   http://dreadnoughtproject.org/tfs/index.php/H.M.S._Dreadnought_(1906)#cite_ref-42, accessed 28 July 2018.

51   Noted by Morris, *Fisher's Face*, p. 90.

52   See, e.g. *Poverty Bay Herald*, 29 May 1905.

53   Quoted in *The Press*, 28 February 1906.

54   Published in *New Zealand Times*, 5 May 1906.

55   *Star* [Christchurch], 8 February 1907.

56   *Evening Star*, 20 October 1906

57   Peter Padfield, *The Great Naval Race: Anglo-German naval rivalry 1900–1914*, Hart-Davis, London, 1974, p. 93.

58   Trainor, pp. 12–15.

59   http://adb.anu.edu.au/biography/creswell-sir-william-rooke-5817, accessed 28 July 2020.

60   G Greenwood and C Grimshad (eds), *Documents on Australian International Affairs*, 1901–1918, Thomas Nelson (Australia) Ltd, Melbourne 1977, p. 109.

61   The Australian Capital Territory was formed in 1911 and work began on the capital, Canberra, in 1913; Parliament House was formally opened there in 1927.

62   Greenwood and Grimshad (ed), p. 114. The *Royal Arthur* was the flagship of the Australasian Squadron.

63   Ibid., pp. 115–16.

64   I H Nish 'Australia and the Anglo Japanese Alliance', *Australian Journal of Politics and History*, Vol. 9 No. 2, Nov 1963, pp. 201–12.

65   *New Zealand Parliamentary Debates* 1909, Vol. 148, p. 809.

66   General Assembly Library (GA), CD 4948 'Conference with the representatives of the self-governing Dominions on the naval and military defence of the Empire, 1909', p. 26.

67   M P Lissington, *New Zealand and Japan 1900–41*, Government Printer, Wellington, 1972, p. 1; see also Meaney, Vol. I, p. 10.

68   Greenwood & Grimshad (eds), p. 143.

69   Ibid., pp. 144–45.

70   Meaney, Vol. I, p. 10.

71 R19162149 ACHK 16603 G48 5 / F/4 G48 'Admiral Fanshawe – Vulnerability of Australia and New Zealand', Confidential Enclosure.

72 The Commander in Chief, Admiral Sir Gerard Noel, became a devout anti-Fisherite.

73 R19162149 ACHK 16603 G48 5 / F/4 G48 'Admiral Fanshawe – Vulnerability of Australia and New Zealand', Confidential Enclosure.

74 *New Zealand Herald*, 1 July 1905, editorial and supplement.

75 Ibid., 3 July 1905.

76 Quoted in Greenwood & Grimshad (eds), p. 205.

77 General Assembly Library (GA), Command Paper CD 3524 'Papers Laid before the Imperial Conference, 1907', p. 48, Document 1 "Report of the Committee of Imperial Defence on the Question of a General Scheme of Defence for Australia – May 1906', p. 48.

78 Ibid., p. 40.

79 R19162355 ACHK 16604 G49 17/34 G49 (a) Defence Scheme of New Zealand, 1906 (Copy No. 5) – (b) Defence Scheme of New Zealand, 1908 [with attached correspondence dated 1913].

80 GA Command Paper CD 3524 'Papers Laid before the Imperial Conference, 1907', 'Report of the Committee of Naval officers of the Commonwealth assembled at Melbourne, Victoria, to consider the Memorandum of the Committee of Imperial Defence, and Report as Regards the Naval Defence of Australia', p. 54.

81 G Greenwood & C Grimshad (eds), p. 140.

82 Ibid., p. 143.

83 A R Barclay, 'The Premier and his troubles', S Lister, Printer, Dunedin, 1909, p. 11.

84 Wright, *Illustrated History of New Zealand*, pp. 246–250.

85 Keith Sinclair, *A History of New Zealand*, Pelican, London, 1959, Revised Edition 1969, p. 207.

86 F L W Wood 'Why did New Zealand not join the Australian Commonwealth in 1900–01?' *New Zealand Journal of History*, Vol. 2, No. 2, October 1968, pp. 115–129, p. 121.

87 Trainor, pp. 15–17.

88 GA CD 3524 'Papers', p. 38.

89 Greenwood and Grimshad (eds), p. 149.

90 General Assembly Library (GA), Command Paper CD 3524, 'Minutes of the Proceedings of the Colonial Conference, 1907', pp. 134–36.

91 R A Loughmann, *Life of Sir Joseph Ward*, Dunedin, 1928, pp. 145–46.

92 Ibid., p. 129.

93 GA, Command Paper CD 3524 'Minutes of the Proceedings of the Colonial Conference, 1907', p. 134.

94 ANZ G2/17 Dominions No. 5 'Correspondence relating to the Imperial Conference', pp. 136–37.

95 General Assembly Library (GA), Command Paper CD 4325, 'Correspondence relating to the Naval Defence of Australia and New Zealand', p. 5.

96 ANZ R24501803 ACHK 16558 G2 17/1909/696, 'Imperial Defence Conference. Papers for publication and copies of confidential proceedings, 'Confidential Papers laid before the Imperial Defence Conference 1909', p. 142.

97 Greenwood and Grimshad (eds), p. 160.

98 ANZ R24501803 ACHK 16558 G2 17/1909/696, 'Imperial Defence Conference. Papers for publication and copies of confidential proceedings, 'Confidential Papers laid before

the Imperial Defence', Conference 1909', p. 176.

99   Ibid., p. 69.

100   Ibid.

101   NZPD, Vol. 143 1908, pp. 554–89.

102   Roger Parkinson, *Dreadnought: the ship that changed the world*, I B Tauris, 2015, p. 142.

103   Cited in ibid.

104   Friedman, *The British Battleship 1906–1946*, p. 96.

105   Reproduced in www.dreadnoughtproject.org/tfs/index.php?title=A_Statement_of_Admiralty_Policy&redirect=no#SHIPBUILDING_POLICY., accessed 11 August 2020.

106   See, e.g. Friedman, *The British Battleship 1906–1946*, p. 97.

107   Burt, *British Battleships of World War One*, p. 104.

108   Ibid., p. 106.

109   Ibid., p. 109; see also Fred. T Jane (ed), *Jane's Fighting Ships 1914*, p. 44.

110   Noted by Norman Friedman, *Naval Weapons of World War One*, Seaforth, Barnsley, 2011, imprint page.

111   *Wairarapa Age*, 19 December 1908.

112   Ibid.

113   See Matthew Seligman, 'Intelligence information and the 1909 Naval Scare: the Secret Foundations of a Public Panic', *War in History*, Vol. 17, No. 1, 2010, pp. 45–52.

114   Ibid., p. 51.

115   Peter Padfield, *The Great Naval Race: Anglo-German Naval Rivalry 1900–1914*, Hart-Davis, MacGibbon, London, 1974, p. 200.

116   Mackay, *Fisher of Kilverstone*, pp. 388–390.

117   Seligman, 'Intelligence information and the 1909 Naval Scare', pp. 55–56.

118   Parkinson, p. 144.

119   Robert K Massie, *Dreadnought: Britain, Germany and the Coming of the Great War*, Random House, New York, 1991, p. 613.

120   Sir Edward Grey to Sir Edward Goschen, 4 January 1909, in G P Gooch and Harold Temperley (eds), *British Documents on the Origins of the War 1898–1914, Vol. VI, Anglo-German tension*, H M Stationery Office, London, 1930; Johnson Reprint Corporation, London, p. 237.

121   Parkinson, p. 143.

122   Massie, p. 614.

123   See, e.g. *Wanganui Herald*, 6 February 1909.

124   Seligman, 'Intelligence information and the 1909 Naval Scare: the Secret Foundations of a Public Panic', p. 50.

125   Parkinson, p. 144.

126   Massie, *Dreadnought*, p. 615.

127   Parkinson, p. 144.

128   See, e.g. *Wairarapa Age*, 3 March 1909.

129   'Reginald McKenna introduces the 1909–10 estimates' in W D Handcock and David Charles Douglas (eds), *English Historical Documents 1974–1914*, Routledge, London, 1977, pp. 412–413.

130   Edward William Humphreys, 'Some aspects of the federal political career of Andrew Fisher', MA Thesis, University of Melbourne 2005, pp. 24, 27.

131   *The Age*, 18 March 1909.

132   *Sydney Morning Herald*, 19 March 1909.

133 *Evening Post*, 18 March 1909.

134 *The Age*, 19 March 1909.

135 Ibid.

136 *Appendix to the Journal of the House of Representatives*, 1909 Session I, A-04, 'Despatches regarding the Imperial Conference and the Dreadnought offer', Memo, 20 March 1909.

137 Ibid.

138 Ibid.

139 Ibid., 'In Cabinet' minute by J Hislop, 22 March 1909.

140 Ibid., Despatch from His Excellency the Governor, Kaikoura North, to the Right Hon. The Prime Minister, Wellington, 22 March 1909.

141 *Appendices to the Journal of the House of Representatives*, 1909 Session II, A-01 'Conference with the representatives of the self-governing Dominions on the naval and military defence of the Empire', Governor to Secretary of State, 22 March 1909.

142 Eric Grove, 'The battleship *Dreadnought*: technological, economic and strategic contexts', in Robert J Blyth, Andrew Lambert and Jan Ruger (eds), *The Dreadnought and the Edwardian Age*, National Maritime Museum, Surrey, 2011, p. 166.

Chapter 3: Politics of Construction

1 *Sydney Morning Herald*, 22 March 1909.

2 Ibid., 23 March 1909.

3 Ibid., 25 March 1909.

4 Ibid., 29 March 1909.

5 *Evening Post*, 22–27 March 1909.

6 GA CD 4949 'Conference with the representatives of the self-governing Dominions on the naval and military defence of the Empire, 1909', p. 3.

7 *Sydney Morning Herald*, 25 March 1909.

8 *Evening Post*, 31 March 1909.

9 GA CD 4948 'Conference with the representatives of the self-governing Dominions on the naval and military defence of the Empire, 1909', pp. 3–5.

10 As quoted by the *Evening Post*, 31 March 1909.

11 Ibid., 1 April 1909.

12 For useful summary see Nicholas Tracy (ed), *The Collective Naval Defence of Empire 1900–1940*, Introduction, Routledge for Navy Records Society, New York, 2019, p. xvi.

13 *The Times*, 26 March 1909.

14 Ibid.

15 GA CD 4948 'Conference with the representatives of the self-governing Dominions on the naval and military defence of the Empire, 1909', Secretary of State to the Governor-General, 30 April 1909.

16 ANZ R3485891, ACGO 8394, IA71 1/1913/1661, Box 5, 'Visit of HMS "New Zealand" (ship) – Correspondence concerning the building and equipping of the ship', 'Voice from England: 'Song of the Dreadnought by Harvey Holyoake'.

17 R24751781 AD1 565 D1909/2929, 'New Zealand offer of dreadnoughts – resolution of thanks by Chamber of Commerce, London', Hall-Jones to Acting Prime Minister, 29 July 1909.

18 Frances Porter, 'Scholefield, Guy Hardy', https://teara.govt.nz/en/biographies/4s12/scholefield-guy-hardy, accessed 29 August 2020.

19 *The Times*, 29 March 1909.

20 *Taranaki Herald*, 1 April 1909.

21 *Wairarapa Age*, 5 May 1909.
22 *New Zealand Times*, 7 April 1909.
23 *Press*, 14 May 1909.
24 *Manawatu Standard*, 16 April 1909.
25 *Wairarapa Age*, 16 April 1909.
26 *The Times*, 15 April 1909.
27 Ibid., 29 March 1909.
28 Ibid.
29 *The Times*, 3 April 1909.
30 According to Hankey, p. 20, the issues arose from an incident in 1900 when Fisher was Commander in Chief of the Mediterranean Fleet, and Beresford his second-in-command.
31 The tactic backfired. Noted by Arthur Marder, *From the Dreadnought to Scapa Flow*, Vol. I., Oxford University Press, London, 1961, p. 91.
32 Parkinson, p. 150.
33 Ibid., p. 149.
34 Command Paper 256 (1909), 'Report of the sub-committee of the Committee of Imperial Defence Appointed to Inquire into Certain Questions of Naval Policy raised by Lord Charles Beresford', p. 4.
35 Mackay, *Fisher of Kilverstone*, p. 412.
36 *The Times*, 3 April 1909.
37 Mackay, *Fisher of Kilverstone*, p. 413.
38 GA CD 4948 'Conference with the representatives of the self-governing Dominions on the naval and military defence of the Empire, 1909', Secretary of State to the Governor-General and Governors, 30 April 1909.
39 Ibid., Governor to Secretary of State, 7 May 1909.
40 GA CD 4948 'Conference with the representatives of the self-governing Dominions on the naval and military defence of the Empire, 1909',
41 Fisher to Esher, 13 September 1909, Arthur Marder (ed), *Fear God and Dread Nought*, Vol. II, Jonathan Cape, London, 1956, p. 266.
42 ANZ CO 209/270 Governor's secret quarterly report, May 1909.
43 Ibid.
44 NZPD, Vol. 146, 1909, p. 145.
45 ANZ R3485891, ACGO 8394, IA71 1/1913/1661, Box 1, 'Visit of HMS "New Zealand" (ship) – Correspondence concerning the building and equipping of the ship', Ward 'To editors', telegram, 22 March 1909.
46 NZPD, Vol. 146, 1909, p. 145.
47 Ibid., p. 184.
48 Ibid., pp. 155–69.
49 ANZ R21467087 AAYT 8490 N1 691/22/6/9 N1 'Naval Board and policy – Naval defence – Policy and agreement – New Zealand prior 1914, 1905–1914', 'Naval Defence', statement by Massey.
50 ANZ R3485891, ACGO 8394, IA71 1/1913/1661, Box 1, 'Visit of HMS "New Zealand" (ship) – Correspondence concerning the building and equipping of the ship', Copy of cable sent to Deputy London 154 June 1909.
51 GA CD 4948 'Conference', Acting Governor to the Secretary of State, 30 April 1909.
52 Todd Christopher Campbell, 'Financing the Royal Navy 1905–1914: sound finance in the Dreadnought era', MA Thesis, University of British Columbia, 1994, p. 71.
53 Noted in naval terms in Campbell, 'Financing the Royal Navy 1904–1914', p. 70.

54   Gooch and Temperley (eds), Heath to Goschen, 30 March 1909, p. 255.
55   ANZ, R24501803 ACHK 16558 G2 17/1909/696, 'Imperial Defence Conference. Papers for publication and copies of confidential proceedings', 'Confidential Papers laid before the Imperial Defence Conference 1909', Admiralty Memorandum.
56   Described as such to Gerard Fiennes, 14 April 1910. Arthur Marder (ed) *Fear God and Dread Nought*, Vol. II, Jonathan Cape, London, 1956, p. 321.
57   Mackay, p. 413.
58   Arthur Marder (ed), *Fear God and Dread Nought*, Vol. II, pp. 321–22.
59   ANZ R24501803 ACHK 16558 G2 17/1909/696, 'Imperial Defence Conference. Papers for publication and copies of confidential proceedings', 'Proceedings', p. 50.
60   Ibid., p. 48.
61   Ibid., p. 49.
62   Ibid., p. 48. Ward may have adopted the idea from Fisher, who had expounded such an opinion in 1904.
63   Ibid., p. 47.
64   Fisher to Esher, 13 September 1909, Arthur Marder (ed), *Fear God and Dread Nought*, Vol. II, p. 266. Fisher's italics.
65   Uncle of the author Graham Greene.
66   AJHR 1909 Session I, A-4a 'Naval and Military Defence of the Empire; conference with representatives of the self-governing Dominions on the, 1909', 'Admiralty Memorandum', McKenna to Ward, 18 August 1909, p. 26; Ward to McKenna, 11 August 1909.
67   Ibid., McKenna to Ward, 18 August 1909.
68   Mackay, *Fisher of Kilverstone*, p. 270.
69   Friedman, *The British Battleship 1906–1946*, p. 148.
70   Fisher to Gerard Fiennes, 14 April 1910 in Marder (ed), *Fear God and Dread Nought*, Vol. II, Jonathan Cape, London, 1956, p. 321.
71   Lindgren, p. 290.
72   Fisher to Arnold White, 8 January 1907, in Marder (ed), *Fear God and Dread Nought*, Vol. II, p. 112.
73   Noted in Mackay, p. 324.
74   Friedman, *The British Battleship 1906–1946*, pp. 84–88, offers useful summary.
75   William M McBride, 'Nineteenth century American warships: the pursuit of exceptionalist design', in Don Leggett and Richard Dunn (eds), *Re-inventing the Ship: Science, Technology and the Maritime World, 1800–1918*, Routledge, London, 2012, p. 202.
76   See, e.g. Matthew Seligman, 'Germany's Ocean Greyhounds and the Royal Navy's First Battle Cruisers: An Historiographical Problem', in *Diplomacy & Statecraft*, Vol. 27, No. 1, 2016, esp. pp 167–169.
77   Summarised in Christopher M Bell, 'Sir John Fisher's Naval Revolution Reconsidered: Winston Churchill at the Admiralty, 1911–1914', *War in History*, Vol. 18, No. 3, 2011, pp. 335–336.
78   Noted in Mackay, p. 322.
79   Reproduced in Admiral of the Fleet Lord Fisher, *Records*, Hodder & Stoughton, London, 1919, pp. 107–108. Fisher's intent with this selection of material was openly self-serving, underscoring his words.
80   Mackay, p. 325.
81   Noted in Nicholas A Lambert, 'Righting the scholarship: the battle-cruiser in history and historiography', *The Historical Journal*, Vol. 58 No. 1, March 2015.

82   Friedman, *The British Battleship 1906–1946*, pp. 96–97.
83   Typified by the three *Courageous* class 'large light cruisers', classified such for political reasons, with light-cruiser protection and scantling, but mounting 15 and 18in guns. See Sturton (ed), pp. 85–87.
84   These were *Indefatigable* (1908–09 programme) and *Lion* (1909–10 programme), see e.g. Friedman *The British Battleship 1906–1946*, p. 118.
85   www.navweaps.com/Weapons/WNBR_135-45_mk5.php, accessed 8 September 2020.
86   Friedman, *The British Battleship 1906–1946*, p. 114.
87   The guaranteed four were the 12in/50-calibre armed ships *Colossus* and *Hercules*; the 13.5in armed battleship *Orion*, and the 13.5in armed 'battleship-cruiser' *Lion*, see Friedman, *The British Battleship 1906–1946*, p. 118.
88   Ibid., pp. 114, 117.
89   Only achieved in service with difficulty, see Sturton (ed), p. 63.
90   Fisher to Arnold White, 12 October 1909, in Marder (ed) *Fear God and Dread Nought*, Vol. II, p. 276.
91   For summary compare Sturton (ed) pp. 59–60, 62–63.
92   Fisher to Arnold White, 12 October 1909, in Marder (ed) *Fear God and Dread Nought*, Vol. II, p. 276. Fisher's punctuation and italics.
93   Campbell, 'Financing the Royal Navy 1904–1914', p. 27.
94   Friedman, *The British Battleship 1906–1946*, p. 117.
95   Campbell, 'Financing the Royal Navy 1904–1914', p. 27.
96   These were the four *King George V* class and the battlecruiser *Queen Mary*. Sturton (ed), pp. 66–67.
97   Nicholas Lambert (ed), *Australia's Naval Inheritance*, Royal Australian Navy Maritime Studies Programme, Department of Defence (Navy), Canberra 1998, 'Notes of the proceedings of a conference at the Admiralty on Tuesday, 10 August 1909, p. 181.
98   Ibid., p. 181.
99   Argued by M Briggs, 'The too vast orb: the Admiralty and Australian naval defence 1881–1913', PhD thesis, University of Tasmania, 1991, p. 269.
100 See, e.g. Burt, *British Battleships of World War 1*, p. 111.
101 Friedman, *The British Battleship 1906–1946*, p. 118.
102 See, e.g. GA CD 4948 'Conference with the Representatives of the self-governing Dominions on the Naval and Military Defence of the Empire, 1909', which published transcripts and correspondence.
103 Noted in www.navweaps.com/Weapons/WNBR_12-50_mk11.php, accessed 6 September 2020.
104 For details of programme years see Ian Buxton and Ian Johnston, *The Battleship Builders: Constructing and Arming British Capital Ships*, Seaforth, Barnsley, 2013, p. 16.
105 www.navweaps.com/Weapons/WNBR_12-50_mk11.php, accessed 6 September 2020.
106 Buxton and Johnston, p. 20.
107 Naval Defence Act 1909 (9 EDW VII 1909 No. 9), www.nzlii.org/nz/legis/hist_act/nda19099ev1909n9194, accessed 23 November 2020.
108 *New Zealand Parliamentary Debates*, Second Session, 17th Parliament, November 10 to December 29 1909, Government Printer, 1909, pp. 874–876.
109 Ibid., p. 882.
110 *Wanganui Chronicle*, 10 December 1909.
111 Naval Defence Act 1909 (9 Edw VII 1909, No. 9) www.nzlii.org/nz/legis/hist_act/nda19099ev1909n9194/, accessed 23 November 2020.

112 ANZ R3485891, ACGO 8394, IA71 1/1913/1661, Box 1, 'Visit of HMS "New Zealand" (ship) – Correspondence concerning the building and equipping of the ship', William Hall-Jones to Ward, 4 March 1910,

113 Ibid., Hall-Jones to Ward, cablegram, 12 March 1910.

114 Ibid.

115 Ibid., William Hall-Jones to Ward, 18 March 1910.

116 Kenneth Warren, *Steel, Ships and Men: Cammell Laird, 1824–1993*, Liverpool University Press, Liverpool 1998, pp. 139–140.

117 Ian Buxton and Ian Johnston, *The Battleship Builders: Arming and Constructing British Capital Ships*, Seaforth, Barnsley, 2013, p. 79.

118 ANZ R3485891, ACGO 8394, IA71 1/1913/1661, Box 1, 'Visit of HMS "New Zealand" (ship) – Correspondence concerning the building and equipping of the ship', C I Thomas to Hall-Jones, 30 June 1910.

119 Ibid., William Hall-Jones to Ward, 18 March 1910; attached telegram 16 March 1910.

120 Ibid., C I Thomas to William Hall-Jones, 15 March 1910, Statement X.

121 Ibid., William Hall-Jones to Ward, 18 March 1910.

122 Ibid., noted in extracts from letter, 28 May 1910, from Sir W G Armstrong Whitworth & Co. Ltd.

123 Ibid.

124 Ibid., C I Thomas to William Hall-Jones, 14 March 1910, 'Statement shewing [sic] prices tendered for 12-inch mountings'.

125 Ibid.

126 Ibid.

127 Stephen Broadberry and Carsten Burhop, 'Real wages and labour productivity in Britain and Germany 1871–1938: a unified approach to the international comparison of living standards', University of Warwick, 2009, p. 28.

128 Ibid., p. 35.

129 Ibid., p. 30.

130 ANZ R3485891, ACGO 8394, IA71 1/1913/1661, Box 1, 'Visit of HMS "New Zealand" (ship) – Correspondence concerning the building and equipping of the ship', C I Thomas to Hall-Jones, 19 March 1910.

131 Ibid., Hall-Jones to Ward, 18 March 1910.

132 Wtu fMS-195, *New Zealand* (ship), Captain's Ship's Book.

133 ANZ R3485891, ACGO 8394, IA71 1/1913/1661, Box 1, 'Visit of HMS "New Zealand" (ship) – Correspondence concerning the building and equipping of the ship', Ward to Hall-Jones 14 March 1910.

134 This is contained in ANZ R3485891, ACGO 8394, IA71 1/1913/1661, Box 1–4, 'Visit of HMS "New Zealand" (ship) – Correspondence concerning the building and equipping of the ship', a massive correspondence file.

135 ANZ R3485891 ACGO 8394, IA71 1/1913/1661, Box 1, 'Visit of HMS "New Zealand" (ship) –Correspondence concerning the building and equipping of the ship', Hall-Jones to Ward, 21 April 1911.

136 Ibid., C I Thomas to Hall-Jones, 19 April 1911.

137 Ibid., Hall-Jones to Ward, 19 May 1911.

138 Ibid., C I Thomas to Hall-Jones, 1 April 1910.

139 Ibid., Hall-Jones to Ward, 8 April 1910.

140 https://nzhistory.govt.nz/media/video/hms-new-zealand-great-war-story, accessed 1 April 2021.

141 Figures in *New Zealand Yearbook* 1913,
www3.stats.govt.nz/New_Zealand_Official_Yearbooks/1913/NZOYB_1913.html,
accessed 29 November 2020.

142 ANZ CO 209/270 Governor's Secret Report, 14 June 1909.

143 See, e.g. Wright, *Illustrated History of New Zealand*, pp. 199–222.

144 See Appendix 2.

145 Figures in *New Zealand Yearbook* 1913,
www3.stats.govt.nz/New_Zealand_Official_Yearbooks/1913/NZOYB_1913.html,
accessed 29 November 2020.

146 Calculated from figures in *New Zealand Yearbook* 1913,
www3.stats.govt.nz/New_Zealand_Official_Yearbooks/1913/NZOYB_1913.html,
accessed 29 November 2020.

147 Calculated from ibid.

148 Calculated from ibid.

149 AJHR 1945, Session I, B-1 'Public Accounts for the Financial Year 1944–45', Part II,
p. xiii.

150 See Appendix 2.

151 Ibid., Hall-Jones to Ward, 24 March 1910.

152 Ibid., Hall-Jones to Ward, 3 May 1910.

153 AJHR 1913, Session I, B-06, 'Financial statement (in Committee of Supply 6th August
1913) by the Minister of Finance, The Hon. James Allen, p. xxvii.

154 AJHR 1912, Session II, B-18H, 'Prospectus of the £4,500,000 loan', p. 1.

155 ANZ R11741448 ADAV 16028 A5 141/23/48 Naval Defence Sinking Fund Account
1921–1938, 'Battle-cruiser "New Zealand"', n.d. typescript.

156 AJHR 1913, Session I, B-06, 'Financial statement (in Committee of Supply 6th August
1913) by the Minister of Finance, The Hon. James Allen, p. xxvii.

157 See Appendix 2.

158 ANZ R11741448 ADAV 16028 A5 141/23/48 Naval Defence Sinking Fund Account
1921–1938, 'Naval Defence Act Account'.

159 Ibid.

160 Ibid.

161 For further details see Appendix 2.

162 For discussion see Friedman, *The British Battleship 1906–1946*, pp. 119–121.

163 Cost of HMS *Orion* has been variously stated but is cited at this figure in www.naval-
encyclopedia.com/ww2/UK/orion-class-battleships-1911 accessed 12 February 2020.

164 https://api.parliament.uk/historic-hansard/commons/1910/jun/29/new-australian-
armoured-cruisers#S5CV0018P0_19100629_HOC_56, accessed 8 September 2020.

165 Jane (ed), *Jane's Fighting Ships 1914*, advertising section, pp. I–CX.

166 Ibid., front matter pp. I–CX.

167 Buxton and Johnston, p. 55.

168 Jane (ed), *Jane's Fighting Ships 1914*, advertising section, pp. I–CX.

169 Buxton and Johnston, pp. 79–80.

170 Ibid., p. 80.

171 ANZ R3485891 ACGO 8394, IA71 1/1913/1661, Box 1, 'Visit of HMS "New Zealand"
(ship) – Correspondence concerning the building and equipping of the ship', C. I.
Thomas to Hall-Jones, 1 April 1910.

172 Ibid., Hall-Jones to Ward, 17 June 1910.

173 Ibid., Extracts from letter, 28 May 1910, from Sir W G Armstrong Whitworth & Co. Ltd.

174   Ibid., W Graham-Greene to Hall-Jones, 14 October 1910.

175   www.dreadnoughtproject.org/tfs/index.php/The_Battle_Cruiser_in_the_Royal_Navy, accessed 11 September 2020.

176   Variously noted in ANZ R3485891 ACGO 8394, IA71 1/1913/1661, Box 1, 'Visit of HMS "New Zealand" (ship) – Correspondence concerning the building and equipping of the ship'.

177   See, e.g. www.merriam-webster.com/dictionary/battle%20cruiser, accessed 20 March 2021.

178   ANZ R3485891 ACGO 8394, IA71 1/1913/1661, Box 1, 'Visit of HMS "New Zealand" (ship) –Correspondence concerning the building and equipping of the ship', Wyllie's capitalisations, Wyllie to High Commissioner, 3 May 1910.

179   Ibid., Hall-Jones to Ward, 17 May 1910, citing telegram 10 June.

180   Ibid.

181   Ibid., McKenna to Hall-Jones, 17 June 1910.

182   Ibid., Ward to Hall-Jones, 23 June 1910.

183   Ibid., Hall-Jones to Ward, 1 July 1910.

184   Ibid., Cabinet memo, 2 July 1910.

185   See, e.g. ANZ R3485891 ACGO 8394, IA71 1/1913/1661, Box 2, 'Visit of HMS "New Zealand" (ship) – Correspondence concerning the building and equipping of the ship', Admiralty to British Mannesman Tube, 11 March 1911.

186   Ibid., Hall-Jones to Ward, 19 August 1910.

187   For useful summary see www.navweaps.com/index_nathan/metalprpsept2009.php accessed 24 September 2020.

188   ANZ R3485891 ACGO 8394, IA71 1/1913/1661, Box 1, 'Visit of HMS "New Zealand" (ship) – Correspondence concerning the building and equipping of the ship', W Graham-Greene to High Commissioner, 17 November 1911.

189   ANZ R3485891 ACGO 8394, IA71 1/1913/1661, Box 1, 'Visit of HMS "New Zealand" (ship) – Correspondence concerning the building and equipping of the ship', High Commissioner to Premier, 14 January 1911.

190   Ibid., McKenna to Hall-Jones, 1 December 1910.

191   Ibid., Hall-Jones to McKenna, 6 December 1910.

192   Reported in *New Zealand Times*, 4 July 1911.

193   *Mataura Ensign*, 23 October 1912; see also *New Zealand Times*, 4 July 1911.

194   Reported in the *Marlborough Express*, 3 July 1911.

195   Ibid.

196   R S Churchill, *W S Churchill Vol. II: The Young Statesman, 1901–14*, William Heinemann, London, 1967, p. 518.

197   Massie, *Dreadnought*, pp. 770–775.

198   See, e.g. Christopher M Bell, 'Sir John Fisher's naval revolution reconsidered: Winston Churchill at the Admiralty, 1911–1914', *War in History*, Vol. 18, No. 3, 2011; Nicholas Lambert, 'On Standards: a reply to Christopher Bell', *War in History*, Vol. 19, No. 2, 2012; Christopher M Bell, 'On Standards and Scholarship: A response to Nicholas Lambert', *War in History*, Vol. 20, No. 3, 2013.

199   ANZ R3485891 ACGO 8394, IA71 1/1913/1661, 'Visit of HMS "New Zealand" (ship) – Correspondence concerning the building and equipping of the ship', Box 3, 'Report of Pit Trial of "Q" turret of "New Zealand" (Colonial Cruiser) at Elswick – 20th October 1911."

200   Ibid., 'Report of Pit Trial of the 12-inch gun machinery of "P" turret of H M Battle

Cruiser New Zealand at Elswick Ordnance Works' 'Report of Pit Trial of the 12-inch gun machinery of "X" turret of H M Battle Cruiser New Zealand at Elswick Ordnance Works'; 'Report of Pit Trial of the 12-inch gun machinery of "A" turret of H M Battle Cruiser New Zealand at Elswick Ordnance Works'.

201 Ibid., 'Report of Pit Trial of the 12-inch gun machinery of "P" turret of H M Battle Cruiser New Zealand at Elswick Ordnance Works'.

202 Ibid., 'Report of Pit Trial of the 12-inch gun machinery of "A" turret of H M Battle Cruiser New Zealand at Elswick Ordnance Works'.

203 See Sturton (ed), pp. 29–30, 32, 35, 37–38.

204 Massie, *Dreadnought*, p. 769.

205 See, e.g. memo by Churchill to Cabinet, 22 June 1912, R S Churchill (ed), *W S Churchill Companion Vol. III*, William Heinemann, London, 1969, Part 3, pp. 1570–71.

206 Friedman, *The British Battleship 1906–1946*, p. 127.

207 For analysis see Matthew S Seligman, 'A great American scholar of the Royal Navy? The disputed legacy of Arthur Marder revisited', *The International History Review*, Vol. 38, No. 5, 2016, esp. pp. 1041–1042.

208 Norman Friedman, *Naval Weapons of World War I*, Seaforth, Barnsley, 2011, p. 44.

209 Noted in www.navweaps.com/Weapons/WNBR_15-42_mk1.php, accessed 14 September 2020.

210 Friedman, *The British Battleship 1906–1946*, p. 134.

211 Noted in Massie, *Dreadnought*, p. 784.

212 Friedman, *The British Battleship 1906–1946*, p. 133. They did not achieve this speed in service.

213 Ibid., pp. 136–137.

214 Massie, *Dreadnought*, p. 785.

215 Buxton and Johnston, p. 79.

216 Sturton (ed), p. 71.

217 See, e.g. R S Churchill (ed), *W S Churchill Companion Vol. III*, p. 1508.

218 Ibid., p. 1513.

219 R3485891, ACGO 8394, IA71 1/1913/1661, Box 3, 'Visit of HMS "New Zealand" (ship) – Correspondence concerning the building and equipping of the ship', MacKenzie to Governor, 12 April 1912.

220 AJHR 1912, Session II, A-4, 'Imperial Conference 1911 (papers paid before the, dealing with naval and military defence', Schedule B, p. 3.

221 Jane, *Jane's Fighting Ships 1914*, front matter, pp. I–CX.

222 Ibid.

223 Wtu fMS-195, *New Zealand* (ship), Captain's Ship's Book.

224 Ibid.

225 *The Monthly Naval List*, H M Stationery Office, London, May 1914, pp. 349–350.

226 www.jutlandcrewlists.org/new-zealand, accessed 17 January 2021.

227 Wtu fMS-195, *New Zealand* (ship), Captain's Ship's Book.

228 Ibid., p. 349.

229 These figures are from the official trials report in Wtu fMS-195, *New Zealand* (ship), Captain's Ship's Book. They differ from those given without source in Burt, p. 112.

230 Wtu fMS-195, *New Zealand* (ship), Captain's Ship's Book.

231 For example, Burt, *British Battleships of World War One*, p. 112, noting 26.38 knots.

232 Shallow water reduces ship speed for given power, due to hydrodynamic effects.

233   See, e.g. *Nelson Evening Mail*, 16 October 1912.

234   Jane, *Jane's Fighting Ships 1914*, p. 44.

235   Ibid. In fact *Indefatigable*'s best speed was 26.89 knots, see Burt, p. 112.

236   Fluid dynamics, in terms of ship performance, generally means that power require-
      ments rise by a factor of three relative to linear speed, although this includes many
      detail variables, including specific hull design.

237   https://museum.timaru.govt.nz/explore/scroll/profile?id=3726, accessed 16 October 2020.

238   Press, 13 May 1913.

239   www.jutlandcrewlists.org/new-zealand, accessed 16 October 2020.

240   Wtu fMS-195, *New Zealand* (ship), Captain's Ship's Book.

241   Ibid.

242   *The Monthly Naval List*, H M Stationery Office, London, May 1914, p. 350.

243   Ibid.

244   www.jutlandcrewlists.org/new-zealand, accessed 16 October 2020.

245   Buxton and Johnston, pp. 120, 153.

246   Wtu fMS-195, *New Zealand* (ship), Captain's Ship's Book

247   *The Monthly Naval List*, H M Stationery Office, London, May 1914, p. 350.

248   www.jutlandcrewlists.org/new-zealand, accessed 16 October 2020.

249   Ibid.

250   Friedman, *The British Battleship*, p. 141.

251   *Nelson Evening Mail*, 23 October 1912.

252   *Evening Star*, 20 November 1912.

253   *Dominion*, 21 November 1912.

254   *Mataura Ensign*, 16 October 1912.

255   Ibid., 23 October 1912.

256   Wtu qMS-0545, Coore, E G B, fl. 1913–1914 – Journal, 15 January 1913.

257   Ibid., 24 January.

Chapter 4: Hero of the Day

1   AJHR 1909 Session I, A-4a 'Naval and Military Defence of the Empire; conference
      with representatives of the self-governing Dominions on the, 1909', 'Admiralty
      Memorandum', McKenna to Ward, 18 August 1909.

2   WTu Micro MS Coll 05, ADM 116/1285,1286 Case 177/1, Voyage of HMS *New
      Zealand* to New Zealand and other Dominions and Colonies 1912–13, Halsey to Sir
      Graham (?) 19/10/1912.

3   Ibid., misc. correspondence Admiralty–High Commission -/11/12.

4   Clear from correspondence published about the journey, e.g. in ANZ R21464096 C363
      197 N1 92/6/9, 'Ships and repairs: HMS "New Zealand"– general', 'Correspondence
      relating to the cruise of HMS New Zealand on the occasion of her visit to New
      Zealand 1913'.

5   Ibid., Governor-General of the Union of South Africa to Secretary of State for the
      Colonies, 8 January 1913.

6   Ibid., Minute sheet 17/10/12.

7   fMS-195, *New Zealand* (ship), Captain's Ship's Book.

8   *Ashburton Guardian*, 26 February 1913.

9   ADM 116/1285 Case 177/1, Voyage of HMS *New Zealand* to New Zealand and other
      Dominions and Colonies 1912–13, 'HMS New Zealand as detatched ship', memo
      10 Jan 1910.

10   Ibid.

11   Ibid., Admiralty to Halsey, 4 February 1913 [draft].

12   Ibid., 'HMS New Zealand: Approximate Programme', typescript, 23 December 1912.

13   Ibid., Admiralty to C in C Portsmouth, 13 January 1913.

14   Ibid., Nicholson to C in C Portsmouth, 24 January 1913.

15   Ibid., Secretary to the Department to Secretary, The Admiralty, 20 January 1913.

16   Ibid., W Graham Greene to Hall-Jones, 21 January 1913; W Graham-Greene to Hall-Jones, 23 January 1913.

17   Ibid., 'Revised programme up to arrival in New Zealand'.

18   Ibid., 'HMS New Zealand: Programme of Movements', 19 February 1913.

19   Wtu QMS-0545: Coore, E G B fl. 1913–1914, journal, entry 5 February 1913.

20   Ibid., 6 February.

21   Ibid., 10 February.

22   Ibid., 10–12 February.

23   Ibid., 13 and 14 February.

24   Ibid., 20 February.

25   WTu Micro MS Coll 05, ADM 116/1285,1286 Case 177/1, Voyage of HMS *New Zealand* to New Zealand and other Dominions and Colonies 1912–13, Halsey to Secretary of the Admiralty, 28 February 1913. Halsey's capitalisation.

26   *Otago Daily Times*, 21 February 1913.

27   Wtu QMS-0545: Coore, E G B fl. 1913–1914, journal, entry 3 March.

28   WTu Micro MS Coll 05, ADM 116/1285,1286 Case 177/1, Voyage of HMS *New Zealand* to New Zealand and other Dominions and Colonies 1912–13, Halsey to Secretary of the Admiralty, 7 March 1913.

29   https://teara.govt.nz/en/biographies/2b16/bell-francis-henry-dillon, accessed

30   Wtu MS-Papers-5210-142, Series 3, Sir Francis Henry Dillon Bell – Political Correspondence and Papers, Mayor of Eltham to Bell, n..d; and associated telegrams from Stratford, New Plymouth; C A Wilkinson to Bell, 25 April 1913.

31   Ibid., telegram, 29 April 1913, Heaton Rhodes to Bell.

32   www.clydeships.co.uk/view.php?ref=5977, accessed 21 October 2020.

33   Wtu MS-Papers-5210-142, Series 3, Sir Francis Henry Dillon Bell – Political Correspondence and Papers, Bell to Clark Walker, telegram, 26 April 1913.

34   Matthew Wright, *The History of Hawke's Bay*, Intruder Books, Wellington, 2019 (second edition), p. 127.

35   *Timaru Herald*, 28 May 1913.

36   *Otago Witness*, 4 June 1913. This usage pre-dates Churchill's invocation of the same imagery.

37   See, e.g. *Timaru Herald*, 28 May 1913; *Pelorus Guardian and Miners' Advocate*, 11 April 1913; *New Zealand Times*, 9 May 1913; *Pelorus Guardian and Miners' Advocate*, 22 April 1913. Spelling, capitalisation and hyphenation per source.

38   Enclosure in Wtu fMS-195, *New Zealand* (ship), Captain's Ship's Book, 'Onward HMS *New Zealand*', p. 3.

39   WTu Micro MS Coll 05, ADM 116/1285,1286 Case 177/1, Voyage of HMS *New Zealand* to New Zealand and other Dominions and Colonies 1912–13, Secretary of State for the Colonies to Governor of New Zealand, 28 February 1913, and associated correspondence.

40   Gail Romano, 'A searchlight on New Zealand: what the visit of an Imperial Battlecruiser tells us about the country in 1913', MA Thesis, Massey University,

Palmerston North, 2019, p. 40.

41 Wtu EPH-B-State-1900/1949, 'Luncheon: the captain and officers of HMS *New Zealand* given by the government of New Zealand'.

42 Enclosure in Wtu fMS-195, *New Zealand* (ship), Captain's Ship's Book, 'Onward HMS *New Zealand*', p. 3; see also *Evening Post*, 26 April 1913.

43 *Dominion*, 23 April 1913.

44 WTu Micro MS-99 Halsey, Sir Lionel 1872–1949, personal papers 1905–1923 (Australian Joint Copying Project M1179; Hertfordshire County Record Office, Hertford, England), Halsey to his father, 18 June 1913.

45 *Evening Post*, 28 April 1913.

46 Enclosure in Wtu fMS-195, *New Zealand* (ship), Captain's Ship's Book, 'Onward HMS *New Zealand*', p. 3.

47 Wtu qMS-0545, Coore, E G B, fl.1913–1914: Journal, 28 April 1913.

48 Ibid., 29 April 1913.

49 Ibid., 1 May 1913.

50 Ibid., 28 April 1913.

51 *New Zealand Herald*, 3 May 1913. By CPI measurement this was about $50 in early twenty-first century New Zealand money, see www.rbnz.govt.nz/monetary-policy/inflation-calculator, accessed 29 November 2020.

52 *Nelson Evening Mail*, 27 May 1913.

53 See, e.g. WTu Micro MS Coll 05, ADM 116/1285, 1286 Case 177/1, Voyage of HMS *New Zealand* to New Zealand and other Dominions and Colonies 1912–13, 'HMS *New Zealand*, programme while in New Zealand waters'.

54 Wtu qMS-0545, Coore, E G B, fl.1913–1914: Journal, 14 May 1913.

55 Enclosure in Wtu fMS-195, *New Zealand* (ship), Captain's Ship's Book, 'Onward HMS *New Zealand*', p. 3.

56 WTu Micro MS-99 Halsey, Sir Lionel 1872–1949, personal papers 1905–1923 (Australian Joint Copying Project M1179; Hertfordshire County Record Office, Hertford, England), Lionel Halsey to his father 15 May 1913.

57 Ibid., Halsey to his mother 4 May 1913. Halsey's emphasis.

58 Ibid.

59 *New Zealand Herald*, 4 September 1914.

60 WTu Micro MS-99 Halsey, Sir Lionel 1872–1949, personal papers 1905–1923 (Australian Joint Copying Project M1179; Hertfordshire County Record Office, Hertford, England); Lionel Halsey to his mother 1 June 1913.

61 WTu Micro MS Coll 05, ADM 116/1285,1286 Case 177/1, Voyage of HMS *New Zealand* to New Zealand and other Dominions and Colonies 1912–13, Halsey to Admiralty, 17 June 1913.

62 *Timaru Herald*, 23 April 1913. His surname was Garsia, not Garcia, although the latter spelling is used in some references.

63 *Dominion*, 12 April 1913.

64 *Lyttelton Times*, 12 June 1913.

65 WTu Micro MS Coll 05, ADM 116/1285,1286 Case 177/1, Voyage of HMS *New Zealand* to New Zealand and other Dominions and Colonies 1912–13, Halsey to Admiralty, 26 June 1913.

66 *Lyttelton Times*, 9 May 1913; for the *Alligator* story see Matthew Wright, *Convicts: New Zealand's Hidden Criminal Past*, Penguin, Auckland, 2010, pp. 143–148.

67 WTu Micro MS-99 Halsey, Sir Lionel 1872–1949, personal papers 1905–1923

(Australian Joint Copying Project M1179; Hertfordshire County Record Office, Hertford, England); Halsey to his father, 18 June 1913.

68   Enclosure in Wtu fMS-195, *New Zealand* (ship), Captain's Ship's Book.

69   Subsequently passed to the Canterbury Museum, see www.canterburymuseum.com/research/published-work/taonga-of-hms-new-zealand, accessed 27 October 2020.

70   *New Zealand Times*, 2 April 1913.

71   WTu Micro MS-99 Halsey, Sir Lionel 1872–1949, personal papers 1905–1923 (Australian Joint Copying Project M1179; Hertfordshire County Record Office, Hertford, England); Lionel Halsey to his mother 29 June 1913.

72   Matthew Wright, *Two Peoples, One Land*, Reed, Auckland, 2006, p. 156.

73   Matthew Wright, *Waitangi: A Living Treaty*, Bateman Books, Auckland, 2019, pp. 169–184.

74   See, e.g. WTu Micro MS-99 Halsey, Sir Lionel 1872–1949, personal papers 1905–1923 (Australian Joint Copying Project M1179; Hertfordshire County Record Office, Hertford, England); any letter. Note that all vowels are pronounced in Te Reo Māori.

75   The origins of this term are discussed in Wright, *Waitangi: A Living Treaty*, pp. 22–23.

76   Romano, pp. 62–64.

77   *Otago Daily Times*, 6 May 1913.

78   *Wanganui Chronicle*, 17 June 1913

79   See Wright, *Waitangi: A Living Treaty*, pp. 181–185.

80   For discussion see ibid., pp. 173–180.

81   *New Zealand Herald*, 26 June 1913.

82   *New Zealand Herald*, 7 May 1913; see also ww100.govt.nz/the-taonga-of-hms-new-zealand, accessed 29 March 2021.

83   Noted in Kathryn Street, 'The Colonial Reinvention of the Hei Tiki: Pounamu, Knowledge and Empire, 1860s–1940s, Victoria University of Wellington, MA thesis, 2017, p. 128.

84   *Evening Post*, 22 April 1913.

85   Ken Te Huingarau Gartner, 'Te Heuheu T kino V, T reiti', in https://teara.govt.nz/en/biographies/3t13/te-heuheu-tukino-v-tureiti, accessed 27 October 2020.

86   The Māori language, which became an official language of New Zealand in 1987.

87   This use of Te Reo in formal setting remained true later, on my own experience when sole 'media minder' for the Governor of the Reserve Bank of New Zealand in 1989, visiting Waiwhetu Marae.

88   Wtu qMS-0545, Coore, E G B, fl.1913–1914: Journal, 21 April 1913.

89   Tangiwai: 'lament/remembrance/sadness water', ie: a teardrop.

90   *Evening Post*, 22 April 1913.

91   Ibid.

92   Online investigations have suggested, without identifying source, that it came from Te Arawa or Ngai Tahu See, e.g. https://navymuseum.co.nz/explore/by-collections/ship-items/piupiu, accessed 27 October 2020.

93   Noted in Street, p. 126.

94   Matthew Wright, *Guns and Utu*, Penguin, Auckland, 2011, pp. 61–78, 151–152.

95   Street, p. 128.

96   www.canterburymuseum.com/research/published-work/taonga-of-hms-new-zealand, accessed 27 October 2020. See also *Onward HMS New Zealand*, p. 37.

97   WTu Micro MS-99 Halsey, Sir Lionel 1872–1949, personal papers 1905–1923 (Australian Joint Copying Project M1179; Hertfordshire County Record Office, Hertford, England); Halsey to his father, 23 April 1913.
98   https://teara.govt.nz/en/photograph/6960/a-historic-piupiu, accessed 27 October 2020.
99   WTu Micro MS Coll 05, ADM 116/1285,1286 Case 177/1, Voyage of HMS *New Zealand* to New Zealand and other Dominions and Colonies 1912–13, 'Record of visitors to HMS New Zealand'.
100 WTu Micro MS-99 Halsey, Sir Lionel 1872–1949, personal papers 1905–1923 (Australian Joint Copying Project M1179; Hertfordshire County Record Office, Hertford, England); Lionel Halsey to his mother 29 June 1913.
101 WTu Micro MS Coll 05, ADM 116/1285,1286 Case 177/1, Voyage of HMS *New Zealand* to New Zealand and other Dominions and Colonies 1912–13, Halsey to Admiralty, 25 July 1913.
102 *Onward HMS New Zealand*, p. 4.
103 WTu Micro MS Coll 05, ADM 116/1285,1286 Case 177/1, Voyage of HMS *New Zealand* to New Zealand and other Dominions and Colonies 1912–13, Commander in Charge to Secretary of Admiralty, 20 April 1913.
104 Ibid., Halsey to Admiralty 24 August 1913.
105 Ibid., Halsey to Admiralty 24 August 1913.
106 Ibid., Halsey to Admiralty 8 September 1913.
107 Ibid., HMS *New Zealand*, 'Programme of Movements', typescript.
108 Ibid., consul to Grey, 14 September 1913.
109 Ibid., Halsey to Admiralty, 3 October 1913.
110 Ibid.
111 Ibid., Halsey to Admiralty 27 October 1913.
112 Ibid., Halsey to Admiralty, 1 November 1913.
113 Ibid.
114 Ibid., Admiralty to Halsey, 7 July 1913.
115 *Onward HMS New Zealand*, p. 38.
116 WTu Micro MS Coll 05, ADM 116/1285,1286 Case 177/1, Voyage of HMS *New Zealand* to New Zealand and other Dominions and Colonies 1912–13, 'Record of visitors to HMS New Zealand'.
117 Ibid., Admiralty note, Aug 1912.
118 Ibid., Admiralty to C in C, Devonport, 12 December 1913.
119 *Greymouth Evening Star*, 31 July 1913.
120 *Star* [Christchurch], 24 April 1913.
121 Wright, *Illustrated History of New Zealand*, pp. 246–250.
122 WTu Micro MS Coll 05, ADM 116/1285,1286 Case 177/1, Voyage of HMS *New Zealand* to New Zealand and other Dominions and Colonies 1912–13, M. branch note, 26 March 1913.
123 *New Zealand Times*, November 29 1912.
124 R22319678 ADBQ 16145 ALLEN1 8 / Naval Defence – General, Un-numbered file, letter 12th February 1914 to the Australian Minister of Defence.
125 Sir James Allen, 'New Zealand and Naval Defence', New Zealand Historical Association, Wellington, 1929, p. 5.
126 R S Churchill (ed), *W S Churchill Companion Vol. III*, p. 1759.
127 ANZ R19162214 ACHK 16603 G48 20 /N/17 G48 Naval policy – (a) Conferences between Admiralty and New Zealand Minister of Defence in 1913 – (b) CID Papers

concerning representation of Dominions on the Committee of Imperial Defence (R19162214) 1913–1913 'Extract from the Minutes of the 123rd Meeting of the CID held on 11th April 1913'.

128 Ibid., 'Imperial Naval Policy of New Zealand', CID Paper 25 April 1913, with letter by Harcourt.

129 WTu Micro MS Coll 05, ADM 116/1285,1286 Case 177/1, Voyage of HMS *New Zealand* to New Zealand and other Dominions and Colonies 1912–13, Admiralty to Halsey, 29 March 1912.

130 ANZ R22319678 ADBQ 16145 ALLEN1 8 / Naval Defence – General, Un-numbered file, Allen to Massey, 21 February 1913.

131 R S Churchill (ed), *W S Churchill Companion Vol. III*, p. 1758.

132 ANZ R21464062 AAYT 8490 N1 85 /6/1/11 N1 HM Ships – Administrative and general – Bristol class cruisers, etc. 1906–1914, memo, Liverpool to Massey, 3 October 1913.

133 ANZ R21467087 AAYT 8490 N1 691/22/6/9 N1 'Naval Board and policy – Naval defence – Policy and agreement – New Zealand prior 1914, 1905–1914', 'Naval Defence' statement by Massey, p. 3.

134 T G Weir, 'New Zealand's Naval Policy 1909–14', MA Thesis, Canterbury, 1973.

135 See, e.g. NZPD Vol. 146, 1909, pp. 155–60.

136 ANZ, ANZ R22319678 ADBQ 16145 ALLEN1 8 / Naval Defence – General, Un-numbered file, Creswell to Allen, 13 December 1914.

Chapter 5: First World War

1 'A naval lieutenant' quoted in *Sun* (Christchurch), 4 September 1914. HMS *Princess Royal* was also present but not listed in this account.

2 www.london-weather.eu/article.54.html, accessed 6 December 2020.

3 Massie, *Dreadnought*, p. 846.

4 Ibid., pp. 851–852.

5 A Temple-Patterson, *The Jellicoe Papers*, Navy Records Society, London, 1966, Von Trotha to Jellicoe, 6 July 1914, p. 37.

6 Wtu QMS-0545: Coore, E G B fl. 1913–1914, journal, 14 and 15 June 1914.

7 Ibid., 17 June 1914.

8 Ibid., 26 June 1914.

9 Ibid., 27 June 1914.

10 *Poverty Bay Herald*, 10 September 1914. Aubrey was described as 'Mr A. Williams' by the paper.

11 Wtu QMS-0545: Coore, E G B fl. 1913–1914, journal, 27 June 1914.

12 Haka are a significant class of ceremonial dances or challenges. The haka performed by the All Blacks before rugby matches is *Ka Mate* ('I may die/it is death'), composed by Te Rauparaha around 1820. There are many others. The precise detail of *New Zealand*'s haka has not been recorded.

13 *Poverty Bay Herald*, 10 September 1914.

14 Ibid.

15 Wtu QMS-0545: Coore, E G B fl. 1913–1914, journal, 28 June 1914.

16 Wtu MS-Papers-0283, Barcroft, Mick, Papers, letter, Barcroft to Miss Bell Irving, 10 December 1914.

17 Massie, *Castles of Steel*, pp. 15–16.

18 Ibid., p. 12.

19 Wtu QMS-0545: Coore, E G B fl. 1913–1914, journal, 14 July 1914.

20   Ibid., 16 July 1914.
21   She was recommissioned for the war and used for shore bombardment, renamed *Redoubtable* in August 1915 to free the name for a super-dreadnought.
22   Wtu QMS-0545: Coore, E G B fl. 1913–1914, journal, 19 July 1914.
23   Ibid., 20 July 1914.
24   www.businessinsider.com.au/kissinger-and-albright-world-war-i-2014-7?r=US&IR=T, accessed 24 December 2020.
25   Matthew Wright, The New Zealand Experience at Gallipoli and the Western Front, Oratia Books, Auckland, 2017, pp. 67–71.
26   Viscount Grey of Fallodon, *Twenty Five years, Vol. II: 1892–1916*, Frederick A. Stokes, New York, 1925, pp. 25–26.
27   Winston Churchill, *The World Crisis 1911–1918*, abridged one-volume edition, Four Square, London, 1960, p. 7.
28   Ibid., p. 118.
29   Canterbury Museum, Folder 698, 199/75, Diary of Captain (Lt Commander) A D Boyle, 27 July 1914.
30   Wtu QMS-0545: Coore, E G B fl. 1913–1914, journal, 27 July 1914.
31   Canterbury Museum, Folder 698, 199/75, Diary of Captain (Lt Commander) A D Boyle, 27 July 1914.
32   Wtu QMS-0545: Coore, E G B fl. 1913–1914, journal, 28 July 1914.
33   Canterbury Museum, Folder 698, 199/75, Diary of Captain (Lt Commander) A D Boyle, 28 July 1914.
34   Churchill, *The World Crisis*, pp. 130–131.
35   Wtu QMS-0545: Coore, E G B fl. 1913–1914, journal, 28 July 1914.
36   Canterbury Museum, Folder 698, 199/75, Diary of Captain (Lt Commander) A D Boyle, 29 July 1914.
37   Wtu QMS-0545: Coore, E G B fl. 1913–1914, journal, 29 July 1914.
38   Churchill, *The World Crisis*, pp. 130–131.
39   Massie, *Castles of Steel*, p. 20.
40   Grey, p. 10.
41   Ibid., p. 3.
42   Canterbury Museum, Folder 698, 199/75, Diary of Captain (Lt Commander) A D Boyle, 30 July 1914.
43   Wtu QMS-0545: Coore, E G B fl. 1913–1914, journal, 30 July 1914.
44   Canterbury Museum, Folder 698, 199/75, Diary of Captain (Lt Commander) A D Boyle, 30 July 1914.
45   Wtu QMS-0545: Coore, E G B fl. 1913–1914, journal, 30 July 1914.
46   Canterbury Museum, Folder 698, 199/75, Diary of Captain (Lt Commander) A D Boyle, 31 July 1914.
47   Canterbury Museum, Folder 698, 199/75, Diary of Captain (Lt Commander) A D Boyle, 31 July 1914, 31 July 1914 [entry for 31 July, written 1 August].
48   Wtu QMS-0545: Coore, E G B fl. 1913–1914, journal, 1 August 1914.
49   Canterbury Museum, Folder 698, 199/75, Diary of Captain (Lt Commander) A D Boyle, 1 August 1914.
50   Ibid., 2 August 1914.
51   Wtu QMS-0545: Coore, E G B fl. 1913–1914, journal, 2 August 1914.
52   Quoted in Randolph Churchill, *Winston S. Churchill, Vol. 1: Young Statesman, 1901–1914*, Heinemann, London, 1967, p. 712.

53   Churchill, *The World Crisis*, p. 134.

54   Ibid.

55   Wtu QMS-0545: Coore, E G B fl. 1913–1914, journal, 3 August 1914.

56   Canterbury Museum, Folder 698, 199/75, Diary of Captain (Lt Commander) A D Boyle, 4 August 1914.

57   Wtu QMS-0545: Coore, E G B fl. 1913–1914, journal, 2 August 1914.

58   Canterbury Museum, Folder 698, 199/75, Diary of Captain (Lt Commander) A D Boyle, 4 August 1914.

59   *Evening Post*, 17 August 1914.

60   Noted in, e.g. *Tuapeka Times*, 8 August 1914.

61   *Evening Post*, 6 August 1914.

62   Ibid.

63   Ibid.

64   James Goldrick, 'The Impact of War: matching expectation with reality in the Royal Navy in the first months of the Great War at sea', *War in History*, Vol. 14, No. 1, p. 24.

65   Nicholas Duncan Black, 'The Admiralty War Staff and its influence on the conduct of the naval war between 1914 and 1918', PhD thesis, University College, London, 2005, p. 87.

66   See, e.g. David G. Morgan-Owen, 'An "intermediate blockade"? British North Sea Strategy 1912–1914', *War in History*, Vol. 22, No. 4, 2015, pp. 478–502.

67   Noted by Morgan-Owen, p. 497.

68   Julian Corbett, *History of the Great War: Naval Operations, Vol. 1*, Longmans, Green & Co., London, 1920, pp. 99–100.

69   Ibid., p. 102.

70   Noted in Morgan-Owen, p. 491.

71   Morgan-Owen, pp. 498–499.

72   Noted in Corbett, *History of the Great War: Naval Operations, Vol. 1*, pp. 95–97.

73   For summary narrative see ibid., pp. 97–98.

74   *Naval Staff Monographs (Historical), Fleet Issue*, Monograph 11, 'The Battle of Heligoland Bight, August 28th, 1914', Naval Staff Training and Staff Duties Division, July 1921, p. 113.

75   The Grand Fleet sailed in distant support, see *Naval Staff Monographs (Historical), Fleet Issue*, Monograph 13, 'Summary of the Operations of the Grand Fleet, August 1914 to November 1916', Training and Staff Duties Division, February 1921, p. 6.

76   For summary narrative see Corbett, Vol. I, pp. 99–110.

77   James Goldrick, *Before Jutland: The Naval War in Northern European Waters*, August 1914–February 1915, p. 117.

78   *Naval Staff Monographs (Historical), Fleet Issue*, Monograph 11, 'The Battle of Heligoland Bight, August 28th, 1914', Naval Staff Training and Staff Duties Division, July 1921, p. 151.

79   Goldrick, *Before Jutland*, p. 121.

80   Canterbury Museum, Folder 698, 199/75, Diary of Captain (Lt Commander) A D Boyle, 31 July 1914, Friday 28 August 1914.

81   *Naval Staff Monographs (Historical), Fleet Issue*, Monograph 11, 'The Battle of Heligoland Bight, August 28th, 1914', pp. 127–128, 151.

82   There is a useful summary in Goldrick, *Before Jutland*, pp. 122–123.

83   Canterbury Museum, Folder 698, 199/75, Diary of Captain (Lt Commander) A D Boyle, 31 July 1914, Friday 28 August 1914.

84   Ibid.

85   Goldrick, *Before Jutland*, p. 121.

86   Ibid., pp. 123–124.

87   *Naval Staff Monographs (Historical), Fleet Issue*, Monograph 11, 'The Battle of Heligoland Bight, August 28th, 1914', p. 129.

88   Goldrick, *Before Jutland*, p. 125.

89   Vice-Admiral's Despatch in *Naval Staff Monographs (Historical), Fleet Issue*, Monograph 11, 'The Battle of Heligoland Bight, August 28th, 1914', Naval Staff Training and Staff Duties Division, July 1921, p. 132.

90   *Naval Staff Monographs (Historical), Fleet Issue*, Monograph 11, 'The Battle of Heligoland Bight, August 28th, 1914', Naval Staff Training and Staff Duties Division, July 1921, p. 136.

91   Boyle diary, 28 August 1914.

92   Noted by Goldrick, p. 128.

93   Boyle diary, 28 August 1914.

94   Goldrick, *Before Jutland*, pp. 125–127.

95   Ibid. Boyle thought this was around noon.

96   Boyle, 28 August 1914.

97   The official record was 12 rounds from that mounting.

98   Boyle, 28 August 1914.

99   Goldrick, *Before Jutland*, p. 129.

100   Noted by Boyle, 28 August 1914.

101   Ibid.

102   Boyle, 28 August 1914.

103   Ibid.

104   See, e.g. *Naval Staff Monographs (Historical), Fleet Issue*, Monograph 11, 'The Battle of Heligoland Bight, August 28th, 1914', Naval Staff Training and Staff Duties Division, July 1921, p. 132.

105   *Marlborough Express*, 10 September 1914.

106   WTu MS-Papers 0283, Barcroft, Mick, Papers: enclosed card.

107   *Sun* (Christchurch), 4 September 1914.

108   *Sun* (Christchurch), 4 September 1914.

109   See, e.g. *Lyttelton Times*, 11 September 1914.

110   *Fielding Star*, 31 August 1914.

111   *West Coast Times*, 1 September 1914.

112   Boyle, 28 August 1914.

113   Boyle, 28 August 1914.

114   For instance, Rodrigo Garcia y Robertson, 'The failure of the heavy gun at sea 1898–1922', *Technology and Culture*, Vol. 28, No. 3, esp. pp. 550–554.

115   H C Wright, personal communication. H C Wright (1896–1996), my great uncle, was a Marine Rangetaker during the First World War.

116   John Brooks, 'Fire Control for British Dreadnoughts – Choices of Technology and Supply', PhD thesis, Department of War Studies, King's College, London, 2001, p. 52.

117   R3485891, ACGO 8394, IA71 1/1913/1661, Box 3, 'Visit of HMS "New Zealand" (ship) – Correspondence concerning the building and equipping of the ship', W Graham Greene to High Commissioner, 14 February 1912.

118   Brooks, p. 56.

119   Ibid., p. 37.

120 Ibid., p. 56.

121 H C Wright, personal communication.

122 Brooks, pp. 8–9.

123 Ibid., p. 2.

124 R3485891, ACGO 8394, IA71 1/1913/1661, Box 3, 'Visit of HMS "New Zealand" (ship) – Correspondence concerning the building and equipping of the ship', Hall-Jones to Prime Minister, 4 April 1912.

125 Noted in Brooks, p. 58.

126 Ibid., p. 57.

127 Wtu fMS-195, *New Zealand* (ship), Captain's Ship's Book.

128 Ibid.

129 Brooks, pp. 62–63.

130 Ibid., p. 192.

131 William Schliehauf, 'A concentrated effort: Royal Navy gunnery exercises at the end of the Great War', *Warship International*, Vol. 35, No. 2, 1998, p. 125.

132 Coore, 26 October 1914.

133 Ibid.

134 Ibid.

135 Massie, *Castles of Steel*, pp. 141–142.

136 Coore, 5 November 1914.

137 Massie, *Castles of Steel*, pp. 300–301.

138 Ibid., pp. 315–316.

139 Goldrick, *Before Jutland*, pp. 201–203.

140 Churchill, *The World Crisis*, pp. 298–299.

141 H C Wright, personal communication.

142 Goldrick, *Before Jutland*, pp. 204–205.

143 Coore, 16 December 1914.

144 Ibid.

145 Ibid.

146 Ibid.

147 Massey, *Castles of Steel*, p. 355.

148 Sea speed is a product of issues such as water depth, hull condition and boiler condition. A squadron was not merely limited by the speed of its slowest ship, but by the fact that ships had to retain a reserve for station-keeping.

149 www.navweaps.com/Weapons/WNGER_827-45_skc05.php, 21 cm/45 (8.27") SK L/45, accessed 21 January 2021.

150 Churchill, *The World Crisis*, p. 377.

151 Ibid., pp. 379–380.

152 Reproduced in *Onward HMS New Zealand*, p. 13.

153 Goldrick, *Before Jutland*, p. 258.

154 Reproduced in *Onward HMS New Zealand*, p. 13.

155 Times here, if not otherwise qualified, are from *Naval Staff Monographs, Fleet Issue,* Monograph 12, 'The action of Dogger Bank, January 24th, 1915', Naval Staff Training and Staff Duties Division, July 1921, which attempted to reconcile the variations.

156 Goldrick, *Before Jutland*, p. 259.

157 Log reproduced in *Onward HMS New Zealand*, p. 14.

158 *Naval Staff Monographs, Fleet Issue,* Monograph 12, 'The action of Dogger Bank, January 24th, 1915', p. 212.

159   Goldrick, p. 261.
160   *Naval Staff Monographs, Fleet Issue,* Monograph 12, 'The action of Dogger Bank, January 24th, 1915', p. 221.
161   www.jutlandcrewlists.org/new-zealand, accessed 22 January 2021.
162   Log reproduced in *Onward HMS New Zealand*, p. 14.
163   Folder 698, 199/75, Diary of Captain (Lt Commander) A D Boyle, 24 January 1915.
164   Cited in Goldrick, *Before Jutland*, p. 269.
165   www.jutlandcrewlists.org/new-zealand, accessed 22 January 2021.
166   Log reproduced in *Onward HMS New Zealand*, p. 16.
167   www.jutlandcrewlists.org/new-zealand, accessed 22 January 2021.
168   Log reproduced in *Onward HMS New Zealand*, p. 14.
169   Noted in Goldrick, *Before Jutland*, p. 268.
170   Log reproduced in *Onward HMS New Zealand*, p. 14.
171   Folder 698, 199/75, Diary of Captain (Lt Commander) A D Boyle, 24 January 1915.
172   Ibid.
173   Ibid.
174   Paul Schmalenbach, 'SMS *Blucher*', *Warship International*, No. 2, June 30, 1971, p. 180. Schmalenbach times it to 11.30: German time was one hour ahead of British.
175   Compare log summary in *Onward HMS New Zealand*, pp. 14–15 with *Naval Staff Monographs, Fleet Issue,* Monograph 12, 'The action of Dogger Bank, January 24th, 1915', p. 215.
176   Goldrick, *Before Jutland*, p. 275.
177   *Naval Staff Monographs, Fleet Issue,* Monograph 12, 'The action of Dogger Bank, January 24th, 1915', p. 214.
178   Goldrick, *Before Jutland*, p. 275.
179   Ibid., p. 277.
180   Paul Kennedy 'Dogger Bank: Clash of the Battle Cruisers' Bernard Fitzsimons (ed), *Warships and Sea Battles of the First World War*, Ure Smith, Sydney, 1973, p. 48.
181   Goldrick, *Before Jutland*, p. 278.
182   Ibid., p. 274.
183   Log reproduced in *Onward HMS New Zealand*, p. 16.
184   Folder 698, 199/75, Diary of Captain (Lt Commander) A D Boyle, 24 January 1915.
185   *Naval Staff Monographs, Fleet Issue,* Monograph 12, 'The action of Dogger Bank, January 24th, 1915', p. 222.
186   Log reproduced in *Onward HMS New Zealand*, p. 16.
187   Ibid., p. 17.
188   Reported in the *Evening Post*, 5 February 1915; *Poverty Bay Herald*, 5 February 1915.
189   *Naval Staff Monographs, Fleet Issue,* Monograph 12, 'The action of Dogger Bank, January 24th, 1915', p. 225.
190   Log reproduced in *Onward HMS New Zealand*, p. 17.
191   See, e.g. *Wanganui Chronicle*, 26 January 1915.
192   *Evening Post*, 27 January 1915.
193   *Evening Post*, 2 February 1915.
194   *London Gazette*, 3 March 1915.
195   Fisher to Beatty, 27 January 1915, in *Fear God and Dread Nought*, Vol. III, pp. 146–147.
196   Neil Mackay, Chris Price and Jamie Wood, 'Dogger Bank: Weighing the Fog of War', *Significance*, Royal Statistical Society, June 2017, pp. 14–19.
197   *Naval Staff Monographs, Fleet Issue,* Monograph 12, 'The action of Dogger Bank,

January 24th, 1915', p. 225.

198 David K. Brown and Iain McCallum, 'Ammunition explosions in World War I: a re-examination of the evidence', *Warship International*, Vol. 38, No. 1, 2001, p. 61.

199 Ott, p. 29.

200 Carsten Reinhardt and Anthony S. Travis, *Heinrich Caro and the Creation of Modern Chemical Industry*, Springer Science + Business Media Dordrecht, 2000, p. 83.

201 Ott, p. 28.

202 See, e.g. Friedman, *The British Battleship*, pp. 192–193.

203 Ott, p. 29.

204 He is sometimes referred to as a 'Dagger Gunner', a specialist position delineated by a dagger badge; but was not.

205 Alexander Grant, *Through the Hawsepipe* (MS), extract reproduced at www.worldwar1.co.uk/grant.htm, accessed 21 January 2021.

206 Churchill, *The World Crisis*, pp. 374–375.

207 Fisher to Beatty, 25 January 1915, *Fear God and Dread Nought*, Vol. III, p. 146.

208 Mackay, *Fisher of Kilverstone*, pp. 497–505.

209 The battleships *Lord Nelson* and *Agamemnon*, together with lighter forces, were considered sufficient to secure the Dardanelles against a sortie by the ex-German battlecruiser *Goeben*.

210 Goldrick, 'The Impact of War: matching expectation with reality in the Royal Navy in the first months of the Great War at sea', p. 31.

Chapter 6: Jutland

1 Wtu MS-Papers-0283, Barcroft, Mick, Papers, letter, Barcroft to Miss Bell Irving, 15 June 1916.

2 Nigel Steel and Peter Hart, *Jutland 1916: Death in the Grey Wastes*, Cassell, London, 2004, p. 7.

3 For names see www.naval-history.net/xDKCas1916–05May-Jutland1.htm, accessed 22 January 2021.

4 Per account in www.navyhistory.org.au/battle-cruisers-in-collision/, accessed 17 January 2021.

5 *Press*, 22 November 1918.

6 Jellicoe's battleships were: *Dreadnought*, three *Bellerophons*, three *St Vincents*, *Neptune*, two *Colossus* class, four *Orions*, three *King George Vs*, four *Iron Dukes*, five *Queen Elizabeths*, two *Revenge* class (plus one more completed, but not worked up to Jellicoe's satisfaction by May 1916), *Erin*, *Agincourt* and *Canada*.

7 See, e.g. Massey, *Castles of Steel*, pp. 558–559.

8 Discussed in Ryan Alexander Peeks, '"The Cavalry of the Fleet", organisation, doctrine and battlecruisers in the United States and the United Kingdom, 1904–1922, PhD thesis, University of North Carolina, Chapel Hill, 2015, pp. 297–298. Moore was referring to *Invincible*, *Inflexible*, *Indomitable*, *Indefatigable*, *New Zealand* and *Australia*.

9 Noted in Massey, *Castles of Steel*, p. 569.

10 www.jutlandcrewlists.org/new-zealand, accessed 17 January 2021.

11 *Kia Ora New Zealand*, p. 15.

12 Ibid.

13 *Battle of Jutland, 30th May to 1st June 1916, Official Despatches*, HMSO, London, 1920, Despatch from the Commander in Chief, 18 June 1916, Enclosure 1, Narrative 31 May, p. 5.

14   Massie, *Castles of Steel*, p. 577.
15   Ibid., p. 580.
16   *Battle of Jutland, 30th May to 1st June 1916, Official Despatches*, Despatch from the Commander in Chief, 18 June 1916, Enclosure 1, Narrative 31 May, p. 7.
17   Campbell, p. 32.
18   *Battle of Jutland, 30th May to 1st June 1916, Official Despatches*, Despatch from the Commander in Chief, 18 June 1916, Enclosure 1, Narrative 31 May, p. 7. Compare this time with that given in Campbell, p. 33.
19   Ibid.
20   Nicholas Jellicoe, *Jutland: the unfinished battle*, Seaforth, Barnsley, 2016, p. 55.
21   *Battle of Jutland, 30th May to 1st June 1916, Official Despatches*, Appendix II, p. 445.
22   Ibid., p. 444.
23   Ibid., p. 445.
24   Ibid., p. 446.
25   Admiral Viscount Jellicoe of Scapa, *The Grand Fleet 1914–16: its creation, development and work*, Cassell & Company, London, 1919, p. 332.
26   Massie, *Castles of Steel*, pp. 584–585; compare John Campbell, *Jutland: an analysis of the fighting*, Lyons Press, New York, 1998, p. 32.
27   Campbell, *Jutland*, p. 35.
28   Ibid., p. 34.
29   *Battle of Jutland, 30th May to 1st June 1916, Official Despatches*, Appendix II, p. 446.
30   www.jutlandcrewlists.org/new-zealand, accessed 28 January 2021.
31   H W Fawcett and G W W Hooper, *The Fighting at Jutland* (abridged edition), Macmillan & Co., London, 1921, p. 15.
32   https://navymuseum.co.nz/explore/by-themes/world-war-one/battle-of-jutland-lieutenant-a-d-boyles-account-from-hms-new-zealand, A D Boyle, letter 6 June 1916, accessed 4 April 2021.
33   Ibid.
34   Log entry in *Kia Ora New Zealand*, p. 16.
35   Ibid., p. 447.
36   Ibid., Despatch from the Commander in Chief, 18 June 1916, Enclosure 1, Narrative 31 May, pp. 7–8.
37   www.jutlandcrewlists.org/reports-from-new-zealand, Report by James John Eames, accessed 28 January 2021.
38   Fawcett and Hooper, p. 17.
39   Michael Wynd 'HMS New Zealand in World WaR i', IN Andrew Forbes (ed), *The War At Sea, proceedings of the King-Hall Naval History Conference 2013*, Sea Power Centre, Canberra, p .120.
40   Street, pp. 129–130.
41   Fawcett and Hooper., p. 15.
42   https://navymuseum.co.nz/explore/by-themes/world-war-one/battle-of-jutland-lieutenant-a-d-boyles-account-from-hms-new-zealand/, A D Boyle, letter 6 June 1916, accessed 4 April 2021.
43   Ibid.
44   http://216.92.248.253/tfs/index.php/Kenelm_Everard_Lane_Creighton, accessed 28 January 2021.
45   Fawcett and Hooper, p. 17.
46   *Battle of Jutland, 30th May to 1st June 1916, Official Despatches*, 'Action with German

Fleet, 31st May 1916, Record of Ranges', p. 393.

47   Noted by Campbell, *Jutland*, p. 48.

48   *Battle of Jutland, 30th May to 1st June 1916, Official Despatches*, 'Captain's Report on Action of 31st May 1916, HMS New Zealand', p. 162.

49   *Battle of Jutland, 30th May to 1st June 1916, Official Despatches*, 'Action with German Fleet, 31st May 1916, 'Appendix 1: time-table compiled by Captain and Officers of HMS *New Zealand*', p. 160.

50   *Battle of Jutland, 30th May to 1st June 1916, Official Despatches*, Appendix II.

51   Campbell, *Jutland*, p. 39.

52   Ibid., 'Action with German Fleet, 31st May 1916, Record of Ranges', p. 393.

53   Campbell, *Jutland*, p. 40.

54   *Battle of Jutland, 30th May to 1st June 1916, Official Despatches*, 'Action with German Fleet, 31st May 1916, Record of Ranges', p. 393.

55   Figures in www.dreadnoughtproject.org/tfs/index.php/H.M.S._New_Zealand_(1911), accessed 21 January 2021.

56   Wtu MS-Papers-0283, Barcroft, Mick, Papers, letter, Barcroft to Miss Bell Irving, 15 June 1916.

57   Campbell, *Jutland*, p. 39.

58   *Battle of Jutland, 30th May to 1st June 1916, Official Despatches*, 'Action with German Fleet, 31st May 1916, Record of Ranges', p. 393.

59   Fawcett and Hooper, p. 17.

60   Ibid.

61   *Battle of Jutland, 30th May to 1st June 1916, Official Despatches*, HMSO, London, 1920, 'Report of Rear-Admiral Second Battle Cruiser Squadron', p. 158.

62   www.jutlandcrewlists.org/new-zealand, accessed 21 January 2021.

63   Innes McCartney, *Jutland 1916: the archaeology of a naval battlefield*, Conway, London, 2016, pp. 36–37. Question has been raised as to whether this image was later 'doctored'.

64   By McCartney, *Jutland 1916*, p. 35.

65   Fawcett and Hooper, pp. 17–18.

66   *Battle of Jutland, 30th May to 1st June 1916, Official Despatches*, 'Captain's Report on Action of 31st May 1916, HMS New Zealand', p. 158.

67   McCartney, *Jutland 1916*, pp. 42–43.

68   Only two survived.

69   https://navymuseum.co.nz/explore/by-themes/world-war-one/battle-of-jutland-lieutenant-a-d-boyles-account-from-hms-new-zealand, A D Boyle, letter 6 June 1916, accessed 4 April 2021.

70   Fawcett and Hooper, p. 15.

71   Arthur Douglas Wales Smith, MS, from papers of Commander James Pipon, at https://battleofjutlandcrewlists.miraheze.org/wiki/Smith,_Arthur_Douglas_Wales, accessed 21 March 2021.

72   See, e.g. Campbell, p. 94.

73   Ibid.

74   Fawcett and Hooper, p. 17.

75   *Battle of Jutland, 30th May to 1st June 1916, Official Despatches*, 'Captain's Report on Action of 31st May 1916, HMS New Zealand', p. 158.

76   Wtu MS-Papers-0283, Barcroft, Mick, Papers, letter, Barcroft to Miss Bell Irving, 15 June 1916.

77   On the displacement of the day, *Barham* was able to make 23.8 knots, see, e.g.

Campbell, *Jutland*, pp. 102–103.

78   Campbell, *Jutland*, p. 46.

79   Quoted in Gary Staff, *Skagerrak: the Battle of Jutland through German eyes*, Pen and Sword Maritime, Barnsley, 2016, p. 65.

80   Fawcett and Hooper, p. 18.

81   Ibid., p. 15.

82   Campbell, *Jutland*, pp. 87–92.

83   *Battle of Jutland, 30th May to 1st June 1916, Official Despatches*, 'Captain's Report on Action of 31st May 1916, HMS New Zealand', p. 162.

84   Campbell, *Jutland*, p. 48.

85   *Battle of Jutland, 30th May to 1st June 1916, Official Despatches*, 'Captain's Report on Action of 31st May 1916, HMS New Zealand', p. 162; see also *Kia Ora New Zealand*, p. 24.

86   Fawcett and Hooper, p. 15.

87   Notes in *Kia Ora HMS New Zealand*, p. 24.

88   Ibid., p. 20.

89   https://navymuseum.co.nz/explore/by-themes/world-war-one/battle-of-jutland-lieutenant-a-d-boyles-account-from-hms-new-zealand, A D Boyle, letter 6 June 1916, accessed 4 April 2021.

90   Fawcett and Hooper, p. 15.

91   Ibid., 19.

92   McCartney, pp. 61–63. McCartney also found evidence of illegal salvage on the wreck, a war grave.

93   Bill Jurens, personal communication 14 February 2021.

94   Fawcett and Hooper, p. 19.

95   Ibid., p. 19.

96   www.jutlandcrewlists.org/reports-from-new-zealand, accessed 29 January 2021.

97   https://navymuseum.co.nz/explore/by-themes/world-war-one/battle-of-jutland-lieutenant-a-d-boyles-account-from-hms-new-zealand/, A D Boyle, letter 6 June 1916, accessed 4 April 2021.

98   Fawcett and Hooper, p. 23.

99   Noted by Nicholas Jellicoe, p. 82.

100 Campbell, *Jutland*, p. 64.

101 Bill Jurens, personal communication, 14 February 2021.

102 More or less, assuming a speed of 24–26 knots and a distance of 1,000–1,200yd.

103 McCartney, p. 56.

104 Bill Jurens, personal communication, 15 February 2021.

105 *Chronicles of the NZEF*, May 30 1917, 'Our Ship', p. 137. Only eighteen survived the sinking. Robertson was not among them.

106 Fawcett and Hooper, *The Fighting at Jutland (abridged edition)*, Macmillan & Co., London, 1921, p. 19.

107 https://navymuseum.co.nz/explore/by-themes/world-war-one/battle-of-jutland-lieutenant-a-d-boyles-account-from-hms-new-zealand, A D Boyle, letter 6 June 1916, accessed 4 April 2021.

108 www.jutlandcrewlists.org/reports-from-new-zealand, accessed 29 January 2021.

109 *Battle of Jutland, 30th May to 1st June 1916, Official Despatches*, 'Action with German Fleet, 31st May 1916, Record of Ranges', p. 393.

110 Massie, *Castles of Steel*, pp. 596–597.

111   *Battle of Jutland, 30th May to 1st June 1916, Official Despatches*, 'Action with German Fleet, 31st May 1916, Appendix II, p. 452.

112   Massie, *Castles of Steel*, p. 600.

113   *Battle of Jutland, 30th May to 1st June 1916, Official Despatches*, 'Action with German Fleet, 31st May 1916, 'Appendix 1: time-table compiled by Captain and Officers of HMS *New Zealand*', p. 160.

114   Ibid.

115   Campbell, pp. 96–97.

116   *Battle of Jutland, 30th May to 1st June 1916, Official Despatches*, 'Action with German Fleet, 31st May 1916, 'Appendix 1: time-table compiled by Captain and Officers of HMS *New Zealand*', p. 160. As noted earlier, times between ships' logs varied.

117   Campbell, *Jutland*, p. 98.

118   Ibid., p. 94.

119   Ibid., p. 78.

120   Noted, e.g. www.dreadnoughtproject.org/tfs/index.php/Lion_Class_Battlecruiser_ (1910)#Gunnery_Control , accessed 5 April 2021.

121   Ott, pp. 22–23.

122   Ibid., p. 21.

123   *Battle of Jutland, 30th May to 1st June 1916, Official Despatches*, 'Action with German Fleet, 31st May 1916, Record of Ranges', p. 393.

124   Campbell, *Jutland*, p. 102.

125   *Battle of Jutland, 30th May to 1st June 1916, Official Despatches*, 'Action with German Fleet, 31st May 1916, Appendix II, p. 455.

126   Arthur Douglas Wales Smith, MS, from papers of Commander James Pipon, at https://battleofjutlandcrewlists.miraheze.org/wiki/Smith,_Arthur_Douglas_Wales, accessed 21 March 2021.

127   *Battle of Jutland, 30th May to 1st June 1916, Official Despatches*, 'Time-table compiled by Captain and Officers of HMS *New Zealand*', p. 160.

128   Wtu MS-Papers-0283, Barcroft, Mick, Papers, letter, Barcroft to Miss Bell Irving, 15 June 1916.

129   Arthur Douglas Wales Smith, MS, from papers of Commander James Pipon, at https://battleofjutlandcrewlists.miraheze.org/wiki/Smith,_Arthur_Douglas_Wales, accessed 21 March 2021.

130   *Battle of Jutland, 30th May to 1st June 1916, Official Despatches*, 'Action with German Fleet, 31st May 1916, Appendix II, pp. 455–456.

131   Admiral Sir Reginald Bacon, *The Jutland Scandal*, Hutchison, London, revised edition 1925, pp. 110–113 provides diagrams of the options.

132   *Battle of Jutland, 30th May to 1st June 1916, Official Despatches*, Appendix II, p. 456.

133   Bacon, *The Jutland Scandal*, p. 108.

134   *Battle of Jutland, 30th May to 1st June 1916, Official Despatches*, Appendix II, p. 458.

135   Ibid., 'Record of Ranges', p. 395.

136   Ibid., Appendix II, p. 458.

137   Ibid., p. 457.

138   Massie, pp. 612–613.

139   See, e.g. Bacon, *The Jutland Scandal*, pp. 120–123.

140   *Battle of Jutland, 30th May to 1st June 1916, Official Despatches*, 'Action with German Fleet, 31st May 1916, Record of Ranges', p. 395.

141   Arthur Douglas Wales Smith, MS, from papers of Commander James Pipon, at

https://battleofjutlandcrewlists.miraheze.org/wiki/Smith,_Arthur_Douglas_Wales, accessed 21 March 2021.

142 Noted in *Kia Ora New Zealand*, p. 22.

143 Campbell, p. 152.

144 David K. Brown and Iain McCallum, 'Ammunition explosions in World War I: a re-examination of the evidence', *Warship International*, Vol. 38, No. 1, 2001, p. 63.

145 McCartney, pp. 58–59.

146 The casualty list is here: www.northeastmedals.co.uk/britishguide/jutland/hms_defence_casualty_list_1916.htm , accessed 4 February 2021. According to a post-battle story, one man was eventually rescued, but this was never confirmed in the official record of the day.

147 Campbell, *Jutland*, p. 153.

148 Campbell, *Jutland*, p. 154.

149 Arthur Douglas Wales Smith, MS, from papers of Commander James Pipon, at https://battleofjutlandcrewlists.miraheze.org/wiki/Smith,_Arthur_Douglas_Wales, accessed 21 March 2021.

150 Campbell, *Jutland*, p. 156.

151 Ibid., pp. 158–159.

152 *Battle of Jutland, 30th May to 1st June 1916, Official Despatches*, 'Report of Senior Officer 3rd Battle Cruiser Squadron', p. 165.

153 For details see David K Brown, 'HMS *Invincible*: the explosion at Jutland and its relevance to HMS Hood', *Warship International*, Vol. 40, No. 4, 2003, p. 344.

154 *Battle of Jutland, 30th May to 1st June 1916, Official Despatches*, 'Report of Senior Officer 3rd Battle Cruiser Squadron', p. 165.

155 McCartney, pp. 120–121.

156 www.northeastmedals.co.uk/britishguide/jutland/hms_invincible_casualty_list_ 1916.htm, accessed 4 February 2021.

157 *Battle of Jutland, 30th May to 1st June 1916, Official Despatches*, 'Time-table compiled by Captain and Officers of HMS *New Zealand*', p. 161.

158 Arthur Douglas Wales Smith, MS, from papers of Commander James Pipon, at https://battleofjutlandcrewlists.miraheze.org/wiki/Smith,_Arthur_Douglas_Wales, accessed 21 March 2021.

159 *Battle of Jutland, 30th May to 1st June 1916, Official Despatches*, 'Time-table compiled by Captain and Officers of HMS *New Zealand*', 'Report of Senior Officer 3rd Battle Cruiser Squadron', p. 166.

160 Ibid., 'Time-table compiled by Captain and Officers of HMS *New Zealand*', p. 162.

161 Campbell, *Jutland*, p. 160.

162 *Battle of Jutland, 30th May to 1st June 1916, Official Despatches*, 'Action with German Fleet, 31st May 1916, Record of Ranges', p. 395.

163 www.jutlandcrewlists.org/reports-from-new-zealand, accessed 4 February 2021. Eames' timing was out by an hour.

164 Campbell, *Jutland*, p. 187.

165 *Battle of Jutland, 30th May to 1st June 1916, Official Despatches*, 'Time-table compiled by Captain and Officers of HMS *New Zealand*', p. 161.

166 Ibid.

167 Ibid.

168 Noted in Creighton to J E T Harper, 12 November 1919, at http://216.92.248.253/tfs/ index.php/Creighton_Letter_to_Harper,_12_November,_1919, accessed 4 February 2021.

169　*Battle of Jutland, 30th May to 1st June 1916, Official Despatches*, chart, pp. 393–394.

170　R19162327 ACHK 16604 G49 10 /16j Plate 9a, 'Maps etc accompanying volume: British – Second Battle Cruiser Squadron, 2pm, 31 May 1916 to 4am, 1 June 1916 – Track'.

171　R19162326 ACHK 16604 G49 10 / 16i Plate 8a G49, 'Maps etc accompanying volume: British – Plan of Battle sent by Vice-Admiral Commanding Battle Cruiser Fleet to Commander-in-Chief – 17 July 1916'.

172　Noted by Nicholas Jellicoe, p. 144.

173　Reinhard Scheer, *Germany's High Seas Fleet in the World War*, Cassell & Co., London, 1920, p. 155.

174　Discussed by Nicholas Jellicoe, p. 144.

175　Campbell, p. 210.

176　Churchill, *The World Crisis*, pp. 715–716.

177　Campbell, pp. 205–206.

178　Ibid., p. 208.

179　Jellicoe, *The Grand Fleet*, p. 359.

180　Steel and Hart, p. 252.

181　Ibid.

182　Quoted in Bacon, *The Jutland Scandal*, p. 119.

183　Campbell, p. 246.

184　Massie, *Castles of Steel*, p. 629.

185　Jellicoe, *The Grand Fleet*, p. 361.

186　For discussion see Jon Tetsuro Sumida, 'Expectation, Adaptation and Resignation: British battle fleet tactical planning, August 1914–April 1916', *Naval War College Review*, Vol. 60, No. 3, 2007, pp. 105–106.

187　Churchill, *The World Crisis*, p. 717.

188　Jellicoe, *The Grand Fleet*, p. 362.

189　Bacon, *The Jutland Scandal*, p. 120.

190　*Battle of Jutland, 30th May to 1st June 1916, Official Despatches*, Appendix II, p. 466.

191　Jellicoe, *The Grand Fleet*, p. 366.

192　Massie, *Castles of Steel*, p. 634.

193　*Battle of Jutland, 30th May to 1st June 1916, Official Despatches*, 'Action with German Fleet, 31st May 1916, Record of Ranges', p. 395.

194　Ibid., 'Time-table compiled by Captain and Officers of HMS *New Zealand*', p. 161.

195　Arthur Douglas Wales Smith, MS, from papers of Commander James Pipon, at https://battleofjutlandcrewlists.miraheze.org/wiki/Smith,_Arthur_Douglas_Wales, accessed 21 March 2021.

196　Wtu MS-Papers-0283, Barcroft, Mick, Papers, letter, Barcroft to Miss Bell Irving, 15 June 1916.

197　By German reckoning, 9.28pm: German standard time was one hour ahead of GMT.

198　Campbell, *Jutland*, pp. 268–269.

199　*Battle of Jutland, 30th May to 1st June 1916, Official Despatches*, 'Action with German Fleet, 31st May 1916, 'Captain's Report on Action of 31st May 1916, HMS *New Zealand*', p. 162.

200　Campbell, *Jutland*, pp. 270–71.

201　Ibid., p. 254.

202　*Battle of Jutland, 30th May to 1st June 1916, Official Despatches*, 'Action with German Fleet, 31st May 1916, Record of Ranges', p. 395.

203 www.jutlandcrewlists.org/reports-from-new-zealand, accessed 4 February 2021.

204 *Battle of Jutland, 30th May to 1st June 1916, Official Despatches*, 'Time-table compiled by Captain and Officers of HMS *New Zealand*', p. 161.

205 Ibid., chart, pp. 394–395.

206 I am grateful to Bill Jurens for pointing this out, personal communication, 14 February 2021.

207 Jellicoe, *The Grand Fleet*, pp. 372–373.

208 Ibid., p. 372.

209 *Battle of Jutland, 30th May to 1st June 1916, Official Despatches*, Appendix II, p. 471.

210 Ibid., p. 472; see also Massie, *Castles of Steel*, pp. 636–637.

211 https://navymuseum.co.nz/explore/by-themes/world-war-one/battle-of-jutland-lieutenant-a-d-boyles-account-from-hms-new-zealand/, A D Boyle, letter 6 June 1916, accessed 4 April 2021

212 Argued by Nicholas Jellicoe, p. 182.

213 *Battle of Jutland, 30th May to 1st June 1916, Official Despatches*, Appendix II, p. 474.

214 Ibid., p. 475.

215 For detail summary see Nicholas Jellicoe, pp. 182–183.

216 Massie, *Castles of Steel*, pp. 641–642; Nicholas Jellicoe, pp. 182–183.

217 Jellicoe, *The Grand Fleet*, p. 384.

218 Nicholas Jellicoe, p. 209.

219 Massie, *Castles of Steel*, p. 654. She had been abandoned and deliberately sunk.

220 www.jutlandcrewlists.org/reports-from-new-zealand, accessed 4 February 2021.

221 www.jutlandcrewlists.org/reports-from-new-zealand, accessed 4 February 2021.

222 *Kia Ora New Zealand*, p. 24.

223 See, e.g. https://collections.tepapa.govt.nz/topic/1049, accessed 23 March 2021.

224 *Kia Ora New Zealand*, p. 24.

225 Wtu MS-Papers-0283, Barcroft, Mick, Papers, letter, Barcroft to Miss Bell Irving, 15 June 1916. Period usage was to pluralise 'Māori': actually all nouns in Te Reo Māori are mass nouns.

226 *Chronicles of the NZEF*, May 30 1917, 'Our Ship', p. 137.

227 McCartney, p. 166.

228 For discussion see Wright, *The New Zealand Experience at Gallipoli and the Western Front*, pp. 161–166.

229 Massey to Green, via Mackenzie, 10 June 1916, in *Kia Ora New Zealand*, p. 26.

230 Green to Massey in ibid., p. 27: see also *Evening Post*, 9 June 1916.

231 See, e.g. *Evening Post*, 14 June 1916; *New Zealand Times*, 15 June 1916, etc.

232 *Star* (Christchurch), 14 June 1916.

233 *Feilding Star*, 30 November 1916.

234 *Evening Post*, 8 December 1916.

235 *Auckland Star*, 29 November 1916.

236 Summarised in Massie, *Castles of Steel*, pp. 660–663.

237 Usefully summarised up to 2001 in Louis D Rubin, Jr, 'The continuing argument over Jutland', *The Virginia Quarterly Review*, Vol. 77, No. 4, Autumn 2001.

238 For useful summary see Nicholas Jellicoe, pp. 290–316.

239 Wtu MS-Papers-0283, Barcroft, Mick, Papers, letter, Barcroft to Miss Bell Irving, 15 June 1916.

240 Arthur Douglas Wales Smith, MS, from papers of Commander James Pipon, at https://battleofjutlandcrewlists.miraheze.org/wiki/Smith,_Arthur_Douglas_Wales,

accessed 21 March 2021.
241 *Kia Ora New Zealand*, p. 24.
242 Bo Ejstrud, 'A near miss: heavy gun efficiency at Jutland', *Warship International*, Vol. 41, No. 2, 2004.
243 Jellicoe, *The Grand Fleet*, p. 419.
244 Quoted in Massie, *Castles of Steel*, p. 596.
245 Discussed in Peeks, pp. 297–298.
246 *Battle of Jutland, 30th May to 1st June 1916, Official Despatches*, 'Despatch from the Commander in Chief' dated 18 June 1916, p. 2.
247 David K. Brown and Iain McCallum, 'Ammunition explosions in World War I: a re-examination of the evidence', *Warship International*, Vol. 38, No. 1, 2001, p. 65.
248 Friedman, *The British Battleship 1906–1945*, p. 194.
249 Ibid., p. 195.
250 Jellicoe, *The Grand Fleet*, p. 418.
251 www.dreadnoughtproject.org/tfs/index.php/A_Direct_Train_of_Cordite, Beatty to W Graham Greene, 14 July 1916, accessed 5 February 2021.
252 Ibid., Beatty to W Graham Greene, 14 July 1916, accessed 5 February 2021. See also David K Brown and Iain McCallum, 'Ammunition explosions in World War I: a re-examination of the evidence', *Warship International*, Vol. 38, No. 1, 2001, p. 65.
253 Brown and McCallum, p. 61.
254 He changed his original surname, Jones, to his middle name, by deed poll in 1890.
255 See www.dreadnoughtproject.org/tfs/index.php/A_Direct_Train_of_Cordite, accessed 5 February 2021.
256 Jellicoe, *The Grand Fleet*, p. 418.
257 Brown and McCallum, p. 65.
258 Friedman, *The British Battleship 1906–1946*, p. 193.
259 Campbell, p. 385.
260 Ibid., p. 128.
261 www.dreadnoughtproject.org/tfs/index.php/A_Direct_Train_of_Cordite, d'Eyncourt, memorandum 7 October 1916, accessed 5 February 2021: see also Friedman, *The British Battleship 1906–1946*, p. 195.
262 Which he maintained, see Jellicoe, *The Grand Fleet*, p. 418.
263 www.dreadnoughtproject.org/tfs/index.php/A_Direct_Train_of_Cordite, d'Eyncourt, memorandum 7 October 1916, accessed 5 February 2021, p. 196.
264 Jellicoe, *The Grand Fleet*, p. 419.
265 fMS-195 New Zealand (ship), Captain's Ship's Book.
266 Jellicoe, *The Grand Fleet*, p. 420.

Chapter 7: The Last Voyage

1 Clutha McKenzie (ed), 'The History of HMS *New Zealand*', Navy League, Wellington, 1919, p. 12.
2 *Kia Ora New Zealand*, p. 37.
3 Ibid., p. 38.
4 Jellicoe, *The Grand Fleet*, p. 420.
5 Ibid., p. 31.
6 *Evening Post*, 25 November 1918.
7 McKenzie (ed), p. 27; also *Stratford Evening Post*, 17 December 1918.
8 For detail and discussion see Nicholas Jellicoe, pp. 224–254; also S W Roskill, 'The

dismissal of AdmiraL Jellicoe', *Journal of Contemporary History*, Vol. 1, No. 4, 1966.

9   John Dunmore, introduction, in Frederick Kelso, *The Last Voyage of HMS New Zealand*, New Zealand Books, Palmerston North 1972, p. 7.

10 McKenzie, p 27: *Dominion*, 21 August 1919.

11 https://knowledgebank.org.nz/person/maud-airini-tiakitai-perry-1879-1944, accessed 7 February 2021.

12 Kelso, p. 17.

13 Ibid., pp. 8–9.

14 fMS-195, New Zealand (ship), Captain's Ship's Book.

15 Kelso, p. 19.

16 Ibid.

17 Ibid.

18 Kelso, p. 21.

19 Ibid., p. 25.

20 Kelso, p. 27.

21 Kelso, p. 40.

22 Ibid., p. 41.

23 *Rangiteiki Advocate and Manawatu Argus*, 20 August 1919.

24 Kelso, p. 42.

25 *Evening Post*, 21 August 1919.

26 Kelso, p. 44.

27 Ibid., p. 44.

28 For discussion see Wright, *The New Zealand Experience at Gallipoli and the Western Front*, pp. 285–316.

29 See, e.g. Micro-MS-Coll-05-5905, United Kingdom, Admiralty: records relating to the Pacific, 1714–1910 (collection), Naval missions – Lord Jellicoe to Australia and New Zealand (Cases 1099/1, 1099/4, 1099/5, 732) (ADM 116/ 1831, 1834, 1835, 1871A), ADM 116/1831ADM 116-191, Jellicoe to Secretary of the Admiralty, 21 August 1919.

30 Bacon, *The Life of John Rushworth, Earl Jellicoe*, pp. 408–11.

31 Micro-MS-Coll-05-5905, United Kingdom, Admiralty: records relating to the Pacific, 1714–1910 (collection), Naval missions – Lord Jellicoe to Australia and New Zealand (Cases 1099/1, 1099/4, 1099/5, 732) (ADM 116/ 1831, 1834, 1835, 1871A), ADM 116/1831, D of P to Jellicoe, 9 July 1919.

32 Ibid., typed minute 29 September 1919.

33 ANZ R21467044 AAYT 8490 N1 680/22/5 Missions – Lord Jellicoe's visit to New Zealand, 1919, 'Secret — New Zealand Naval Estimates'.

34 Wright, *Blue Water Kiwis*, pp. 62–66.

35 Kelso, p. 49.

36 Ibid., p. 72.

37 See, e.g. *Otago Witness*, 27 September 1920.

38 Kelso, p. 72.

39 Ibid.

40 *Navy List*, HMSO, London, January 1921, p. 816.

41 ANZ R21463719 AAYT 8490 N1 18 /1/34 N1, 'Accounts – Naval Benevolent Fund, New Zealand – HMS New Zealand prizes fund – General – Correspondence', Winston Churchill to Jellicoe, 7 February 1921.

42 'Limitation of Naval Armament (Five Power Treaty or Washington Treaty), at www.loc.gov/law/help/us-treaties/bevans/m-ust000002-0351.pdf, accessed 8 February

2021.

43 *Hercules* and *Bellerophon* were sold on 8 November 1921, *St Vincent* on 1 December and *Temeraire* on 8 December, after due negotiations with scrappers. These sale dates were during the discussions in Washington but came ahead of final agreement, and were in any event the last step in a lengthy process.

44 Robert Stern, *The Battleship Holiday*, Seaforth, Barnsley, 2017, p. 86.

45 Norman Friedman 'How promise turned to disappointment', *Naval History Magazine*, Vol. 30, No. 4, August 2016.

46 https://mises.org/library/forgotten-depression-1920, accessed 13 January 2020.

47 Stern, pp. 98–99.

48 'Limitation of Naval Armament (Five Power Treaty or Washington Treaty), at www.loc.gov/law/help/us-treaties/bevans/m-ust000002-0351.pdf, accessed 8 February 2021.

49 Ibid., Section II, p. 364. *Colossus* was kept as a training ship until 1928, disarmed.

50 *Auckland Star*, 6 March 1922.

51 ANZ, R22430265 AAYS 8638 AD1 760 /17/69, 'Shipping – HMS "New Zealand" (ship) – Correspondence re-1911–1927', Rhodes to High Commissioner, 25 March 1922.

52 www.dreadnoughtproject.org/tfs/index.php/John_Frederick_Ernest_Green, accessed 3 April 2021.

53 Ibid., Under-Secretary Department of Internal Affairs to General Officer Administration, Defence Department, 4 April 1922.

54 *Evening Star*, 13 April 1922.

55 ANZ, R22430265 AAYS 8638 AD1 760 /17/69, 'Shipping – HMS "New Zealand" (ship) – Correspondence re-1911–1927', Massey to Rhodes, 21 April 1922.

56 *Gisborne Times*, 19 April 1922.

57 *New Zealand Herald*, 27 April 1922. At this time it was the 'Auckland War Museum', not 'Auckland War Memorial Museum'.

58 ANZ, R22430265 AAYS 8638 AD1 760 /17/69, 'Shipping – HMS "New Zealand" (ship) – Correspondence re-1911–1927', Jellicoe to Rhodes, 27 April 1922.

59 Ibid., Commodore Commanding to GO i/c Administration, NZ Military Headquarters, 28 June 1922.

60 Ibid., Lt-Colonel, Staff Q Duties, to Engineer in Chief, PWD, [obscured] July 1922.

61 Ibid., Furkert to Staff Officer Q Duties, 13 July 1922.

62 Ibid., 'List of plate, pictures etc, HMS *New Zealand*'.

63 Ibid., Allen to Defence Department, 16 November 1922.

64 Ibid., Allen to Defence Department, 23 March 1922.

65 Ibid., Chief staff Officer to GOC, New Zealand Military Forces, 15 September 1923.

66 Ibid., H E Avery, Quartermaster General, to Under Secretary, Department of Internal Affairs, 14 July 1924.

67 ANZ R1836075 ABFK W3947 3/ The Rosyth Shipbreaking Co. Ltd, album, A Wallace Cowan, 'Lecture to the Edinburgh University Commerce Association', 10 February 1936.

68 *New Zealand Yearbook*, 1926, www3.stats.govt.nz/New_Zealand_Official_Yearbooks/1926/NZOYB_1926.html?_ga =2.123762893.63746472.1614892679-1598441439.1614892679#idsect1_1_232106, accessed 4 March 2021.

69 Ibid.

70   Ibid.

71   ANZ R1836075 ABFK W3947 3/ The Rosyth Shipbreaking Co. Ltd, album.

72   *Auckland Star*, 23 January 1924.

73   ANZ R1836075 ABFK W3947 3/ The Rosyth Shipbreaking Co. Ltd, album, A Wallace Cowan, 'Lecture to the Edinburgh University Commerce Association', 10 February 1936.

74   See, e.g. ANZ ANZ R21463719 AAYT 8490 N1 18 /1/34 N1, 'Accounts – Naval Benevolent Fund, New Zealand – HMS New Zealand prizes fund – General – Correspondence', Naval Secretary to Commodore Commanding, 7 May 1937.

75   https://collections.tepapa.govt.nz/topic/1049, accessed 1 April 2021.

76   AJHR 1913, Session I, B-06, 'Financial statement (in Committee of Supply 6th August 1913) by the Minister of Finance, The Hon. James Allen, p. xxvii.

77   ANZ R11741448 ADAV 16028 A5 141/23/48 Naval Defence Sinking Fund Account 1921–1938, 'Battle-cruiser "New Zealand"'.

78   ANZ R11741448 ADAV 16028 A5 141/23/48 Naval Defence Sinking Fund Account 1921–1938, Controller and Auditor-General to Secretary of the Treasury, 26 March 1924.

79   *New Zealand Yearbook* 1926, www3.stats.govt.nz/New_Zealand_Official_Yearbooks/1926/NZOYB_1926.html?_ga =2.123762893.63746472.1614892679-1598441439.1614892679#idsect1_1_232106, accessed 4 March 2021.

80   ANZ R11741448 ADAV 16028 A5 141/23/48 Naval Defence Sinking Fund Account 1921–1938, Controller and Auditor-General to Secretary of the Treasury, 26 March 1924.

81   AJHR 1926, B-8, 'The Naval Defence Act Sinking Fund', p. 1.

82   A function of the 1912 arrangement to raise up to £4.5 million.

83   ANZ R11741448 ADAV 16028 A5 141/23/48 Naval Defence Sinking Fund Account 1921–1938, 'Battle-cruiser "New Zealand"'.

84   Michael Reddell, 'The New Zealand Debt Conversion Act 1933: a case study in coercive domestic public debt restructuring', Reserve Bank of New Zealand *Bulletin*, Vol. 75, No. 1, March 2012.

85   For background, see Matthew Wright, 'The Policy Origins of the Reserve Bank of New Zealand', Reserve Bank of New Zealand *Bulletin*, Vol. 69, No. 3, September 2006.

86   AJHR 1932 Session I-II, B-01, Part 3, 'Public accounts for the financial year 1931–1932, Part 3', p. 21.

87   See, e.g. AJHR 1943 Session I, B-01, Part 2, 'Public accounts for the financial year 1942–43, Part 2, p. xi.

88   Ibid., p. xi.

89   AJHR 1944, Session I, B-02, 'Repayment of the public debt: report and accounts of the public debt commission for the year ended 31st March 1944', p. 2.

90   AJHR 1945, Session I, B-02, 'Repayment of the public debt: report and accounts of the public debt commission for the year ended 31st March 1945', p. 2.

91   ANZ R11741448 ADAV 16028 A5 141/23/48 Naval Defence Sinking Fund Account 1921–1938, 'Naval Defence Sinking Fund'.

92   For explanation of how inflation 'repays' debt, see Matthew Wright and Graham Howard, 'The Reserve Bank Inflation Calculator', Reserve Bank of New Zealand *Bulletin*, Vol. 66, No. 4, December 2003.

93   See www.rbnz.govt.nz/monetary-policy/inflation-calculator , comparing Q4 1913 with Q1 1945. Figures rounded.
94   Ibid., comparing Q4 1913 with Q1 1931. Figures rounded. There was a period of deflation during the Great Depression, peaking at 12 per cent in 1932. Price levels had not returned to 1931 values by 1945.
95   Michael Reddell and Cath Sleeman, 'Some perspectives on past recessions', Reserve Bank of New Zealand *Bulletin*, Vol. 71, No. 2, June 2008.
96   For economic analysis of the depression see Matthew Wright, 'Mordacious Years: socio-economic aspects and outcomes of New Zealand's experience in the Great Depression', Reserve Bank of New Zealand *Bulletin*, Vol. 72, No. 3, September 2009.
97   ANZ, R22430265 AAYS 8638 AD1 760 /17/69, 'Shipping – HMS "New Zealand" (ship) – Correspondence re-1911–1927', OC Supplies & Transport to Director of Artillery 25 July 1923
98   ww100.govt.nz/the-taonga-of-hms-new-zealand, accessed 27 March 2021.
99   *Manawatu Standard*, 17 December 1924.
100 https://collections.tepapa.govt.nz/object/58400, accessed 27 March 2021.
101 ww100.govt.nz/the-taonga-of-hms-new-zealand, accessed 27 March 2021.
102 For further discussion see Matthew Wright, *The New Zealand Experience at Gallipoli and the Western Front*, pp. 285–298.

Appendix 1
1   Wtu fMS-195 *HMS New Zealand Captain's Ship's Book*.

Appendix 2
1   ANZ R11741448 ADAV 16028 A5 141/23/48 Naval Defence Sinking Fund Account 1921–1938, 'Naval Defence Act Account'.

INDEX